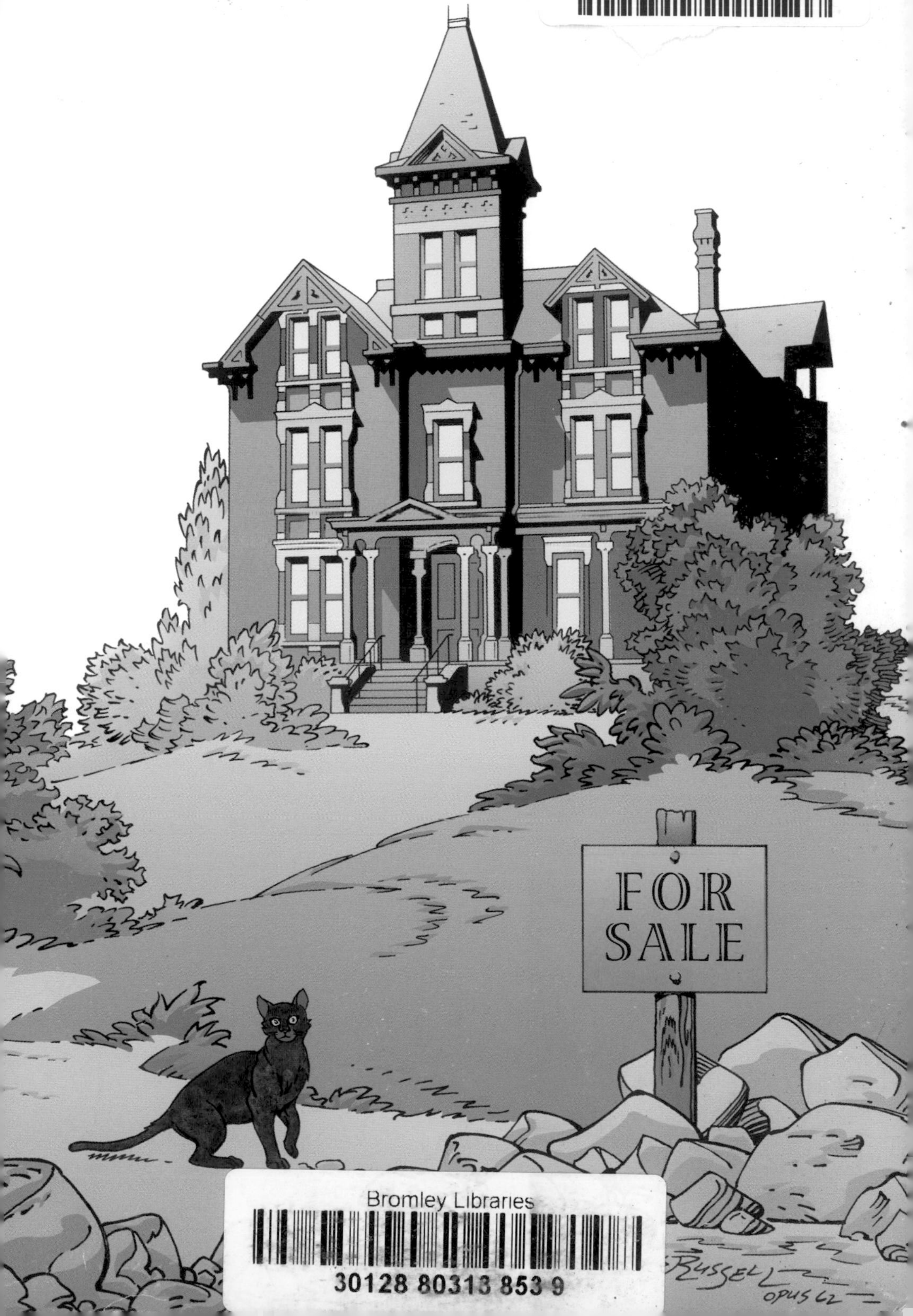
FOR
SALE

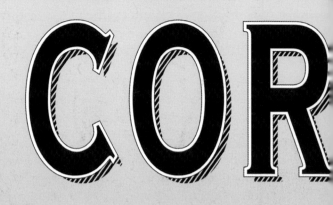

COR

based on the *novel* by

NEIL GAIMAN

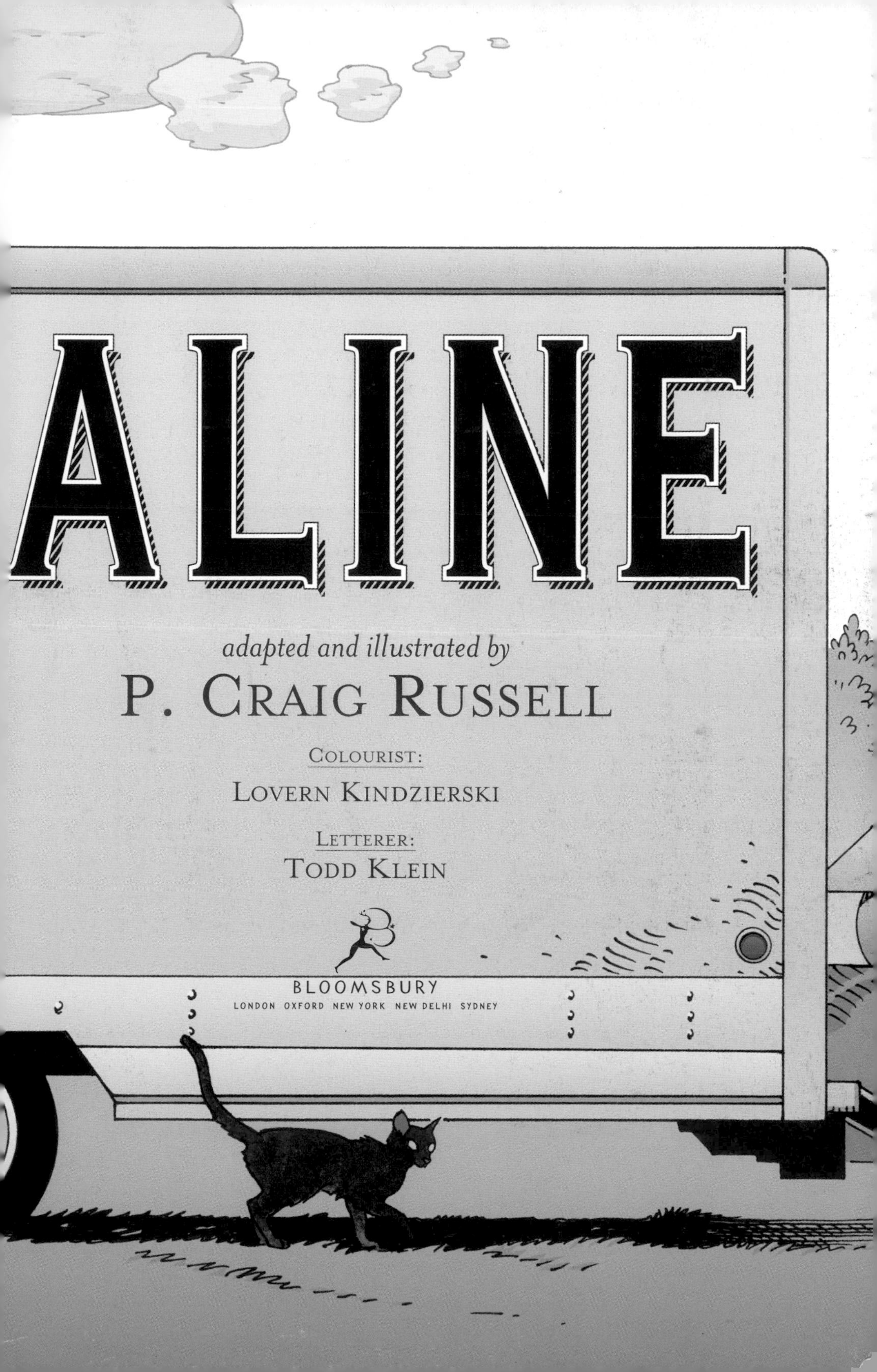
ALINE
adapted and illustrated by
P. CRAIG RUSSELL
COLOURIST:
LOVERN KINDZIERSKI
LETTERER:
TODD KLEIN
BLOOMSBURY
LONDON OXFORD NEW YORK NEW DELHI SYDNEY

FIRST PUBLISHED IN GREAT BRITAIN IN 2008 BY BLOOMSBURY PUBLISHING PLC
50 BEDFORD SQUARE, LONDON WC1B 3DP

PUBLISHED BY ARRANGEMENT WITH HARPERCOLLINS CHILDREN'S BOOKS, A DIVISION OF
HARPERCOLLINS PUBLISHERS

FIRST PUBLISHED IN AMERICA IN 2008 BY HARPERCOLLINS CHILDREN'S BOOKS,
A DIVISION OF HARPERCOLLINS PUBLISHERS, 195 BROADWAY, NEW YORK, NY 10007

WWW.BLOOMSBURY.COM
WWW.NEILGAIMAN.COM

BLOOMSBURY IS A REGISTERED TRADEMARK OF BLOOMSBURY PUBLISHING PLC

A CIP CATALOGUE RECORD OF THIS BOOK IS AVAILABLE FROM THE BRITISH LIBRARY

ISBN 978 0 7475 9406 2

PRINTED IN CHINA

15

ALL PAPERS USED BY BLOOMSBURY PUBLISHING ARE NATURAL, RECYCLABLE PRODUCTS MADE FROM WOOD
GROWN IN WELL-MANAGED FORESTS. THE MANUFACTURING PRODUCTS CONFORM TO THE ENVIRONMENTAL
REGULATIONS OF THE COUNTRY OF ORIGIN

I started this for Holly
I finished it for Maddy — N.G.

To Allison, Sloane, and Ivy — P.C.R.

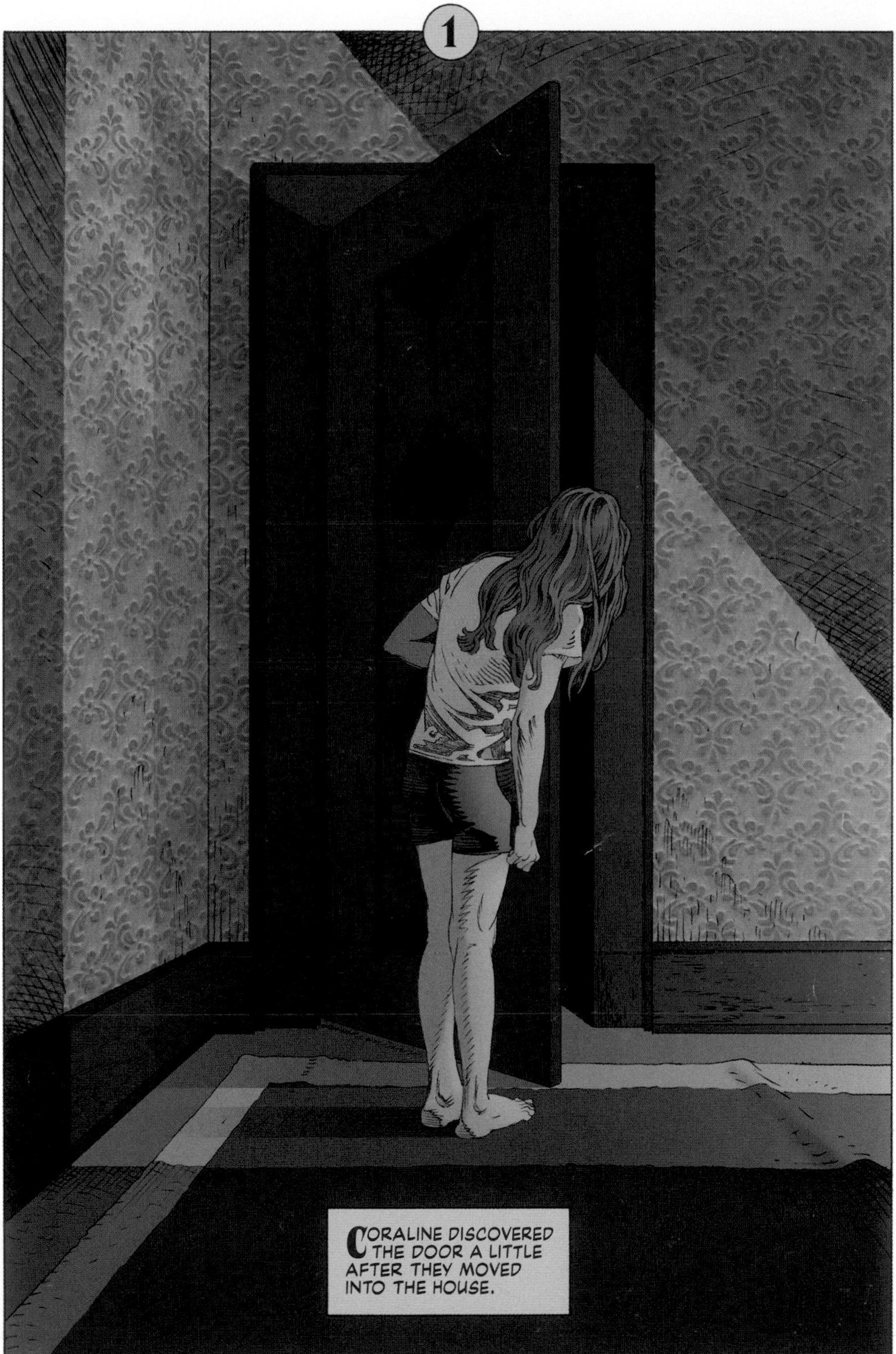
1
CORALINE DISCOVERED THE DOOR A LITTLE AFTER THEY MOVED INTO THE HOUSE.

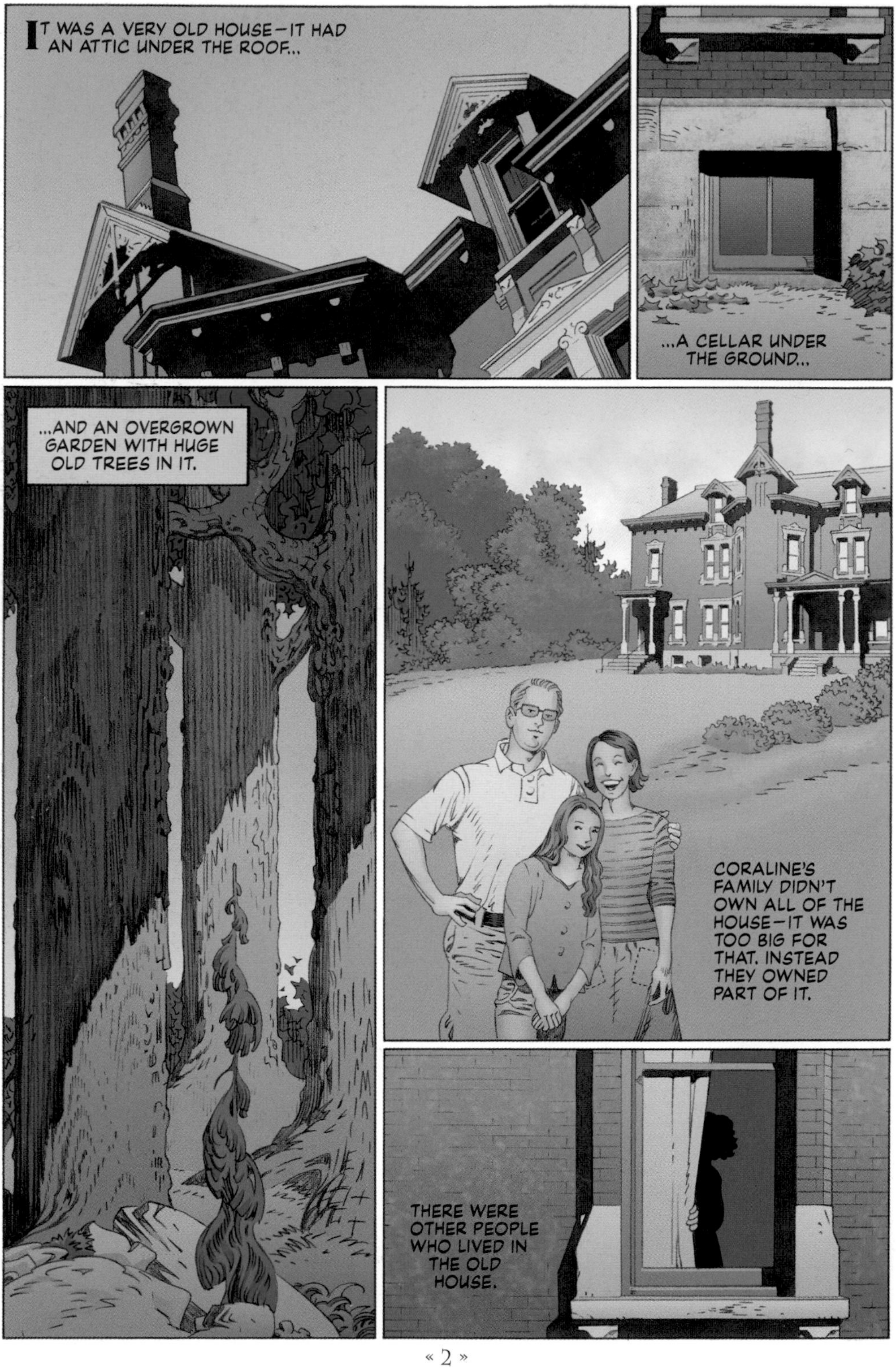
IT WAS A VERY OLD HOUSE—IT HAD AN ATTIC UNDER THE ROOF...
...A CELLAR UNDER THE GROUND...
...AND AN OVERGROWN GARDEN WITH HUGE OLD TREES IN IT.
CORALINE'S FAMILY DIDN'T OWN ALL OF THE HOUSE—IT WAS TOO BIG FOR THAT. INSTEAD THEY OWNED PART OF IT.
THERE WERE OTHER PEOPLE WHO LIVED IN THE OLD HOUSE.

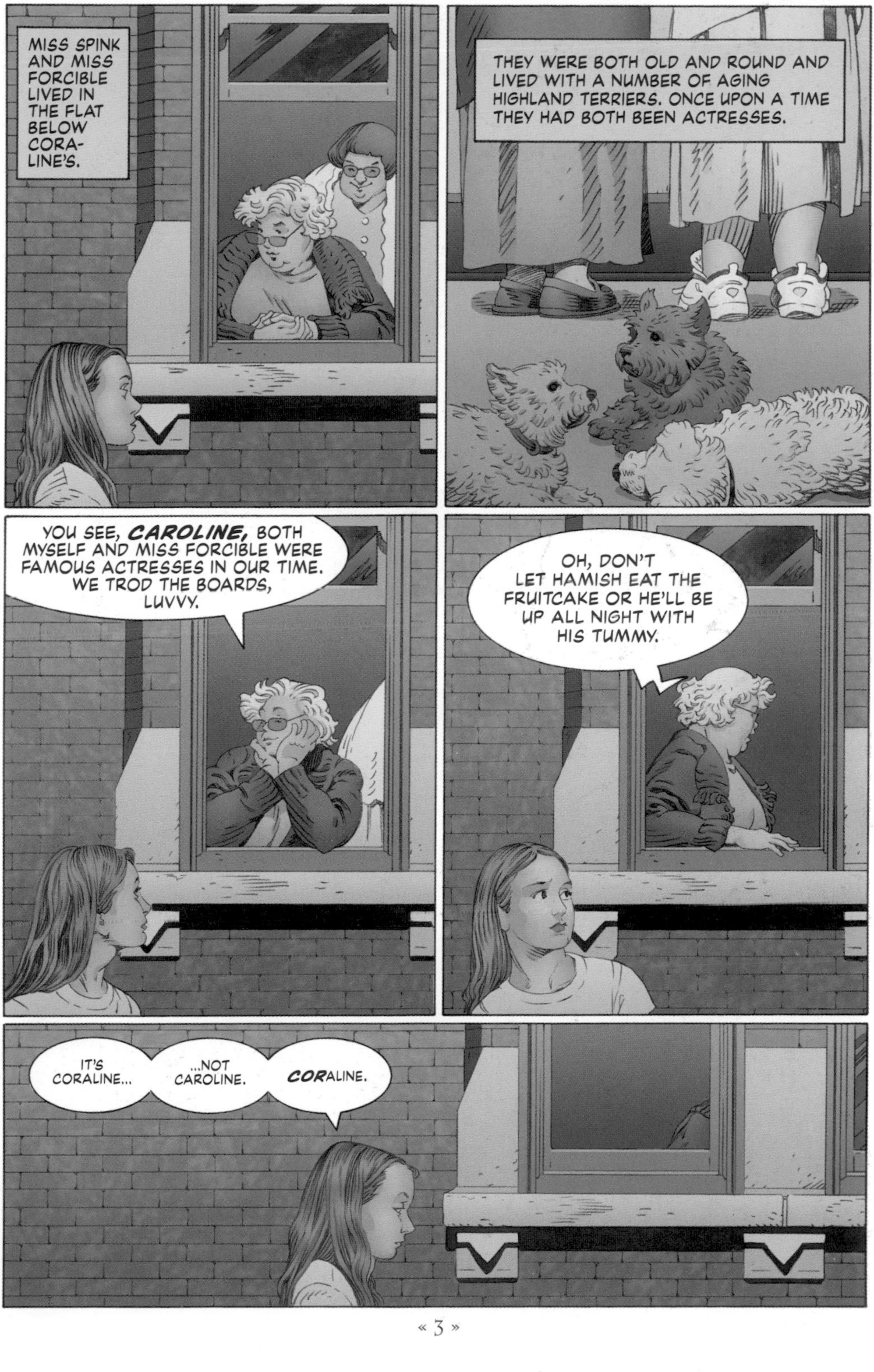
MISS SPINK AND MISS FORCIBLE LIVED IN THE FLAT BELOW CORA-LINE'S.
THEY WERE BOTH OLD AND ROUND AND LIVED WITH A NUMBER OF AGING HIGHLAND TERRIERS. ONCE UPON A TIME THEY HAD BOTH BEEN ACTRESSES.
YOU SEE, ***CAROLINE,*** BOTH MYSELF AND MISS FORCIBLE WERE FAMOUS ACTRESSES IN OUR TIME. WE TROD THE BOARDS, LUVVY.
OH, DON'T LET HAMISH EAT THE FRUITCAKE OR HE'LL BE UP ALL NIGHT WITH HIS TUMMY.
IT'S CORALINE...
...NOT CAROLINE.
CORALINE.

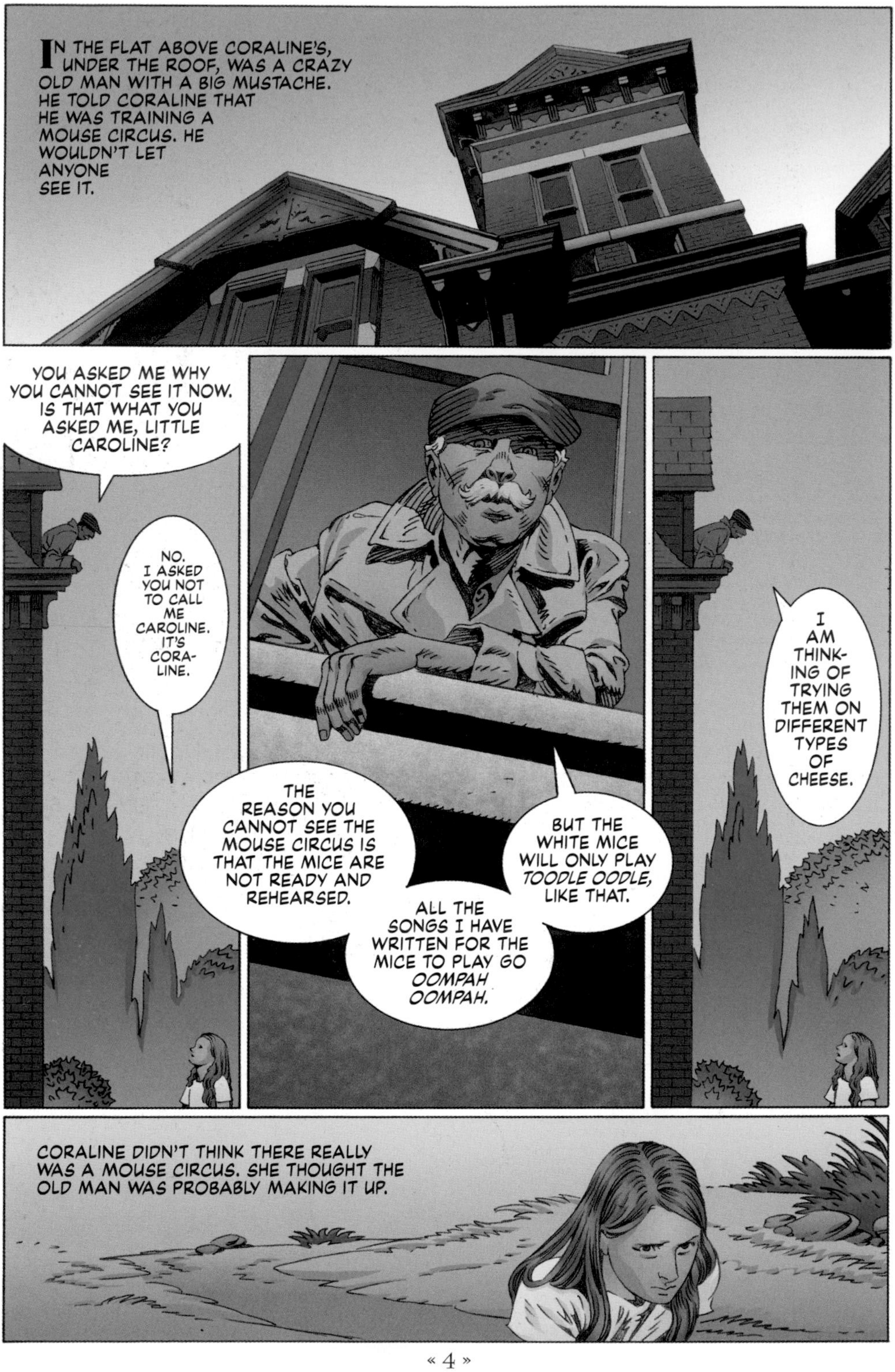
IN THE FLAT ABOVE CORALINE'S, UNDER THE ROOF, WAS A CRAZY OLD MAN WITH A BIG MUSTACHE. HE TOLD CORALINE THAT HE WAS TRAINING A MOUSE CIRCUS. HE WOULDN'T LET ANYONE SEE IT.
YOU ASKED ME WHY YOU CANNOT SEE IT NOW. IS THAT WHAT YOU ASKED ME, LITTLE CAROLINE?
NO. I ASKED YOU NOT TO CALL ME CAROLINE. IT'S CORA-LINE.
THE REASON YOU CANNOT SEE THE MOUSE CIRCUS IS THAT THE MICE ARE NOT READY AND REHEARSED.
ALL THE SONGS I HAVE WRITTEN FOR THE MICE TO PLAY GO *OOMPAH OOMPAH.*
BUT THE WHITE MICE WILL ONLY PLAY *TOODLE OODLE,* LIKE THAT.
I AM THINKING OF TRYING THEM ON DIFFERENT TYPES OF CHEESE.
CORALINE DIDN'T THINK THERE REALLY WAS A MOUSE CIRCUS. SHE THOUGHT THE OLD MAN WAS PROBABLY MAKING IT UP.

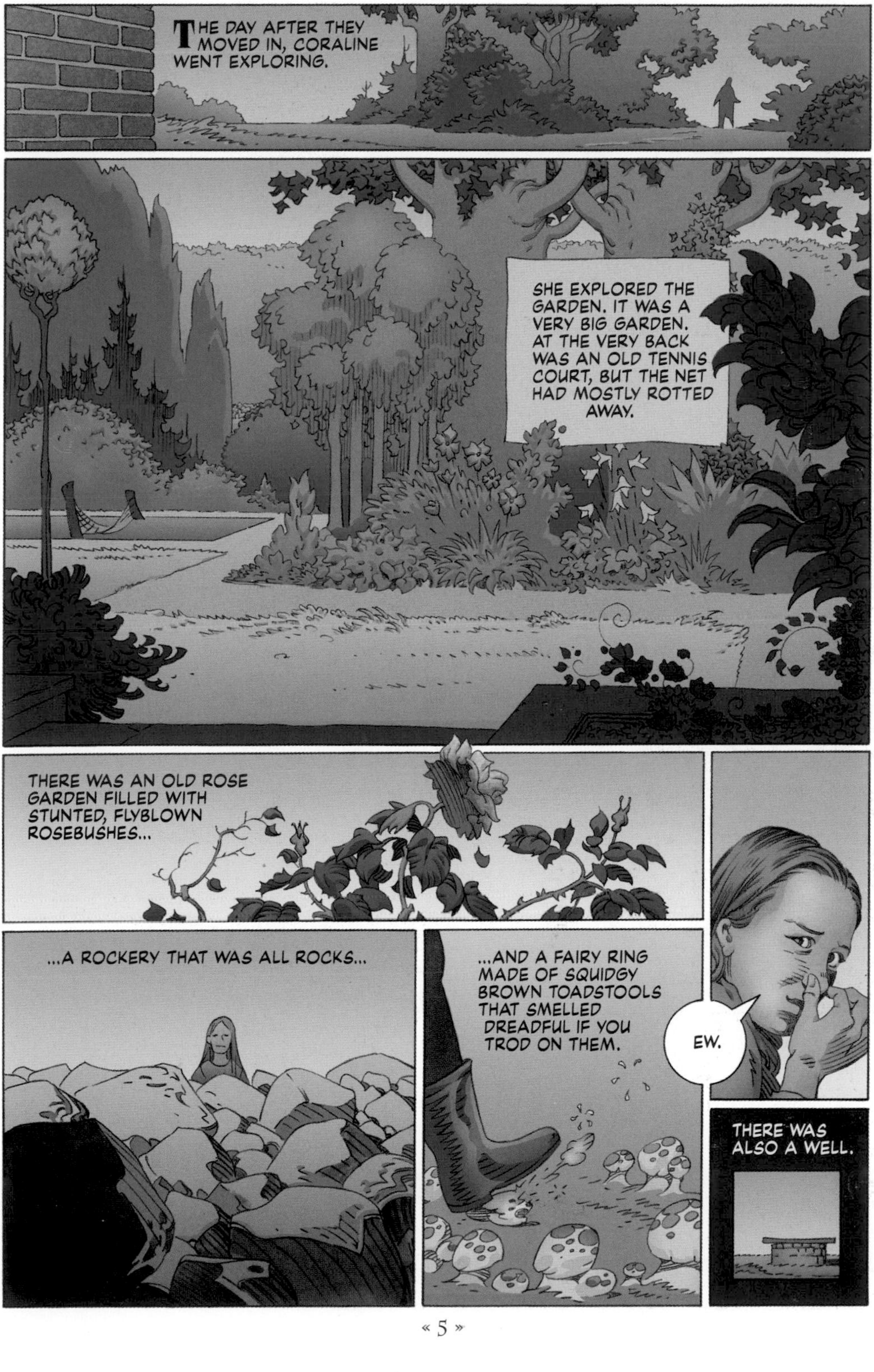
THE DAY AFTER THEY MOVED IN, CORALINE WENT EXPLORING.
SHE EXPLORED THE GARDEN. IT WAS A VERY BIG GARDEN. AT THE VERY BACK WAS AN OLD TENNIS COURT, BUT THE NET HAD MOSTLY ROTTED AWAY.
THERE WAS AN OLD ROSE GARDEN FILLED WITH STUNTED, FLYBLOWN ROSEBUSHES...
...A ROCKERY THAT WAS ALL ROCKS...
...AND A FAIRY RING MADE OF SQUIDGY BROWN TOADSTOOLS THAT SMELLED DREADFUL IF YOU TROD ON THEM.
EW.
THERE WAS ALSO A WELL.

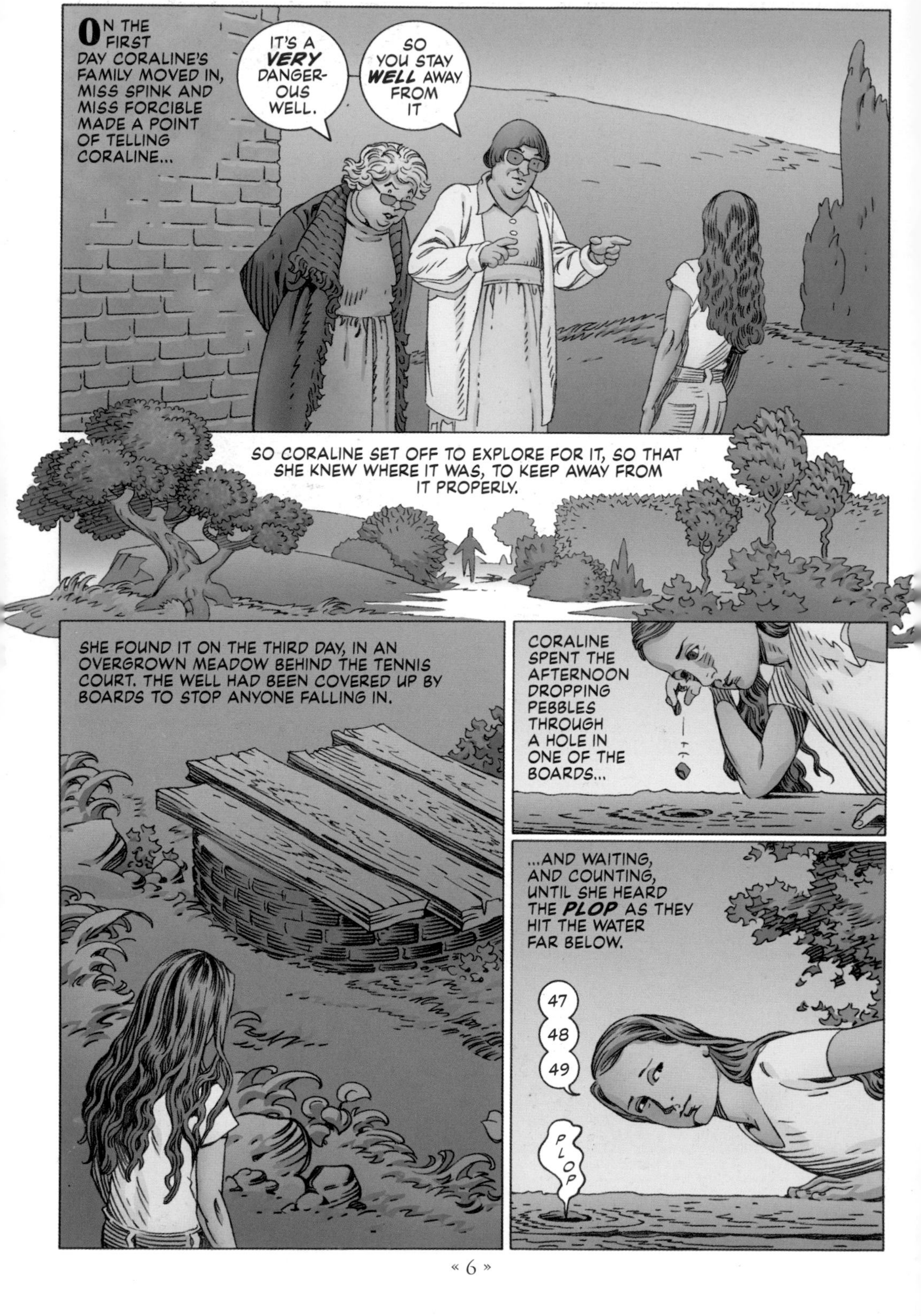
ON THE FIRST DAY CORALINE'S FAMILY MOVED IN, MISS SPINK AND MISS FORCIBLE MADE A POINT OF TELLING CORALINE...
IT'S A VERY DANGEROUS WELL.
SO YOU STAY WELL AWAY FROM IT
SO CORALINE SET OFF TO EXPLORE FOR IT, SO THAT SHE KNEW WHERE IT WAS, TO KEEP AWAY FROM IT PROPERLY.
SHE FOUND IT ON THE THIRD DAY, IN AN OVERGROWN MEADOW BEHIND THE TENNIS COURT. THE WELL HAD BEEN COVERED UP BY BOARDS TO STOP ANYONE FALLING IN.
CORALINE SPENT THE AFTERNOON DROPPING PEBBLES THROUGH A HOLE IN ONE OF THE BOARDS...
...AND WAITING, AND COUNTING, UNTIL SHE HEARD THE PLOP AS THEY HIT THE WATER FAR BELOW.
47
48
49
PLOP

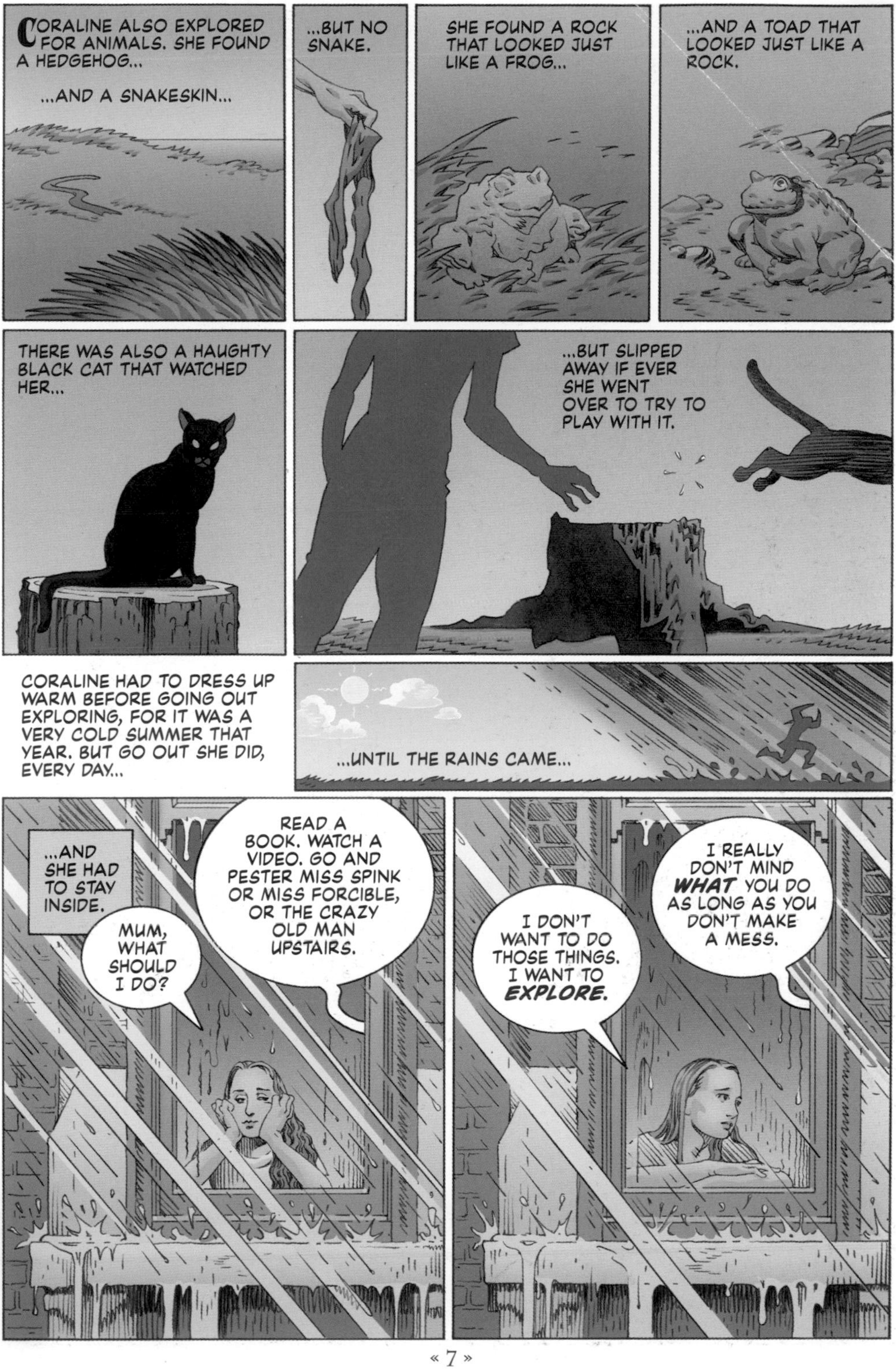
CORALINE ALSO EXPLORED FOR ANIMALS. SHE FOUND A HEDGEHOG...
...AND A SNAKESKIN...
...BUT NO SNAKE.
SHE FOUND A ROCK THAT LOOKED JUST LIKE A FROG...
...AND A TOAD THAT LOOKED JUST LIKE A ROCK.
THERE WAS ALSO A HAUGHTY BLACK CAT THAT WATCHED HER...
...BUT SLIPPED AWAY IF EVER SHE WENT OVER TO TRY TO PLAY WITH IT.
CORALINE HAD TO DRESS UP WARM BEFORE GOING OUT EXPLORING, FOR IT WAS A VERY COLD SUMMER THAT YEAR. BUT GO OUT SHE DID, EVERY DAY...
...UNTIL THE RAINS CAME...
...AND SHE HAD TO STAY INSIDE.
MUM, WHAT SHOULD I DO?
READ A BOOK. WATCH A VIDEO. GO AND PESTER MISS SPINK OR MISS FORCIBLE, OR THE CRAZY OLD MAN UPSTAIRS.
I DON'T WANT TO DO THOSE THINGS. I WANT TO ***EXPLORE.***
I REALLY DON'T MIND ***WHAT*** YOU DO AS LONG AS YOU DON'T MAKE A MESS.

CORALINE WATCHED THE RAIN COME DOWN. IT WAS THE KIND OF RAIN THAT MEANT BUSINESS, AND CURRENTLY ITS BUSINESS WAS TURNING THE GARDEN INTO A MUDDY, WET SOUP.

SHE HAD WATCHED ALL THE VIDEOS...

TOTORO

BABE

...SHE WAS BORED WITH HER TOYS...

...AND SHE'D READ ALL HER BOOKS.

BEVERLY CLEARY

Lily's Ghosts

WARRIOR

The WALL and the WING

IT WAS TIME TO VISIT HER FATHER IN HIS STUDY. SHE WALKED DOWN THE HALL.

HELLO, CORA-LINE.

MMPH. IT'S RAIN-ING.

YUP. IT'S BUCKETING DOWN.

NO, IT'S JUST RAINING. CAN I GO OUTSIDE?

WHAT DOES YOUR MOTHER SAY?

SHE SAYS, "YOU'RE NOT GOING OUT IN WEATHER LIKE THAT, CORALINE JONES."

THEN, NO.

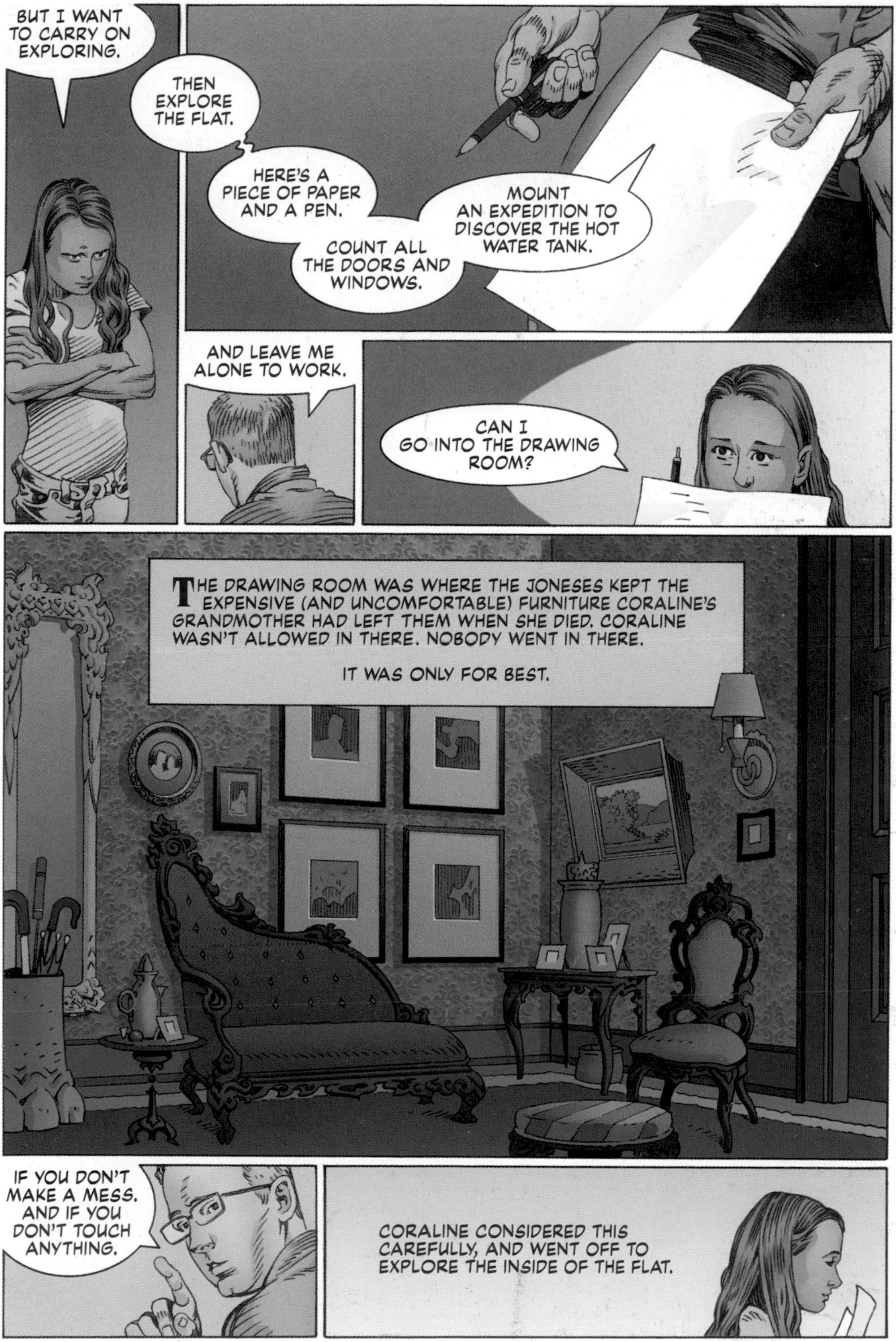
BUT I WANT TO CARRY ON EXPLORING.
THEN EXPLORE THE FLAT.
HERE'S A PIECE OF PAPER AND A PEN.
COUNT ALL THE DOORS AND WINDOWS.
MOUNT AN EXPEDITION TO DISCOVER THE HOT WATER TANK.
AND LEAVE ME ALONE TO WORK.
CAN I GO INTO THE DRAWING ROOM?
THE DRAWING ROOM WAS WHERE THE JONESES KEPT THE EXPENSIVE (AND UNCOMFORTABLE) FURNITURE CORALINE'S GRANDMOTHER HAD LEFT THEM WHEN SHE DIED. CORALINE WASN'T ALLOWED IN THERE. NOBODY WENT IN THERE.
IT WAS ONLY FOR BEST.
IF YOU DON'T MAKE A MESS. AND IF YOU DON'T TOUCH ANYTHING.
CORALINE CONSIDERED THIS CAREFULLY, AND WENT OFF TO EXPLORE THE INSIDE OF THE FLAT.

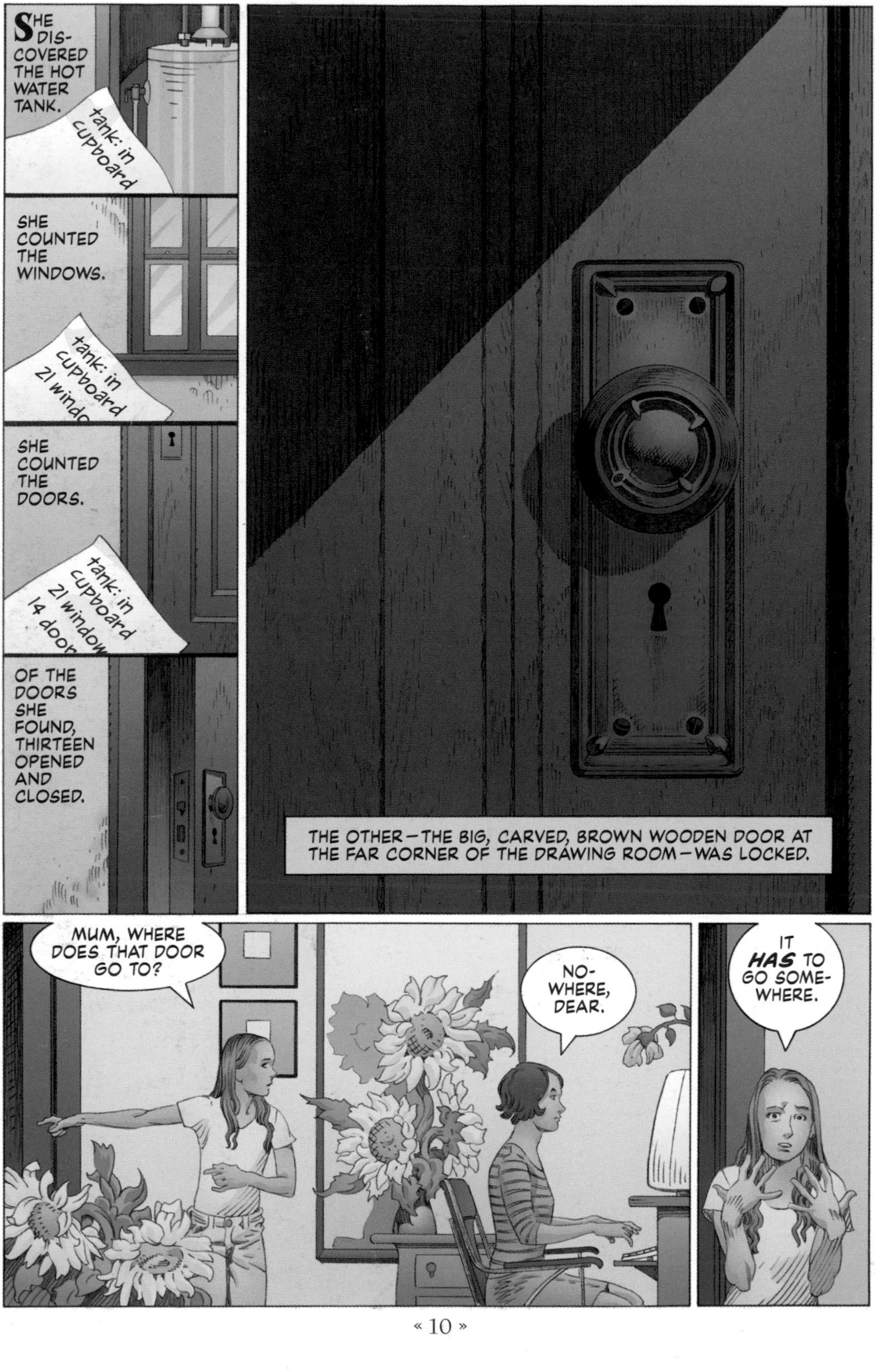
SHE DISCOVERED THE HOT WATER TANK.
tank: in cupboard
SHE COUNTED THE WINDOWS.
tank: in cupboard 21 windo
SHE COUNTED THE DOORS.
tank: in cupboard 21 window 14 door
OF THE DOORS SHE FOUND, THIRTEEN OPENED AND CLOSED.
THE OTHER—THE BIG, CARVED, BROWN WOODEN DOOR AT THE FAR CORNER OF THE DRAWING ROOM—WAS LOCKED.
MUM, WHERE DOES THAT DOOR GO TO?
NOWHERE, DEAR.
IT HAS TO GO SOMEWHERE.

LOOK.

CLUNK

HER MOTHER WAS RIGHT. THE DOOR DIDN'T GO ANYWHERE.

WHEN THIS PLACE WAS JUST ONE HOUSE, THAT DOOR WENT SOME-WHERE.

WHEN THEY TURNED THE HOUSE INTO FLATS, THEY SIMPLY BRICKED IT UP.

THE ONE THAT'S STILL FOR SALE.

THE OTHER SIDE IS THE EMPTY FLAT ON THE OTHER SIDE OF THE HOUSE.

SHE SHUT THE DOOR AND WENT TO PUT THE KEY BACK ON TOP OF THE KITCHEN DOOR FRAME.

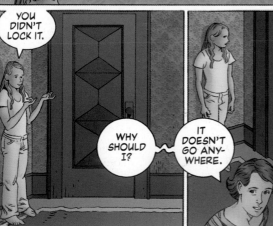

YOU DIDN'T LOCK IT.

WHY SHOULD I?

IT DOESN'T GO ANY-WHERE.

IT WAS REALLY DARK OUT-SIDE NOW, AND THE RAIN WAS STILL COM-ING DOWN.

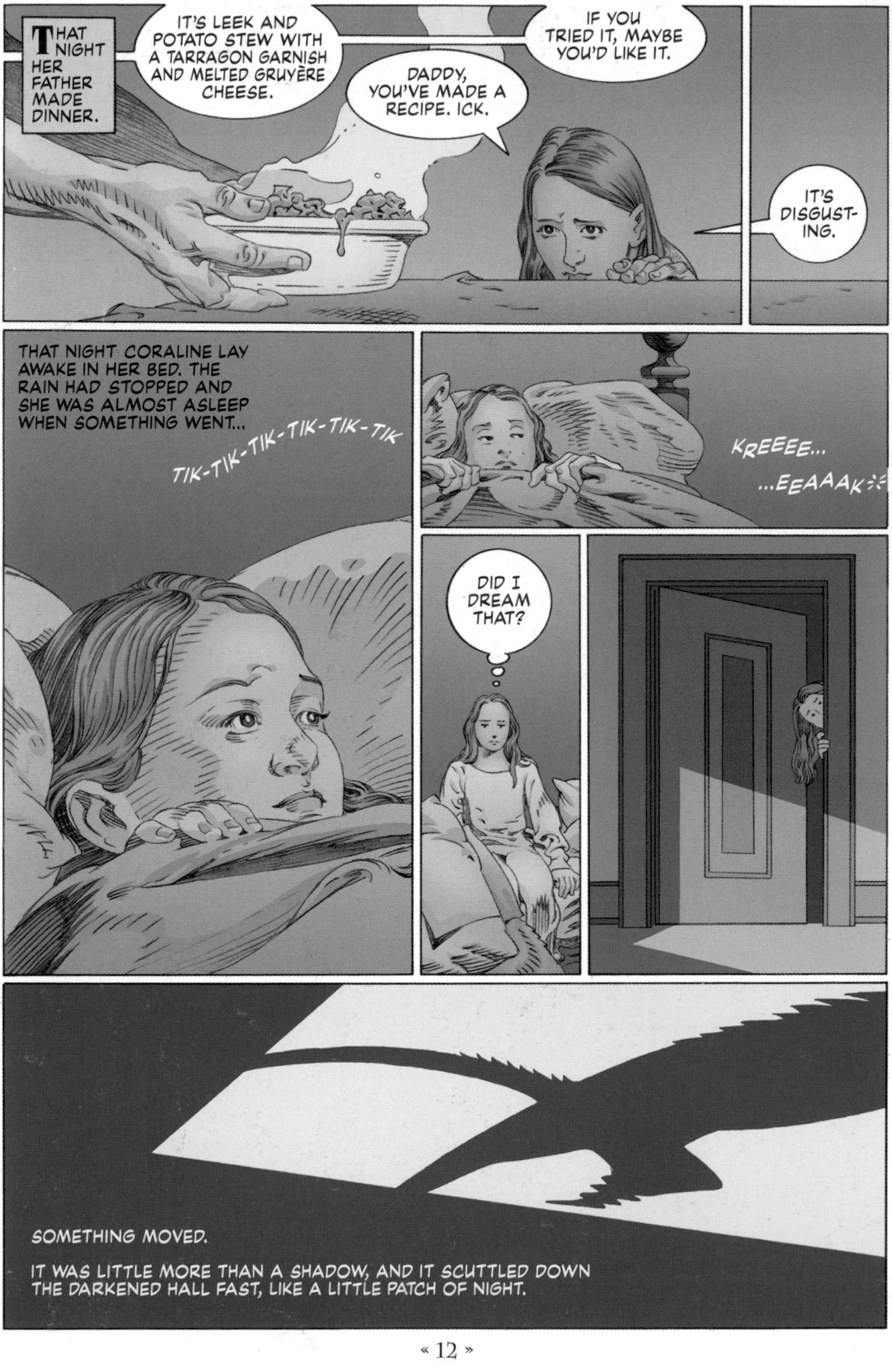

THAT NIGHT HER FATHER MADE DINNER.
IT'S LEEK AND POTATO STEW WITH A TARRAGON GARNISH AND MELTED GRUYÈRE CHEESE.
DADDY, YOU'VE MADE A RECIPE. ICK.
IF YOU TRIED IT, MAYBE YOU'D LIKE IT.
IT'S DISGUST-ING.
THAT NIGHT CORALINE LAY AWAKE IN HER BED. THE RAIN HAD STOPPED AND SHE WAS ALMOST ASLEEP WHEN SOMETHING WENT...
TIK-TIK-TIK-TIK-TIK-TIK
KREEEE...
...EEAAAK
DID I DREAM THAT?
SOMETHING MOVED.
IT WAS LITTLE MORE THAN A SHADOW, AND IT SCUTTLED DOWN THE DARKENED HALL FAST, LIKE A LITTLE PATCH OF NIGHT.

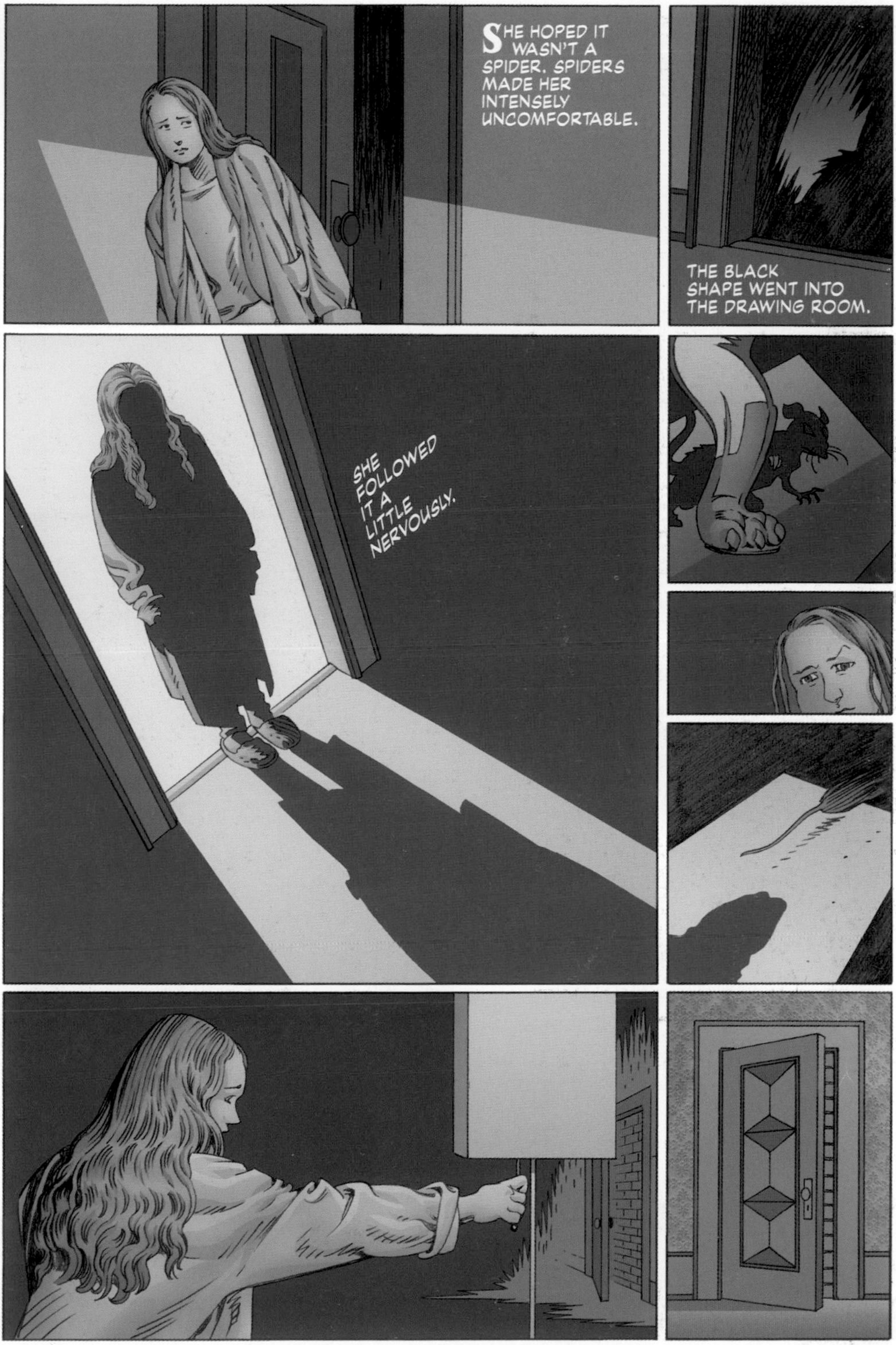
SHE HOPED IT WASN'T A SPIDER. SPIDERS MADE HER INTENSELY UNCOMFORTABLE.
THE BLACK SHAPE WENT INTO THE DRAWING ROOM.
SHE FOLLOWED IT A LITTLE NERVOUSLY.

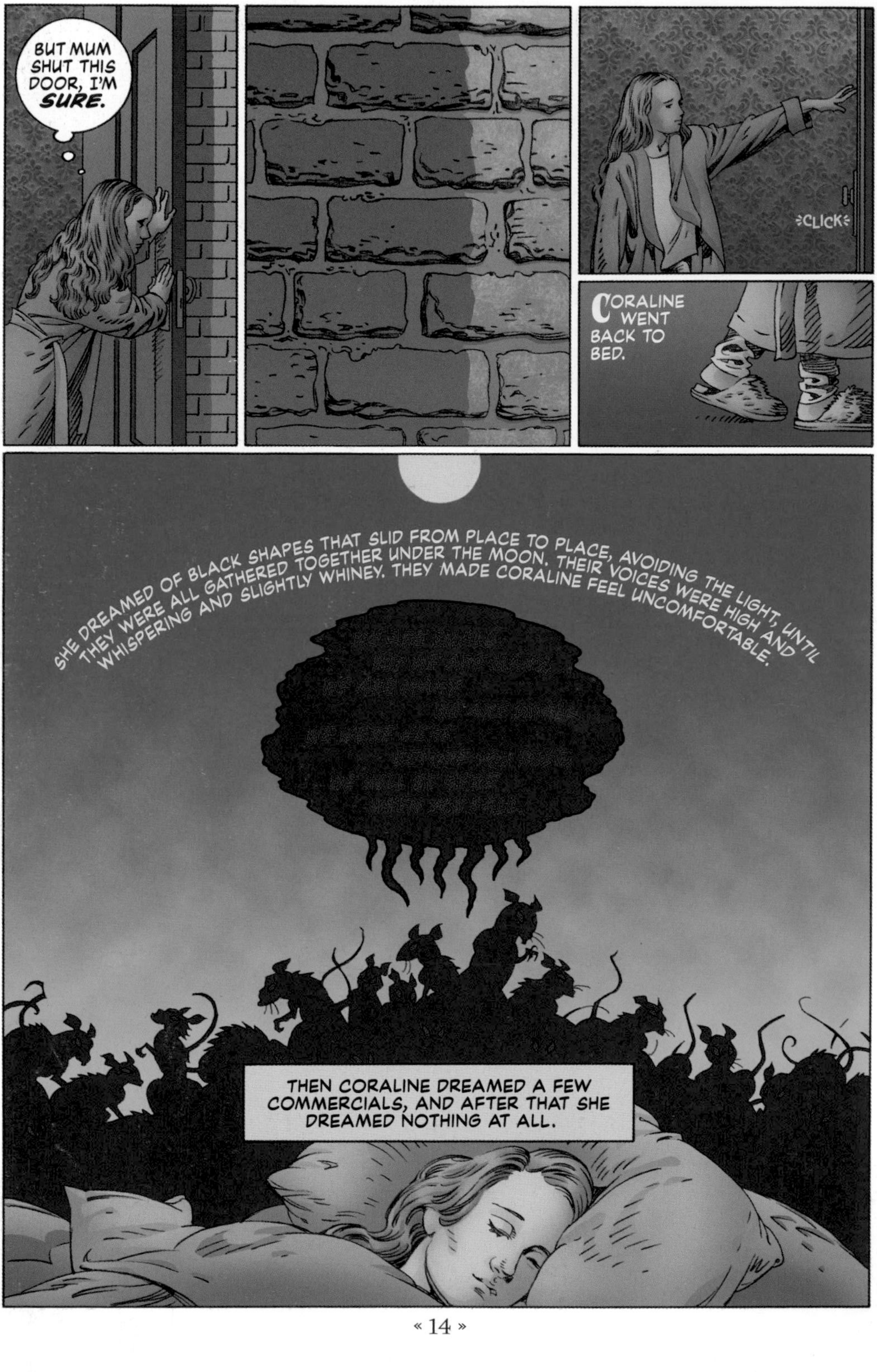
BUT MUM SHUT THIS DOOR, I'M SURE.
CLICK
CORALINE WENT BACK TO BED.
SHE DREAMED OF BLACK SHAPES THAT SLID FROM PLACE TO PLACE, AVOIDING THE LIGHT, UNTIL THEY WERE ALL GATHERED TOGETHER UNDER THE MOON. THEIR VOICES WERE HIGH AND WHISPERING AND SLIGHTLY WHINEY. THEY MADE CORALINE FEEL UNCOMFORTABLE.
THEN CORALINE DREAMED A FEW COMMERCIALS, AND AFTER THAT SHE DREAMED NOTHING AT ALL.

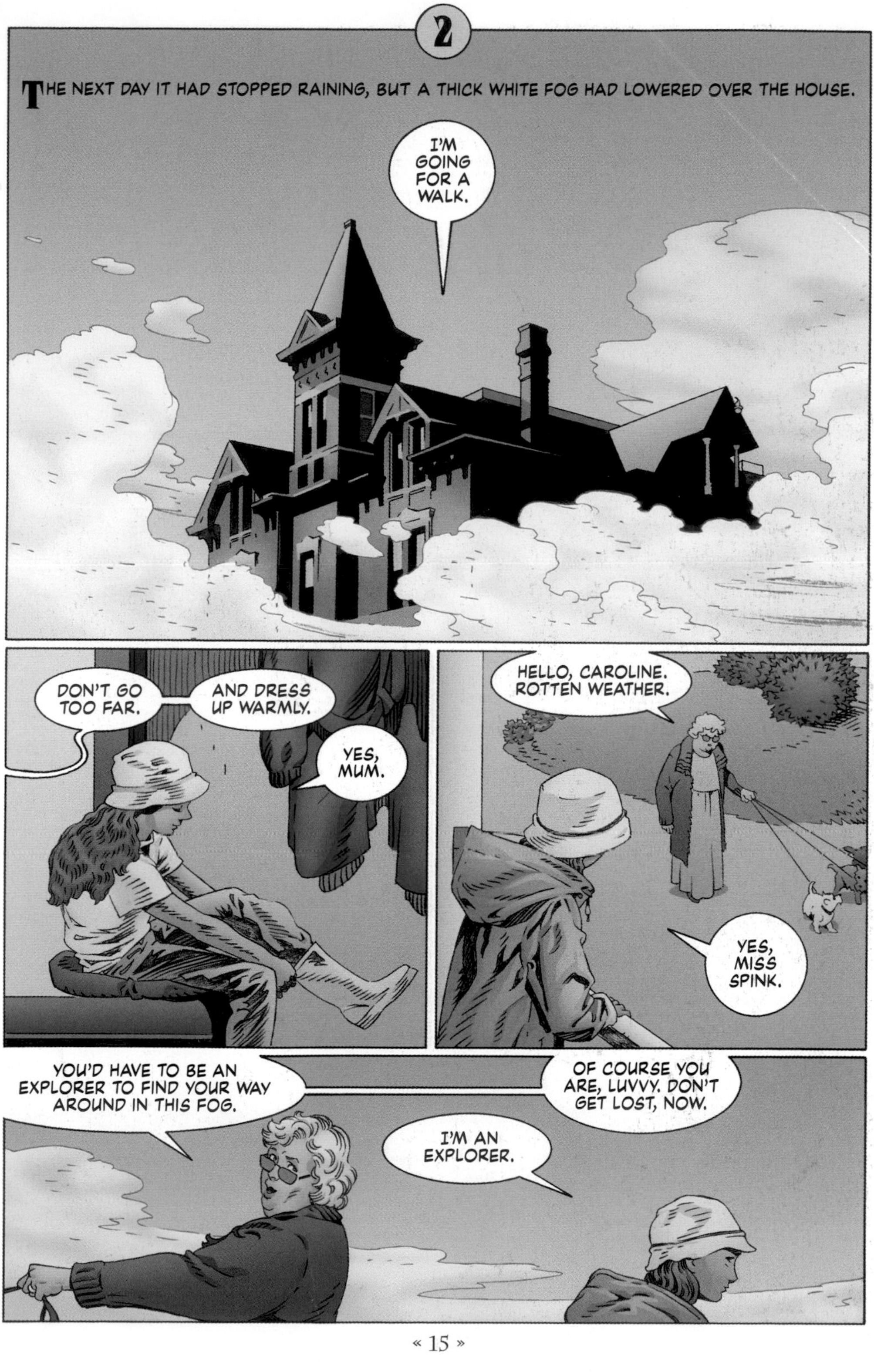
2
THE NEXT DAY IT HAD STOPPED RAINING, BUT A THICK WHITE FOG HAD LOWERED OVER THE HOUSE.
I'M GOING FOR A WALK.
DON'T GO TOO FAR.
AND DRESS UP WARMLY.
YES, MUM.
HELLO, CAROLINE. ROTTEN WEATHER.
YES, MISS SPINK.
YOU'D HAVE TO BE AN EXPLORER TO FIND YOUR WAY AROUND IN THIS FOG.
I'M AN EXPLORER.
OF COURSE YOU ARE, LUVVY. DON'T GET LOST, NOW.

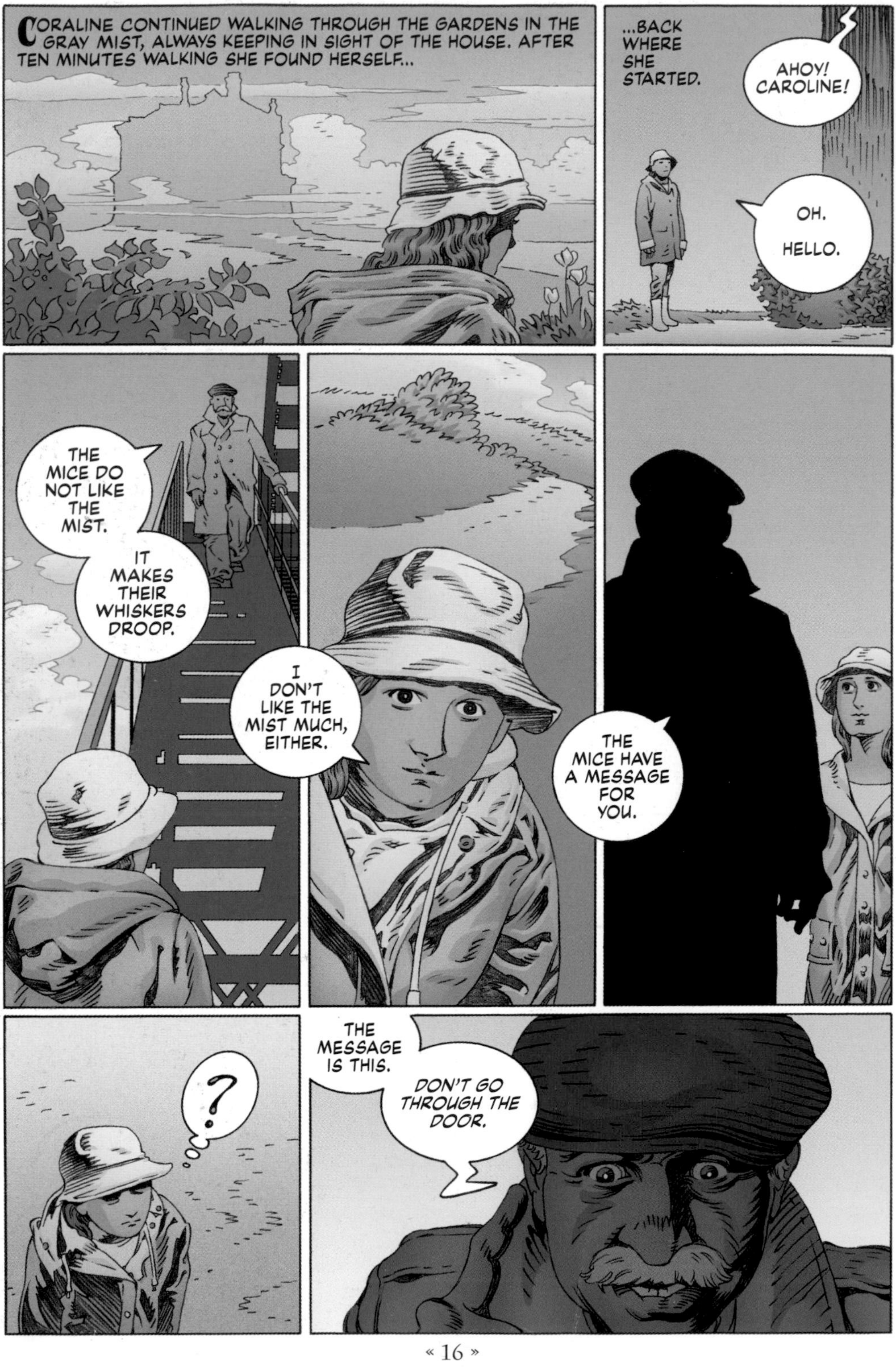
CORALINE CONTINUED WALKING THROUGH THE GARDENS IN THE GRAY MIST, ALWAYS KEEPING IN SIGHT OF THE HOUSE. AFTER TEN MINUTES WALKING SHE FOUND HERSELF...
...BACK WHERE SHE STARTED.
AHOY! CAROLINE!
OH.
HELLO.
THE MICE DO NOT LIKE THE MIST.
IT MAKES THEIR WHISKERS DROOP.
I DON'T LIKE THE MIST MUCH, EITHER.
THE MICE HAVE A MESSAGE FOR YOU.
?
THE MESSAGE IS THIS.
DON'T GO THROUGH THE DOOR.

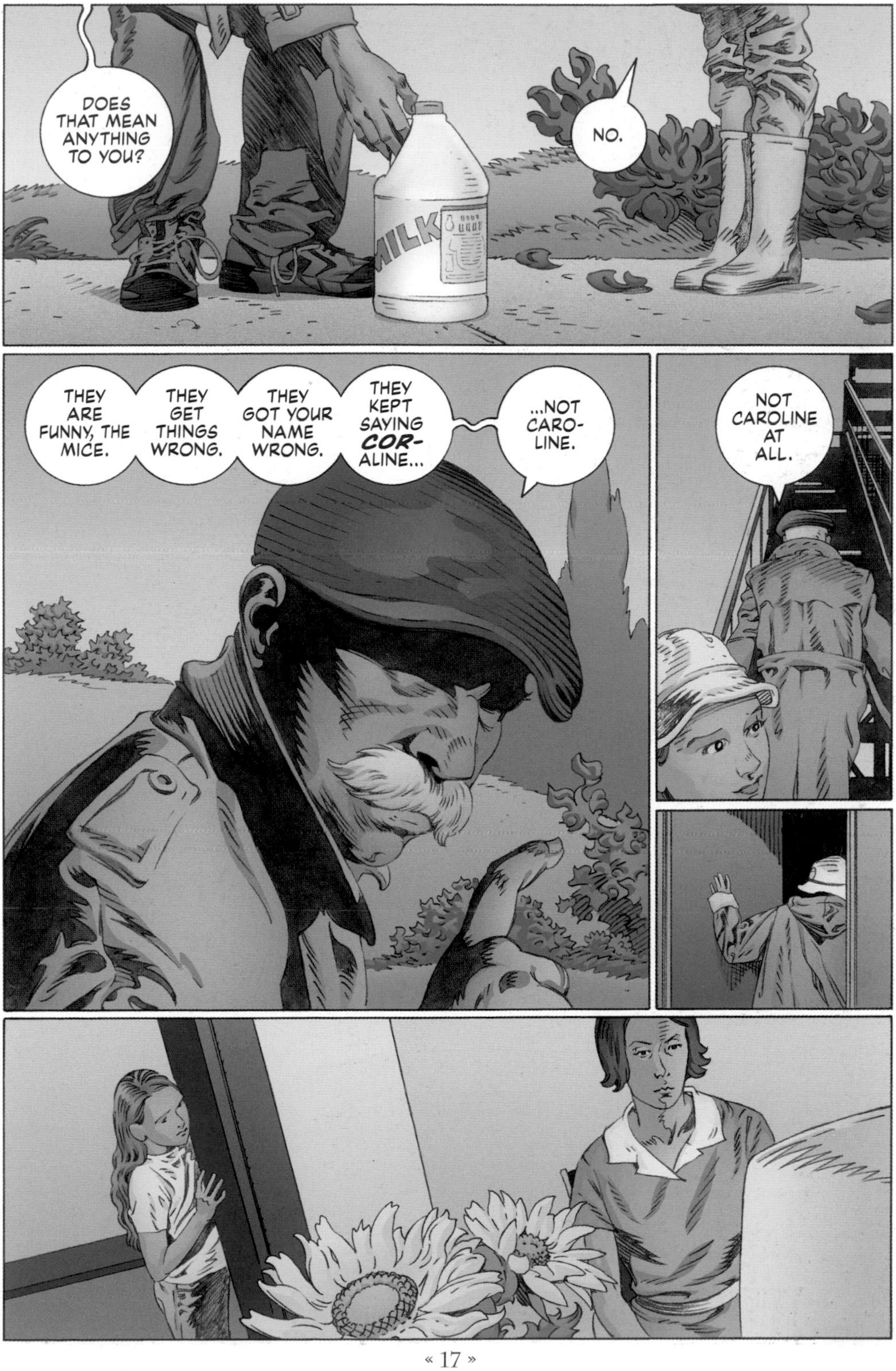
DOES THAT MEAN ANYTHING TO YOU?
NO.
THEY ARE FUNNY, THE MICE.
THEY GET THINGS WRONG.
THEY GOT YOUR NAME WRONG.
THEY KEPT SAYING *COR*-ALINE...
...NOT CARO-LINE.
NOT CAROLINE AT ALL.

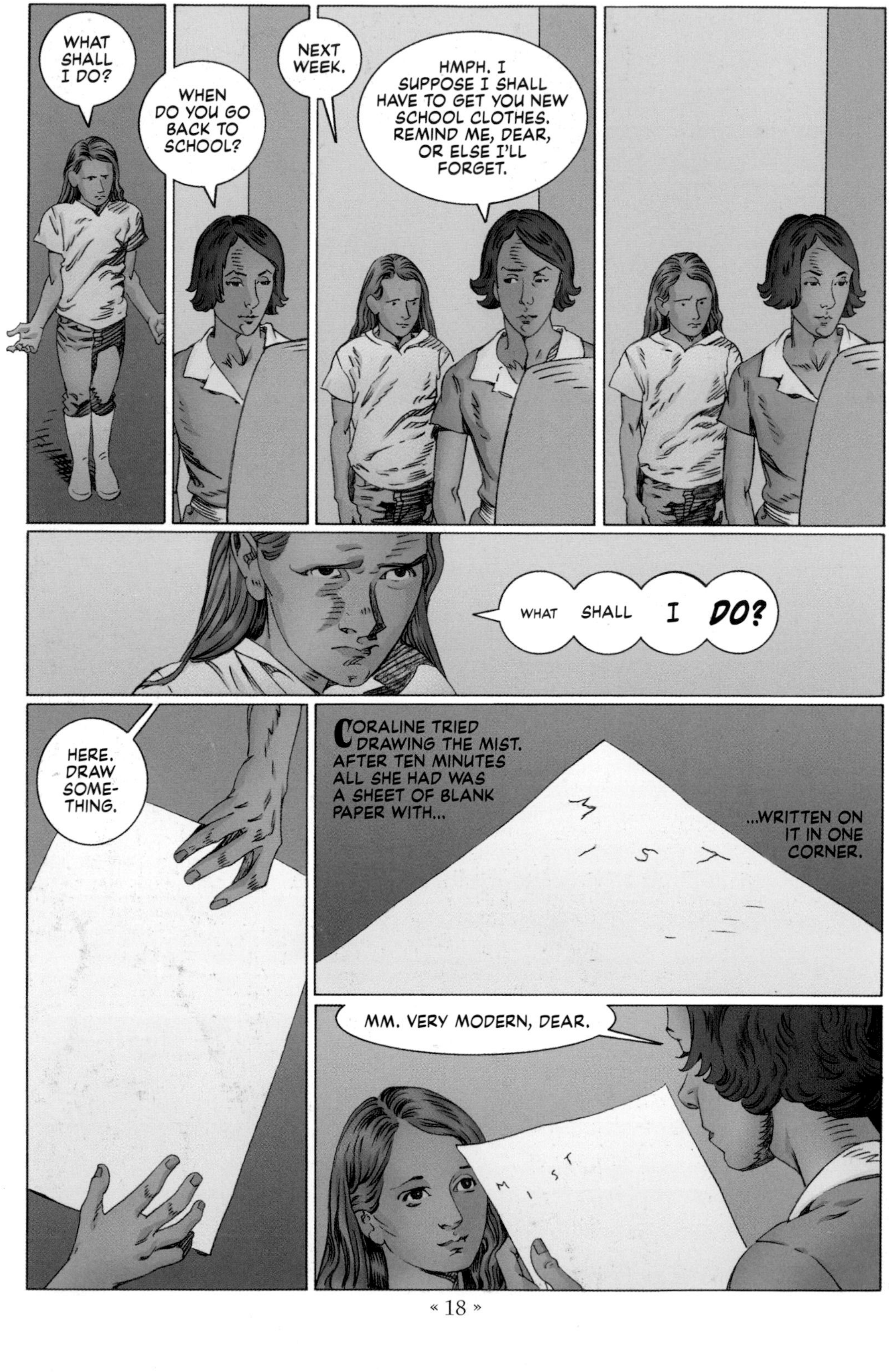
WHAT SHALL I DO?
WHEN DO YOU GO BACK TO SCHOOL?
NEXT WEEK.
HMPH. I SUPPOSE I SHALL HAVE TO GET YOU NEW SCHOOL CLOTHES. REMIND ME, DEAR, OR ELSE I'LL FORGET.
WHAT SHALL I DO?
HERE. DRAW SOME-THING.
CORALINE TRIED DRAWING THE MIST. AFTER TEN MINUTES ALL SHE HAD WAS A SHEET OF BLANK PAPER WITH...
MIST
...WRITTEN ON IT IN ONE CORNER.
MM. VERY MODERN, DEAR.
MIST

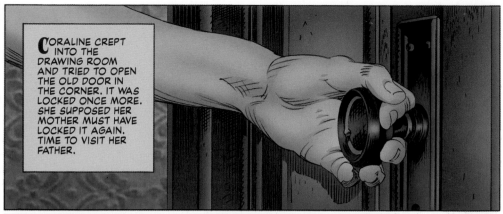

CORALINE CREPT INTO THE DRAWING ROOM AND TRIED TO OPEN THE OLD DOOR IN THE CORNER. IT WAS LOCKED ONCE MORE. SHE SUPPOSED HER MOTHER MUST HAVE LOCKED IT AGAIN. TIME TO VISIT HER FATHER.

GO AWA-AY.

I'M BORED.

LEARN HOW TO TAP DANCE.

WHY DON'T YOU PLAY WITH ME?

BUSY.

WORKING.

WHY DON'T YOU GO BOTHER MISS SPINK AND MISS FORCIBLE?

RINNNNNNG

AROOOOOOO ARKARKARKARROO

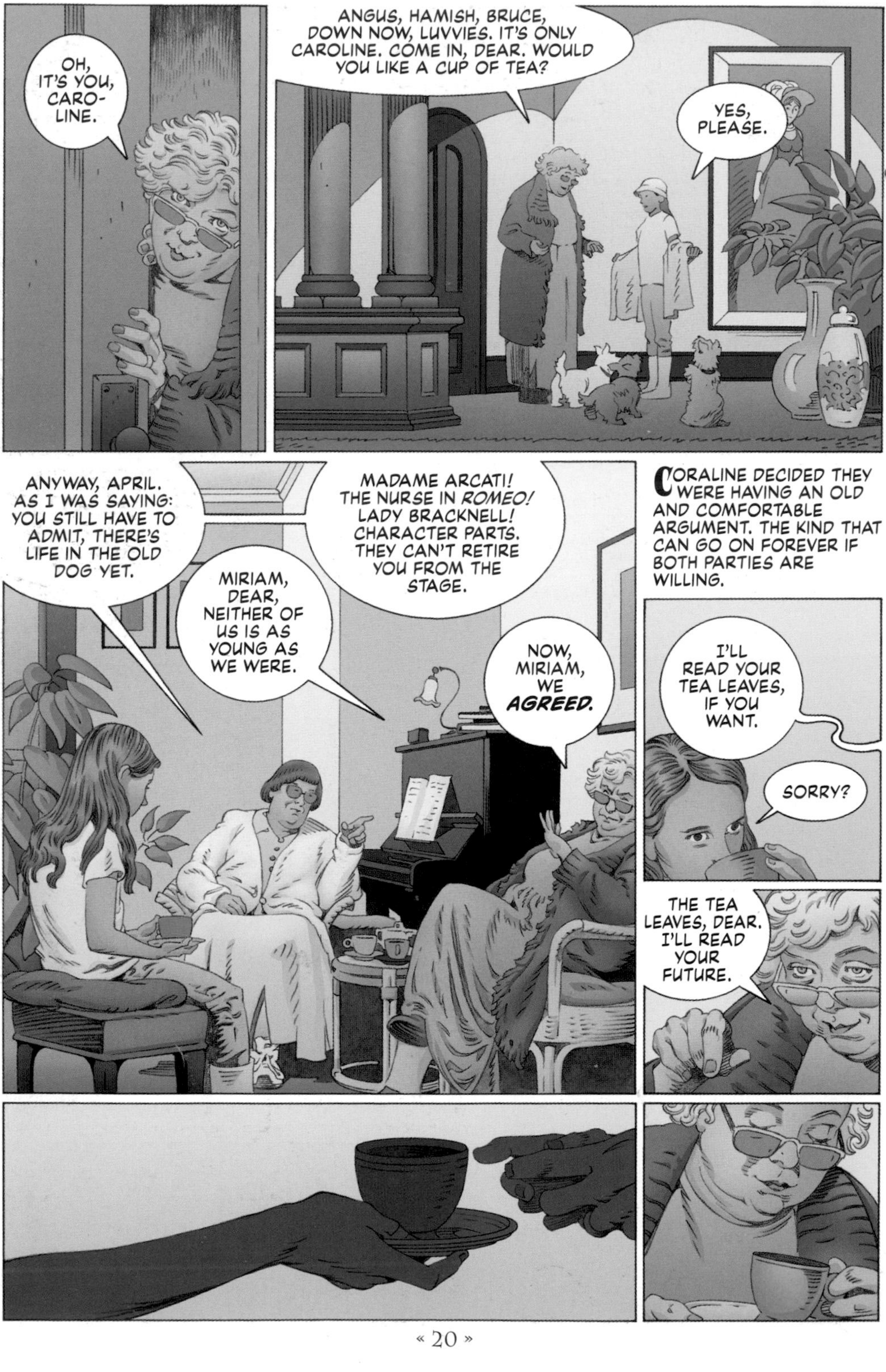
OH, IT'S YOU, CARO-LINE.
ANGUS, HAMISH, BRUCE, DOWN NOW, LUVVIES. IT'S ONLY CAROLINE. COME IN, DEAR. WOULD YOU LIKE A CUP OF TEA?
YES, PLEASE.
ANYWAY, APRIL. AS I WAS SAYING: YOU STILL HAVE TO ADMIT, THERE'S LIFE IN THE OLD DOG YET.
MIRIAM, DEAR, NEITHER OF US IS AS YOUNG AS WE WERE.
MADAME ARCATI! THE NURSE IN *ROMEO!* LADY BRACKNELL! CHARACTER PARTS. THEY CAN'T RETIRE YOU FROM THE STAGE.
NOW, MIRIAM, WE ***AGREED.***
CORALINE DECIDED THEY WERE HAVING AN OLD AND COMFORTABLE ARGUMENT. THE KIND THAT CAN GO ON FOREVER IF BOTH PARTIES ARE WILLING.
I'LL READ YOUR TEA LEAVES, IF YOU WANT.
SORRY?
THE TEA LEAVES, DEAR. I'LL READ YOUR FUTURE.

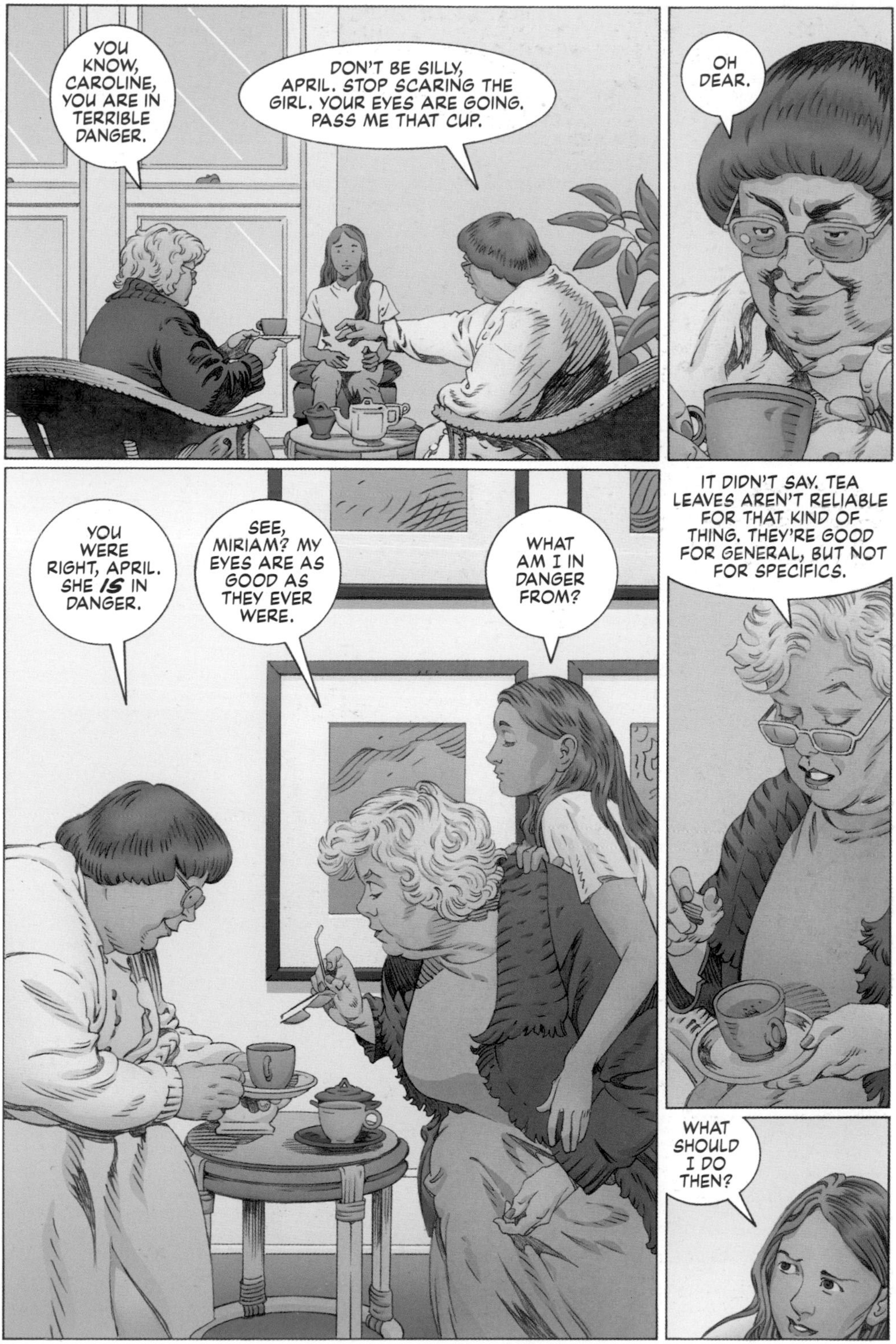
YOU KNOW, CAROLINE, YOU ARE IN TERRIBLE DANGER.
DON'T BE SILLY, APRIL. STOP SCARING THE GIRL. YOUR EYES ARE GOING. PASS ME THAT CUP.
OH DEAR.
YOU WERE RIGHT, APRIL. SHE *IS* IN DANGER.
SEE, MIRIAM? MY EYES ARE AS GOOD AS THEY EVER WERE.
WHAT AM I IN DANGER FROM?
IT DIDN'T SAY. TEA LEAVES AREN'T RELIABLE FOR THAT KIND OF THING. THEY'RE GOOD FOR GENERAL, BUT NOT FOR SPECIFICS.
WHAT SHOULD I DO THEN?

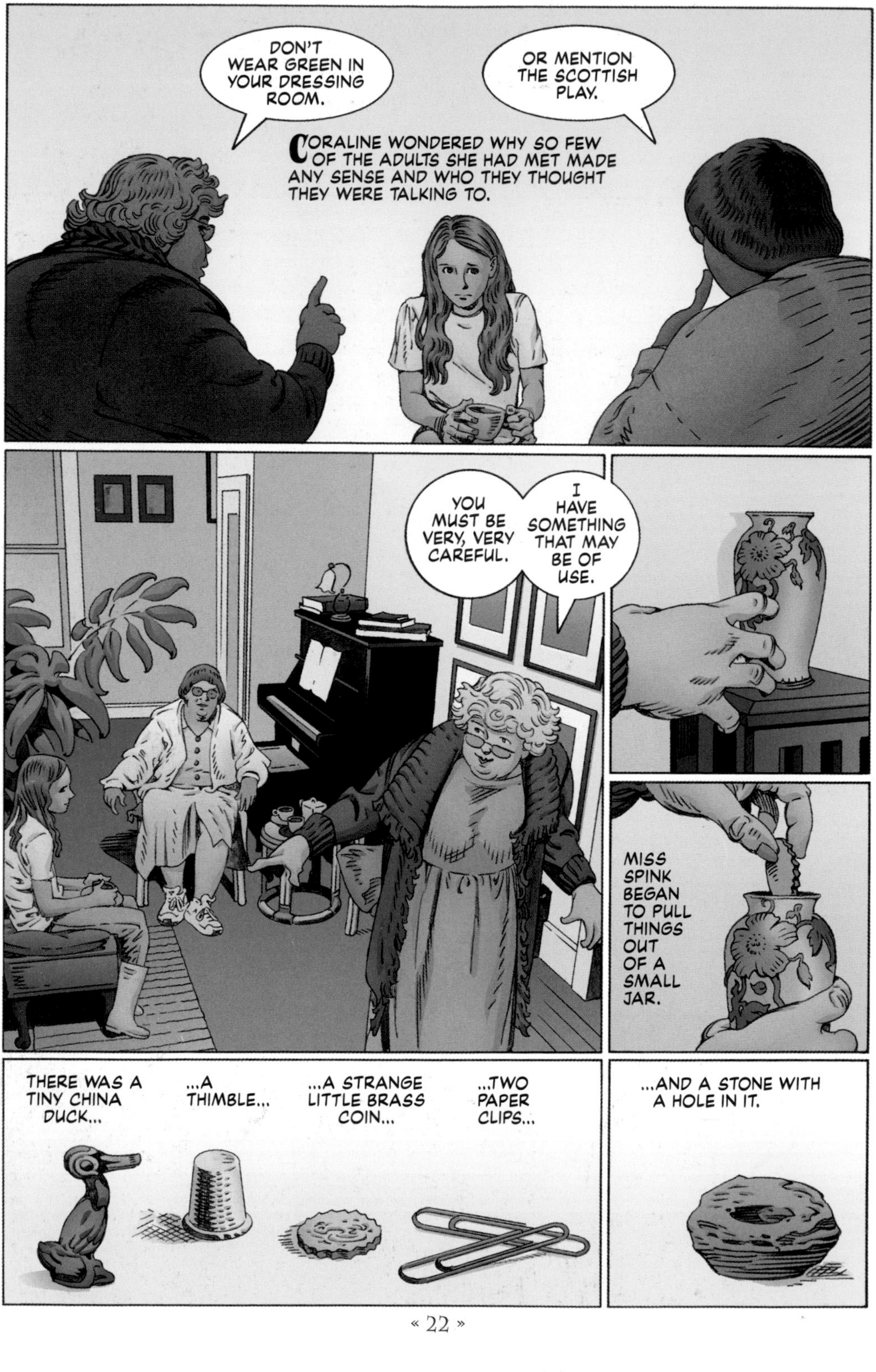
DON'T WEAR GREEN IN YOUR DRESSING ROOM.
OR MENTION THE SCOTTISH PLAY.
CORALINE WONDERED WHY SO FEW OF THE ADULTS SHE HAD MET MADE ANY SENSE AND WHO THEY THOUGHT THEY WERE TALKING TO.
YOU MUST BE VERY, VERY CAREFUL.
I HAVE SOMETHING THAT MAY BE OF USE.
MISS SPINK BEGAN TO PULL THINGS OUT OF A SMALL JAR.
THERE WAS A TINY CHINA DUCK...
...A THIMBLE...
...A STRANGE LITTLE BRASS COIN...
...TWO PAPER CLIPS...
...AND A STONE WITH A HOLE IN IT.

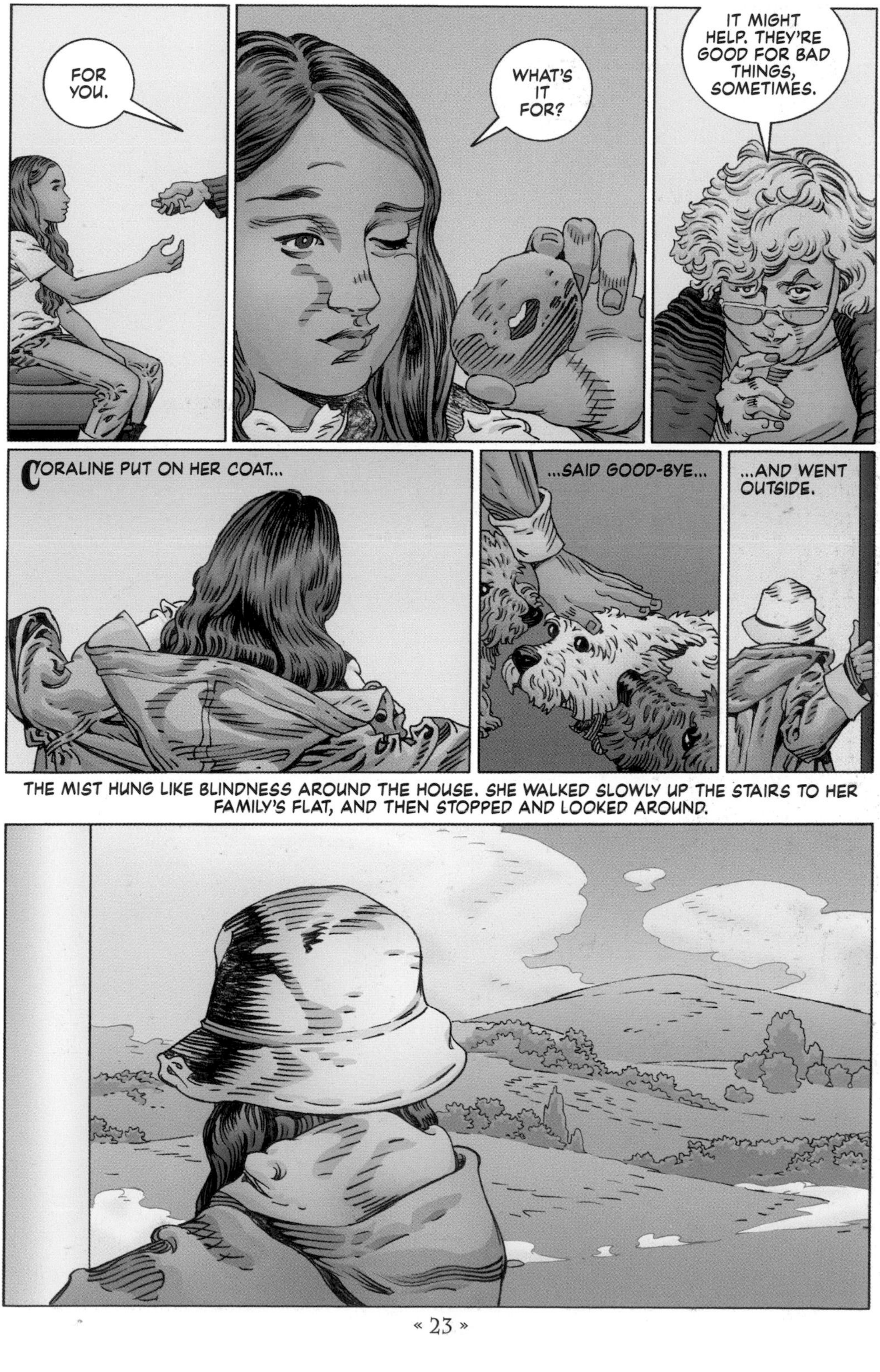
FOR YOU.
WHAT'S IT FOR?
IT MIGHT HELP. THEY'RE GOOD FOR BAD THINGS, SOMETIMES.
CORALINE PUT ON HER COAT...
...SAID GOOD-BYE...
...AND WENT OUTSIDE.
THE MIST HUNG LIKE BLINDNESS AROUND THE HOUSE. SHE WALKED SLOWLY UP THE STAIRS TO HER FAMILY'S FLAT, AND THEN STOPPED AND LOOKED AROUND.

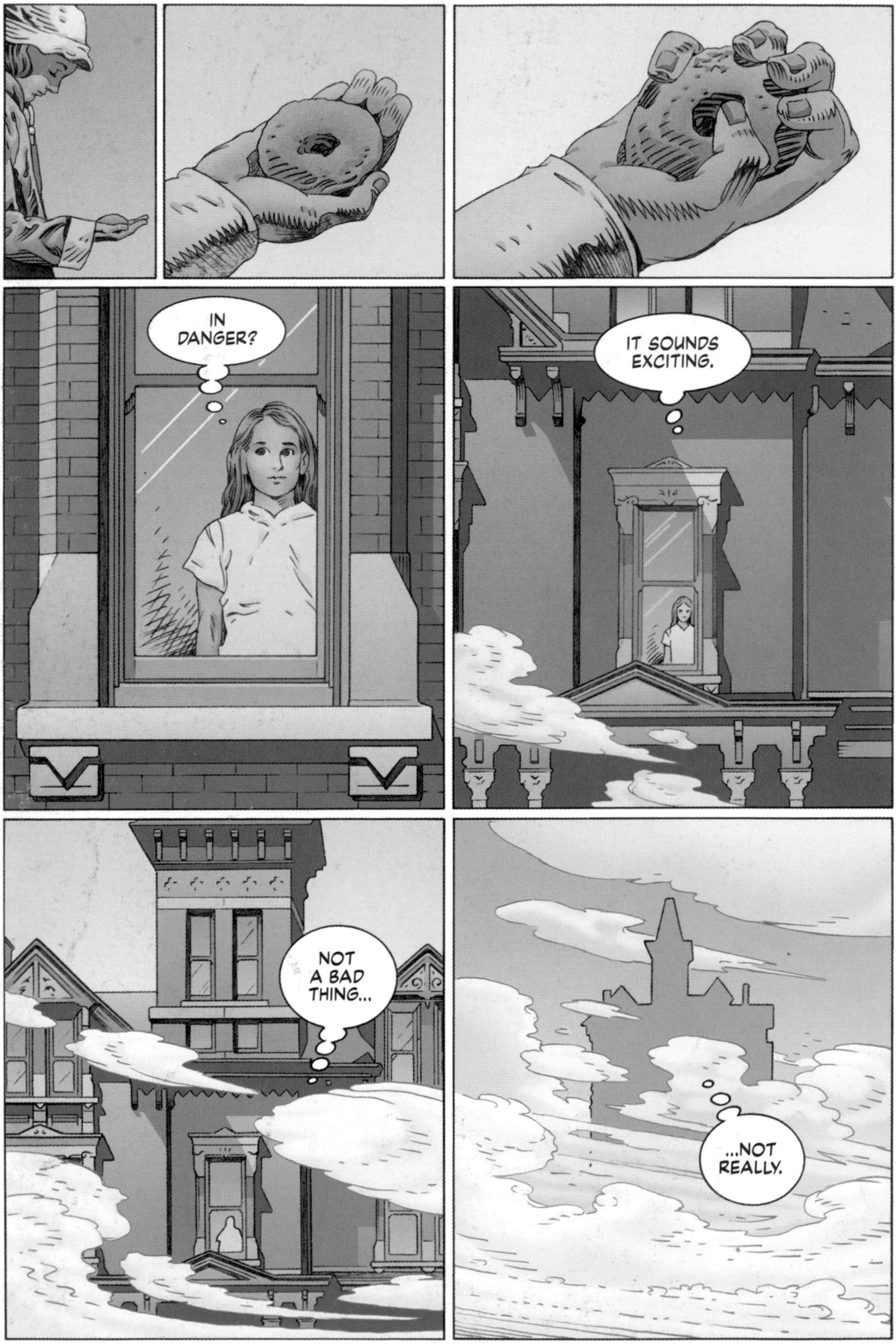
IN DANGER?
IT SOUNDS EXCITING.
NOT A BAD THING...
...NOT REALLY.

3

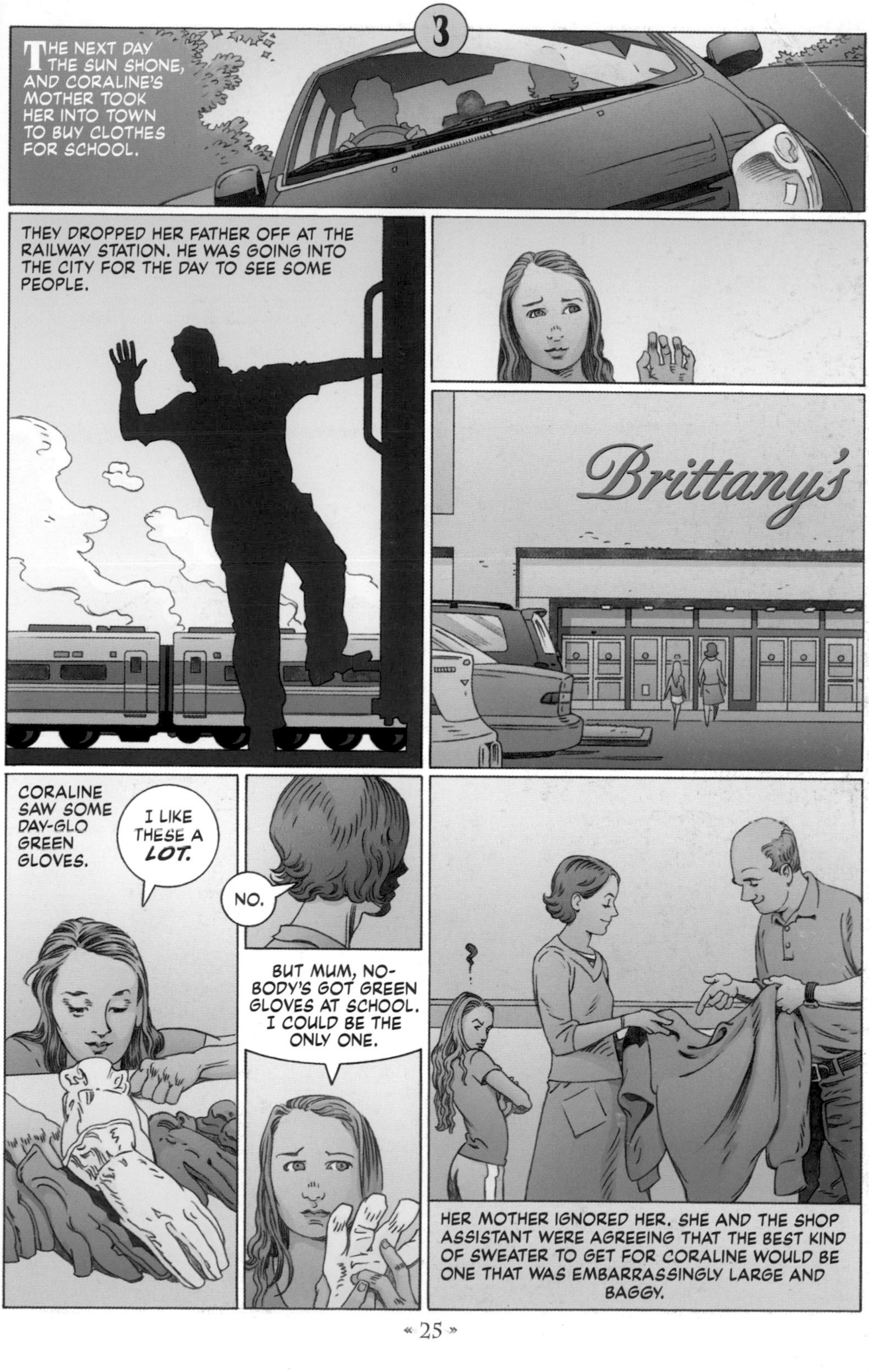
THE NEXT DAY THE SUN SHONE, AND CORALINE'S MOTHER TOOK HER INTO TOWN TO BUY CLOTHES FOR SCHOOL.
THEY DROPPED HER FATHER OFF AT THE RAILWAY STATION. HE WAS GOING INTO THE CITY FOR THE DAY TO SEE SOME PEOPLE.
Brittany's
CORALINE SAW SOME DAY-GLO GREEN GLOVES.
I LIKE THESE A *LOT.*
NO.
BUT MUM, NOBODY'S GOT GREEN GLOVES AT SCHOOL. I COULD BE THE ONLY ONE.
HER MOTHER IGNORED HER. SHE AND THE SHOP ASSISTANT WERE AGREEING THAT THE BEST KIND OF SWEATER TO GET FOR CORALINE WOULD BE ONE THAT WAS EMBARRASSINGLY LARGE AND BAGGY.

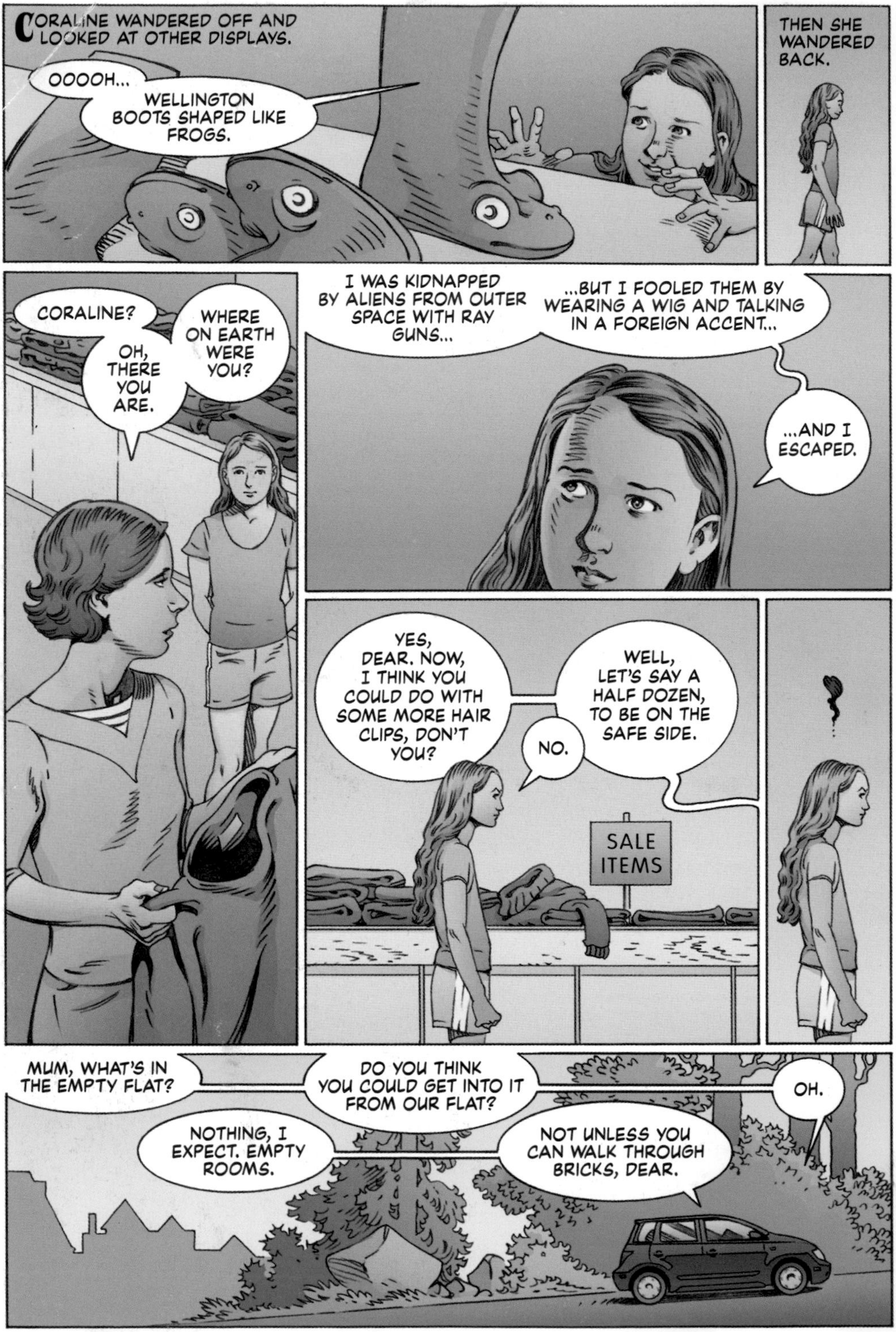
CORALINE WANDERED OFF AND LOOKED AT OTHER DISPLAYS.
OOOOH...
WELLINGTON BOOTS SHAPED LIKE FROGS.
THEN SHE WANDERED BACK.
CORALINE?
OH, THERE YOU ARE.
WHERE ON EARTH WERE YOU?
I WAS KIDNAPPED BY ALIENS FROM OUTER SPACE WITH RAY GUNS...
...BUT I FOOLED THEM BY WEARING A WIG AND TALKING IN A FOREIGN ACCENT...
...AND I ESCAPED.
YES, DEAR. NOW, I THINK YOU COULD DO WITH SOME MORE HAIR CLIPS, DON'T YOU?
NO.
WELL, LET'S SAY A HALF DOZEN, TO BE ON THE SAFE SIDE.
SALE ITEMS
MUM, WHAT'S IN THE EMPTY FLAT?
NOTHING, I EXPECT. EMPTY ROOMS.
DO YOU THINK YOU COULD GET INTO IT FROM OUR FLAT?
NOT UNLESS YOU CAN WALK THROUGH BRICKS, DEAR.
OH.

THEY GOT HOME AROUND LUNCHTIME. IN THE FRIDGE WERE ONLY A SAD LITTLE TOMATO AND A PIECE OF CHEESE WITH GREEN STUFF GROWING ON IT.

I'D BETTER DASH DOWN TO THE SHOPS TO GET SOME FISH FINGERS OR SOMETHING. DO YOU WANT TO COME?

NO.

SUIT YOUR-SELF.

THEN SHE WENT OUT AGAIN.

CORALINE WAS BORED.

PEOPLE IN DISTANT COUNTRIES

SHE FLIPPED THROUGH A BOOK ABOUT PEOPLE IN A DISTANT COUNTRY; HOW EVERY DAY THEY WOULD TAKE PIECES OF WHITE SILK AND DRAW ON THEM IN WAX, THEN DIP THE SILKS IN DYE, AND THEN FINALLY THROW THE NOW BEAUTIFUL CLOTHES IN A FIRE AND BURN THEM TO ASHES.

IT SEEMED POINTLESS TO CORALINE, BUT SHE HOPED THE PEOPLE ENJOYED IT.

SHE WAS *STILL* BORED.

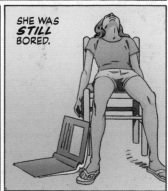

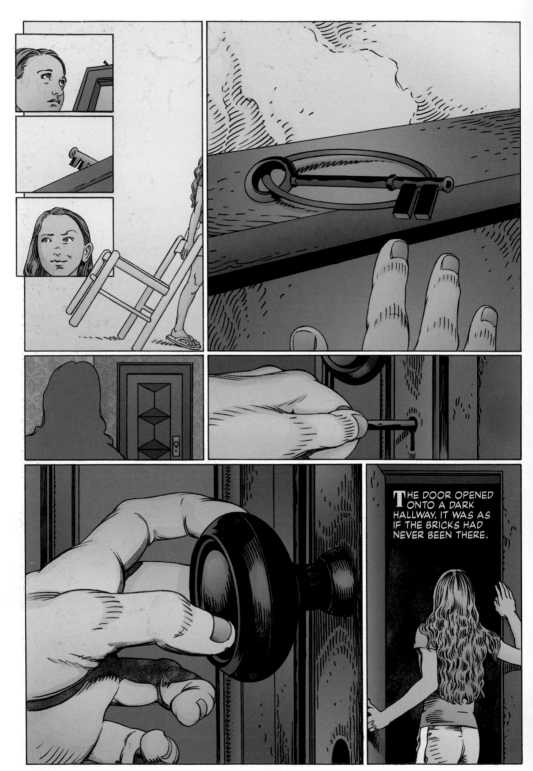

THE DOOR OPENED ONTO A DARK HALLWAY. IT WAS AS IF THE BRICKS HAD NEVER BEEN THERE.

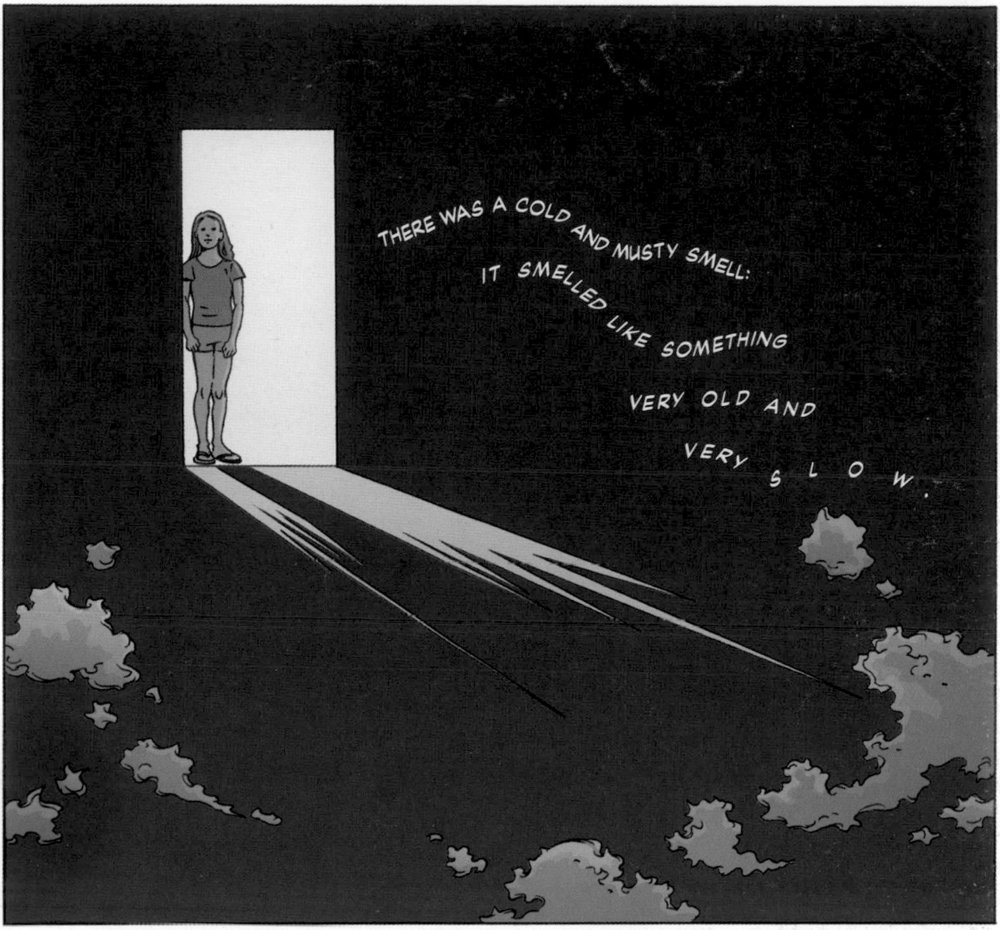
THERE WAS A COLD AND MUSTY SMELL:
IT SMELLED LIKE SOMETHING
VERY OLD AND
VERY S L O W.

CORALINE WENT THROUGH THE DOOR.

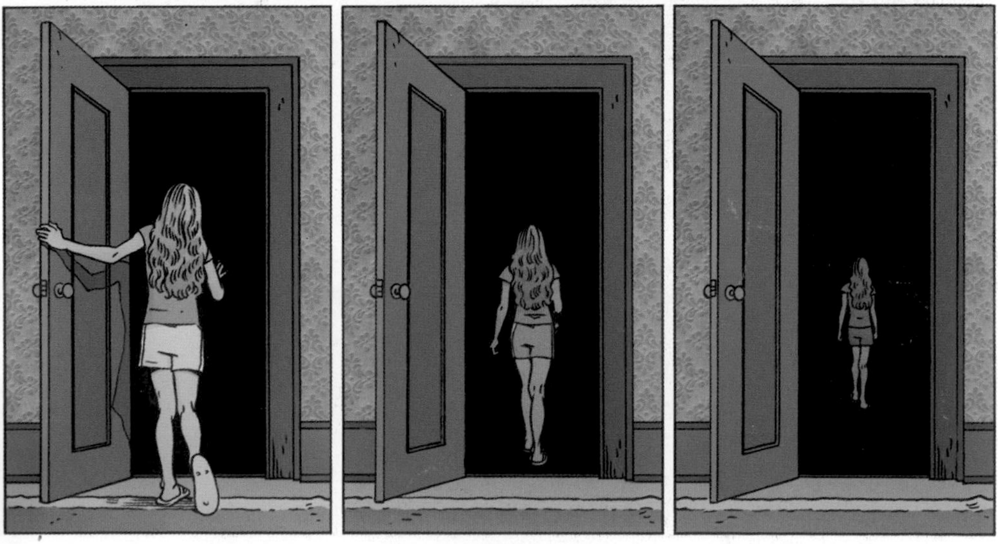

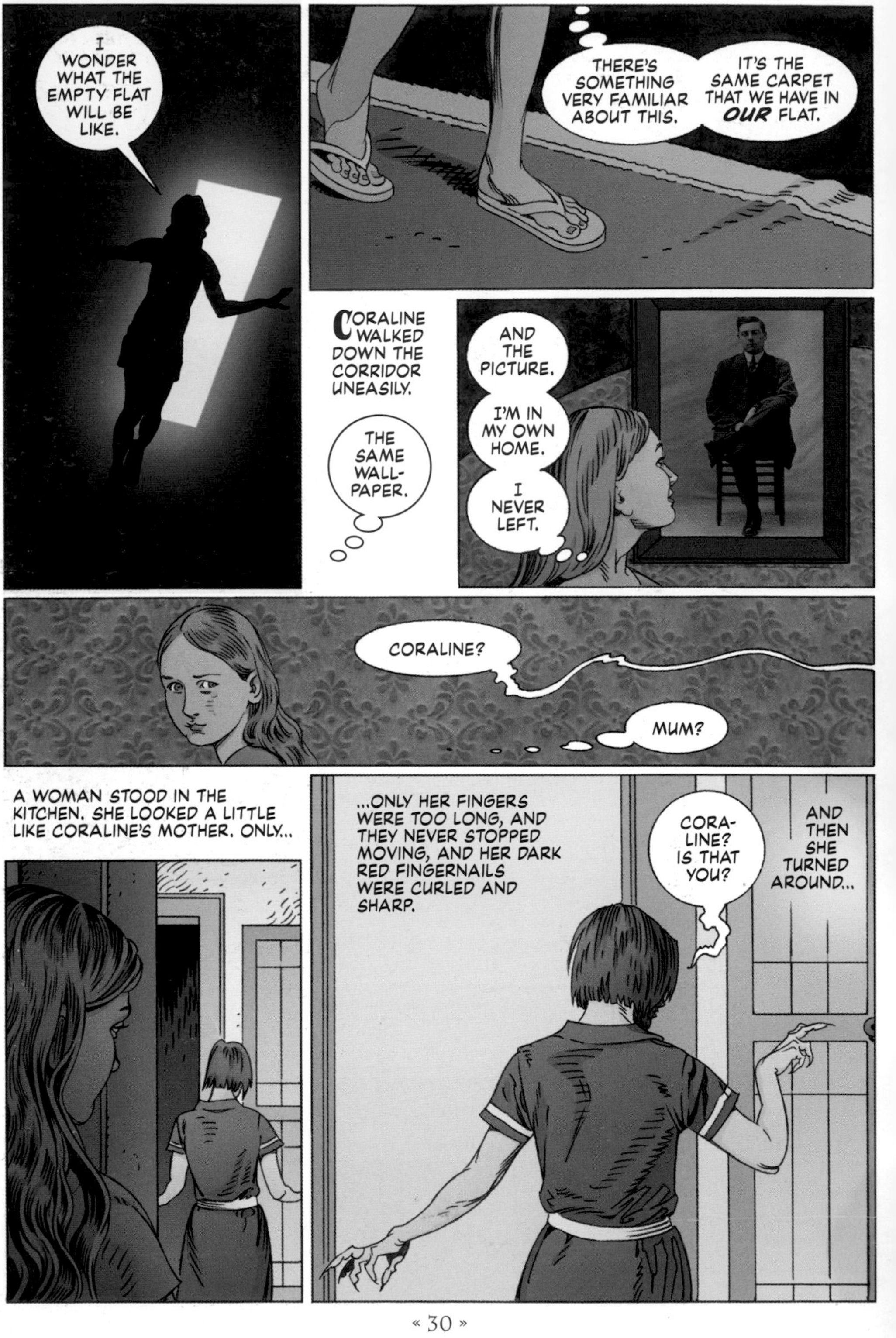
I WONDER WHAT THE EMPTY FLAT WILL BE LIKE.
THERE'S SOMETHING VERY FAMILIAR ABOUT THIS.
IT'S THE SAME CARPET THAT WE HAVE IN OUR FLAT.
CORALINE WALKED DOWN THE CORRIDOR UNEASILY.
THE SAME WALL-PAPER.
AND THE PICTURE.
I'M IN MY OWN HOME.
I NEVER LEFT.
CORALINE?
MUM?
A WOMAN STOOD IN THE KITCHEN. SHE LOOKED A LITTLE LIKE CORALINE'S MOTHER. ONLY...
...ONLY HER FINGERS WERE TOO LONG, AND THEY NEVER STOPPED MOVING, AND HER DARK RED FINGERNAILS WERE CURLED AND SHARP.
CORA-LINE? IS THAT YOU?
AND THEN SHE TURNED AROUND...

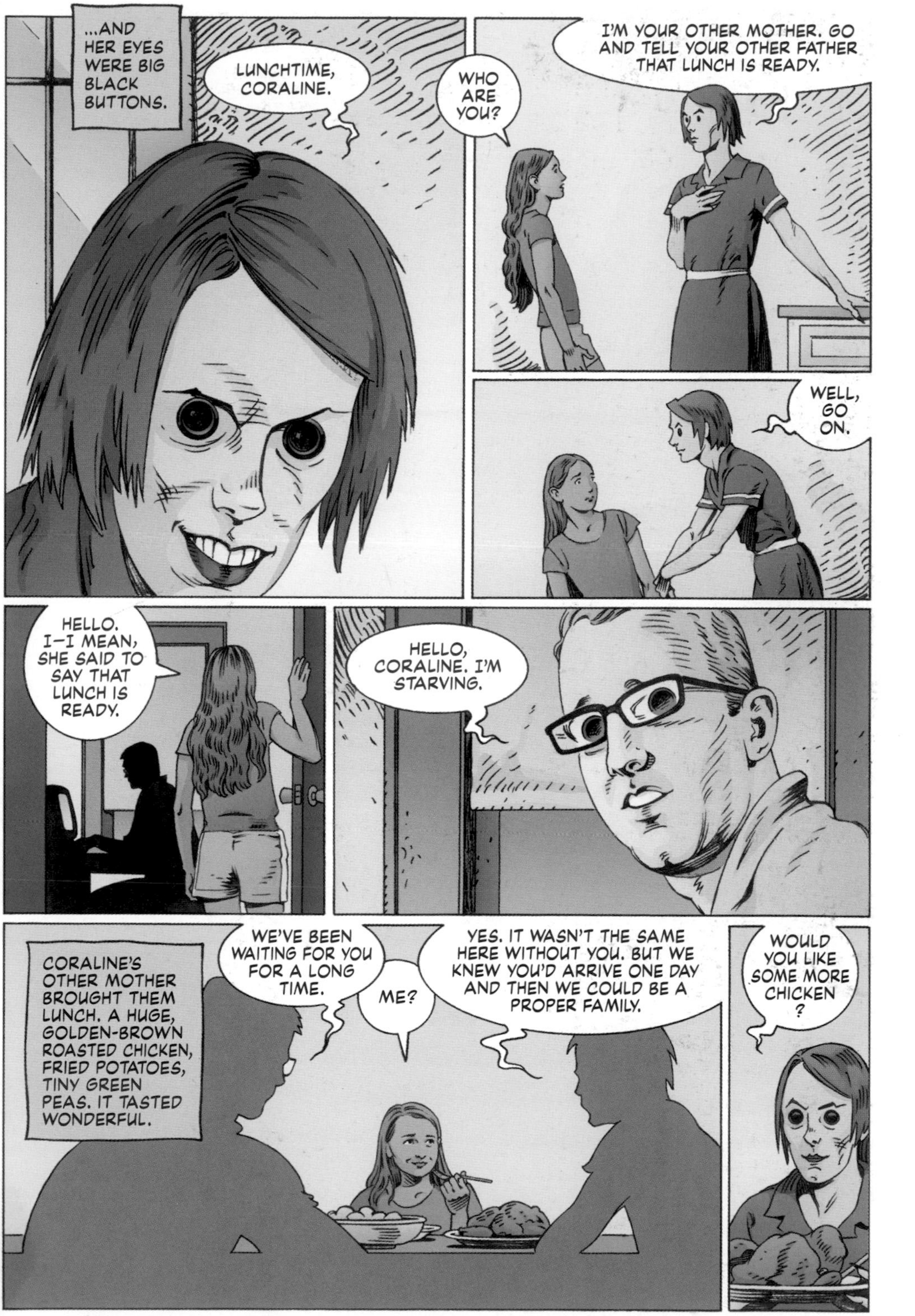
...AND HER EYES WERE BIG BLACK BUTTONS.
LUNCHTIME, CORALINE.
WHO ARE YOU?
I'M YOUR OTHER MOTHER. GO AND TELL YOUR OTHER FATHER THAT LUNCH IS READY.
WELL, GO ON.
HELLO. I—I MEAN, SHE SAID TO SAY THAT LUNCH IS READY.
HELLO, CORALINE. I'M STARVING.
CORALINE'S OTHER MOTHER BROUGHT THEM LUNCH. A HUGE, GOLDEN-BROWN ROASTED CHICKEN, FRIED POTATOES, TINY GREEN PEAS. IT TASTED WONDERFUL.
WE'VE BEEN WAITING FOR YOU FOR A LONG TIME.
ME?
YES. IT WASN'T THE SAME HERE WITHOUT YOU. BUT WE KNEW YOU'D ARRIVE ONE DAY AND THEN WE COULD BE A PROPER FAMILY.
WOULD YOU LIKE SOME MORE CHICKEN ?

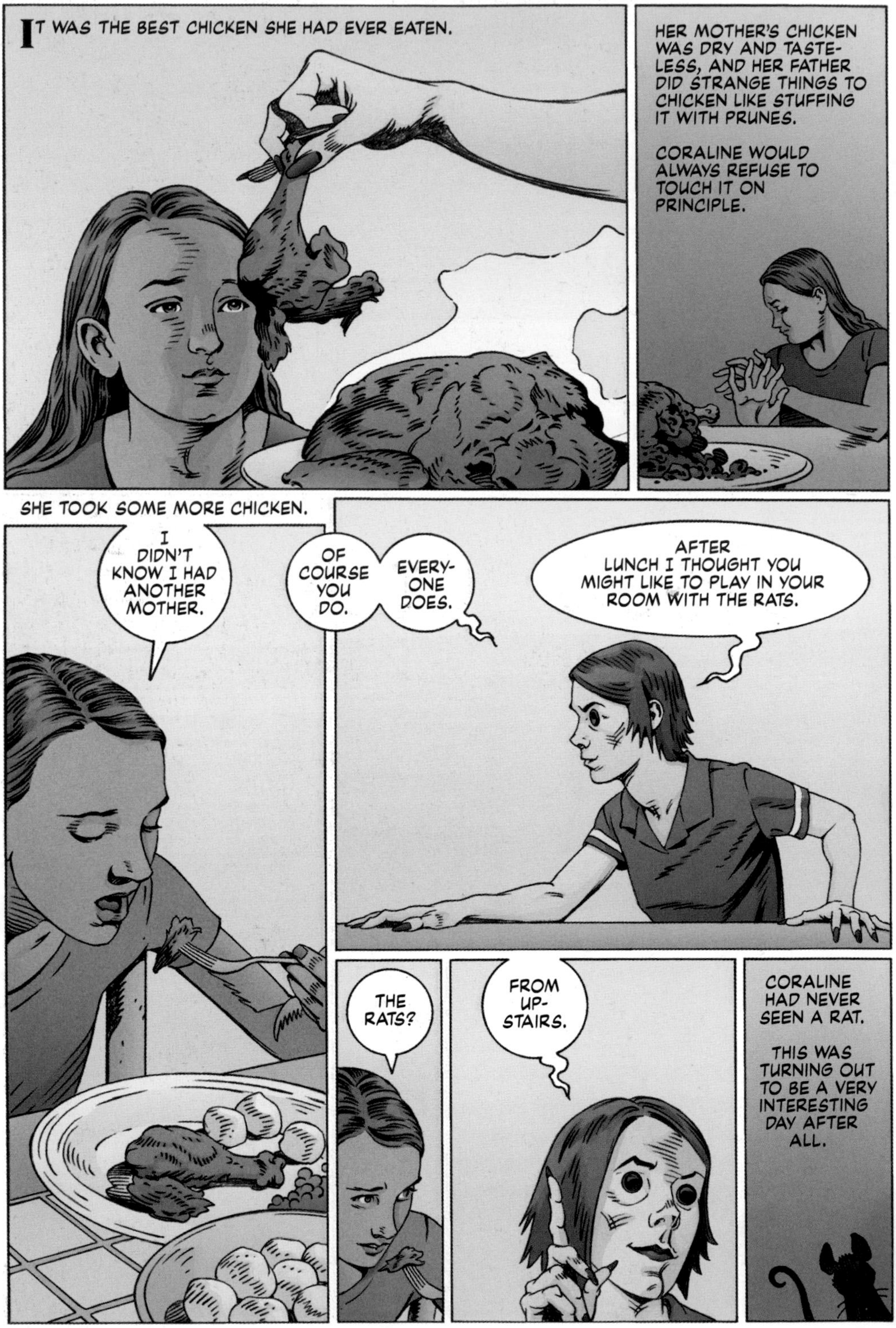
IT WAS THE BEST CHICKEN SHE HAD EVER EATEN.
HER MOTHER'S CHICKEN WAS DRY AND TASTELESS, AND HER FATHER DID STRANGE THINGS TO CHICKEN LIKE STUFFING IT WITH PRUNES.
CORALINE WOULD ALWAYS REFUSE TO TOUCH IT ON PRINCIPLE.
SHE TOOK SOME MORE CHICKEN.
I DIDN'T KNOW I HAD ANOTHER MOTHER.
OF COURSE YOU DO.
EVERYONE DOES.
AFTER LUNCH I THOUGHT YOU MIGHT LIKE TO PLAY IN YOUR ROOM WITH THE RATS.
THE RATS?
FROM UPSTAIRS.
CORALINE HAD NEVER SEEN A RAT.
THIS WAS TURNING OUT TO BE A VERY INTERESTING DAY AFTER ALL.

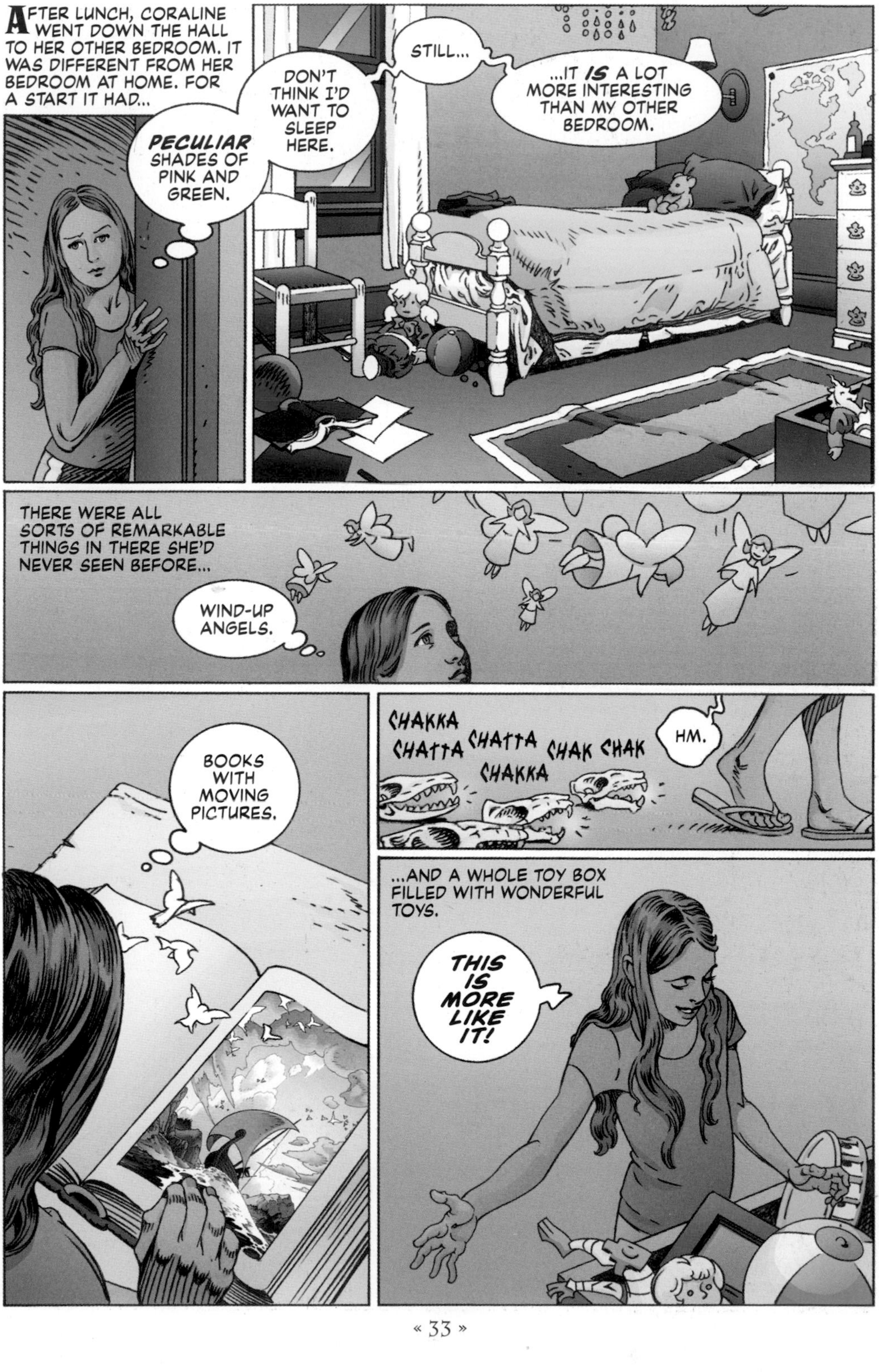
AFTER LUNCH, CORALINE WENT DOWN THE HALL TO HER OTHER BEDROOM. IT WAS DIFFERENT FROM HER BEDROOM AT HOME. FOR A START IT HAD...
PECULIAR SHADES OF PINK AND GREEN.
DON'T THINK I'D WANT TO SLEEP HERE.
STILL...
...IT IS A LOT MORE INTERESTING THAN MY OTHER BEDROOM.
THERE WERE ALL SORTS OF REMARKABLE THINGS IN THERE SHE'D NEVER SEEN BEFORE...
WIND-UP ANGELS.
BOOKS WITH MOVING PICTURES.
CHAKKA CHATTA CHATTA CHAKKA CHAK CHAK
HM.
...AND A WHOLE TOY BOX FILLED WITH WONDERFUL TOYS.
THIS IS MORE LIKE IT!

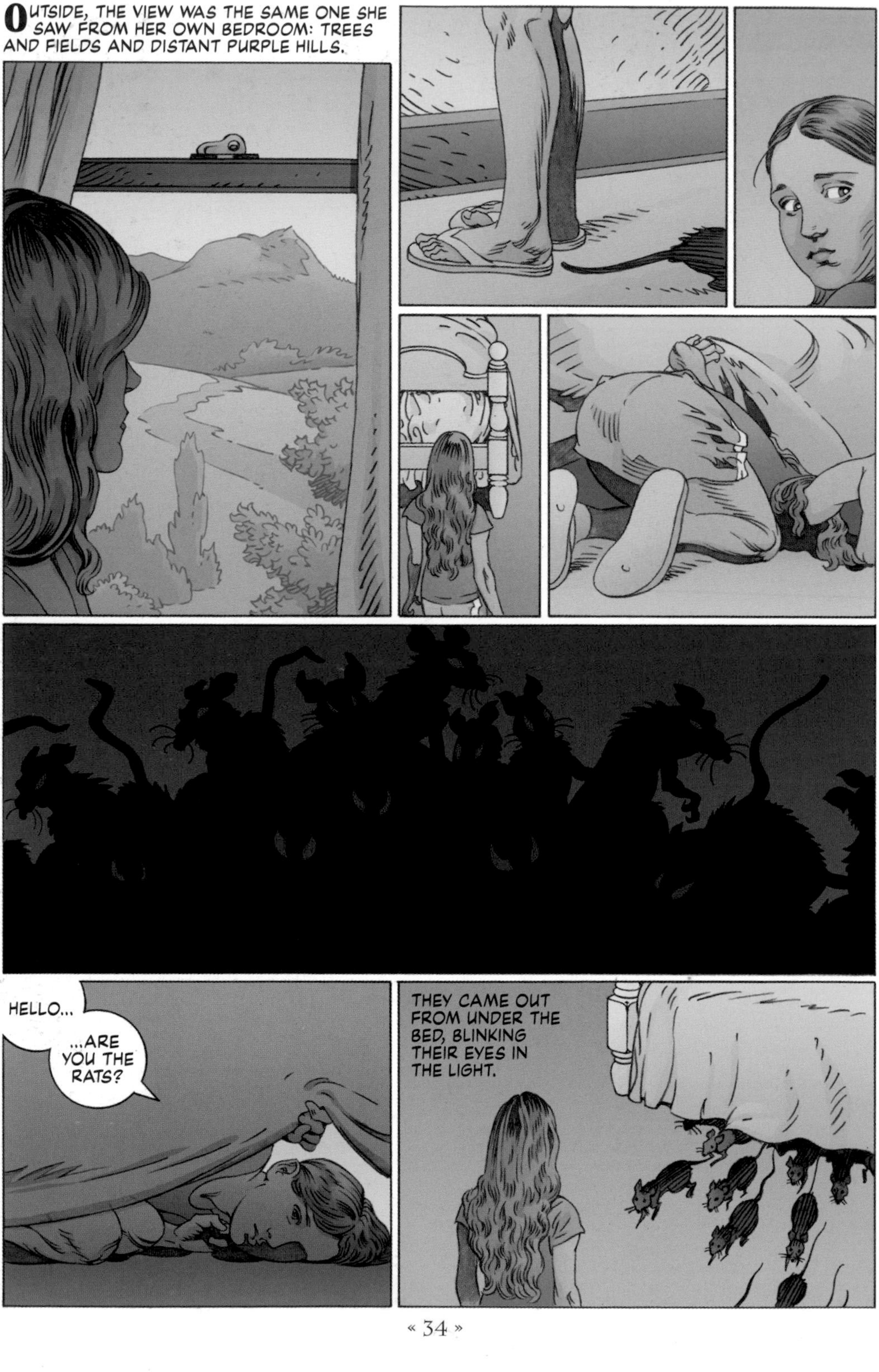
OUTSIDE, THE VIEW WAS THE SAME ONE SHE SAW FROM HER OWN BEDROOM: TREES AND FIELDS AND DISTANT PURPLE HILLS.
HELLO...
...ARE YOU THE RATS?
THEY CAME OUT FROM UNDER THE BED, BLINKING THEIR EYES IN THE LIGHT.

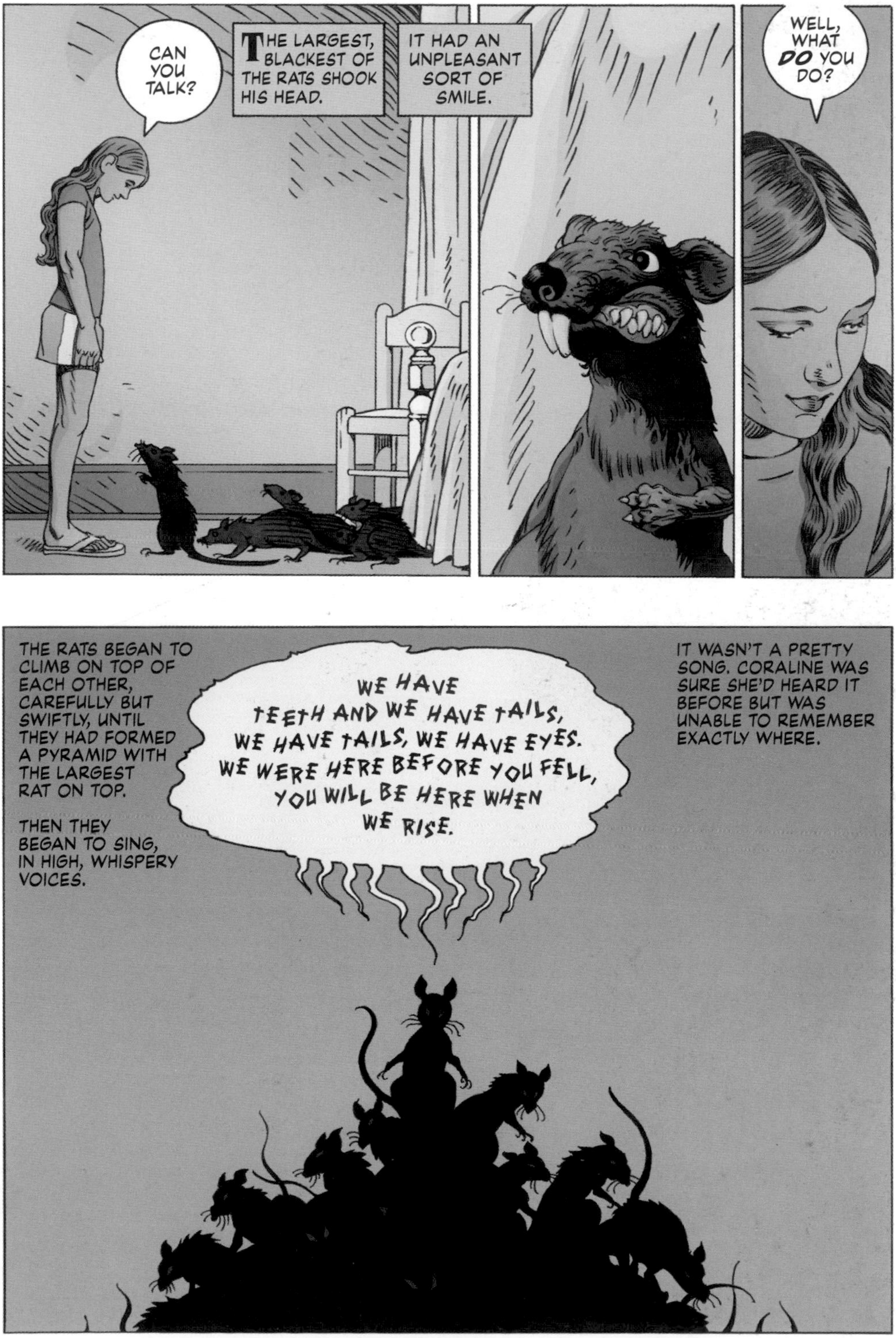
CAN YOU TALK?
THE LARGEST, BLACKEST OF THE RATS SHOOK HIS HEAD.
IT HAD AN UNPLEASANT SORT OF SMILE.
WELL, WHAT DO YOU DO?
THE RATS BEGAN TO CLIMB ON TOP OF EACH OTHER, CAREFULLY BUT SWIFTLY, UNTIL THEY HAD FORMED A PYRAMID WITH THE LARGEST RAT ON TOP.
THEN THEY BEGAN TO SING, IN HIGH, WHISPERY VOICES.
WE HAVE TEETH AND WE HAVE TAILS, WE HAVE TAILS, WE HAVE EYES. WE WERE HERE BEFORE YOU FELL, YOU WILL BE HERE WHEN WE RISE.
IT WASN'T A PRETTY SONG. CORALINE WAS SURE SHE'D HEARD IT BEFORE BUT WAS UNABLE TO REMEMBER EXACTLY WHERE.

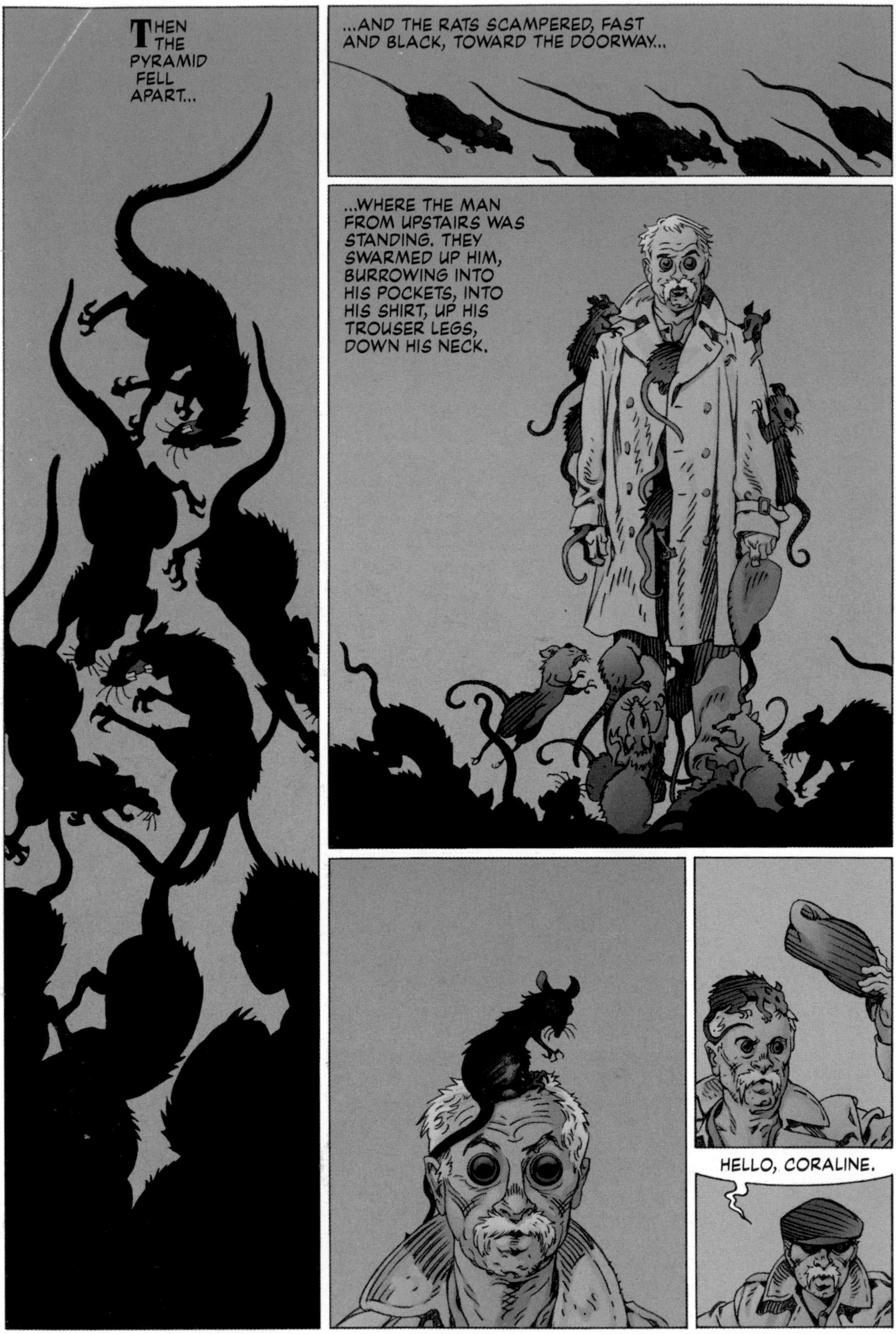
THEN THE PYRAMID FELL APART...
...AND THE RATS SCAMPERED, FAST AND BLACK, TOWARD THE DOORWAY...
...WHERE THE MAN FROM UPSTAIRS WAS STANDING. THEY SWARMED UP HIM, BURROWING INTO HIS POCKETS, INTO HIS SHIRT, UP HIS TROUSER LEGS, DOWN HIS NECK.
HELLO, CORALINE.

I HEARD YOU WERE HERE. IT IS TIME FOR THE RATS TO HAVE THEIR DINNER. BUT YOU CAN COME UP WITH ME IF YOU LIKE, AND WATCH THEM FEED.

THERE WAS SOMETHING HUNGRY IN THE OLD MAN'S BUTTON EYES THAT MADE CORALINE FEEL UNCOMFORTABLE.

NO, THANK YOU. I'M GOING OUTSIDE TO EXPLORE.

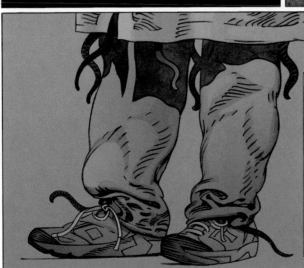

CORALINE COULD HEAR THE RATS WHISPERING TO EACH OTHER. SHE WAS NOT CERTAIN THAT SHE WANTED TO KNOW WHAT THEY WERE SAYING.

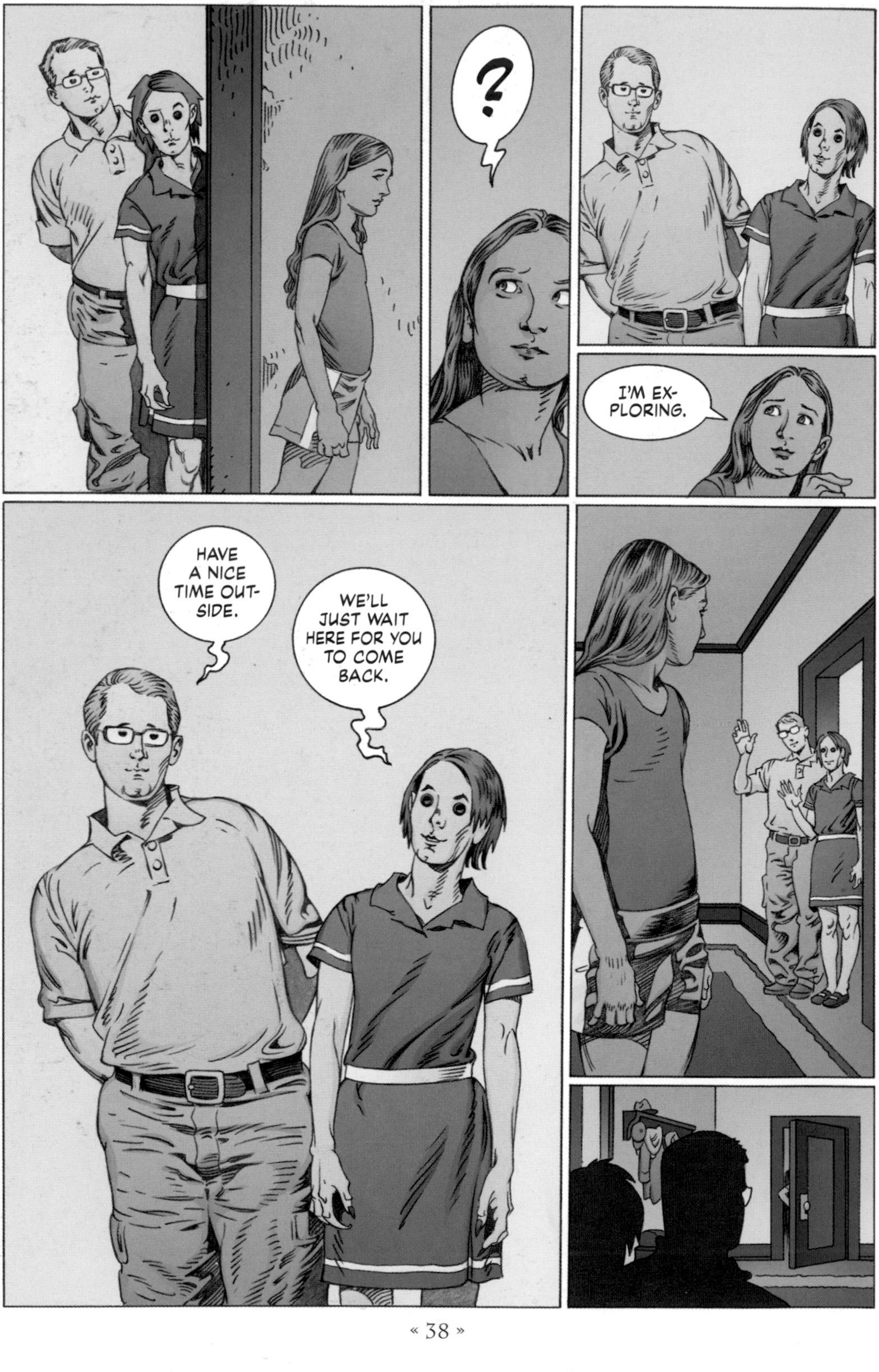
?
I'M EX-PLORING.
HAVE A NICE TIME OUT-SIDE.
WE'LL JUST WAIT HERE FOR YOU TO COME BACK.

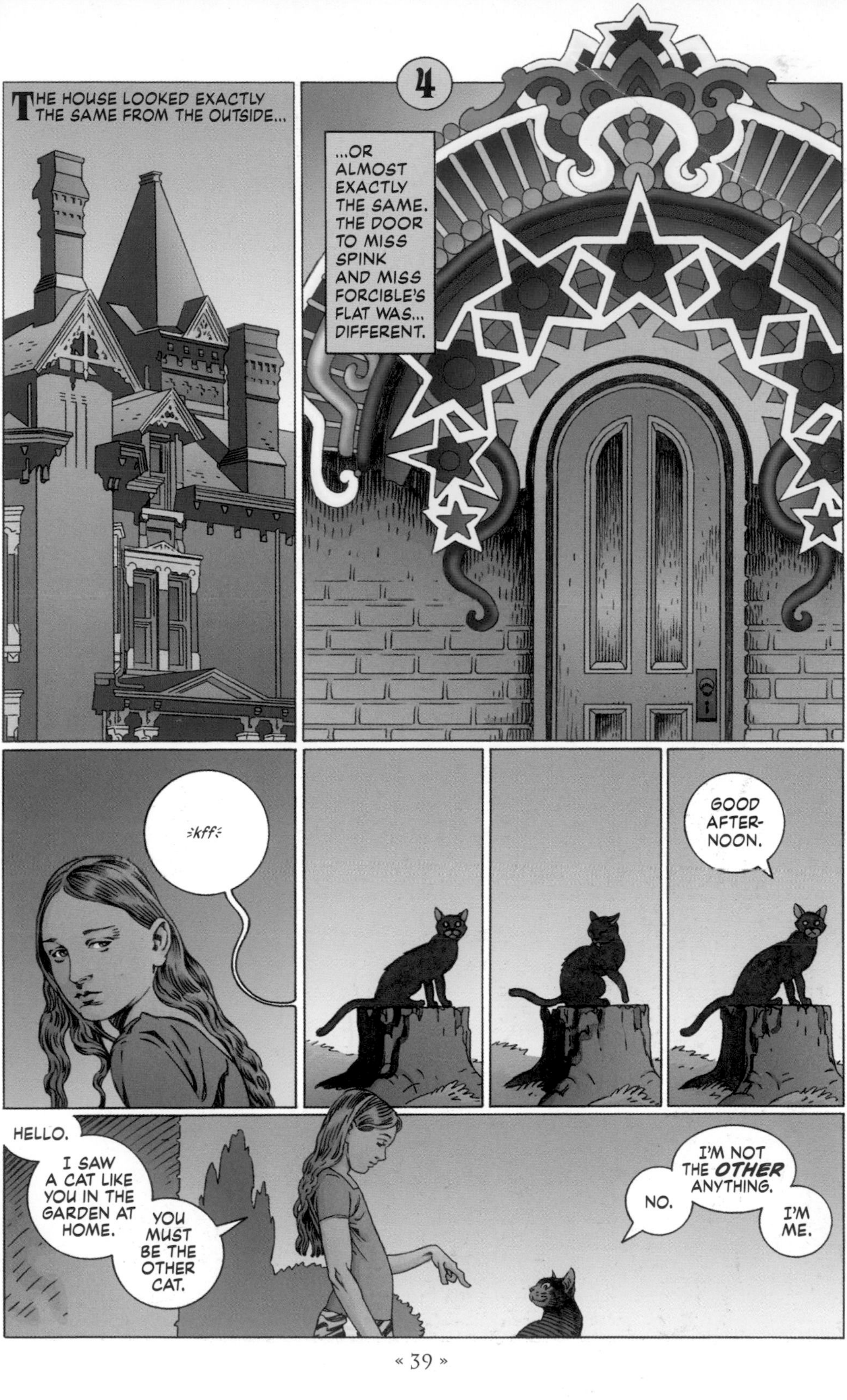
THE HOUSE LOOKED EXACTLY THE SAME FROM THE OUTSIDE...
4
...OR ALMOST EXACTLY THE SAME. THE DOOR TO MISS SPINK AND MISS FORCIBLE'S FLAT WAS... DIFFERENT.
kff
GOOD AFTER-NOON.
HELLO.
I SAW A CAT LIKE YOU IN THE GARDEN AT HOME.
YOU MUST BE THE OTHER CAT.
NO.
I'M NOT THE OTHER ANYTHING.
I'M ME.

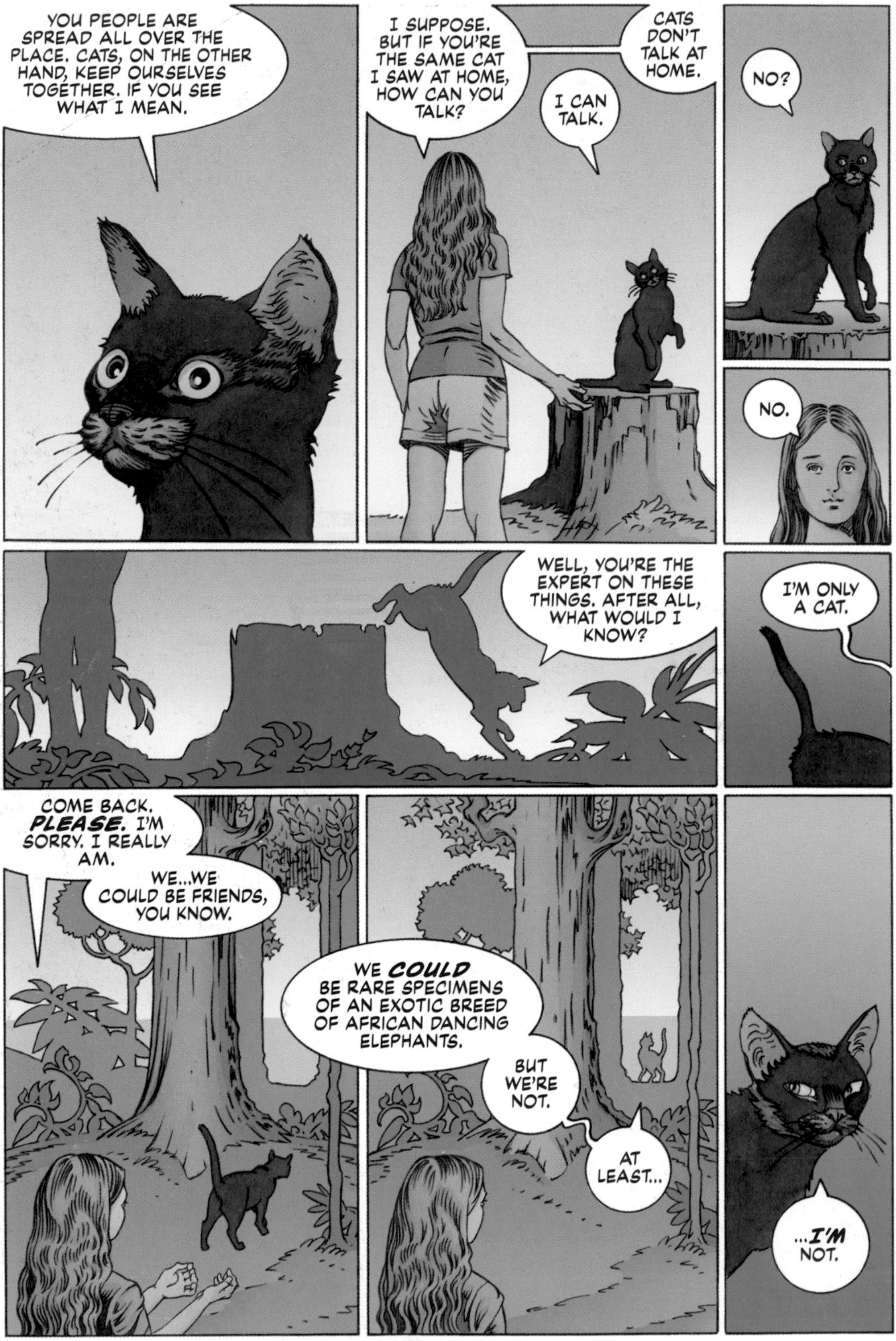
YOU PEOPLE ARE SPREAD ALL OVER THE PLACE. CATS, ON THE OTHER HAND, KEEP OURSELVES TOGETHER. IF YOU SEE WHAT I MEAN.
I SUPPOSE. BUT IF YOU'RE THE SAME CAT I SAW AT HOME, HOW CAN YOU TALK?
CATS DON'T TALK AT HOME.
I CAN TALK.
NO?
NO.
WELL, YOU'RE THE EXPERT ON THESE THINGS. AFTER ALL, WHAT WOULD I KNOW?
I'M ONLY A CAT.
COME BACK. PLEASE. I'M SORRY. I REALLY AM.
WE...WE COULD BE FRIENDS, YOU KNOW.
WE COULD BE RARE SPECIMENS OF AN EXOTIC BREED OF AFRICAN DANCING ELEPHANTS.
BUT WE'RE NOT.
AT LEAST...
...I'M NOT.

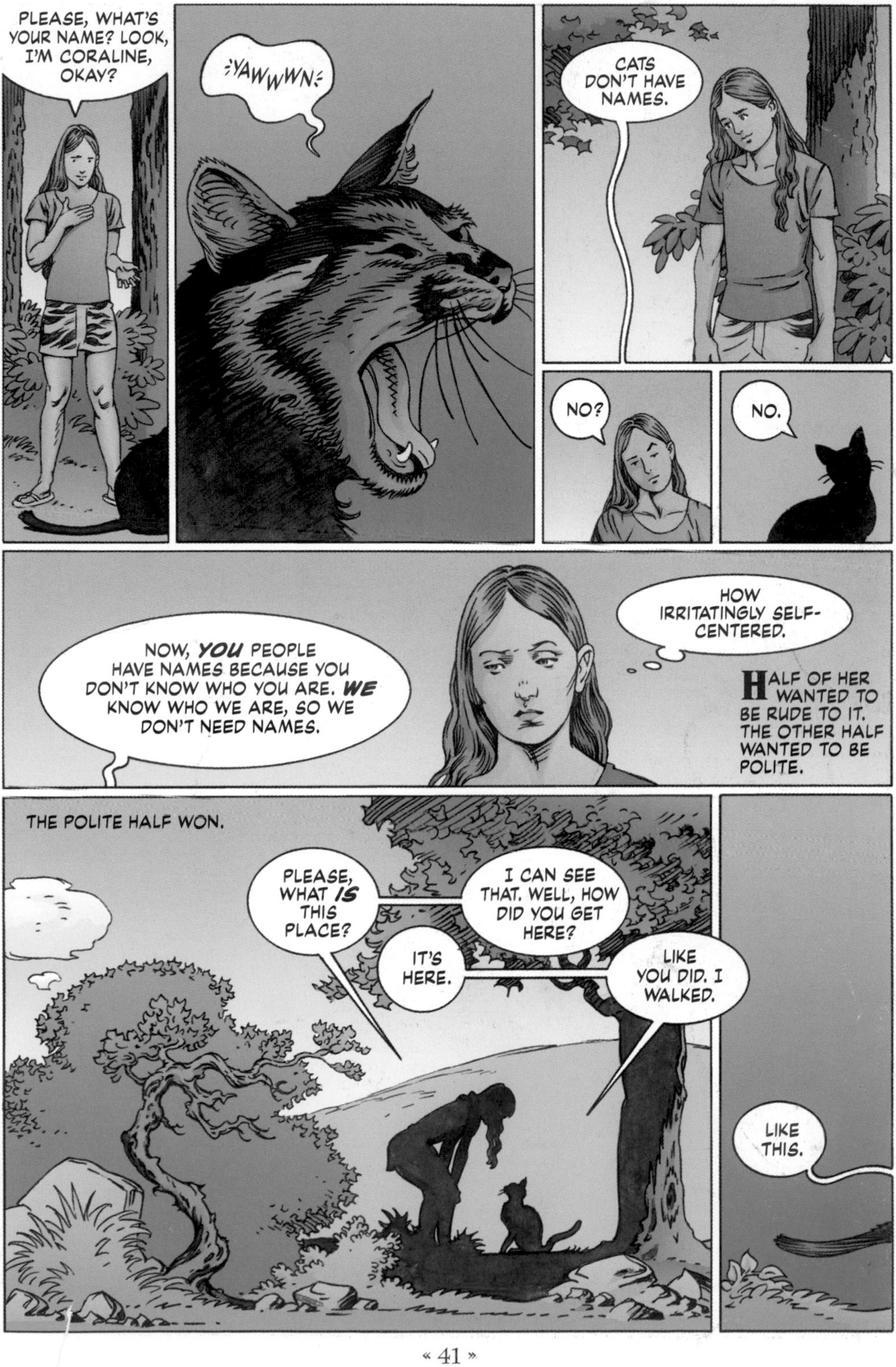
PLEASE, WHAT'S YOUR NAME? LOOK, I'M CORALINE, OKAY?
YAWWWN
CATS DON'T HAVE NAMES.
NO?
NO.
NOW, YOU PEOPLE HAVE NAMES BECAUSE YOU DON'T KNOW WHO YOU ARE. WE KNOW WHO WE ARE, SO WE DON'T NEED NAMES.
HOW IRRITATINGLY SELF-CENTERED.
HALF OF HER WANTED TO BE RUDE TO IT. THE OTHER HALF WANTED TO BE POLITE.
THE POLITE HALF WON.
PLEASE, WHAT IS THIS PLACE?
IT'S HERE.
I CAN SEE THAT. WELL, HOW DID YOU GET HERE?
LIKE YOU DID. I WALKED.
LIKE THIS.

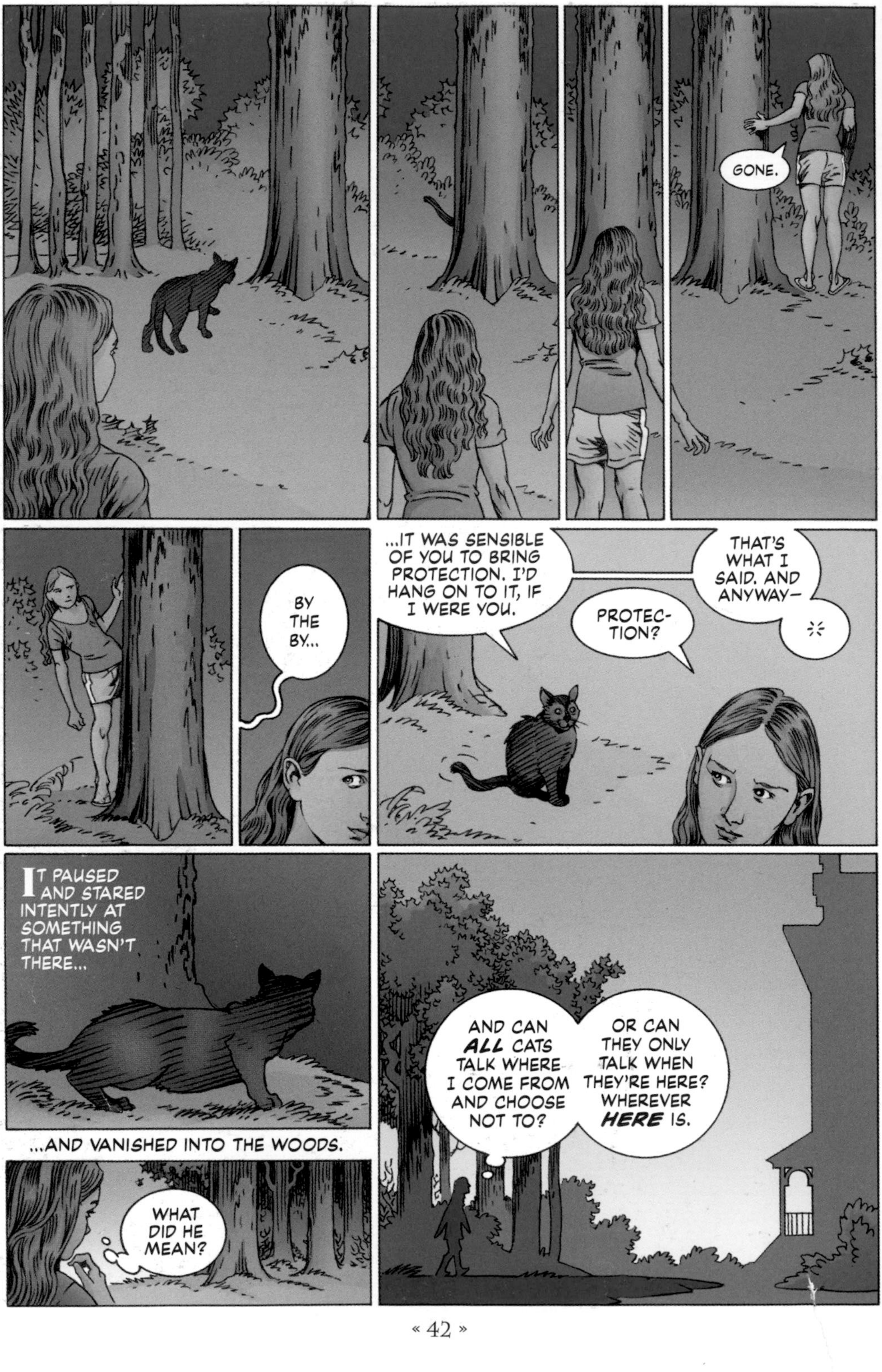
GONE.
BY THE BY...
...IT WAS SENSIBLE OF YOU TO BRING PROTECTION. I'D HANG ON TO IT, IF I WERE YOU.
PROTECTION?
THAT'S WHAT I SAID. AND ANYWAY—
IT PAUSED AND STARED INTENTLY AT SOMETHING THAT WASN'T THERE...
...AND VANISHED INTO THE WOODS.
WHAT DID HE MEAN?
AND CAN ALL CATS TALK WHERE I COME FROM AND CHOOSE NOT TO?
OR CAN THEY ONLY TALK WHEN THEY'RE HERE? WHEREVER HERE IS.

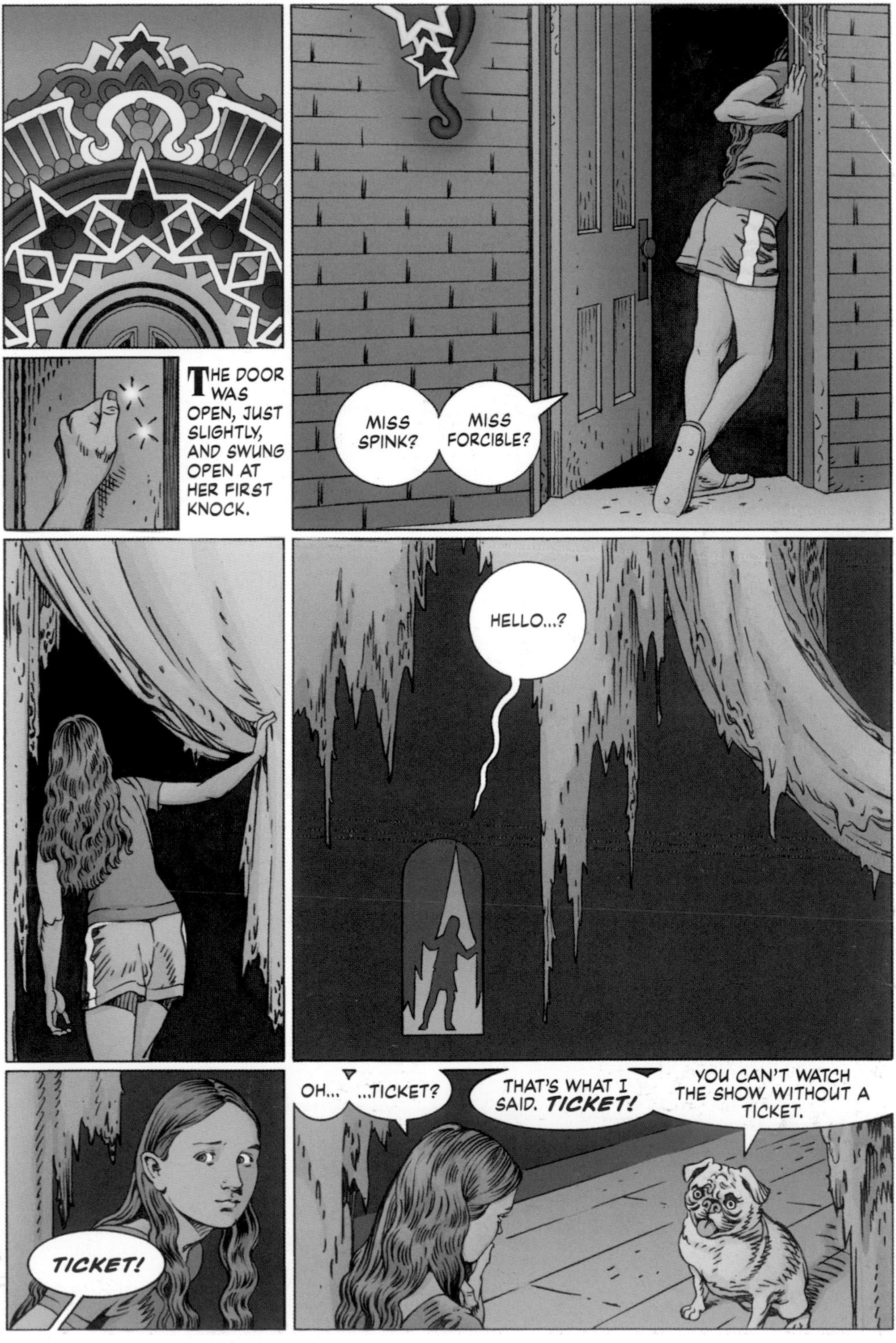
THE DOOR WAS OPEN, JUST SLIGHTLY, AND SWUNG OPEN AT HER FIRST KNOCK.
MISS SPINK?
MISS FORCIBLE?
HELLO...?
TICKET!
OH...
...TICKET?
THAT'S WHAT I SAID. TICKET!
YOU CAN'T WATCH THE SHOW WITHOUT A TICKET.

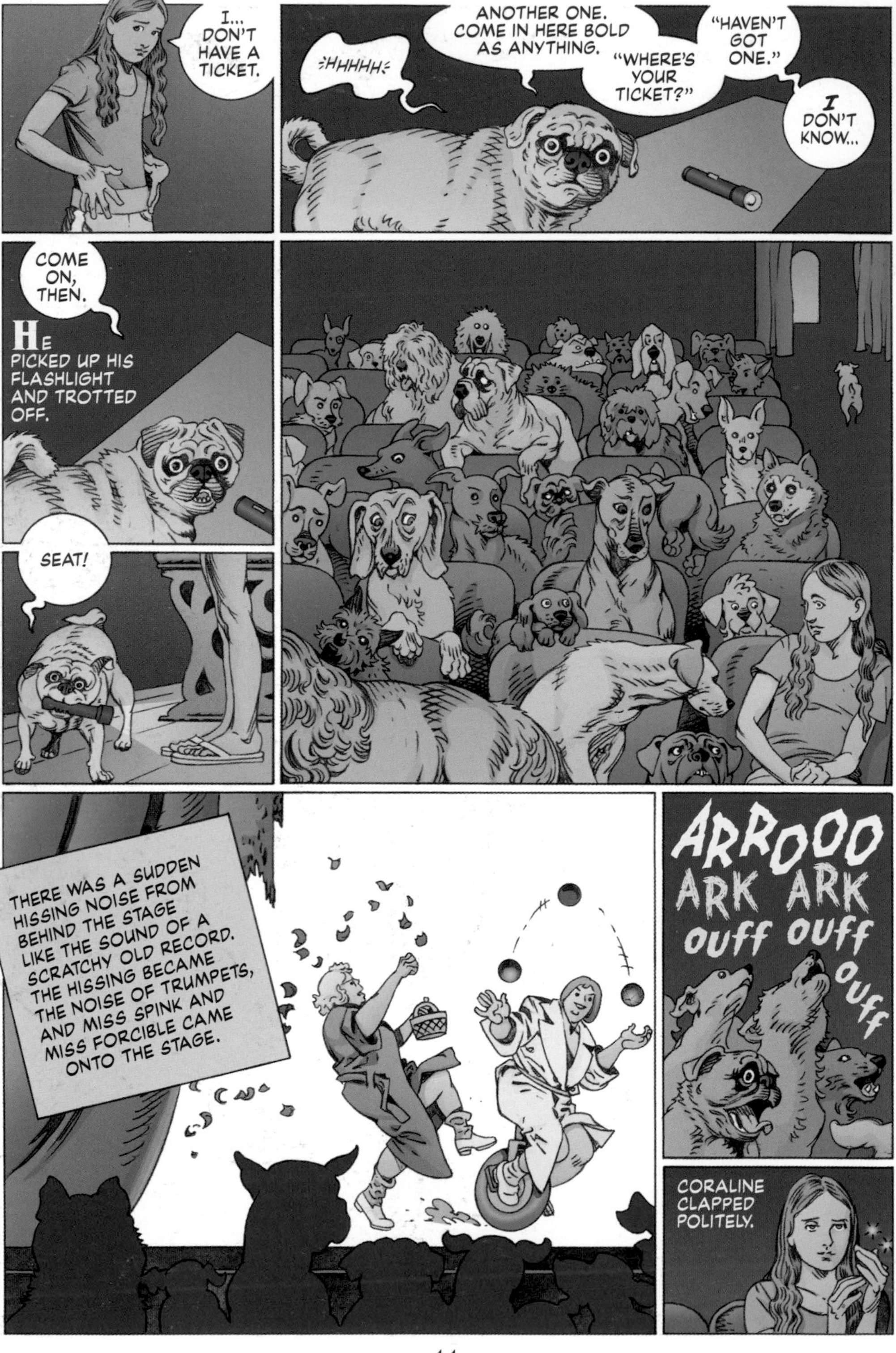
I... DON'T HAVE A TICKET.
HHHHH
ANOTHER ONE. COME IN HERE BOLD AS ANYTHING.
"WHERE'S YOUR TICKET?"
"HAVEN'T GOT ONE."
I DON'T KNOW...
COME ON, THEN.
HE PICKED UP HIS FLASHLIGHT AND TROTTED OFF.
SEAT!
THERE WAS A SUDDEN HISSING NOISE FROM BEHIND THE STAGE LIKE THE SOUND OF A SCRATCHY OLD RECORD. THE HISSING BECAME THE NOISE OF TRUMPETS, AND MISS SPINK AND MISS FORCIBLE CAME ONTO THE STAGE.
ARROOO
ARK ARK
ouff ouff
ouff
CORALINE CLAPPED POLITELY.

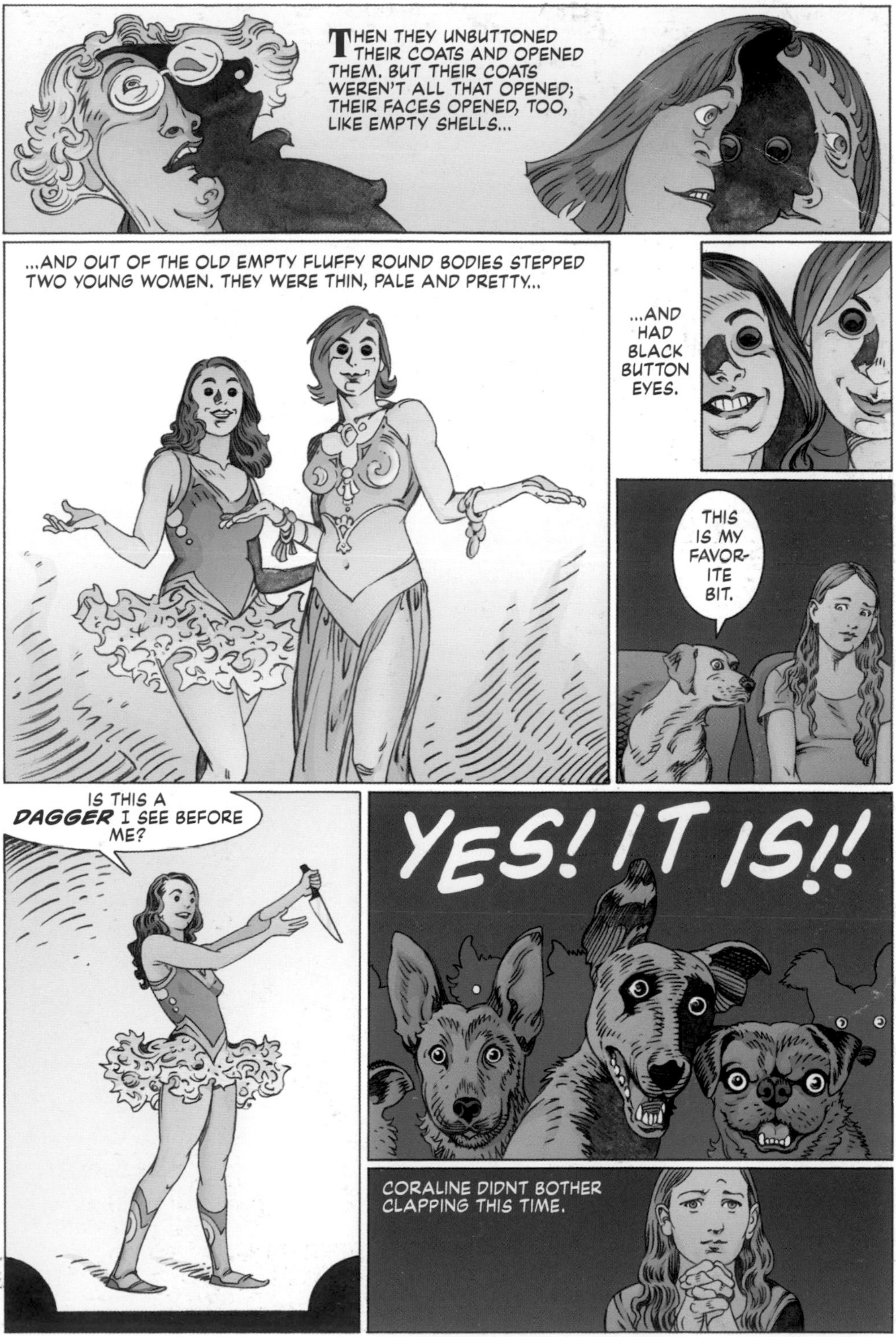
THEN THEY UNBUTTONED THEIR COATS AND OPENED THEM. BUT THEIR COATS WEREN'T ALL THAT OPENED; THEIR FACES OPENED, TOO, LIKE EMPTY SHELLS...
...AND OUT OF THE OLD EMPTY FLUFFY ROUND BODIES STEPPED TWO YOUNG WOMEN. THEY WERE THIN, PALE AND PRETTY...
...AND HAD BLACK BUTTON EYES.
THIS IS MY FAVOR-ITE BIT.
IS THIS A DAGGER I SEE BEFORE ME?
YES! IT IS!!
CORALINE DIDNT BOTHER CLAPPING THIS TIME.

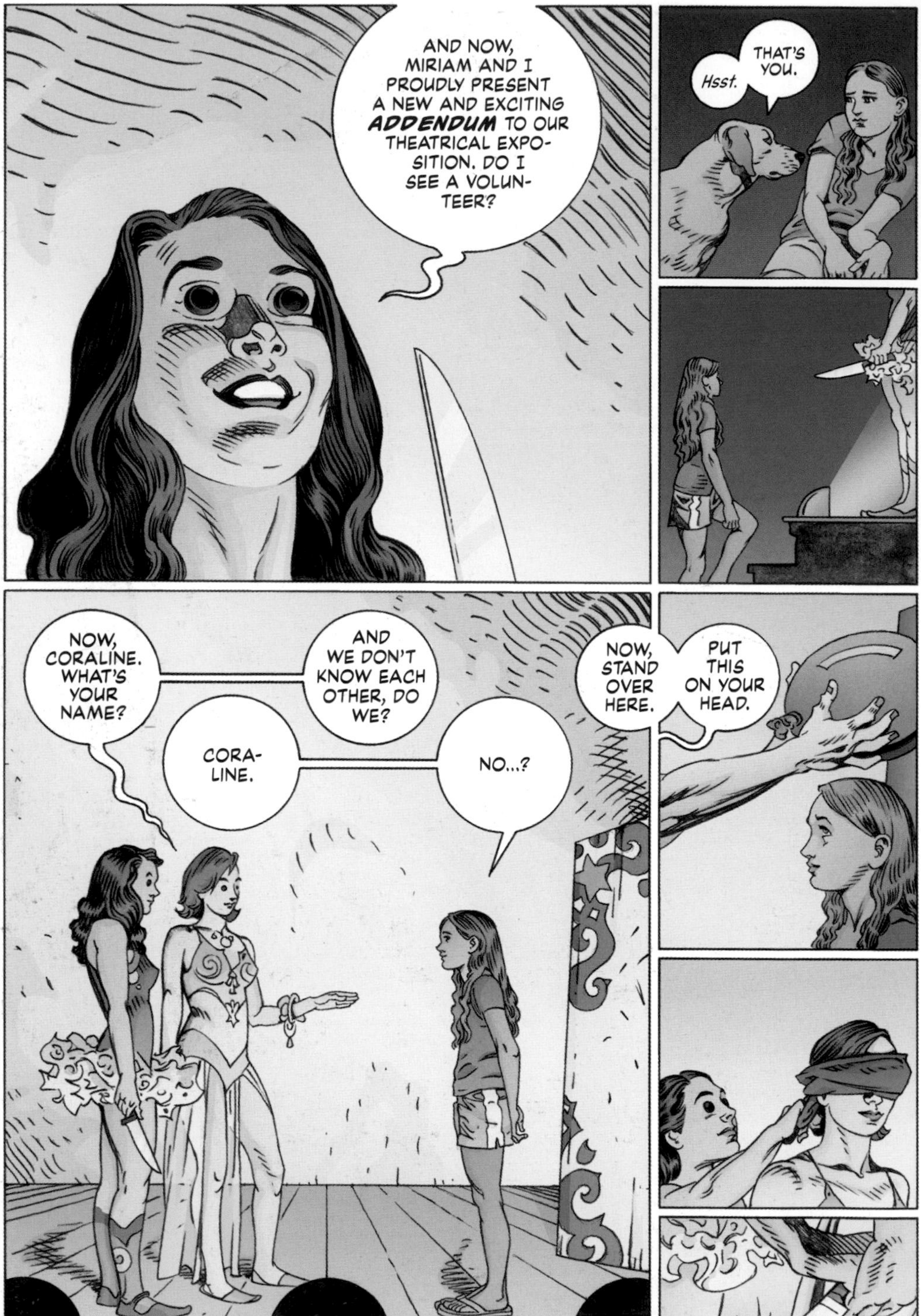
AND NOW, MIRIAM AND I PROUDLY PRESENT A NEW AND EXCITING ADDENDUM TO OUR THEATRICAL EXPO-SITION. DO I SEE A VOLUN-TEER?
THAT'S YOU.
Hsst.
NOW, CORALINE. WHAT'S YOUR NAME?
CORA-LINE.
AND WE DON'T KNOW EACH OTHER, DO WE?
NO...?
NOW, STAND OVER HERE.
PUT THIS ON YOUR HEAD.

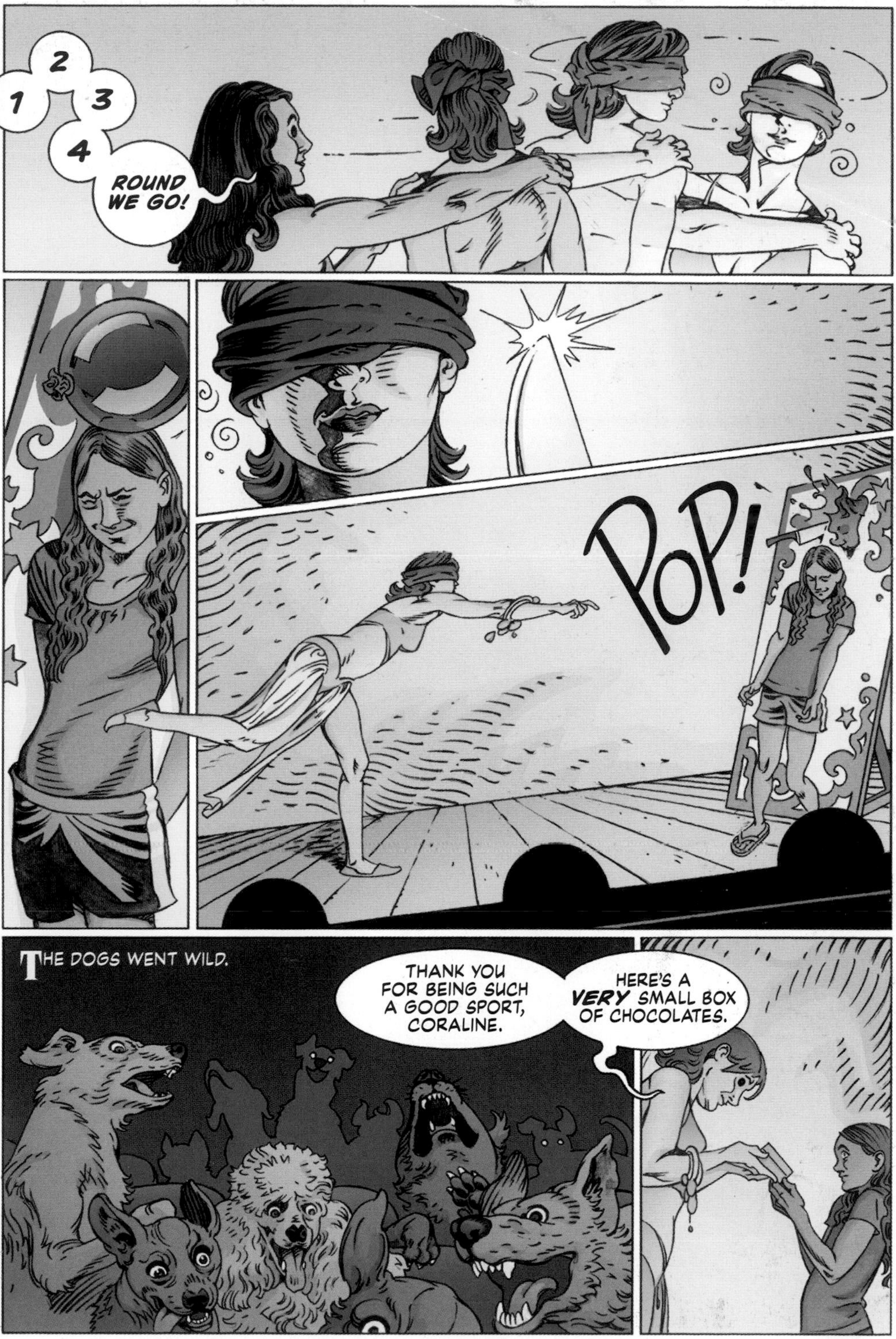
1
2
3
4
ROUND WE GO!
POP!
THE DOGS WENT WILD.
THANK YOU FOR BEING SUCH A GOOD SPORT, CORALINE.
HERE'S A VERY SMALL BOX OF CHOCOLATES.

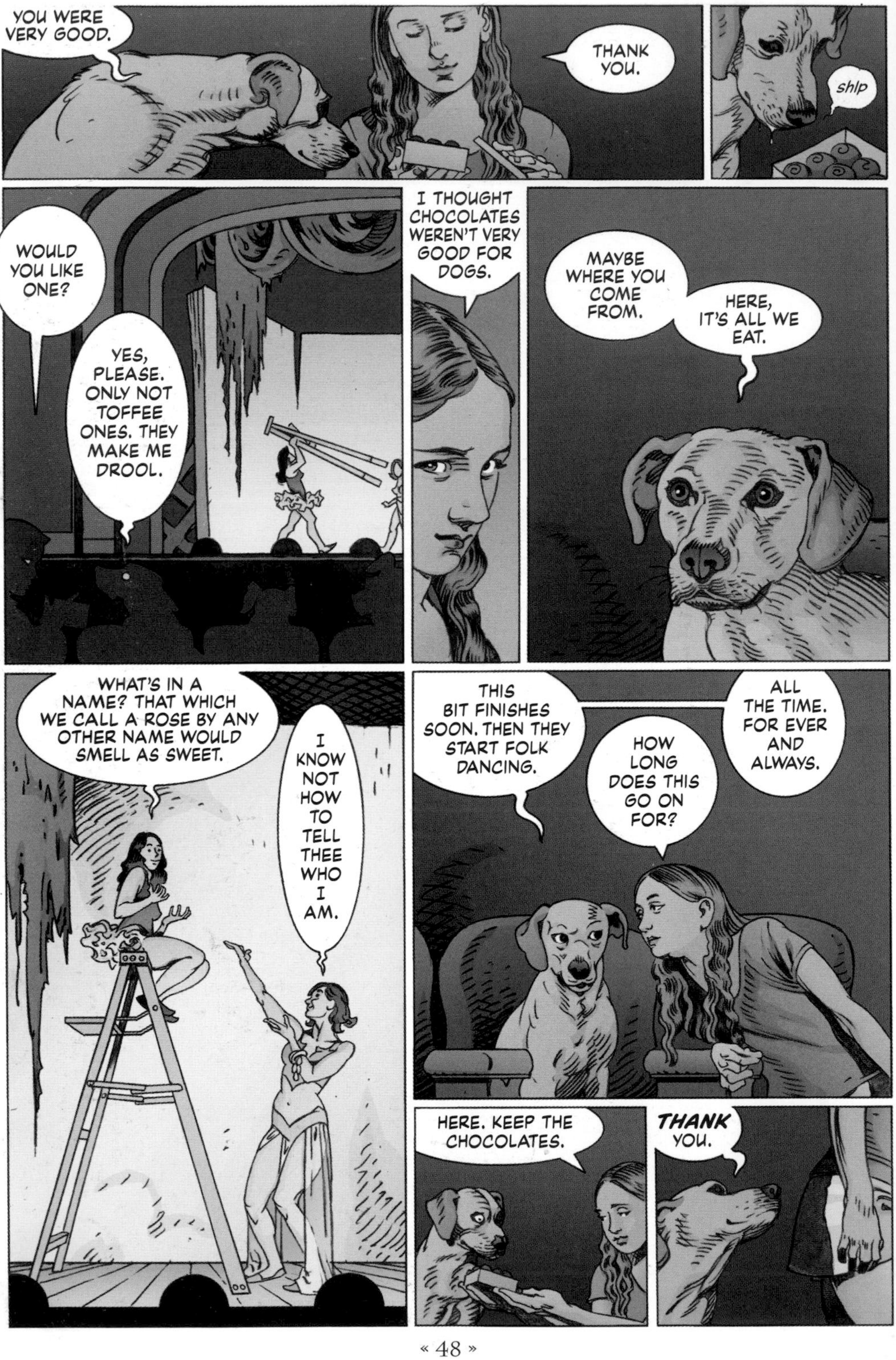
YOU WERE VERY GOOD.
THANK YOU.
shlp
WOULD YOU LIKE ONE?
YES, PLEASE. ONLY NOT TOFFEE ONES. THEY MAKE ME DROOL.
I THOUGHT CHOCOLATES WEREN'T VERY GOOD FOR DOGS.
MAYBE WHERE YOU COME FROM.
HERE, IT'S ALL WE EAT.
WHAT'S IN A NAME? THAT WHICH WE CALL A ROSE BY ANY OTHER NAME WOULD SMELL AS SWEET.
I KNOW NOT HOW TO TELL THEE WHO I AM.
THIS BIT FINISHES SOON. THEN THEY START FOLK DANCING.
HOW LONG DOES THIS GO ON FOR?
ALL THE TIME. FOR EVER AND ALWAYS.
HERE. KEEP THE CHOCOLATES.
THANK YOU.

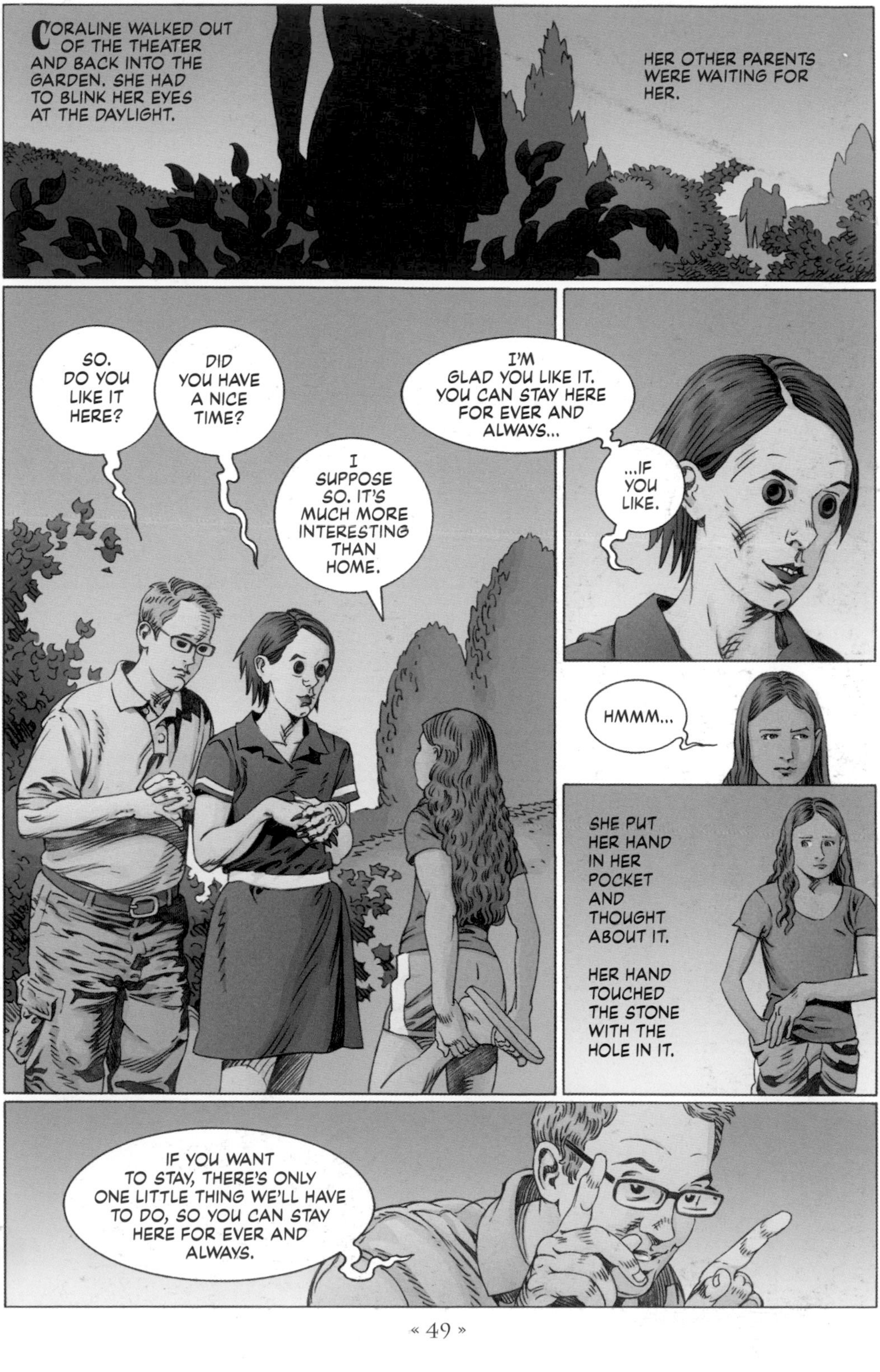
CORALINE WALKED OUT OF THE THEATER AND BACK INTO THE GARDEN. SHE HAD TO BLINK HER EYES AT THE DAYLIGHT.
HER OTHER PARENTS WERE WAITING FOR HER.
SO. DO YOU LIKE IT HERE?
DID YOU HAVE A NICE TIME?
I SUPPOSE SO. IT'S MUCH MORE INTERESTING THAN HOME.
I'M GLAD YOU LIKE IT. YOU CAN STAY HERE FOR EVER AND ALWAYS...
...IF YOU LIKE.
HMMM...
SHE PUT HER HAND IN HER POCKET AND THOUGHT ABOUT IT.
HER HAND TOUCHED THE STONE WITH THE HOLE IN IT.
IF YOU WANT TO STAY, THERE'S ONLY ONE LITTLE THING WE'LL HAVE TO DO, SO YOU CAN STAY HERE FOR EVER AND ALWAYS.

They went into the kitchen. On the table was a spool of black cotton, and a long silver needle, and beside them, two large black buttons.

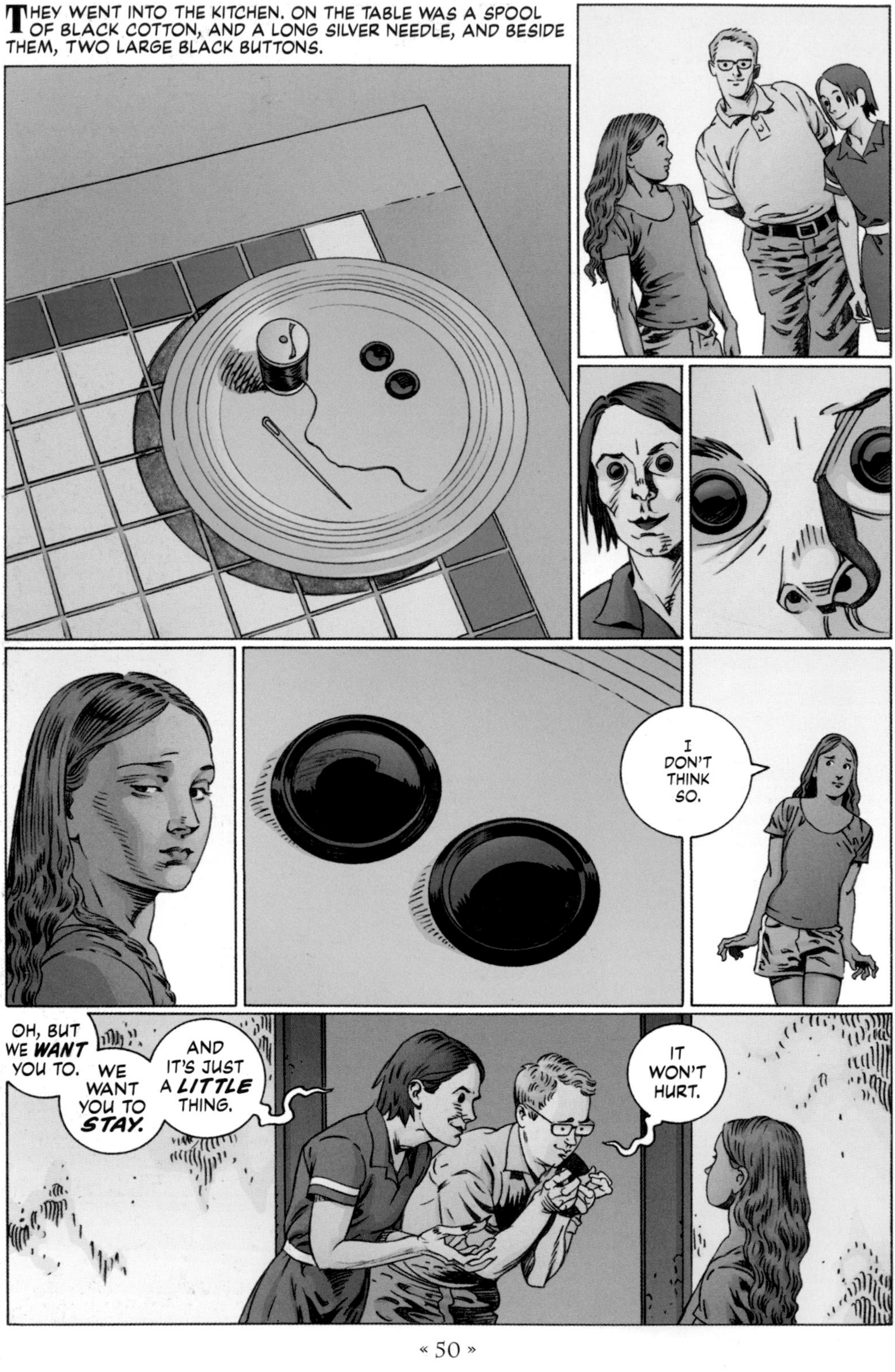

I DON'T THINK SO.
OH, BUT WE WANT YOU TO.
WE WANT YOU TO STAY.
AND IT'S JUST A LITTLE THING.
IT WON'T HURT.

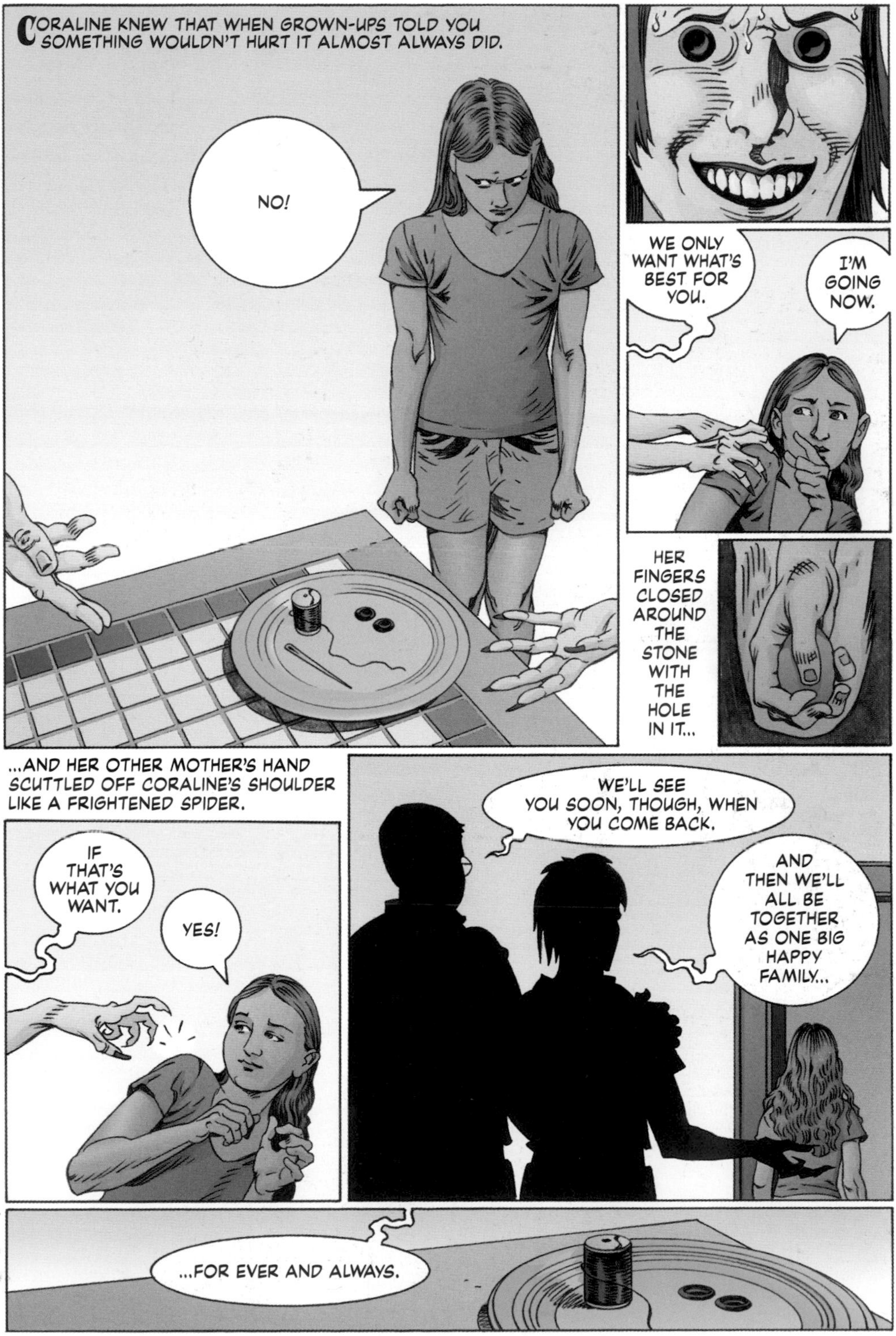
CORALINE KNEW THAT WHEN GROWN-UPS TOLD YOU SOMETHING WOULDN'T HURT IT ALMOST ALWAYS DID.
NO!
WE ONLY WANT WHAT'S BEST FOR YOU.
I'M GOING NOW.
HER FINGERS CLOSED AROUND THE STONE WITH THE HOLE IN IT...
...AND HER OTHER MOTHER'S HAND SCUTTLED OFF CORALINE'S SHOULDER LIKE A FRIGHTENED SPIDER.
IF THAT'S WHAT YOU WANT.
YES!
WE'LL SEE YOU SOON, THOUGH, WHEN YOU COME BACK.
AND THEN WE'LL ALL BE TOGETHER AS ONE BIG HAPPY FAMILY...
...FOR EVER AND ALWAYS.

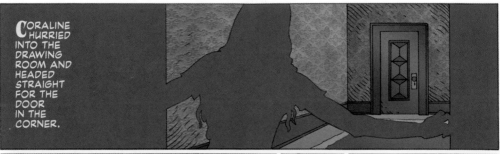

CORALINE HURRIED INTO THE DRAWING ROOM AND HEADED STRAIGHT FOR THE DOOR IN THE CORNER.

THERE WAS NO BRICK WALL THERE NOW—JUST DARKNESS. A DARKNESS THAT SEEMED AS IF THINGS IN IT MIGHT BE MOVING.

COME BACK SOON.

SHE TOOK A DEEP BREATH...

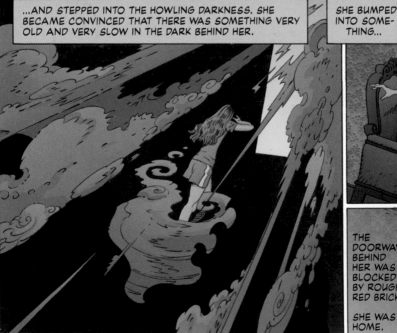

...AND STEPPED INTO THE HOWLING DARKNESS. SHE BECAME CONVINCED THAT THERE WAS SOMETHING VERY OLD AND VERY SLOW IN THE DARK BEHIND HER.

SHE BUMPED INTO SOME-THING...

...AN ARM-CHAIR.

THE DOORWAY BEHIND HER WAS BLOCKED BY ROUGH RED BRICKS.

SHE WAS HOME.

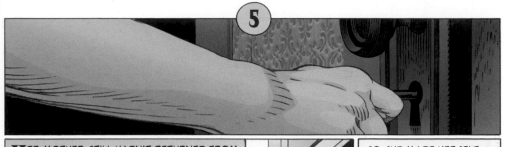

5

HER MOTHER STILL HADN'T RETURNED FROM HER SHOPPING EXPEDITION.

HUNGRY.

SO SHE MADE HERSELF SOME TOAST...

...WITH JAM AND PEANUT BUTTER...

...AND DRANK A GLASS OF WATER.

WHEN IT BEGAN TO GET DARK SHE MICROWAVED HERSELF A FROZEN PIZZA.

SHE WAITED FOR HER PARENTS TO GET BACK.

DING

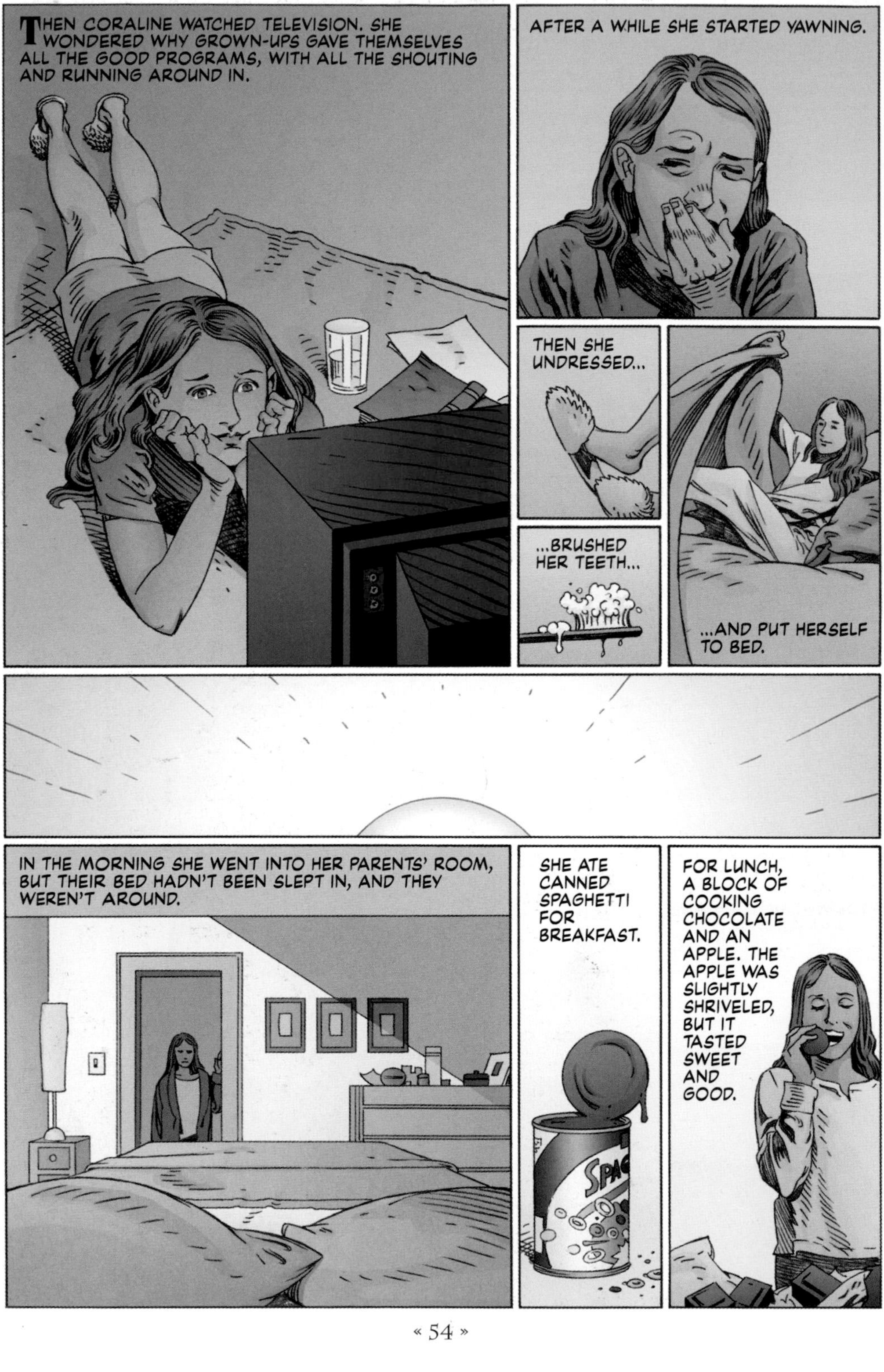
THEN CORALINE WATCHED TELEVISION. SHE WONDERED WHY GROWN-UPS GAVE THEMSELVES ALL THE GOOD PROGRAMS, WITH ALL THE SHOUTING AND RUNNING AROUND IN.
AFTER A WHILE SHE STARTED YAWNING.
THEN SHE UNDRESSED...
...BRUSHED HER TEETH...
...AND PUT HERSELF TO BED.
IN THE MORNING SHE WENT INTO HER PARENTS' ROOM, BUT THEIR BED HADN'T BEEN SLEPT IN, AND THEY WEREN'T AROUND.
SHE ATE CANNED SPAGHETTI FOR BREAKFAST.
FOR LUNCH, A BLOCK OF COOKING CHOCOLATE AND AN APPLE. THE APPLE WAS SLIGHTLY SHRIVELED, BUT IT TASTED SWEET AND GOOD.

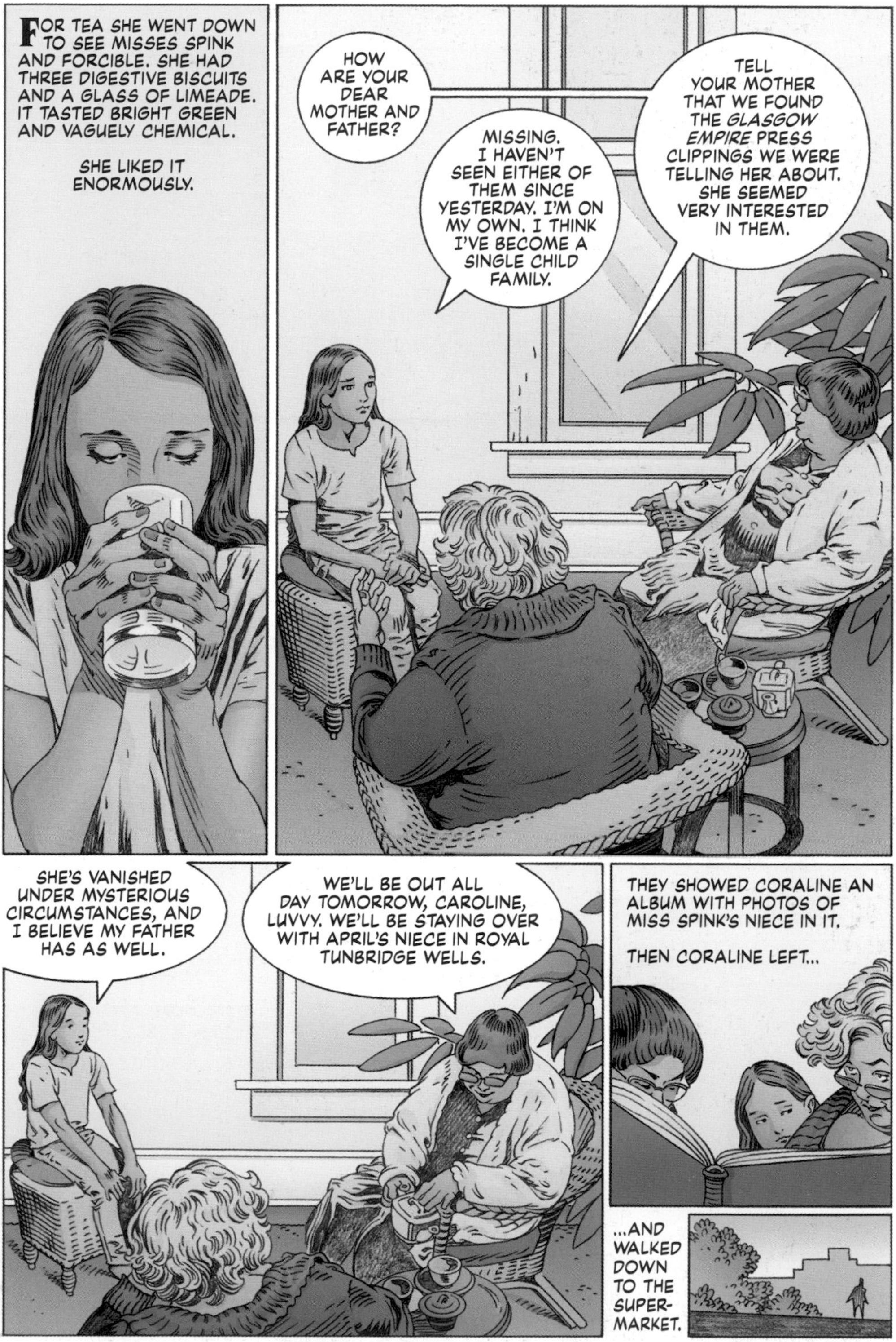
FOR TEA SHE WENT DOWN TO SEE MISSES SPINK AND FORCIBLE. SHE HAD THREE DIGESTIVE BISCUITS AND A GLASS OF LIMEADE. IT TASTED BRIGHT GREEN AND VAGUELY CHEMICAL.
SHE LIKED IT ENORMOUSLY.
HOW ARE YOUR DEAR MOTHER AND FATHER?
MISSING. I HAVEN'T SEEN EITHER OF THEM SINCE YESTERDAY. I'M ON MY OWN. I THINK I'VE BECOME A SINGLE CHILD FAMILY.
TELL YOUR MOTHER THAT WE FOUND THE *GLASGOW EMPIRE* PRESS CLIPPINGS WE WERE TELLING HER ABOUT. SHE SEEMED VERY INTERESTED IN THEM.
SHE'S VANISHED UNDER MYSTERIOUS CIRCUMSTANCES, AND I BELIEVE MY FATHER HAS AS WELL.
WE'LL BE OUT ALL DAY TOMORROW, CAROLINE, LUVVY. WE'LL BE STAYING OVER WITH APRIL'S NIECE IN ROYAL TUNBRIDGE WELLS.
THEY SHOWED CORALINE AN ALBUM WITH PHOTOS OF MISS SPINK'S NIECE IN IT.
THEN CORALINE LEFT...
...AND WALKED DOWN TO THE SUPER-MARKET.

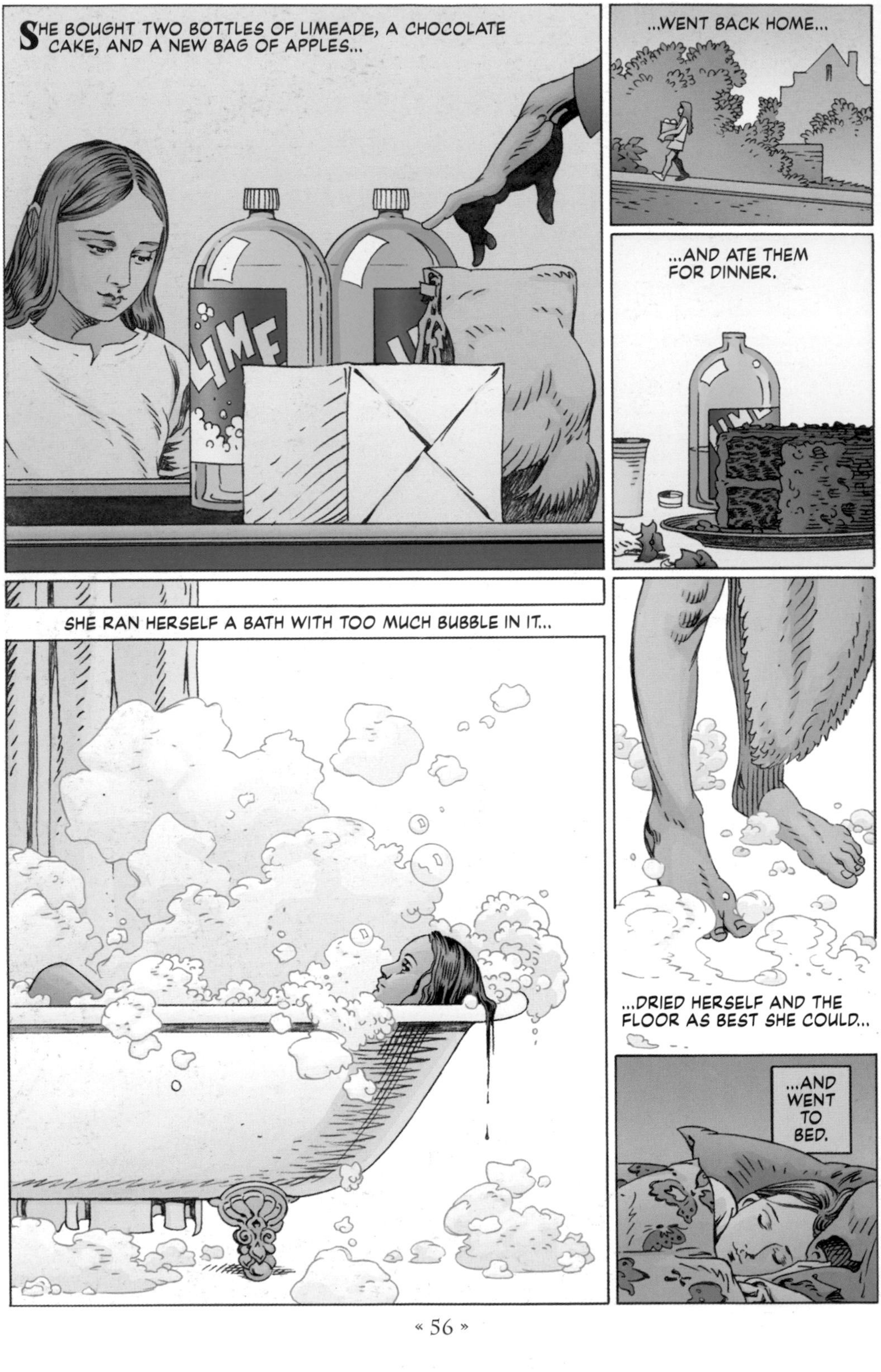
SHE BOUGHT TWO BOTTLES OF LIMEADE, A CHOCOLATE CAKE, AND A NEW BAG OF APPLES...
LIME
...WENT BACK HOME...
...AND ATE THEM FOR DINNER.
SHE RAN HERSELF A BATH WITH TOO MUCH BUBBLE IN IT...
...DRIED HERSELF AND THE FLOOR AS BEST SHE COULD...
...AND WENT TO BED.

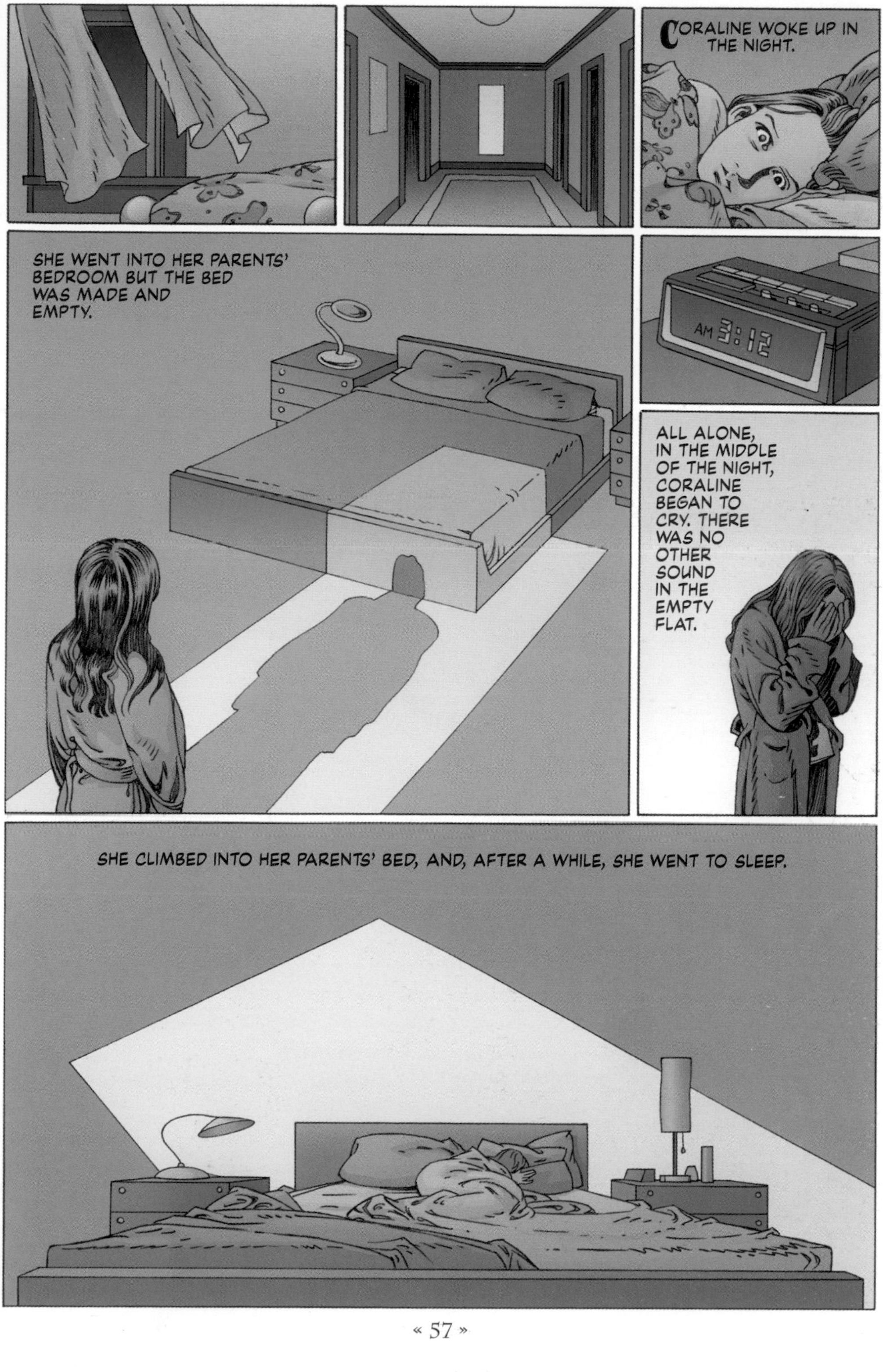
CORALINE WOKE UP IN THE NIGHT.
SHE WENT INTO HER PARENTS' BEDROOM BUT THE BED WAS MADE AND EMPTY.
AM 3:12
ALL ALONE, IN THE MIDDLE OF THE NIGHT, CORALINE BEGAN TO CRY. THERE WAS NO OTHER SOUND IN THE EMPTY FLAT.
SHE CLIMBED INTO HER PARENTS' BED, AND, AFTER A WHILE, SHE WENT TO SLEEP.

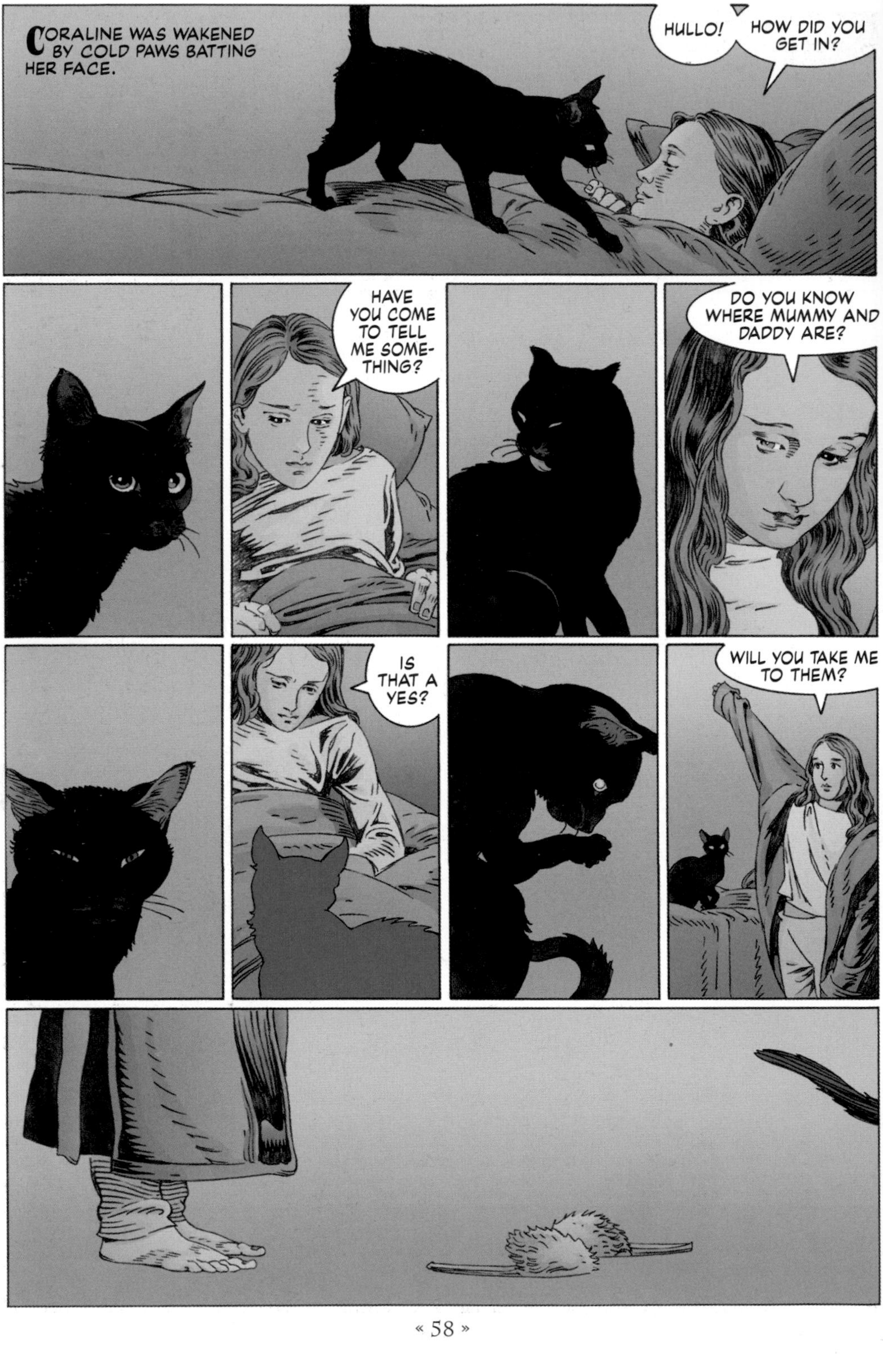
CORALINE WAS WAKENED BY COLD PAWS BATTING HER FACE.
HULLO!
HOW DID YOU GET IN?
HAVE YOU COME TO TELL ME SOME-THING?
DO YOU KNOW WHERE MUMMY AND DADDY ARE?
IS THAT A YES?
WILL YOU TAKE ME TO THEM?

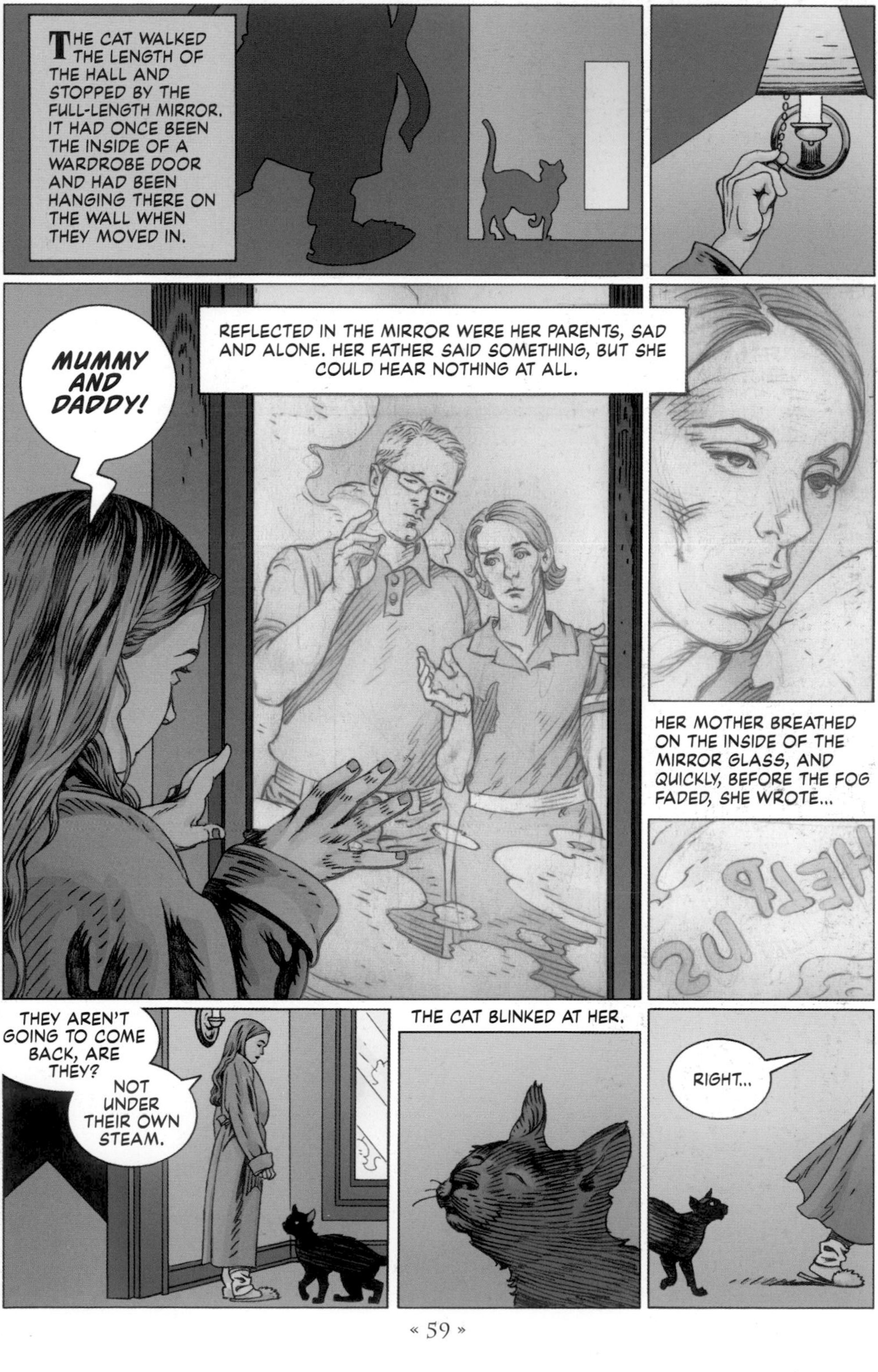
THE CAT WALKED THE LENGTH OF THE HALL AND STOPPED BY THE FULL-LENGTH MIRROR. IT HAD ONCE BEEN THE INSIDE OF A WARDROBE DOOR AND HAD BEEN HANGING THERE ON THE WALL WHEN THEY MOVED IN.
REFLECTED IN THE MIRROR WERE HER PARENTS, SAD AND ALONE. HER FATHER SAID SOMETHING, BUT SHE COULD HEAR NOTHING AT ALL.
MUMMY AND DADDY!
HER MOTHER BREATHED ON THE INSIDE OF THE MIRROR GLASS, AND QUICKLY, BEFORE THE FOG FADED, SHE WROTE...
HELP US
THEY AREN'T GOING TO COME BACK, ARE THEY?
NOT UNDER THEIR OWN STEAM.
THE CAT BLINKED AT HER.
RIGHT...

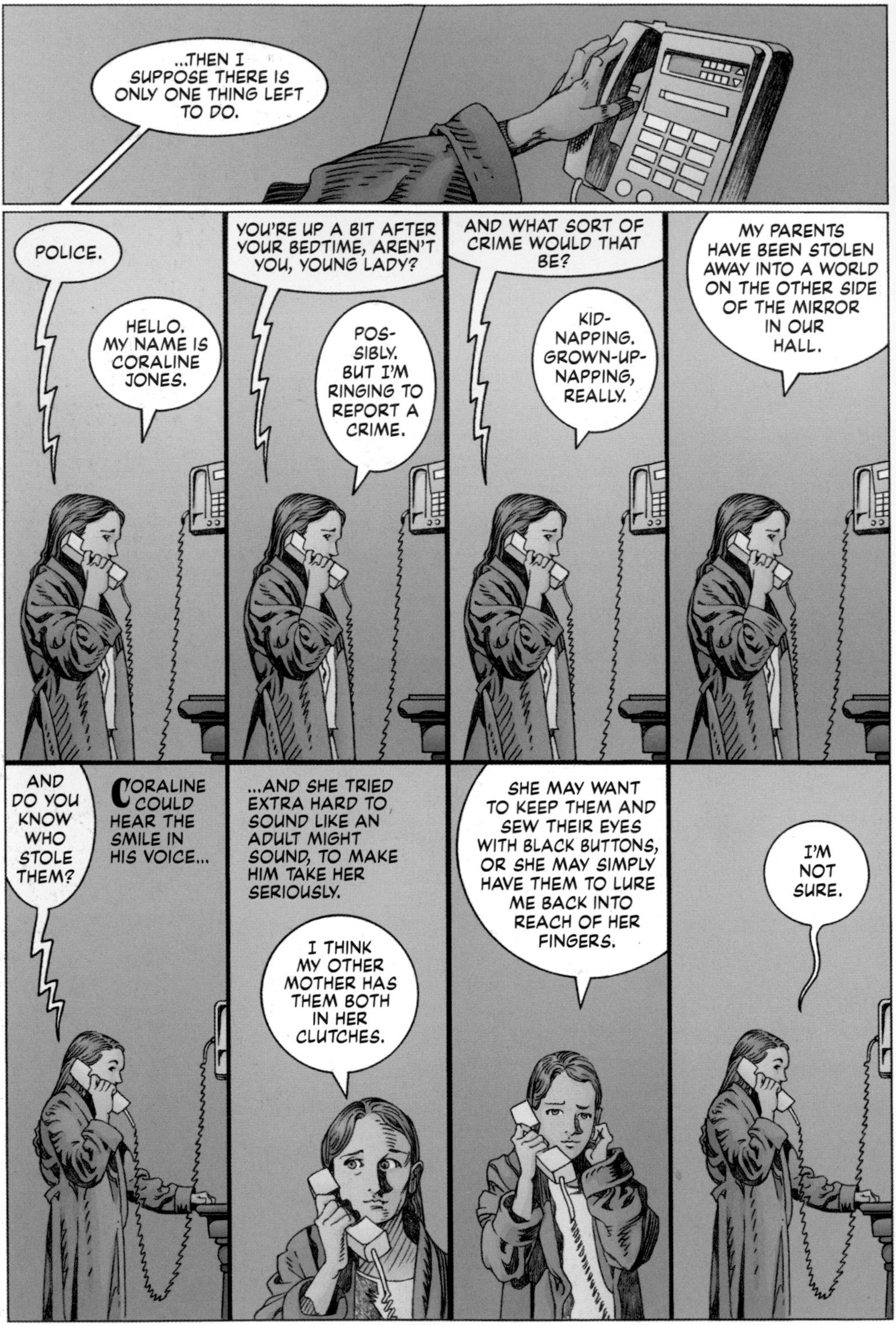
...THEN I SUPPOSE THERE IS ONLY ONE THING LEFT TO DO.
POLICE.
HELLO. MY NAME IS CORALINE JONES.
YOU'RE UP A BIT AFTER YOUR BEDTIME, AREN'T YOU, YOUNG LADY?
POS-SIBLY. BUT I'M RINGING TO REPORT A CRIME.
AND WHAT SORT OF CRIME WOULD THAT BE?
KID-NAPPING. GROWN-UP-NAPPING, REALLY.
MY PARENTS HAVE BEEN STOLEN AWAY INTO A WORLD ON THE OTHER SIDE OF THE MIRROR IN OUR HALL.
AND DO YOU KNOW WHO STOLE THEM?
CORALINE COULD HEAR THE SMILE IN HIS VOICE...
...AND SHE TRIED EXTRA HARD TO SOUND LIKE AN ADULT MIGHT SOUND, TO MAKE HIM TAKE HER SERIOUSLY.
I THINK MY OTHER MOTHER HAS THEM BOTH IN HER CLUTCHES.
SHE MAY WANT TO KEEP THEM AND SEW THEIR EYES WITH BLACK BUTTONS, OR SHE MAY SIMPLY HAVE THEM TO LURE ME BACK INTO REACH OF HER FINGERS.
I'M NOT SURE.

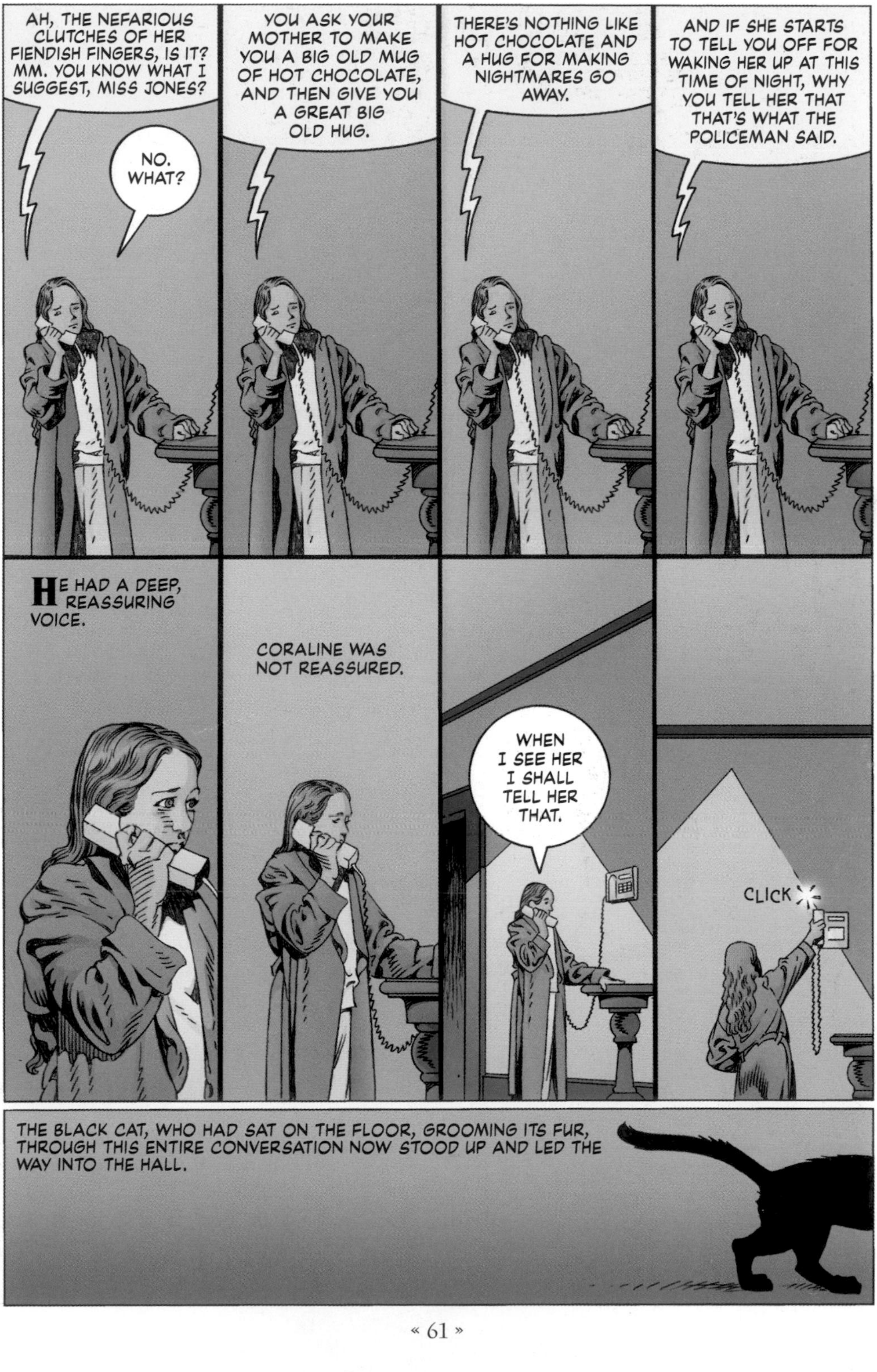
AH, THE NEFARIOUS CLUTCHES OF HER FIENDISH FINGERS, IS IT? MM. YOU KNOW WHAT I SUGGEST, MISS JONES?
NO. WHAT?
YOU ASK YOUR MOTHER TO MAKE YOU A BIG OLD MUG OF HOT CHOCOLATE, AND THEN GIVE YOU A GREAT BIG OLD HUG.
THERE'S NOTHING LIKE HOT CHOCOLATE AND A HUG FOR MAKING NIGHTMARES GO AWAY.
AND IF SHE STARTS TO TELL YOU OFF FOR WAKING HER UP AT THIS TIME OF NIGHT, WHY YOU TELL HER THAT THAT'S WHAT THE POLICEMAN SAID.
HE HAD A DEEP, REASSURING VOICE.
CORALINE WAS NOT REASSURED.
WHEN I SEE HER I SHALL TELL HER THAT.
CLICK
THE BLACK CAT, WHO HAD SAT ON THE FLOOR, GROOMING ITS FUR, THROUGH THIS ENTIRE CONVERSATION NOW STOOD UP AND LED THE WAY INTO THE HALL.

CORALINE WENT INTO THE KITCHEN AND FOUND A BOX OF EMERGENCY WHITE CANDLES...

...PUT AN APPLE INTO EACH POCKET...

...AND TOOK THE OLD BLACK KEY OFF THE RING.

BACK IN HER BED-ROOM SHE RUM-MAGED IN THE POCKET OF HER JEANS...

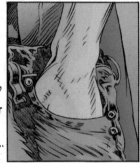

...FOUND THE STONE WITH THE HOLE IN IT...

...PUT IT INTO HER POCKET...

...AND WALKED INTO THE DRAWING ROOM.

SHE HAD THE FEELING THAT THE DOOR WAS LOOKING AT HER, WHICH SHE KNEW WAS SILLY, AND KNEW ON A DEEPER LEVEL WAS SOMEHOW TRUE.

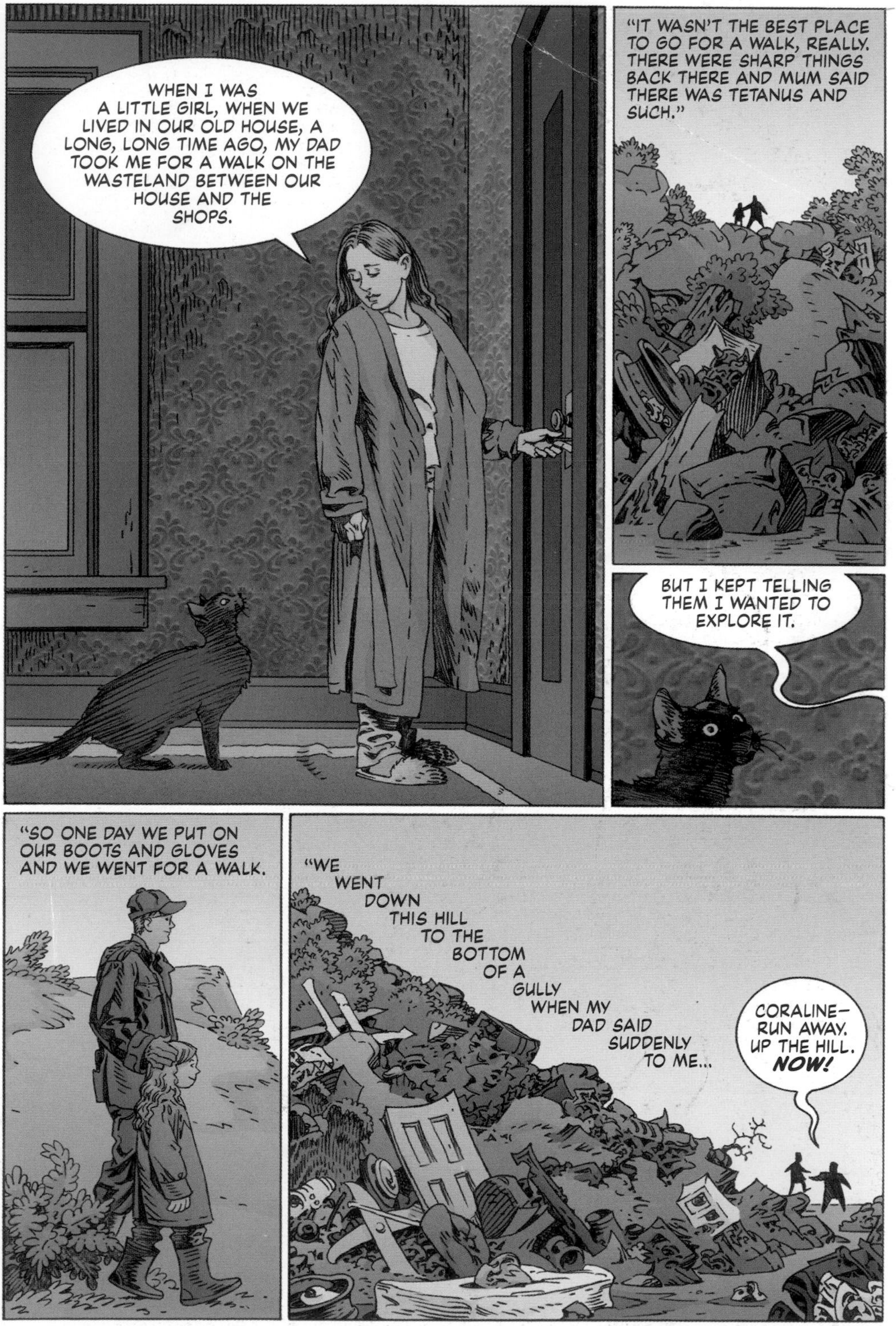
WHEN I WAS A LITTLE GIRL, WHEN WE LIVED IN OUR OLD HOUSE, A LONG, LONG TIME AGO, MY DAD TOOK ME FOR A WALK ON THE WASTELAND BETWEEN OUR HOUSE AND THE SHOPS.
"IT WASN'T THE BEST PLACE TO GO FOR A WALK, REALLY. THERE WERE SHARP THINGS BACK THERE AND MUM SAID THERE WAS TETANUS AND SUCH."
BUT I KEPT TELLING THEM I WANTED TO EXPLORE IT.
"SO ONE DAY WE PUT ON OUR BOOTS AND GLOVES AND WE WENT FOR A WALK.
"WE WENT DOWN THIS HILL TO THE BOTTOM OF A GULLY WHEN MY DAD SAID SUDDENLY TO ME...
CORALINE— RUN AWAY. UP THE HILL. ***NOW!***

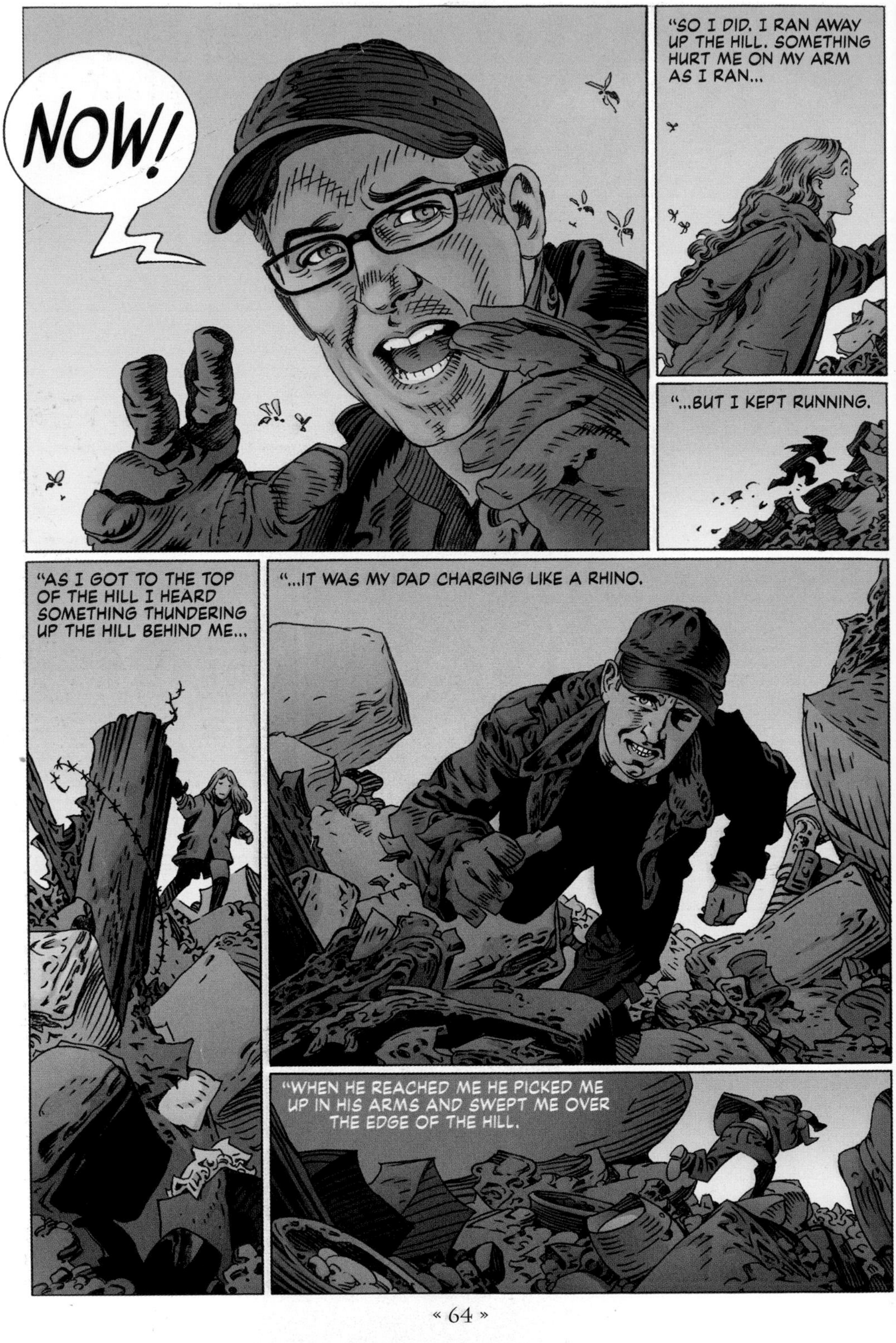
NOW!
"SO I DID. I RAN AWAY UP THE HILL. SOMETHING HURT ME ON MY ARM AS I RAN...
"...BUT I KEPT RUNNING.
"AS I GOT TO THE TOP OF THE HILL I HEARD SOMETHING THUNDERING UP THE HILL BEHIND ME...
"...IT WAS MY DAD CHARGING LIKE A RHINO.
"WHEN HE REACHED ME HE PICKED ME UP IN HIS ARMS AND SWEPT ME OVER THE EDGE OF THE HILL.

"THE AIR WAS ALIVE WITH YELLOW WASPS. MY DAD STAYED AND GOT STUNG TO GIVE ME TIME TO RUN AWAY.

"HIS GLASSES HAD FALLEN OFF WHEN HE RAN.

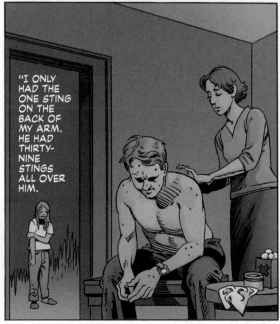

"I ONLY HAD THE ONE STING ON THE BACK OF MY ARM. HE HAD THIRTY-NINE STINGS ALL OVER HIM.

"SO LATER THAT AFTERNOON MY DAD WENT BACK AGAIN TO THE WASTELAND TO GET HIS GLASSES BACK. HE SAID IF HE LEFT IT ANOTHER DAY HE WOULDN'T BE ABLE TO REMEMBER WHERE THEY'D FALLEN."

AND SOON HE GOT HOME, WEARING HIS GLASSES.

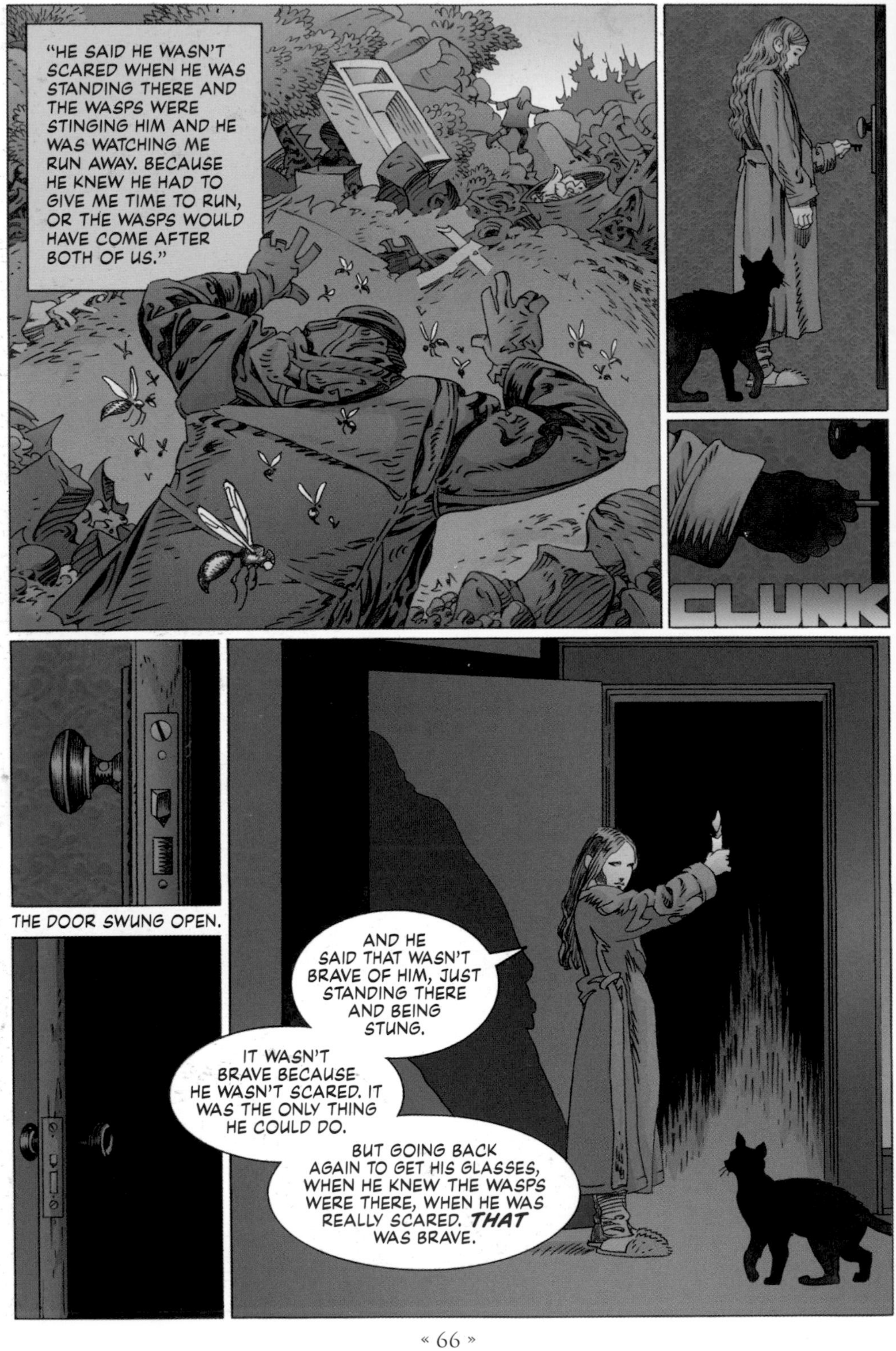
"HE SAID HE WASN'T SCARED WHEN HE WAS STANDING THERE AND THE WASPS WERE STINGING HIM AND HE WAS WATCHING ME RUN AWAY. BECAUSE HE KNEW HE HAD TO GIVE ME TIME TO RUN, OR THE WASPS WOULD HAVE COME AFTER BOTH OF US."
CLUNK
THE DOOR SWUNG OPEN.
AND HE SAID THAT WASN'T BRAVE OF HIM, JUST STANDING THERE AND BEING STUNG.
IT WASN'T BRAVE BECAUSE HE WASN'T SCARED. IT WAS THE ONLY THING HE COULD DO.
BUT GOING BACK AGAIN TO GET HIS GLASSES, WHEN HE KNEW THE WASPS WERE THERE, WHEN HE WAS REALLY SCARED. ***THAT*** WAS BRAVE.

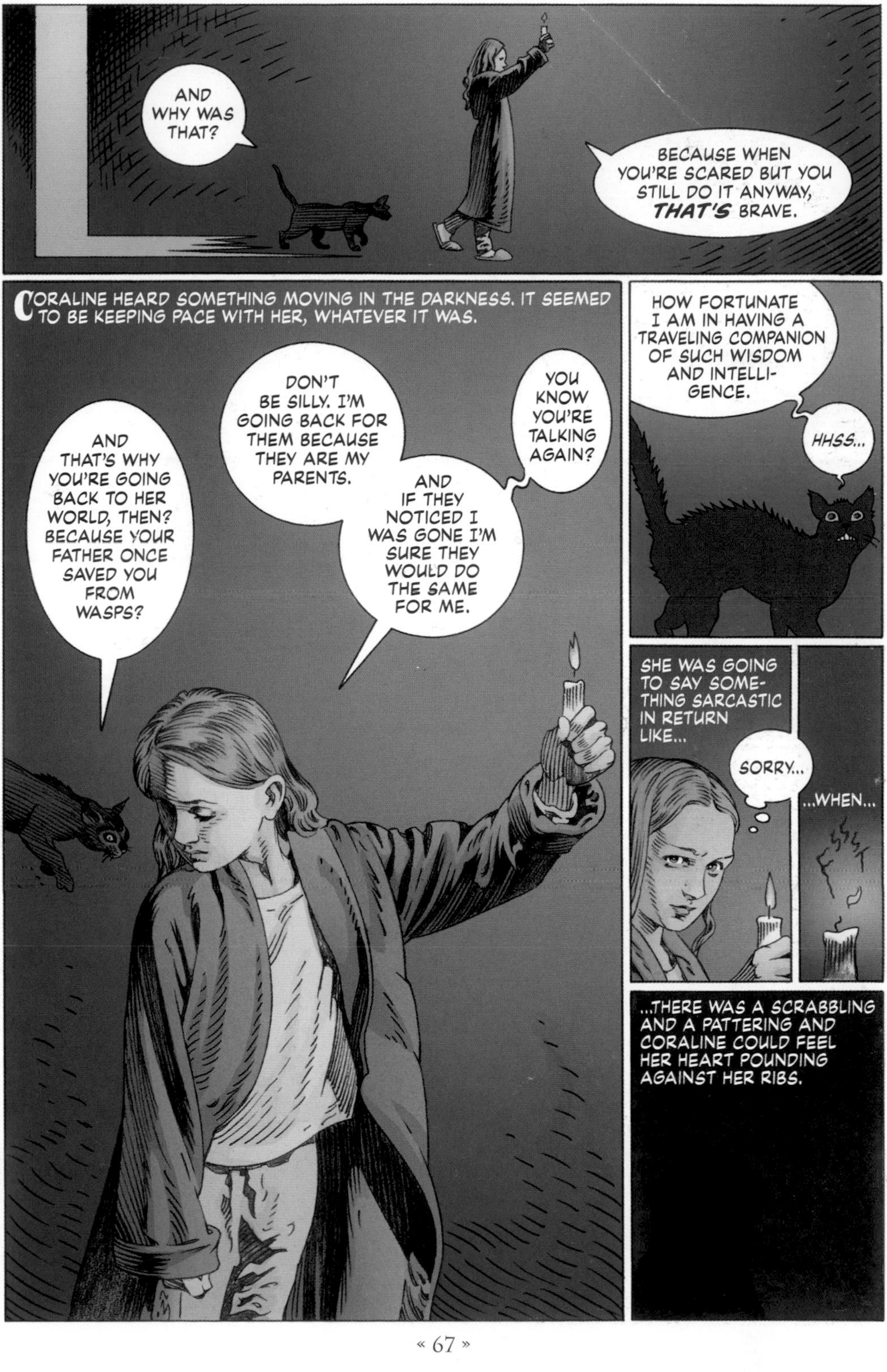
AND WHY WAS THAT?
BECAUSE WHEN YOU'RE SCARED BUT YOU STILL DO IT ANYWAY, THAT'S BRAVE.
CORALINE HEARD SOMETHING MOVING IN THE DARKNESS. IT SEEMED TO BE KEEPING PACE WITH HER, WHATEVER IT WAS.
AND THAT'S WHY YOU'RE GOING BACK TO HER WORLD, THEN? BECAUSE YOUR FATHER ONCE SAVED YOU FROM WASPS?
DON'T BE SILLY. I'M GOING BACK FOR THEM BECAUSE THEY ARE MY PARENTS.
AND IF THEY NOTICED I WAS GONE I'M SURE THEY WOULD DO THE SAME FOR ME.
YOU KNOW YOU'RE TALKING AGAIN?
HOW FORTUNATE I AM IN HAVING A TRAVELING COMPANION OF SUCH WISDOM AND INTELLI-GENCE.
HHSS...
SHE WAS GOING TO SAY SOME-THING SARCASTIC IN RETURN LIKE...
SORRY...
...WHEN...
...THERE WAS A SCRABBLING AND A PATTERING AND CORALINE COULD FEEL HER HEART POUNDING AGAINST HER RIBS.

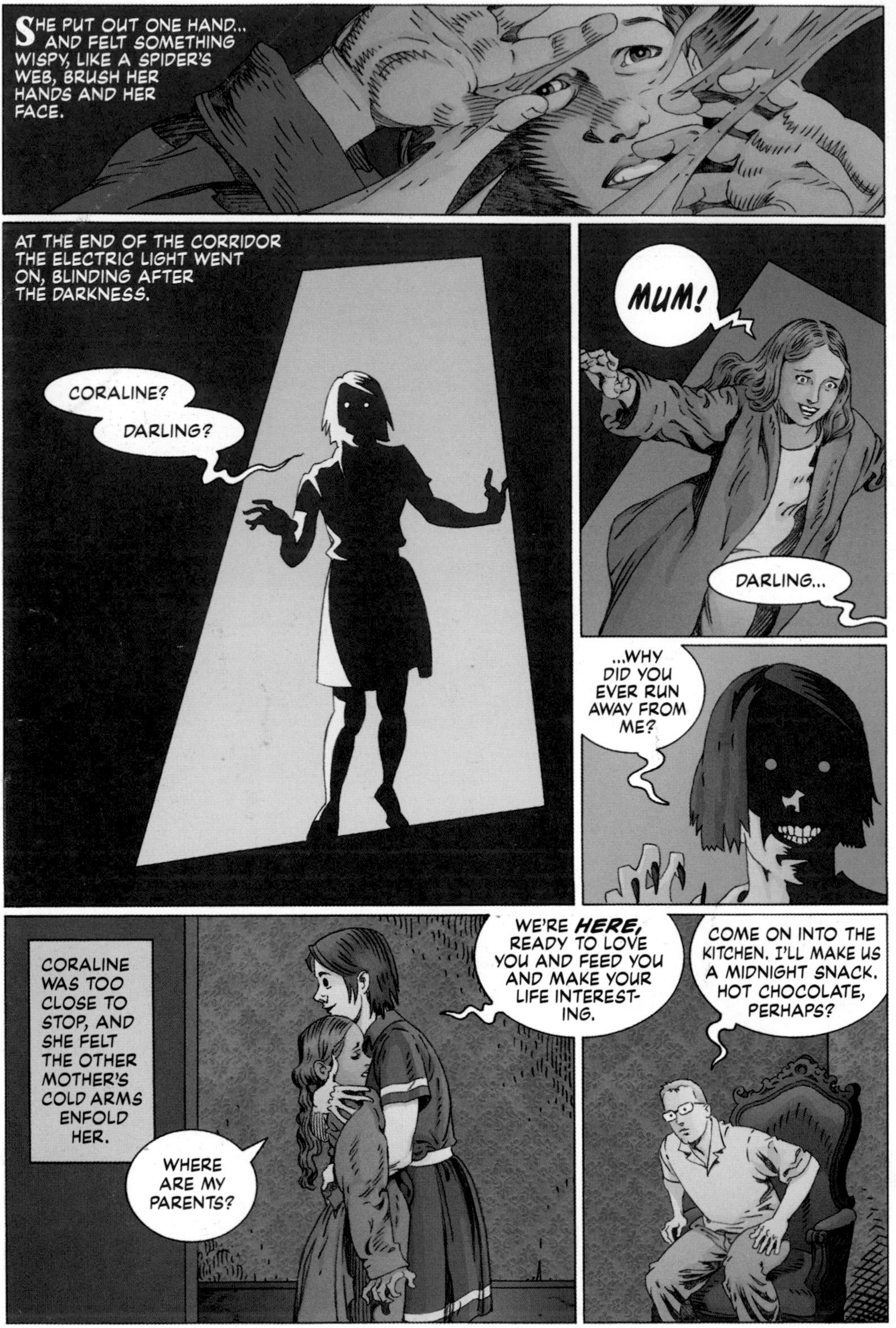
SHE PUT OUT ONE HAND... AND FELT SOMETHING WISPY, LIKE A SPIDER'S WEB, BRUSH HER HANDS AND HER FACE.
AT THE END OF THE CORRIDOR THE ELECTRIC LIGHT WENT ON, BLINDING AFTER THE DARKNESS.
CORALINE?
DARLING?
MUM!
DARLING...
...WHY DID YOU EVER RUN AWAY FROM ME?
CORALINE WAS TOO CLOSE TO STOP, AND SHE FELT THE OTHER MOTHER'S COLD ARMS ENFOLD HER.
WHERE ARE MY PARENTS?
WE'RE HERE, READY TO LOVE YOU AND FEED YOU AND MAKE YOUR LIFE INTEREST-ING.
COME ON INTO THE KITCHEN. I'LL MAKE US A MIDNIGHT SNACK. HOT CHOCOLATE, PERHAPS?

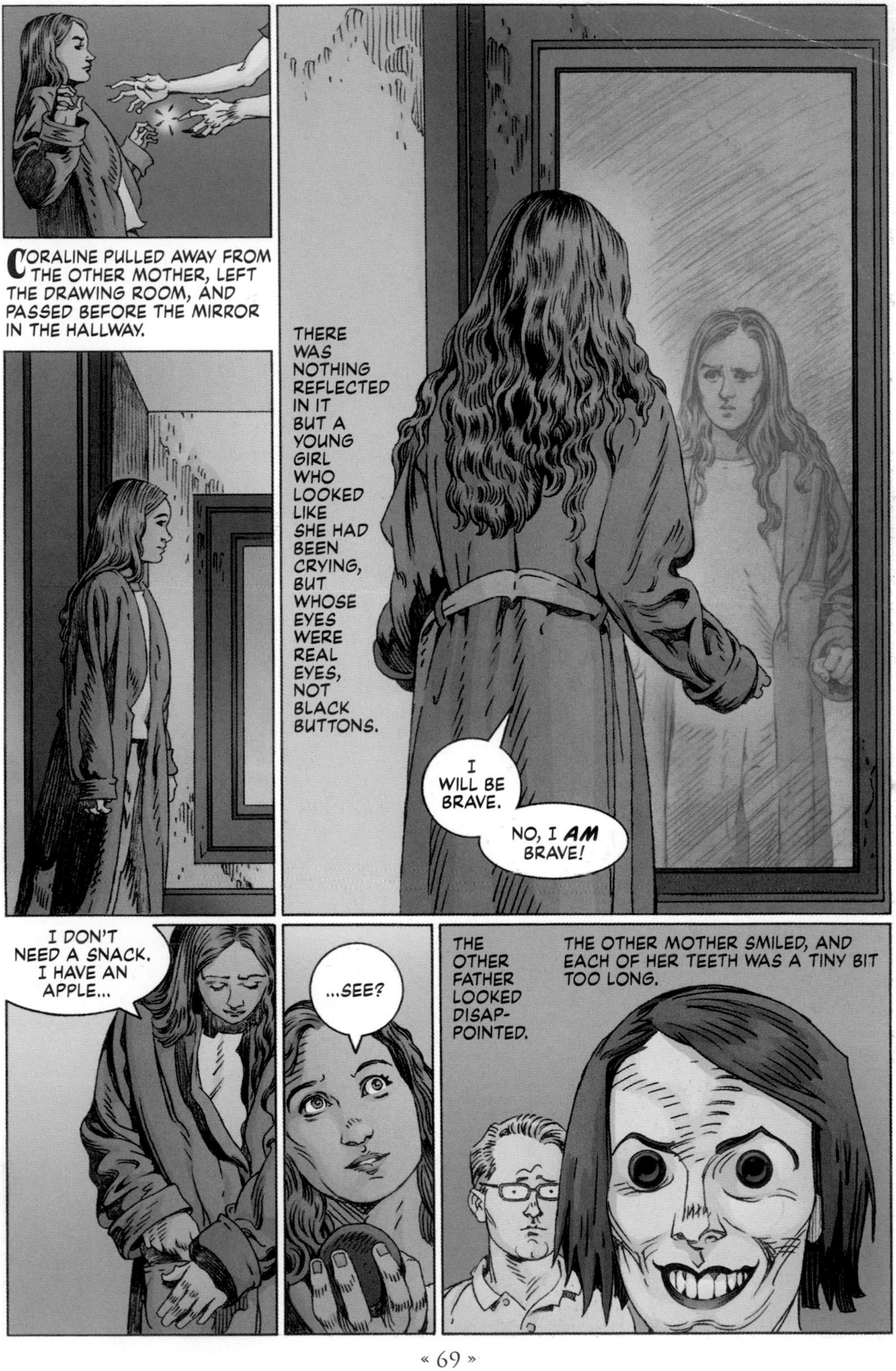
CORALINE PULLED AWAY FROM THE OTHER MOTHER, LEFT THE DRAWING ROOM, AND PASSED BEFORE THE MIRROR IN THE HALLWAY.
THERE WAS NOTHING REFLECTED IN IT BUT A YOUNG GIRL WHO LOOKED LIKE SHE HAD BEEN CRYING, BUT WHOSE EYES WERE REAL EYES, NOT BLACK BUTTONS.
I WILL BE BRAVE.
NO, I ***AM*** BRAVE!
I DON'T NEED A SNACK. I HAVE AN APPLE...
...SEE?
THE OTHER FATHER LOOKED DISAP-POINTED.
THE OTHER MOTHER SMILED, AND EACH OF HER TEETH WAS A TINY BIT TOO LONG.

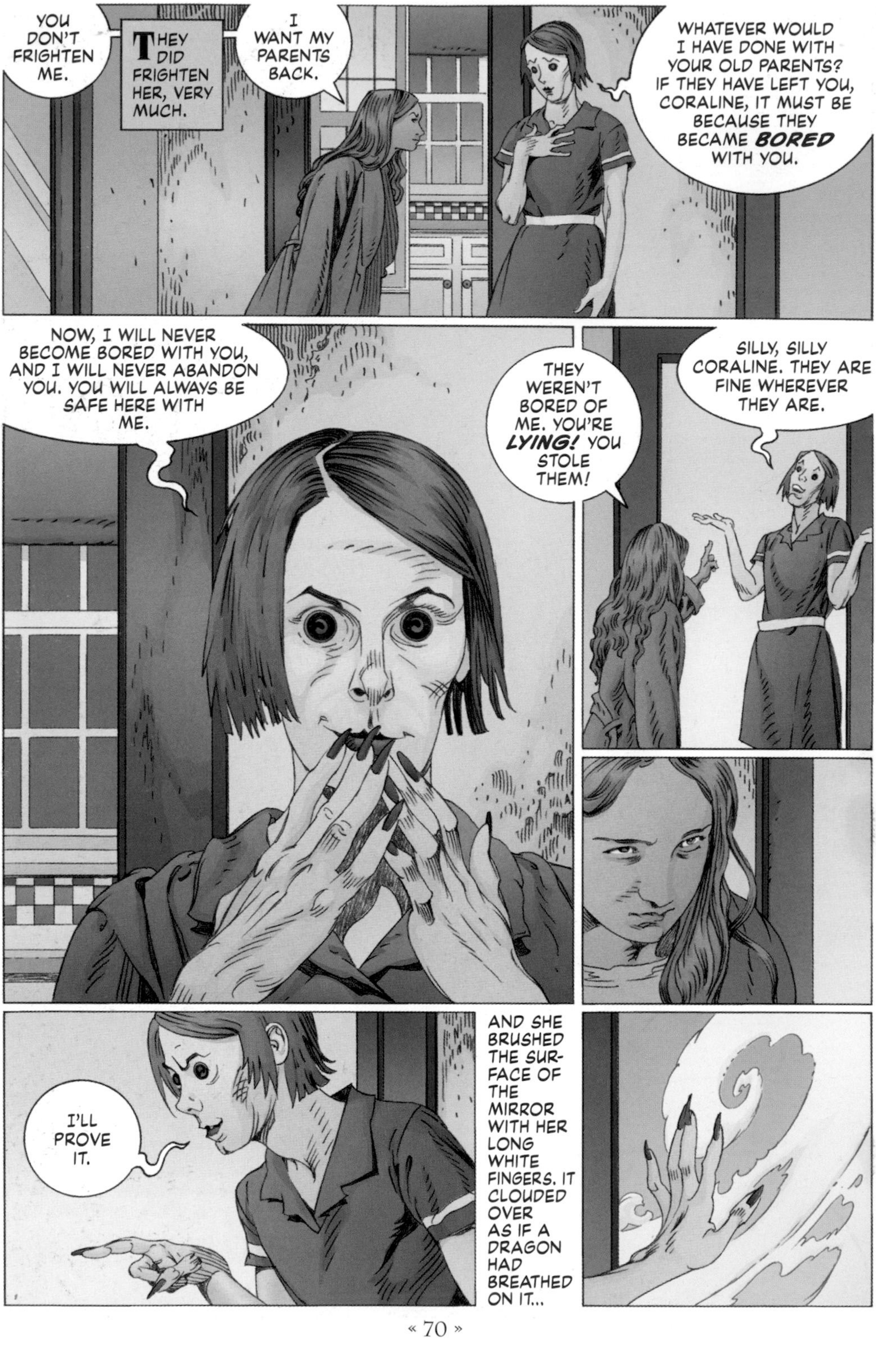
YOU DON'T FRIGHTEN ME.
THEY DID FRIGHTEN HER, VERY MUCH.
I WANT MY PARENTS BACK.
WHATEVER WOULD I HAVE DONE WITH YOUR OLD PARENTS? IF THEY HAVE LEFT YOU, CORALINE, IT MUST BE BECAUSE THEY BECAME BORED WITH YOU.
NOW, I WILL NEVER BECOME BORED WITH YOU, AND I WILL NEVER ABANDON YOU. YOU WILL ALWAYS BE SAFE HERE WITH ME.
THEY WEREN'T BORED OF ME. YOU'RE LYING! YOU STOLE THEM!
SILLY, SILLY CORALINE. THEY ARE FINE WHEREVER THEY ARE.
I'LL PROVE IT.
AND SHE BRUSHED THE SURFACE OF THE MIRROR WITH HER LONG WHITE FINGERS. IT CLOUDED OVER AS IF A DRAGON HAD BREATHED ON IT...

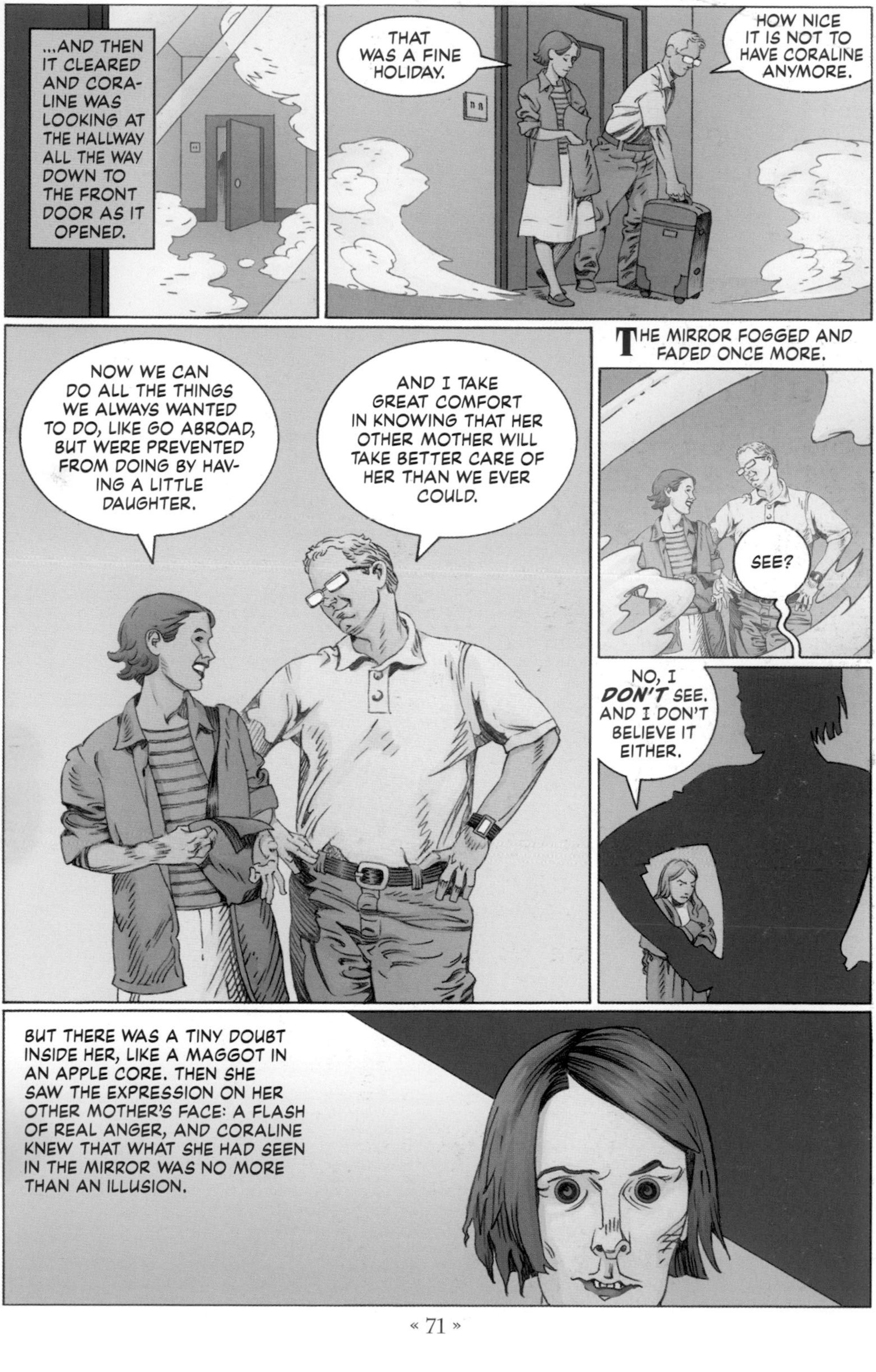

...AND THEN IT CLEARED AND CORALINE WAS LOOKING AT THE HALLWAY ALL THE WAY DOWN TO THE FRONT DOOR AS IT OPENED.
THAT WAS A FINE HOLIDAY.
HOW NICE IT IS NOT TO HAVE CORALINE ANYMORE.
NOW WE CAN DO ALL THE THINGS WE ALWAYS WANTED TO DO, LIKE GO ABROAD, BUT WERE PREVENTED FROM DOING BY HAVING A LITTLE DAUGHTER.
AND I TAKE GREAT COMFORT IN KNOWING THAT HER OTHER MOTHER WILL TAKE BETTER CARE OF HER THAN WE EVER COULD.
THE MIRROR FOGGED AND FADED ONCE MORE.
SEE?
NO, I DON'T SEE. AND I DON'T BELIEVE IT EITHER.
BUT THERE WAS A TINY DOUBT INSIDE HER, LIKE A MAGGOT IN AN APPLE CORE. THEN SHE SAW THE EXPRESSION ON HER OTHER MOTHER'S FACE: A FLASH OF REAL ANGER, AND CORALINE KNEW THAT WHAT SHE HAD SEEN IN THE MIRROR WAS NO MORE THAN AN ILLUSION.

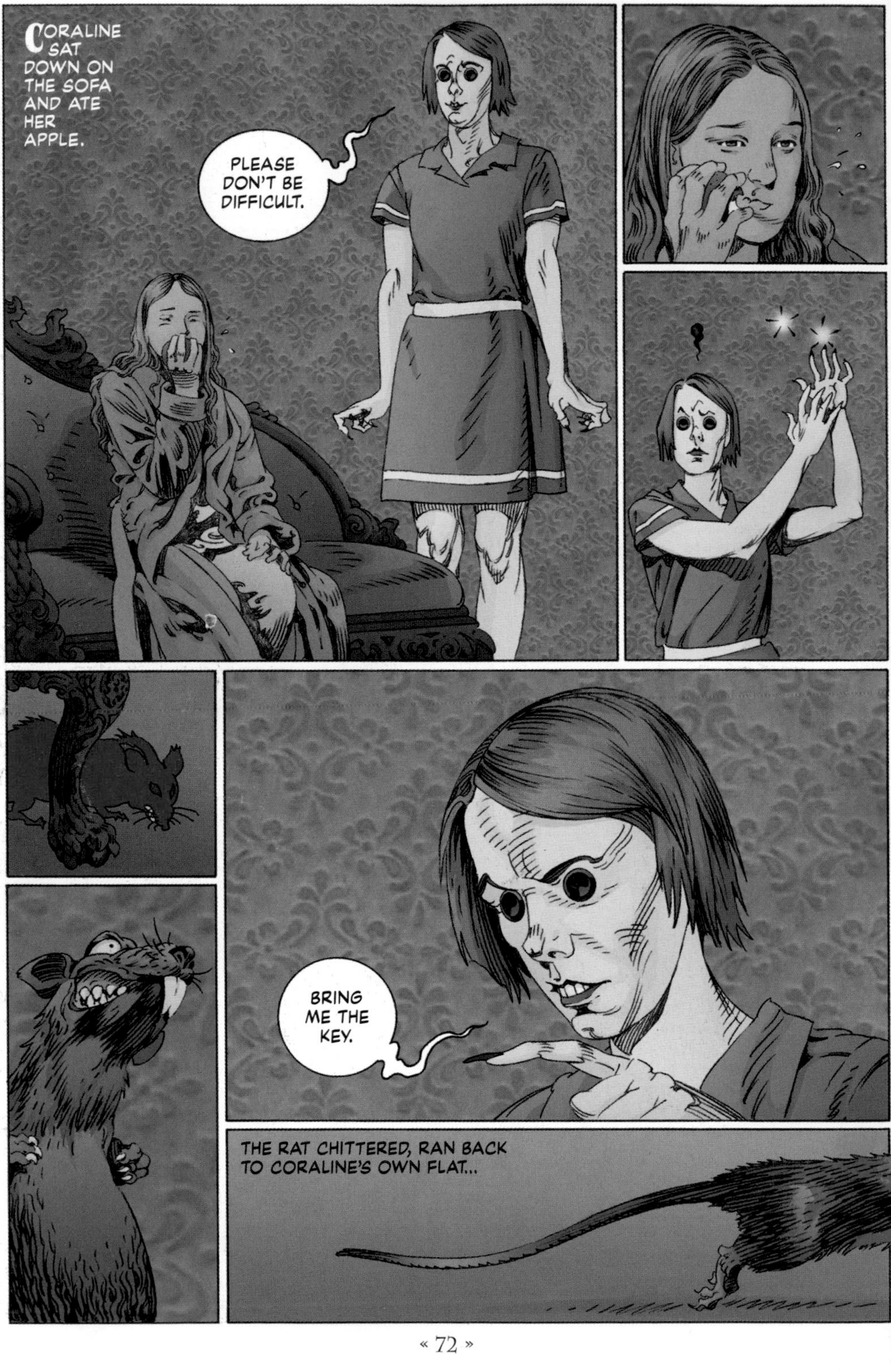
CORALINE SAT DOWN ON THE SOFA AND ATE HER APPLE.
PLEASE DON'T BE DIFFICULT.
BRING ME THE KEY.
THE RAT CHITTERED, RAN BACK TO CORALINE'S OWN FLAT...

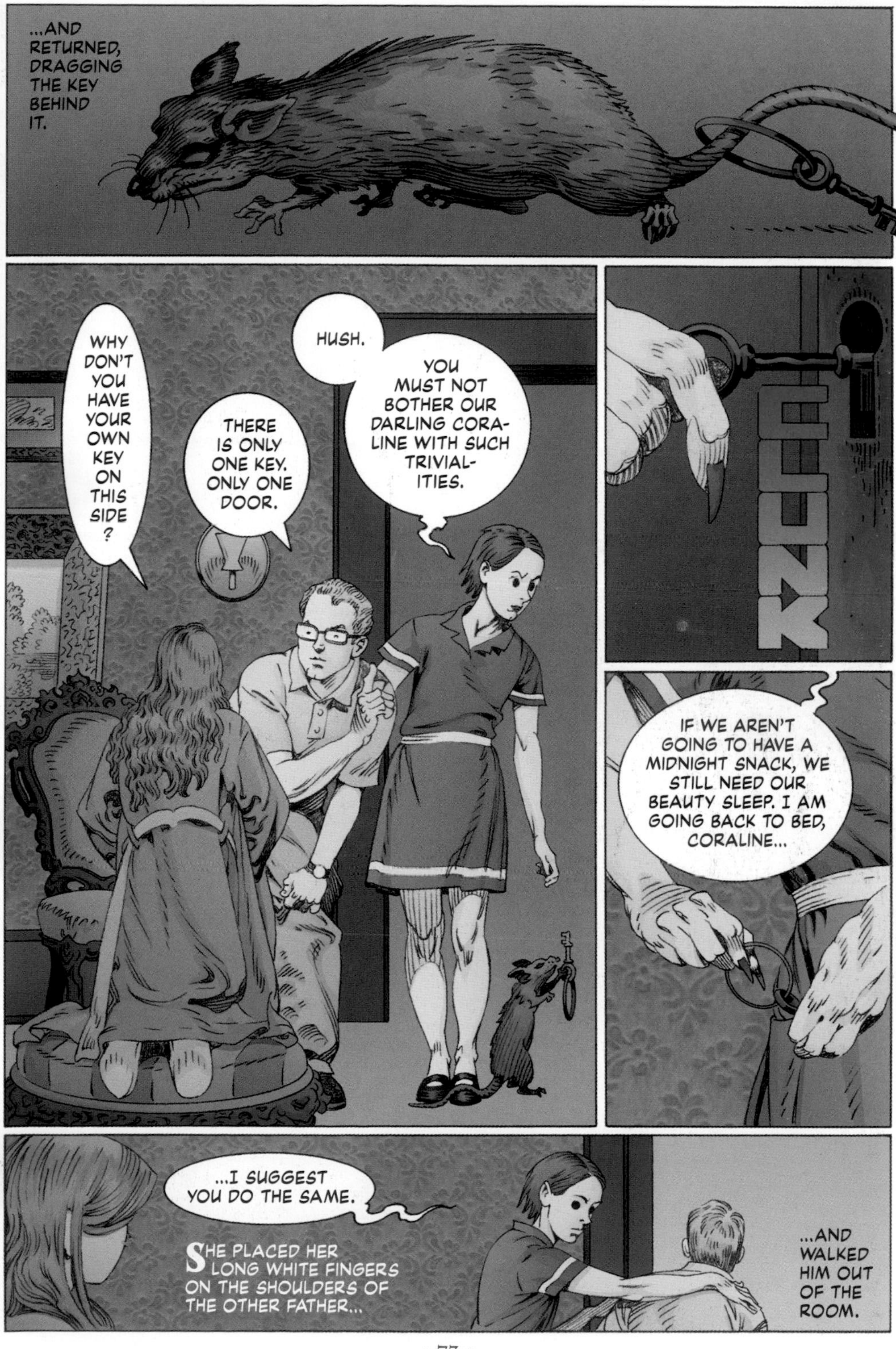
...AND RETURNED, DRAGGING THE KEY BEHIND IT.
WHY DON'T YOU HAVE YOUR OWN KEY ON THIS SIDE ?
THERE IS ONLY ONE KEY. ONLY ONE DOOR.
HUSH.
YOU MUST NOT BOTHER OUR DARLING CORALINE WITH SUCH TRIVIALITIES.
CLUNK
IF WE AREN'T GOING TO HAVE A MIDNIGHT SNACK, WE STILL NEED OUR BEAUTY SLEEP. I AM GOING BACK TO BED, CORALINE...
...I SUGGEST YOU DO THE SAME.
SHE PLACED HER LONG WHITE FINGERS ON THE SHOULDERS OF THE OTHER FATHER...
...AND WALKED HIM OUT OF THE ROOM.

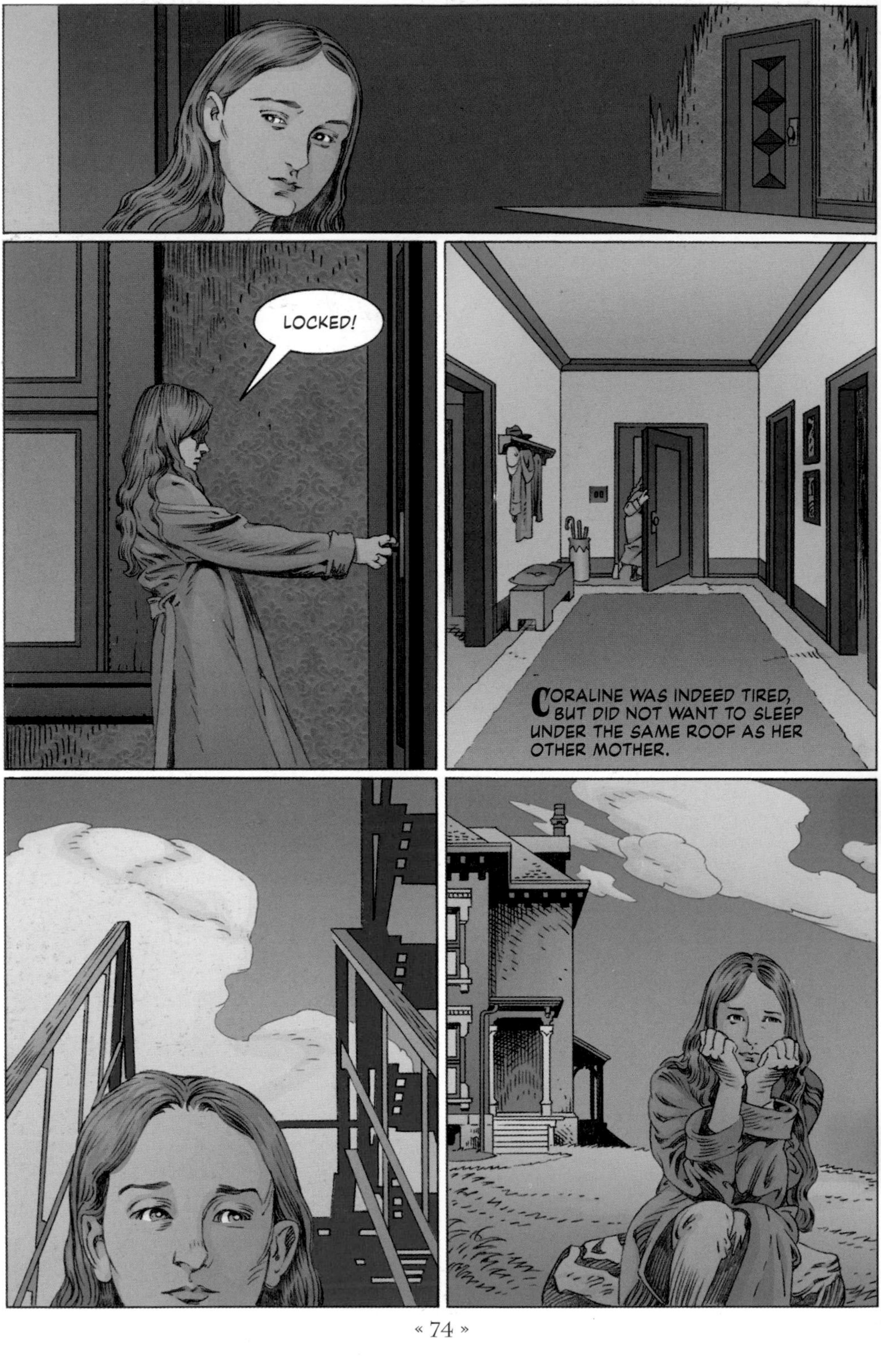
LOCKED!
CORALINE WAS INDEED TIRED, BUT DID NOT WANT TO SLEEP UNDER THE SAME ROOF AS HER OTHER MOTHER.

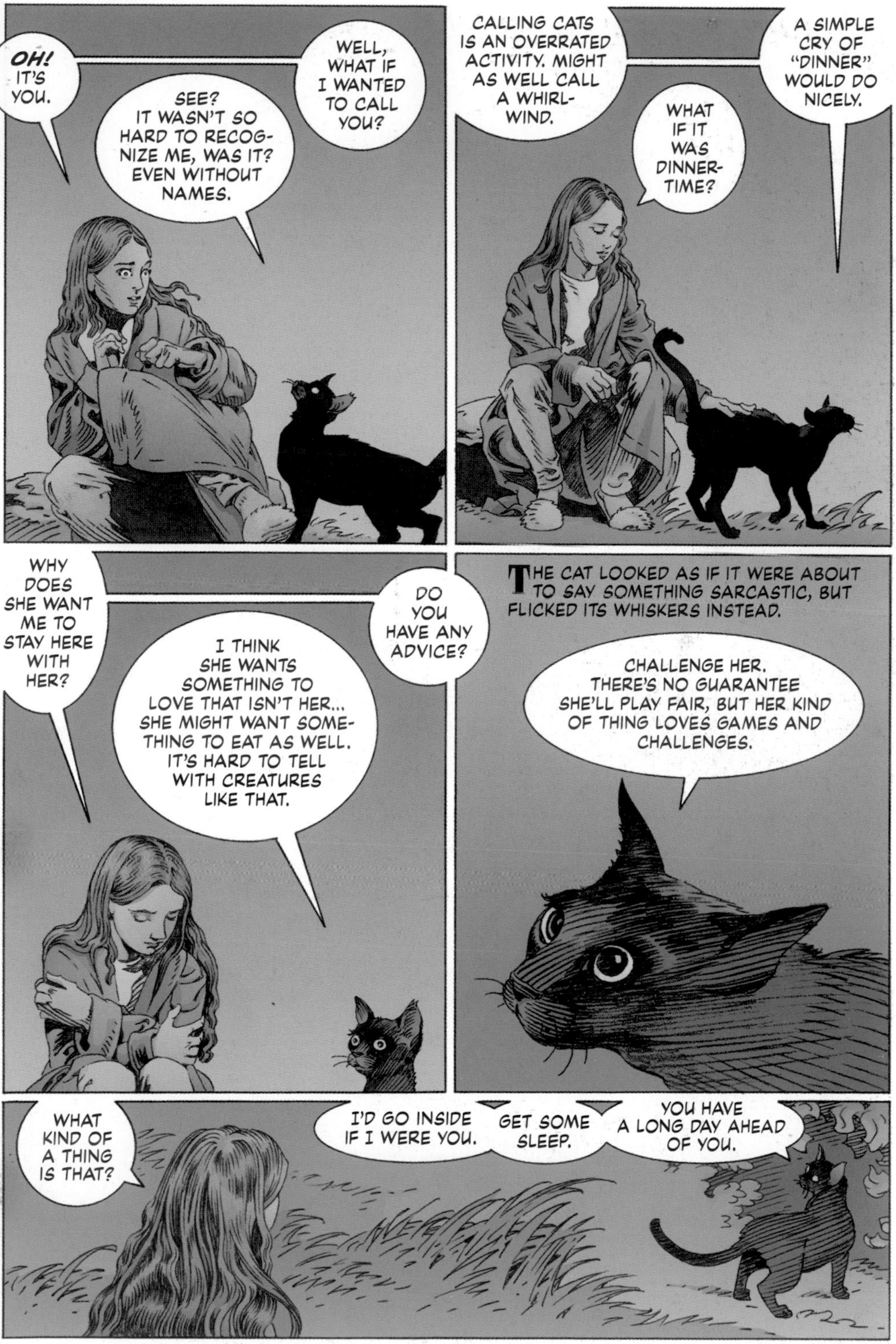
OH! IT'S YOU.
WELL, WHAT IF I WANTED TO CALL YOU?
SEE? IT WASN'T SO HARD TO RECOGNIZE ME, WAS IT? EVEN WITHOUT NAMES.
CALLING CATS IS AN OVERRATED ACTIVITY. MIGHT AS WELL CALL A WHIRLWIND.
A SIMPLE CRY OF "DINNER" WOULD DO NICELY.
WHAT IF IT WAS DINNERTIME?
WHY DOES SHE WANT ME TO STAY HERE WITH HER?
DO YOU HAVE ANY ADVICE?
I THINK SHE WANTS SOMETHING TO LOVE THAT ISN'T HER... SHE MIGHT WANT SOMETHING TO EAT AS WELL. IT'S HARD TO TELL WITH CREATURES LIKE THAT.
THE CAT LOOKED AS IF IT WERE ABOUT TO SAY SOMETHING SARCASTIC, BUT FLICKED ITS WHISKERS INSTEAD.
CHALLENGE HER. THERE'S NO GUARANTEE SHE'LL PLAY FAIR, BUT HER KIND OF THING LOVES GAMES AND CHALLENGES.
WHAT KIND OF A THING IS THAT?
I'D GO INSIDE IF I WERE YOU.
GET SOME SLEEP.
YOU HAVE A LONG DAY AHEAD OF YOU.

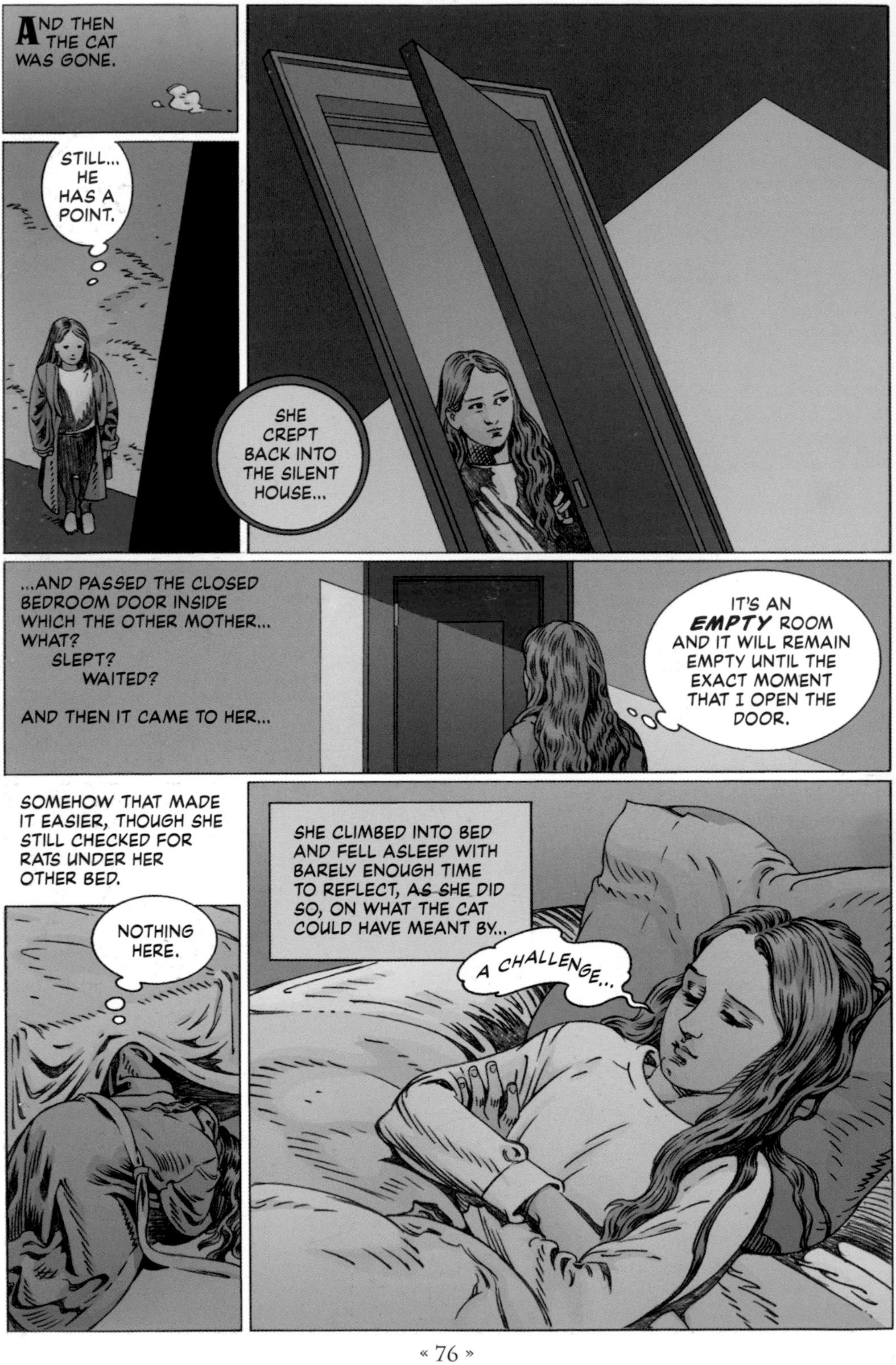
AND THEN THE CAT WAS GONE.
STILL... HE HAS A POINT.
SHE CREPT BACK INTO THE SILENT HOUSE...
...AND PASSED THE CLOSED BEDROOM DOOR INSIDE WHICH THE OTHER MOTHER... WHAT? SLEPT? WAITED?
AND THEN IT CAME TO HER...
IT'S AN EMPTY ROOM AND IT WILL REMAIN EMPTY UNTIL THE EXACT MOMENT THAT I OPEN THE DOOR.
SOMEHOW THAT MADE IT EASIER, THOUGH SHE STILL CHECKED FOR RATS UNDER HER OTHER BED.
NOTHING HERE.
SHE CLIMBED INTO BED AND FELL ASLEEP WITH BARELY ENOUGH TIME TO REFLECT, AS SHE DID SO, ON WHAT THE CAT COULD HAVE MEANT BY...
A CHALLENGE...

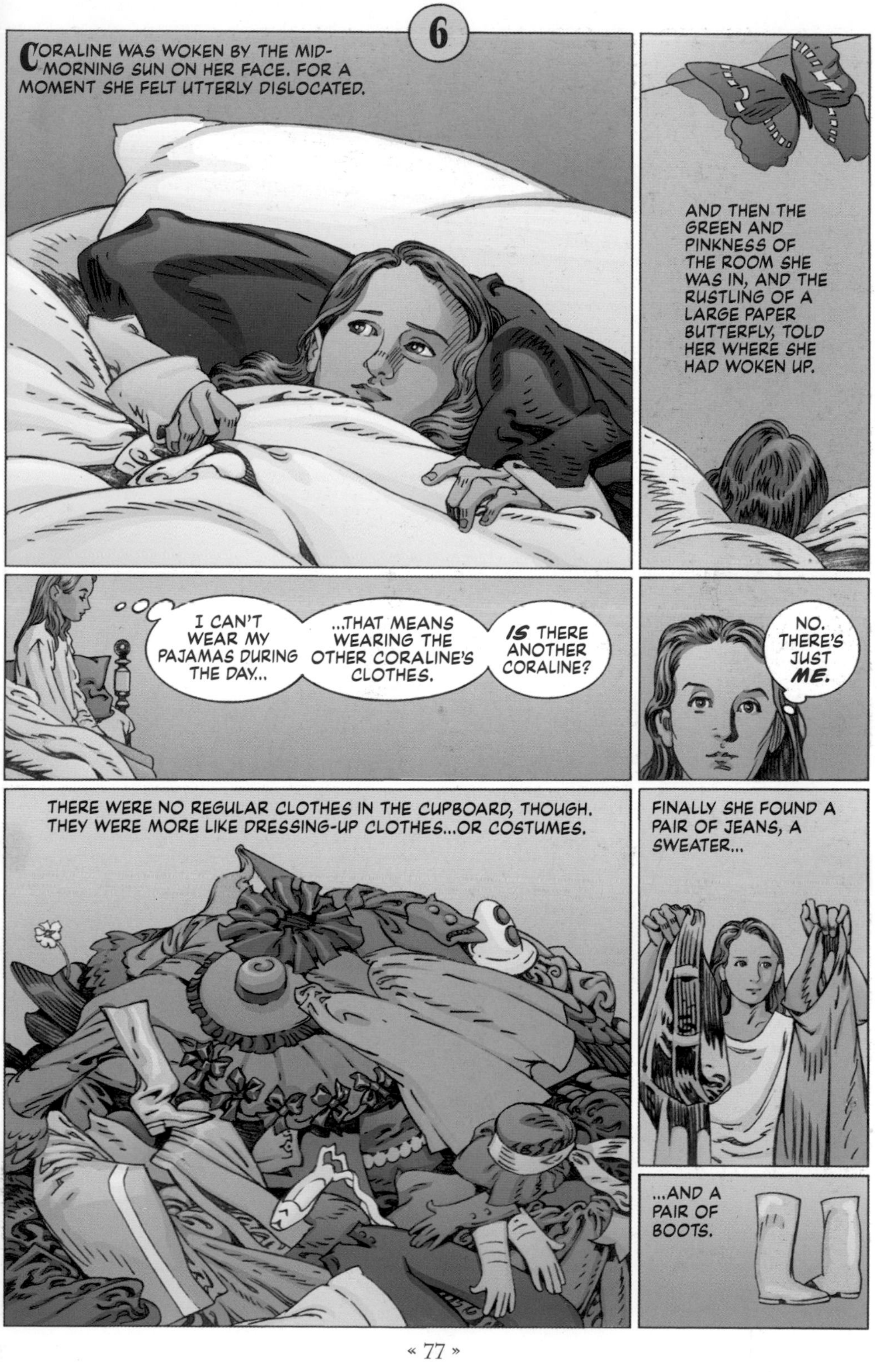
6
CORALINE WAS WOKEN BY THE MID-MORNING SUN ON HER FACE. FOR A MOMENT SHE FELT UTTERLY DISLOCATED.
AND THEN THE GREEN AND PINKNESS OF THE ROOM SHE WAS IN, AND THE RUSTLING OF A LARGE PAPER BUTTERFLY, TOLD HER WHERE SHE HAD WOKEN UP.
I CAN'T WEAR MY PAJAMAS DURING THE DAY...
...THAT MEANS WEARING THE OTHER CORALINE'S CLOTHES.
IS THERE ANOTHER CORALINE?
NO. THERE'S JUST *ME.*
THERE WERE NO REGULAR CLOTHES IN THE CUPBOARD, THOUGH. THEY WERE MORE LIKE DRESSING-UP CLOTHES...OR COSTUMES.
FINALLY SHE FOUND A PAIR OF JEANS, A SWEATER...
...AND A PAIR OF BOOTS.

FROM OUT OF HER POCKET SHE TOOK HER LAST APPLE AND THE STONE WITH A HOLE IN IT.

SHE PUT THE STONE BACK INTO HER POCKET AND IT WAS AS IF HER HEAD HAD CLEARED A LITTLE...

...LIKE COMING OUT OF A FOG.

SHE WENT INTO THE KITCHEN, BUT IT WAS DESERTED.

STILL, SHE WAS SURE THAT THERE WAS SOMEONE IN THE FLAT. SHE WALKED DOWN THE HALL.

THE OTHER FATHER WAS SITTING AT A DESK JUST LIKE HER FATHER'S, BUT HE WAS ONLY PRETENDING TO BE WORKING.

WHERE'S THE OTHER MOTHER?

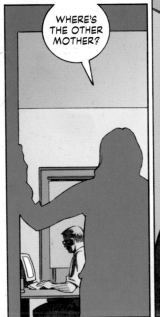

OUT. FIXING THE DOORS. THERE ARE SOME VERMIN PROBLEMS.

THE RATS, YOU MEAN?

NO, THE RATS ARE OUR FRIENDS. THIS IS THE OTHER KIND. BIG BLACK FELLOW WITH HIS TAIL HIGH.

THE CAT, YOU MEAN?

THAT'S THE ONE.

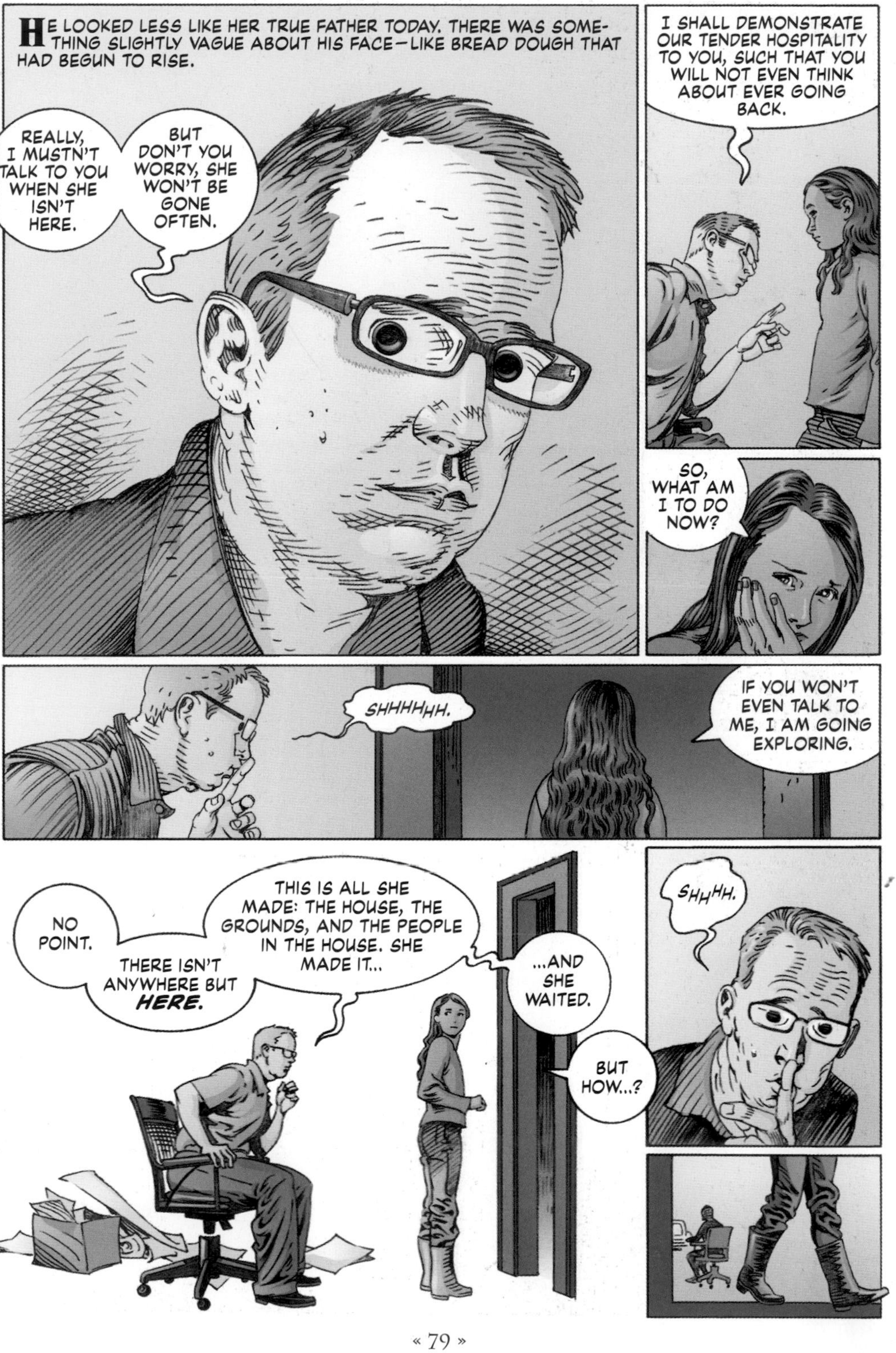
HE LOOKED LESS LIKE HER TRUE FATHER TODAY. THERE WAS SOMETHING SLIGHTLY VAGUE ABOUT HIS FACE—LIKE BREAD DOUGH THAT HAD BEGUN TO RISE.
REALLY, I MUSTN'T TALK TO YOU WHEN SHE ISN'T HERE.
BUT DON'T YOU WORRY, SHE WON'T BE GONE OFTEN.
I SHALL DEMONSTRATE OUR TENDER HOSPITALITY TO YOU, SUCH THAT YOU WILL NOT EVEN THINK ABOUT EVER GOING BACK.
SO, WHAT AM I TO DO NOW?
SHHHHHH.
IF YOU WON'T EVEN TALK TO ME, I AM GOING EXPLORING.
NO POINT.
THERE ISN'T ANYWHERE BUT HERE.
THIS IS ALL SHE MADE: THE HOUSE, THE GROUNDS, AND THE PEOPLE IN THE HOUSE. SHE MADE IT...
...AND SHE WAITED.
BUT HOW...?
SHHHH.

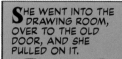

SHE WENT INTO THE DRAWING ROOM, OVER TO THE OLD DOOR, AND SHE PULLED ON IT.

RATS! IT'S LOCKED FAST...

...AND THE OTHER MOTHER HAS THE KEY.

SHE LOOKED AROUND THE ROOM. IT WAS SO FAMILIAR—THAT WAS WHAT MADE IT FEEL SO TRULY STRANGE. EVERYTHING WAS EXACTLY THE SAME AS SHE REMEMBERED...

...BUT THERE WAS SOMETHING ELSE...

...SOMETHING SHE DID NOT REMEMBER SEEING BEFORE.

A BALL OF GLASS, UP ON THE MANTELPIECE.

A SNOW GLOBE WITH TWO LITTLE PEOPLE IN IT.

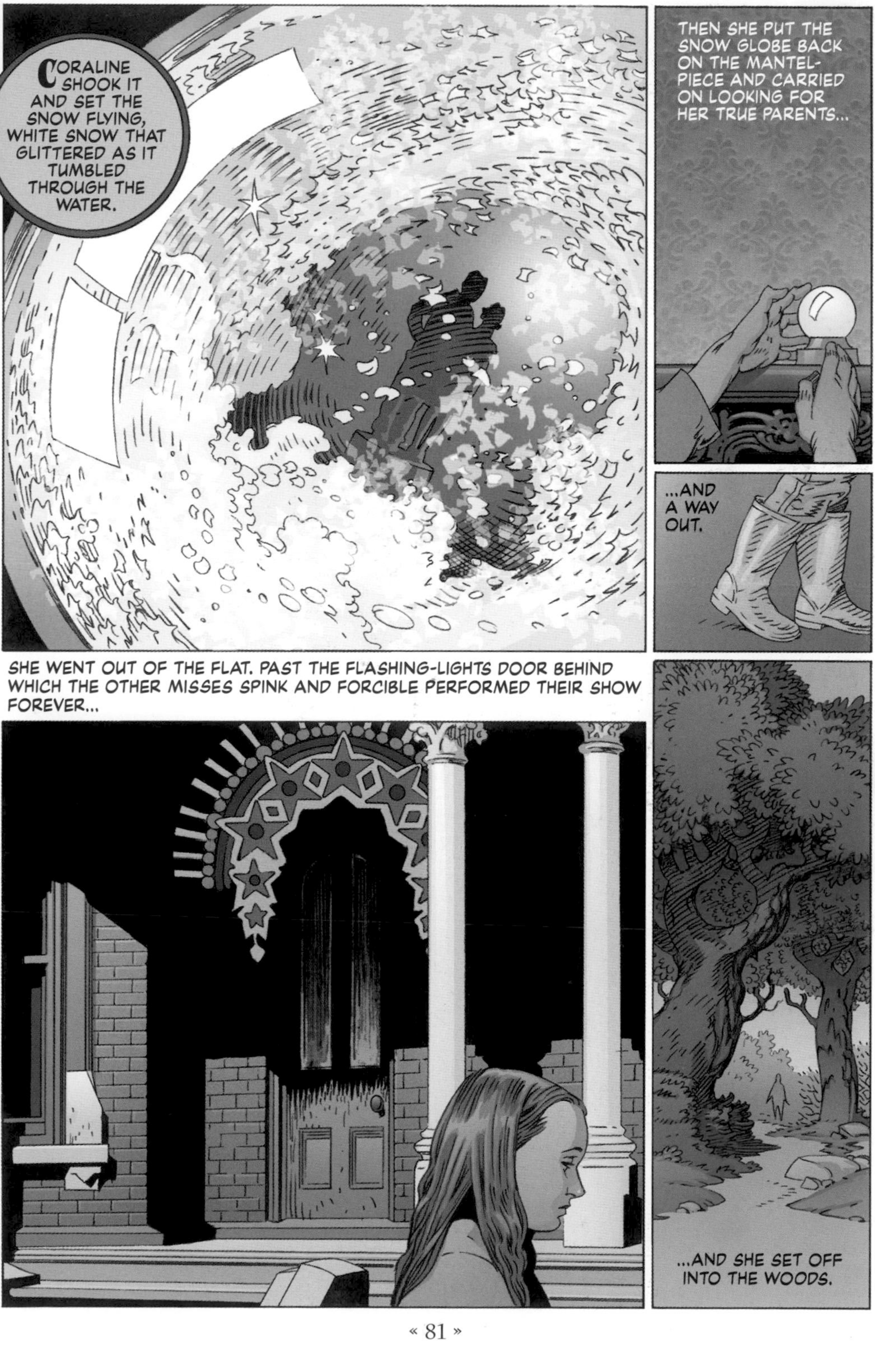
CORALINE SHOOK IT AND SET THE SNOW FLYING, WHITE SNOW THAT GLITTERED AS IT TUMBLED THROUGH THE WATER.
THEN SHE PUT THE SNOW GLOBE BACK ON THE MANTEL-PIECE AND CARRIED ON LOOKING FOR HER TRUE PARENTS...
...AND A WAY OUT.
SHE WENT OUT OF THE FLAT. PAST THE FLASHING-LIGHTS DOOR BEHIND WHICH THE OTHER MISSES SPINK AND FORCIBLE PERFORMED THEIR SHOW FOREVER...
...AND SHE SET OFF INTO THE WOODS.

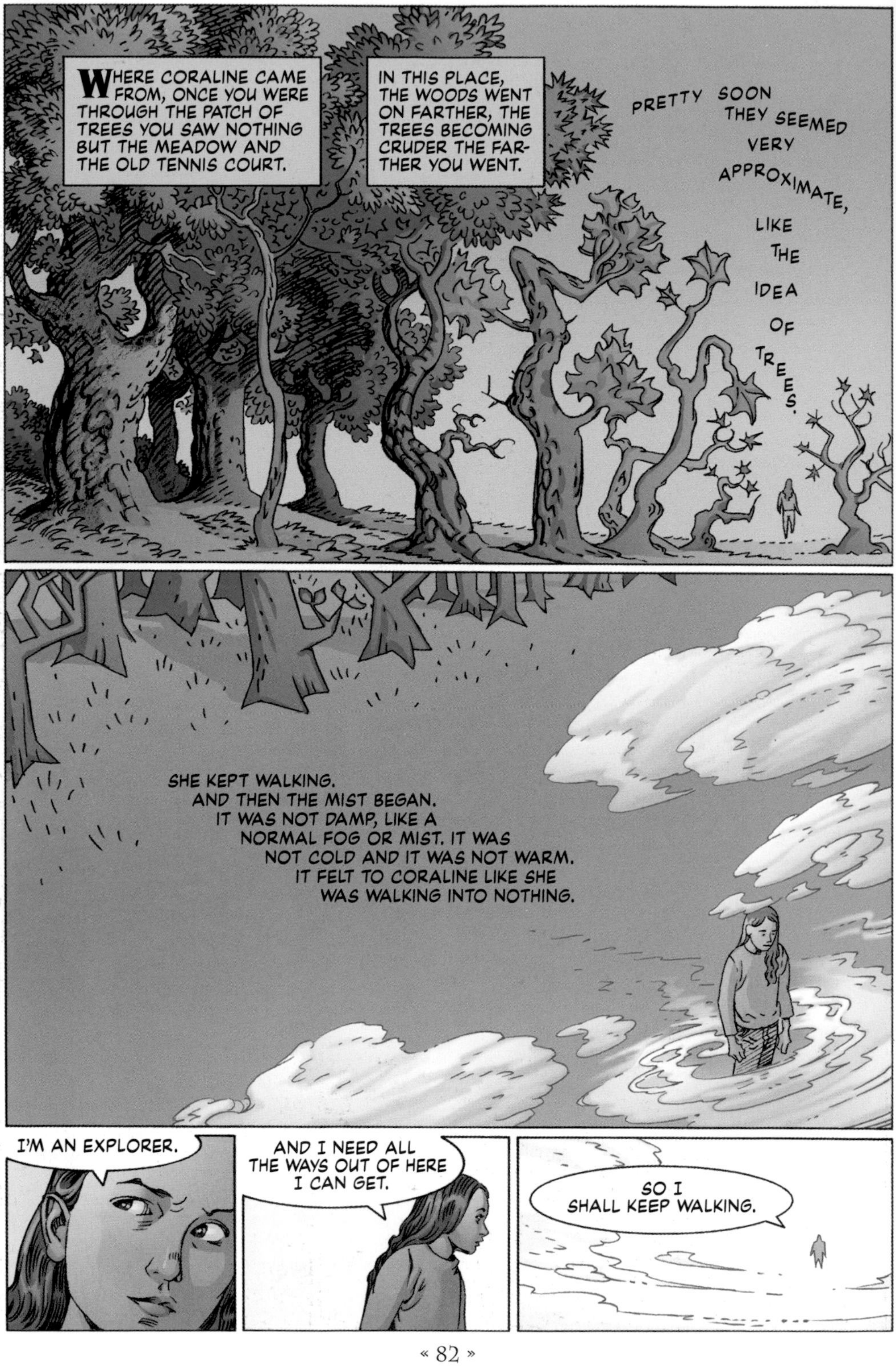

WHERE CORALINE CAME FROM, ONCE YOU WERE THROUGH THE PATCH OF TREES YOU SAW NOTHING BUT THE MEADOW AND THE OLD TENNIS COURT.
IN THIS PLACE, THE WOODS WENT ON FARTHER, THE TREES BECOMING CRUDER THE FARTHER YOU WENT.
PRETTY SOON THEY SEEMED VERY APPROXIMATE, LIKE THE IDEA OF TREES.
SHE KEPT WALKING. AND THEN THE MIST BEGAN. IT WAS NOT DAMP, LIKE A NORMAL FOG OR MIST. IT WAS NOT COLD AND IT WAS NOT WARM. IT FELT TO CORALINE LIKE SHE WAS WALKING INTO NOTHING.
I'M AN EXPLORER.
AND I NEED ALL THE WAYS OUT OF HERE I CAN GET.
SO I SHALL KEEP WALKING.

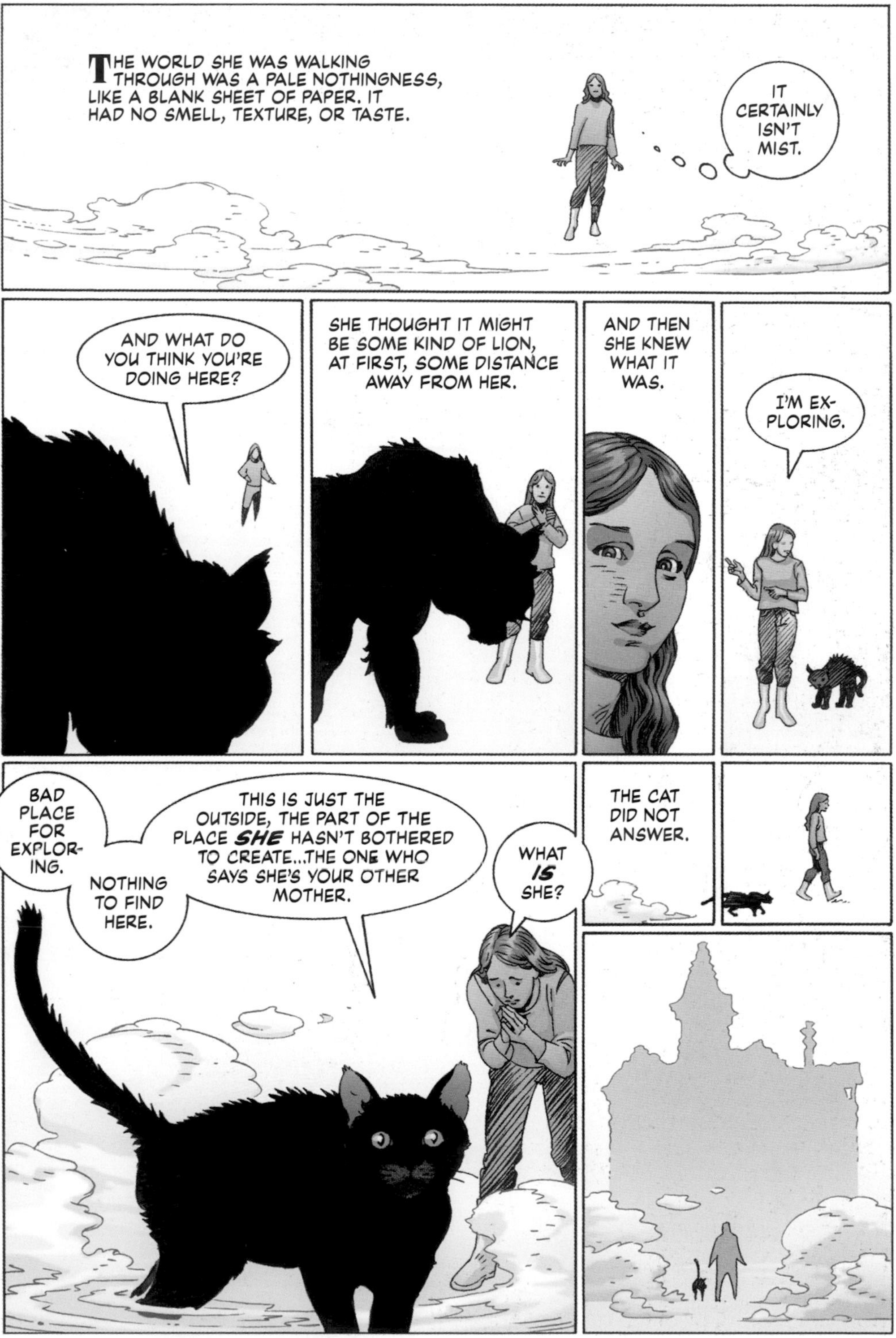
THE WORLD SHE WAS WALKING THROUGH WAS A PALE NOTHINGNESS, LIKE A BLANK SHEET OF PAPER. IT HAD NO SMELL, TEXTURE, OR TASTE.
IT CERTAINLY ISN'T MIST.
AND WHAT DO YOU THINK YOU'RE DOING HERE?
SHE THOUGHT IT MIGHT BE SOME KIND OF LION, AT FIRST, SOME DISTANCE AWAY FROM HER.
AND THEN SHE KNEW WHAT IT WAS.
I'M EXPLORING.
BAD PLACE FOR EXPLORING.
NOTHING TO FIND HERE.
THIS IS JUST THE OUTSIDE, THE PART OF THE PLACE SHE HASN'T BOTHERED TO CREATE...THE ONE WHO SAYS SHE'S YOUR OTHER MOTHER.
WHAT IS SHE?
THE CAT DID NOT ANSWER.

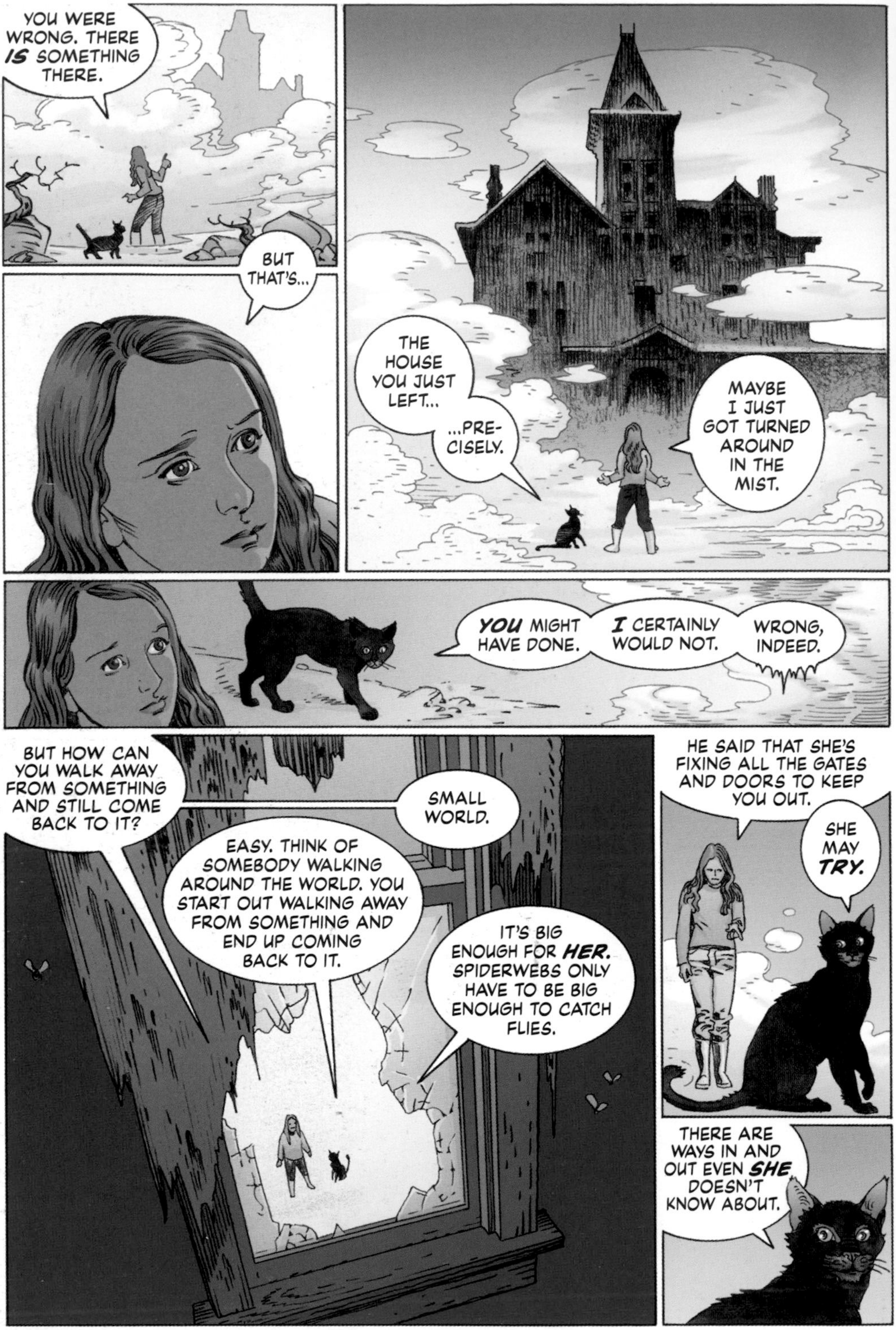
YOU WERE WRONG. THERE IS SOMETHING THERE.
BUT THAT'S...
THE HOUSE YOU JUST LEFT...
...PRE-CISELY.
MAYBE I JUST GOT TURNED AROUND IN THE MIST.
YOU MIGHT HAVE DONE.
I CERTAINLY WOULD NOT.
WRONG, INDEED.
BUT HOW CAN YOU WALK AWAY FROM SOMETHING AND STILL COME BACK TO IT?
SMALL WORLD.
EASY. THINK OF SOMEBODY WALKING AROUND THE WORLD. YOU START OUT WALKING AWAY FROM SOMETHING AND END UP COMING BACK TO IT.
IT'S BIG ENOUGH FOR HER. SPIDERWEBS ONLY HAVE TO BE BIG ENOUGH TO CATCH FLIES.
HE SAID THAT SHE'S FIXING ALL THE GATES AND DOORS TO KEEP YOU OUT.
SHE MAY TRY.
THERE ARE WAYS IN AND OUT EVEN SHE DOESN'T KNOW ABOUT.

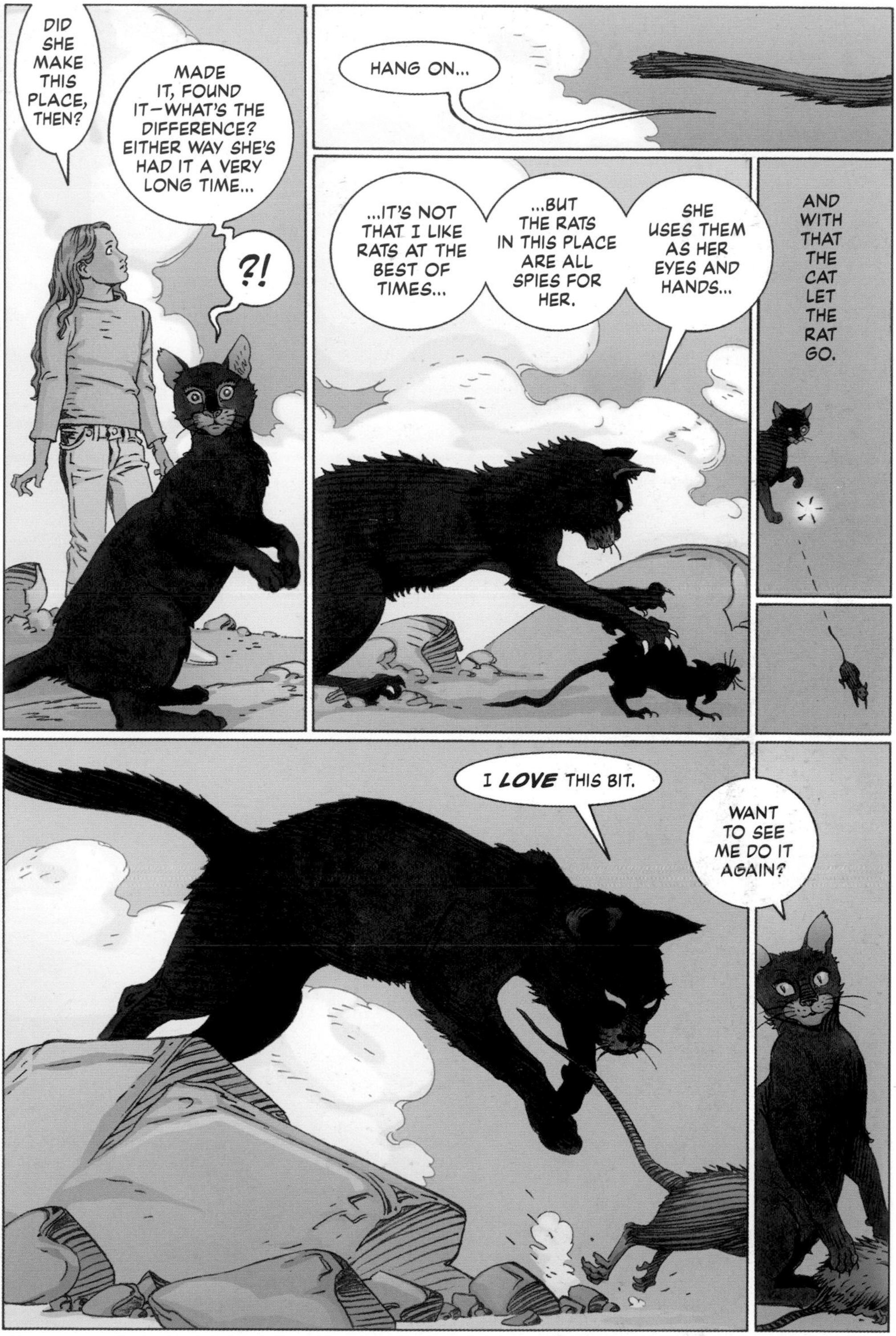
DID SHE MAKE THIS PLACE, THEN?
MADE IT, FOUND IT—WHAT'S THE DIFFERENCE? EITHER WAY SHE'S HAD IT A VERY LONG TIME...
?!
HANG ON...
...IT'S NOT THAT I LIKE RATS AT THE BEST OF TIMES...
...BUT THE RATS IN THIS PLACE ARE ALL SPIES FOR HER.
SHE USES THEM AS HER EYES AND HANDS...
AND WITH THAT THE CAT LET THE RAT GO.
I **LOVE** THIS BIT.
WANT TO SEE ME DO IT AGAIN?

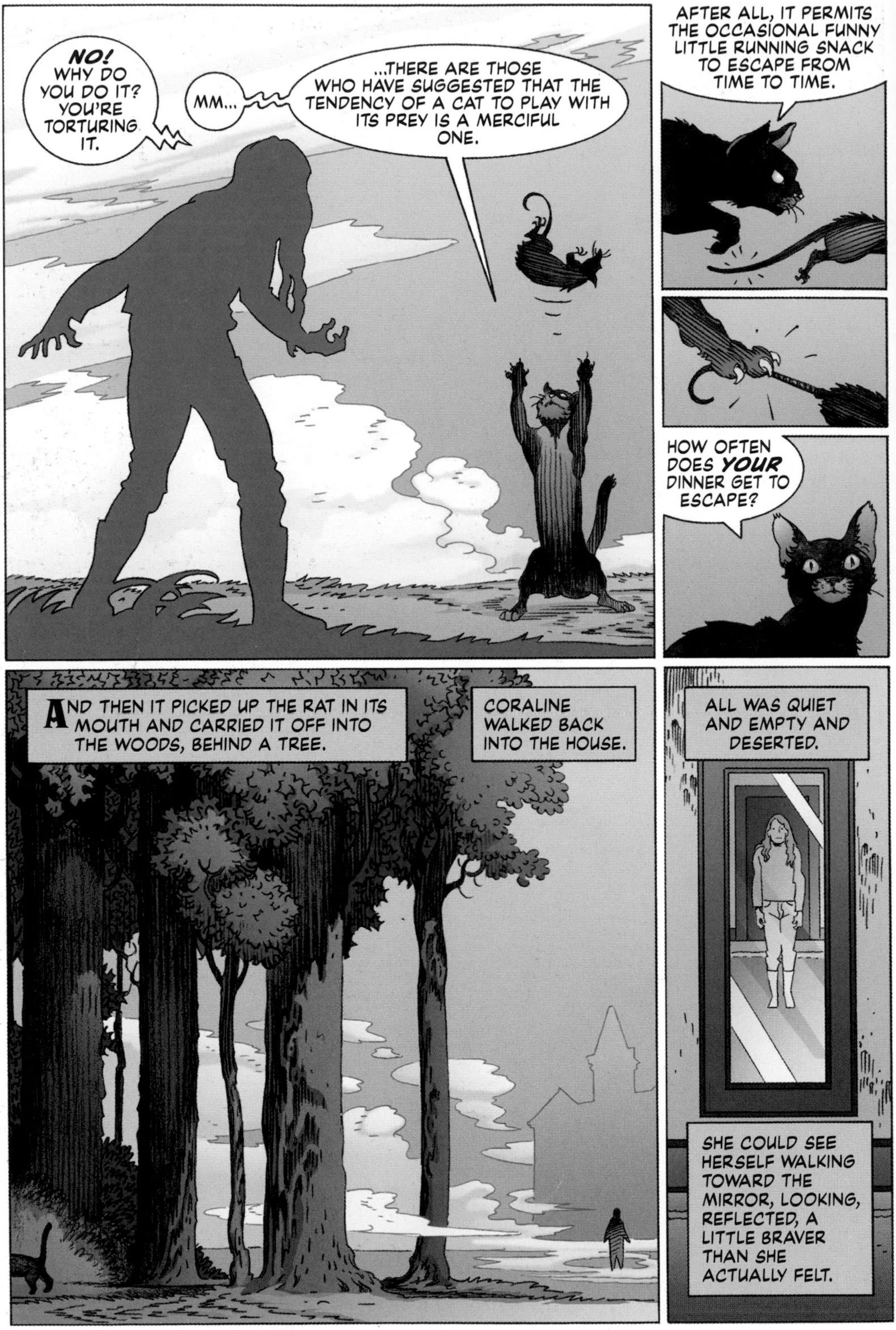
NO! WHY DO YOU DO IT? YOU'RE TORTURING IT.
MM...
...THERE ARE THOSE WHO HAVE SUGGESTED THAT THE TENDENCY OF A CAT TO PLAY WITH ITS PREY IS A MERCIFUL ONE.
AFTER ALL, IT PERMITS THE OCCASIONAL FUNNY LITTLE RUNNING SNACK TO ESCAPE FROM TIME TO TIME.
HOW OFTEN DOES *YOUR* DINNER GET TO ESCAPE?
AND THEN IT PICKED UP THE RAT IN ITS MOUTH AND CARRIED IT OFF INTO THE WOODS, BEHIND A TREE.
CORALINE WALKED BACK INTO THE HOUSE.
ALL WAS QUIET AND EMPTY AND DESERTED.
SHE COULD SEE HERSELF WALKING TOWARD THE MIRROR, LOOKING, REFLECTED, A LITTLE BRAVER THAN SHE ACTUALLY FELT.

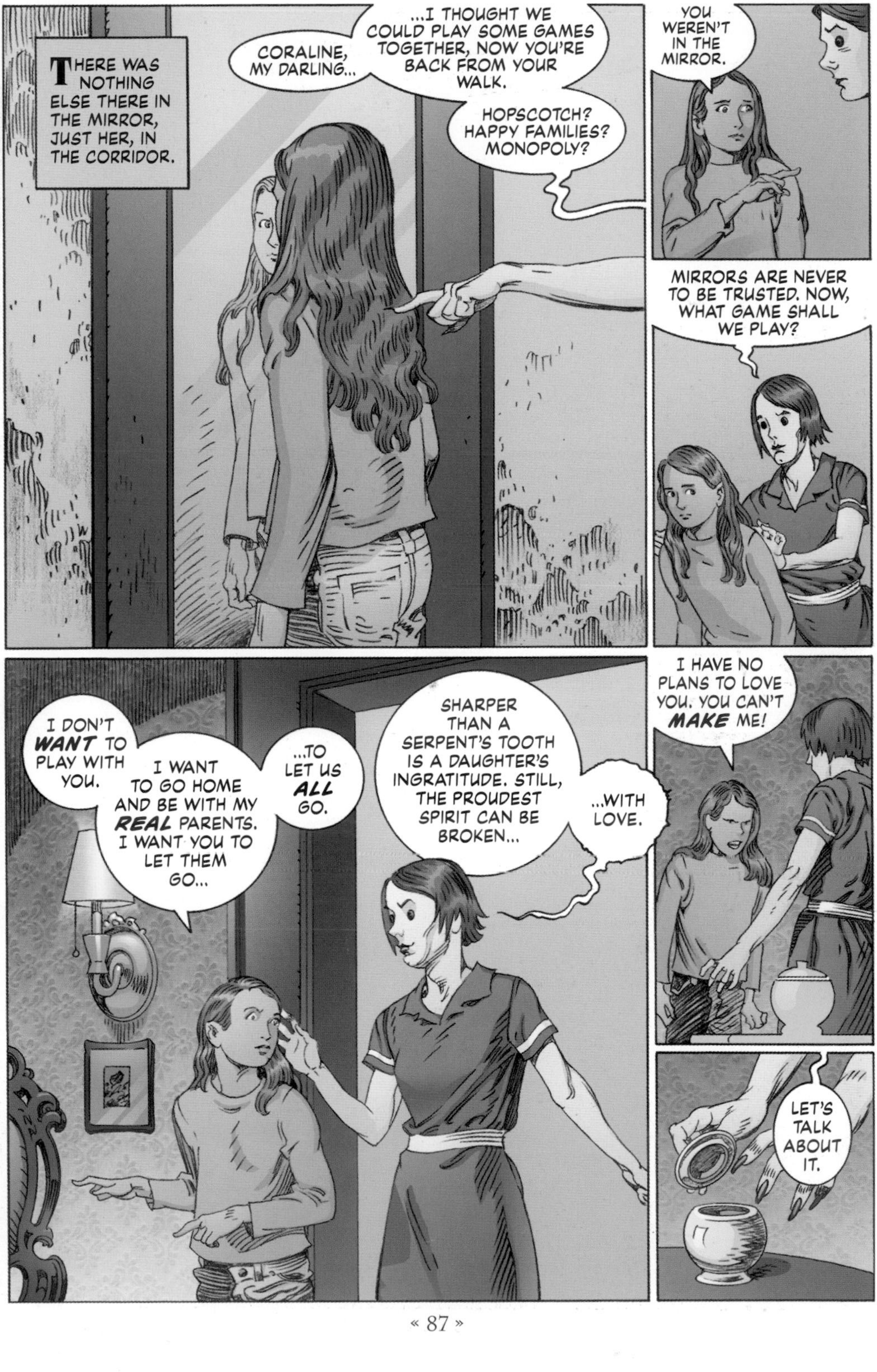
THERE WAS NOTHING ELSE THERE IN THE MIRROR, JUST HER, IN THE CORRIDOR.
CORALINE, MY DARLING...
...I THOUGHT WE COULD PLAY SOME GAMES TOGETHER, NOW YOU'RE BACK FROM YOUR WALK.
HOPSCOTCH? HAPPY FAMILIES? MONOPOLY?
YOU WEREN'T IN THE MIRROR.
MIRRORS ARE NEVER TO BE TRUSTED. NOW, WHAT GAME SHALL WE PLAY?
I DON'T WANT TO PLAY WITH YOU.
I WANT TO GO HOME AND BE WITH MY REAL PARENTS. I WANT YOU TO LET THEM GO...
...TO LET US ALL GO.
SHARPER THAN A SERPENT'S TOOTH IS A DAUGHTER'S INGRATITUDE. STILL, THE PROUDEST SPIRIT CAN BE BROKEN...
...WITH LOVE.
I HAVE NO PLANS TO LOVE YOU. YOU CAN'T MAKE ME!
LET'S TALK ABOUT IT.

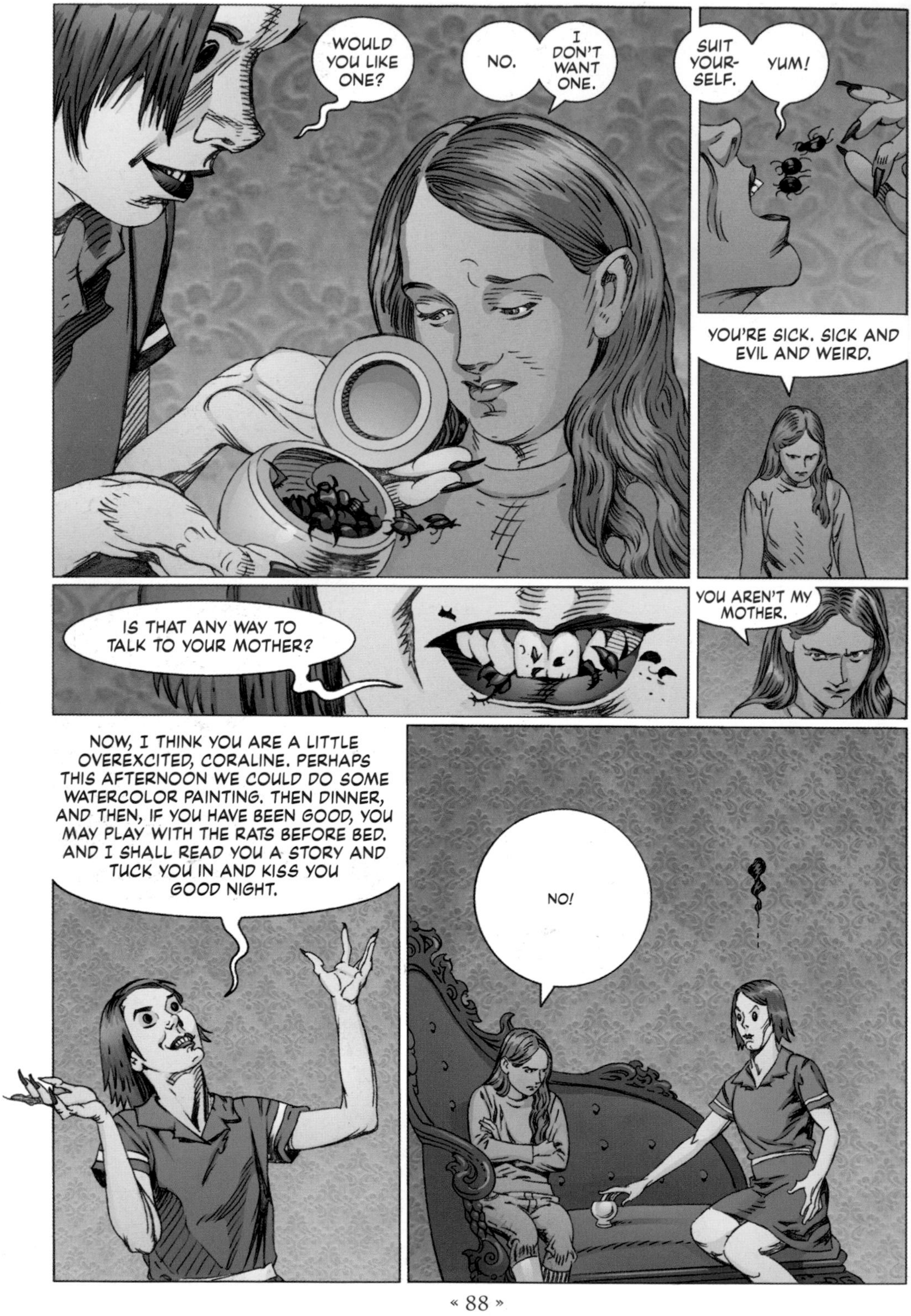
WOULD YOU LIKE ONE?
NO.
I DON'T WANT ONE.
SUIT YOURSELF.
YUM!
YOU'RE SICK. SICK AND EVIL AND WEIRD.
IS THAT ANY WAY TO TALK TO YOUR MOTHER?
YOU AREN'T MY MOTHER.
NOW, I THINK YOU ARE A LITTLE OVEREXCITED, CORALINE. PERHAPS THIS AFTERNOON WE COULD DO SOME WATERCOLOR PAINTING. THEN DINNER, AND THEN, IF YOU HAVE BEEN GOOD, YOU MAY PLAY WITH THE RATS BEFORE BED. AND I SHALL READ YOU A STORY AND TUCK YOU IN AND KISS YOU GOOD NIGHT.
NO!

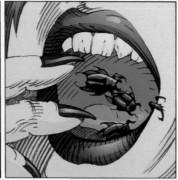

MANNERS!

THERE WE ARE!

THIS IS FOR YOU, CORALINE. FOR YOUR OWN GOOD. BECAUSE I LOVE YOU. TO TEACH YOU MANNERS. *MANNERS MAKETH MAN,* AFTER ALL.

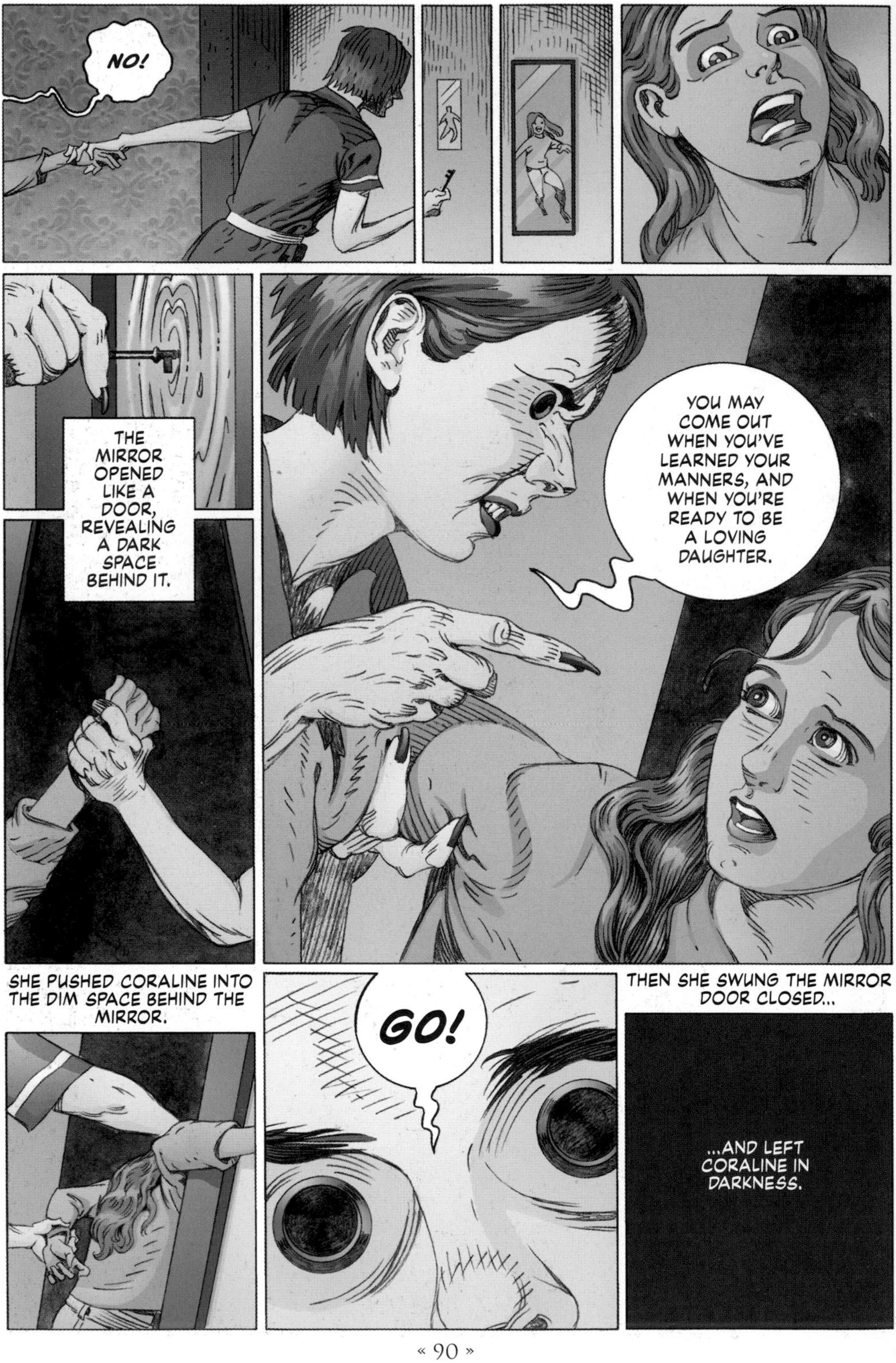
NO!
THE MIRROR OPENED LIKE A DOOR, REVEALING A DARK SPACE BEHIND IT.
YOU MAY COME OUT WHEN YOU'VE LEARNED YOUR MANNERS, AND WHEN YOU'RE READY TO BE A LOVING DAUGHTER.
SHE PUSHED CORALINE INTO THE DIM SPACE BEHIND THE MIRROR.
GO!
THEN SHE SWUNG THE MIRROR DOOR CLOSED...
...AND LEFT CORALINE IN DARKNESS.

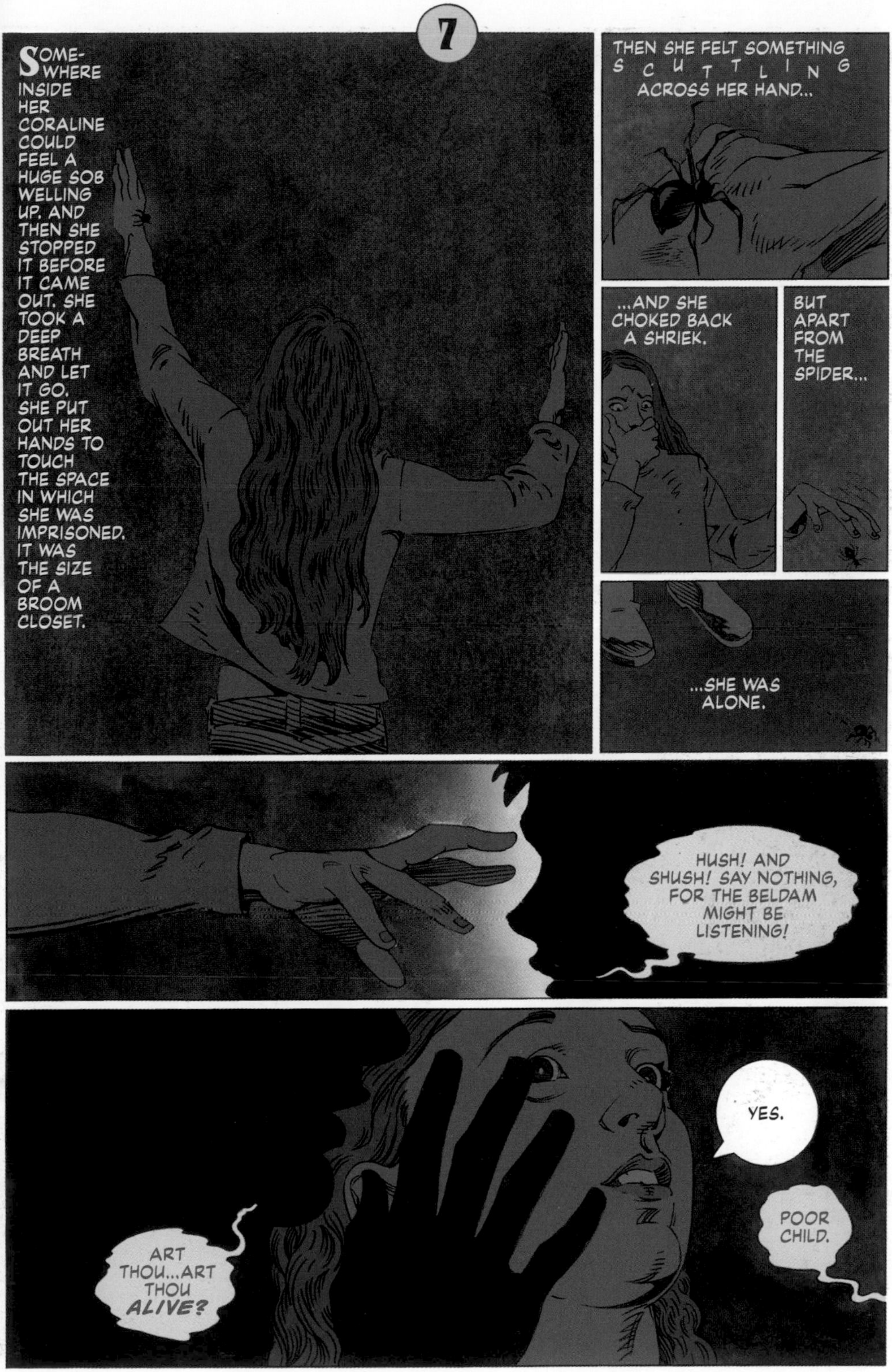
7
SOMEWHERE INSIDE HER CORALINE COULD FEEL A HUGE SOB WELLING UP. AND THEN SHE STOPPED IT BEFORE IT CAME OUT. SHE TOOK A DEEP BREATH AND LET IT GO. SHE PUT OUT HER HANDS TO TOUCH THE SPACE IN WHICH SHE WAS IMPRISONED. IT WAS THE SIZE OF A BROOM CLOSET.
THEN SHE FELT SOMETHING S C U T T L I N G ACROSS HER HAND...
...AND SHE CHOKED BACK A SHRIEK.
BUT APART FROM THE SPIDER...
...SHE WAS ALONE.
HUSH! AND SHUSH! SAY NOTHING, FOR THE BELDAM MIGHT BE LISTENING!
ART THOU...ART THOU ALIVE?
YES.
POOR CHILD.

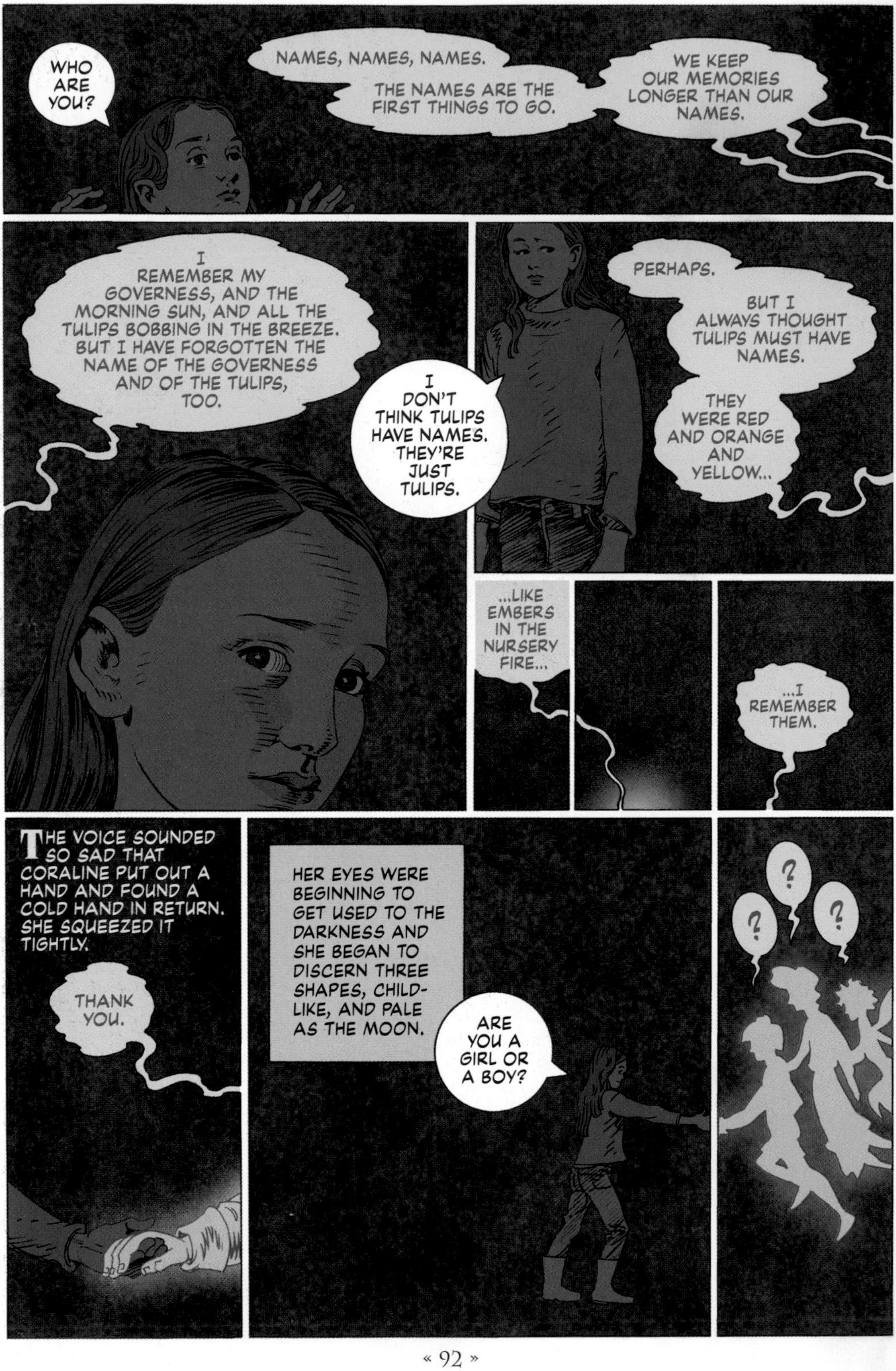
WHO ARE YOU?
NAMES, NAMES, NAMES.
THE NAMES ARE THE FIRST THINGS TO GO.
WE KEEP OUR MEMORIES LONGER THAN OUR NAMES.
I REMEMBER MY GOVERNESS, AND THE MORNING SUN, AND ALL THE TULIPS BOBBING IN THE BREEZE. BUT I HAVE FORGOTTEN THE NAME OF THE GOVERNESS AND OF THE TULIPS, TOO.
I DON'T THINK TULIPS HAVE NAMES. THEY'RE JUST TULIPS.
PERHAPS.
BUT I ALWAYS THOUGHT TULIPS MUST HAVE NAMES.
THEY WERE RED AND ORANGE AND YELLOW...
...LIKE EMBERS IN THE NURSERY FIRE...
...I REMEMBER THEM.
THE VOICE SOUNDED SO SAD THAT CORALINE PUT OUT A HAND AND FOUND A COLD HAND IN RETURN. SHE SQUEEZED IT TIGHTLY.
THANK YOU.
HER EYES WERE BEGINNING TO GET USED TO THE DARKNESS AND SHE BEGAN TO DISCERN THREE SHAPES, CHILD-LIKE, AND PALE AS THE MOON.
ARE YOU A GIRL OR A BOY?
?
?
?

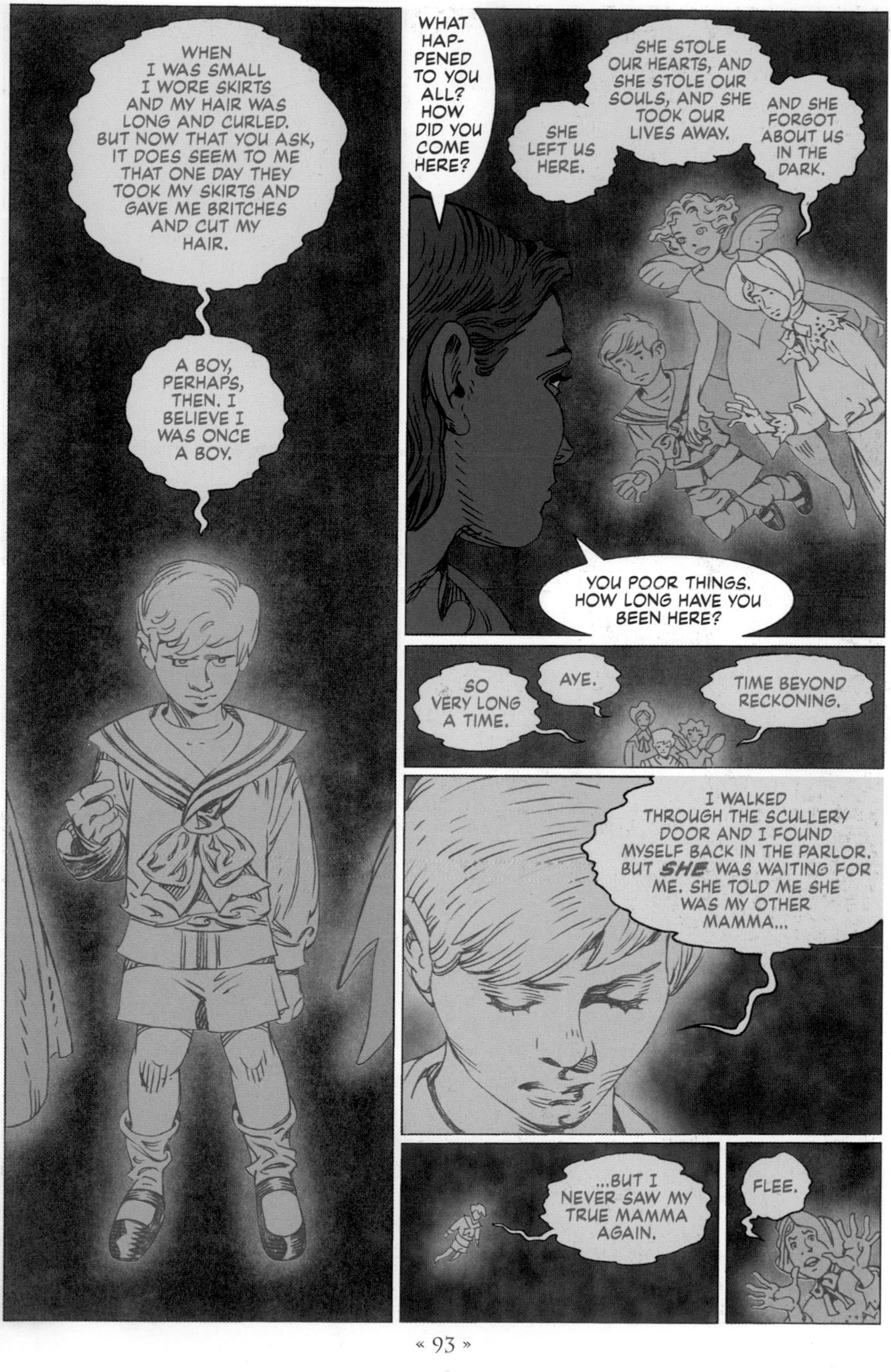
WHEN I WAS SMALL I WORE SKIRTS AND MY HAIR WAS LONG AND CURLED. BUT NOW THAT YOU ASK, IT DOES SEEM TO ME THAT ONE DAY THEY TOOK MY SKIRTS AND GAVE ME BRITCHES AND CUT MY HAIR.
A BOY, PERHAPS, THEN. I BELIEVE I WAS ONCE A BOY.
WHAT HAPPENED TO YOU ALL? HOW DID YOU COME HERE?
SHE LEFT US HERE.
SHE STOLE OUR HEARTS, AND SHE STOLE OUR SOULS, AND SHE TOOK OUR LIVES AWAY.
AND SHE FORGOT ABOUT US IN THE DARK.
YOU POOR THINGS. HOW LONG HAVE YOU BEEN HERE?
SO VERY LONG A TIME.
AYE.
TIME BEYOND RECKONING.
I WALKED THROUGH THE SCULLERY DOOR AND I FOUND MYSELF BACK IN THE PARLOR. BUT SHE WAS WAITING FOR ME. SHE TOLD ME SHE WAS MY OTHER MAMMA...
...BUT I NEVER SAW MY TRUE MAMMA AGAIN.
FLEE.

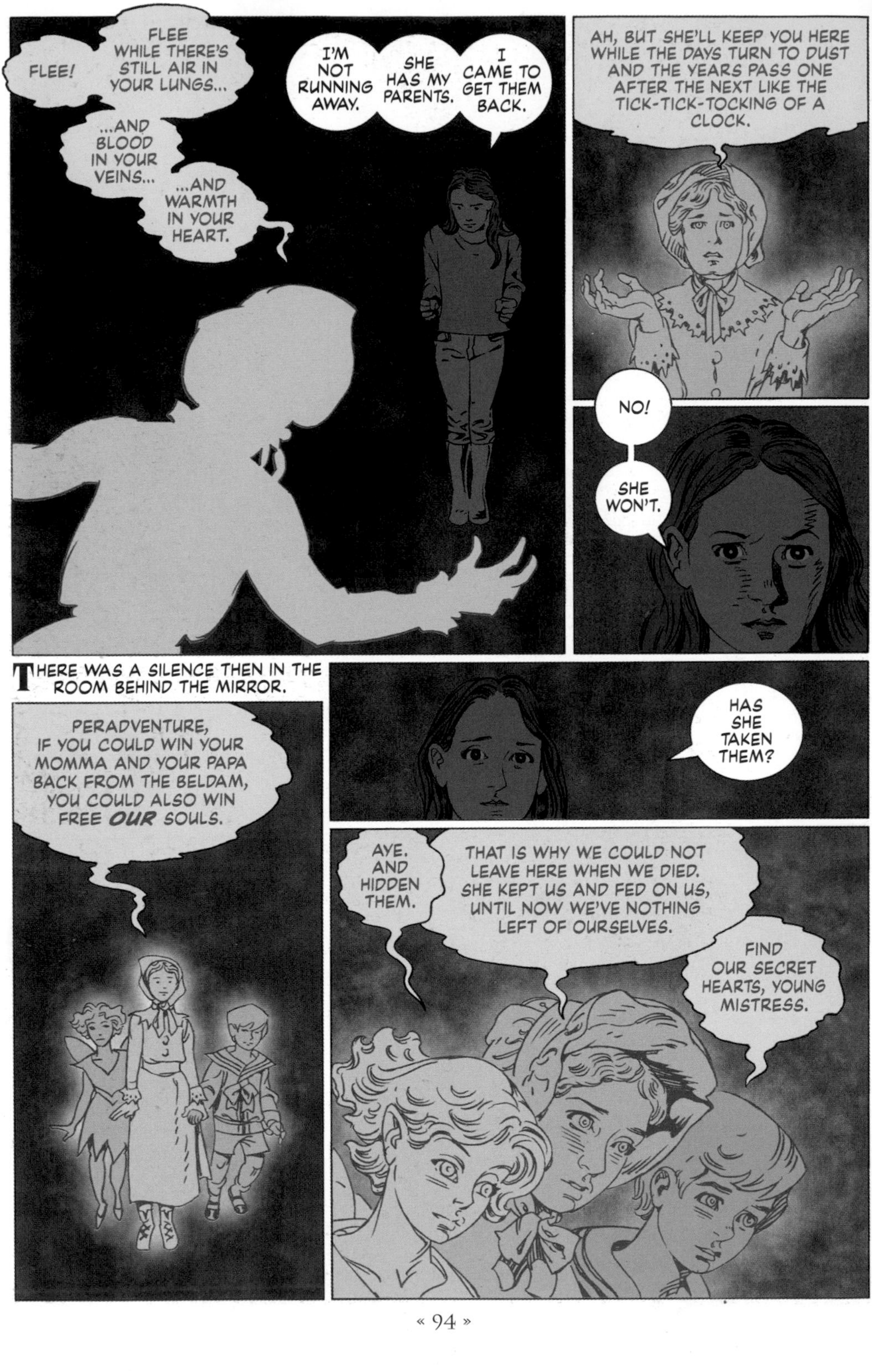
FLEE!
FLEE WHILE THERE'S STILL AIR IN YOUR LUNGS...
...AND BLOOD IN YOUR VEINS...
...AND WARMTH IN YOUR HEART.
I'M NOT RUNNING AWAY.
SHE HAS MY PARENTS.
I CAME TO GET THEM BACK.
AH, BUT SHE'LL KEEP YOU HERE WHILE THE DAYS TURN TO DUST AND THE YEARS PASS ONE AFTER THE NEXT LIKE THE TICK-TICK-TOCKING OF A CLOCK.
NO!
SHE WON'T.
THERE WAS A SILENCE THEN IN THE ROOM BEHIND THE MIRROR.
HAS SHE TAKEN THEM?
PERADVENTURE, IF YOU COULD WIN YOUR MOMMA AND YOUR PAPA BACK FROM THE BELDAM, YOU COULD ALSO WIN FREE *OUR* SOULS.
AYE. AND HIDDEN THEM.
THAT IS WHY WE COULD NOT LEAVE HERE WHEN WE DIED. SHE KEPT US AND FED ON US, UNTIL NOW WE'VE NOTHING LEFT OF OURSELVES.
FIND OUR SECRET HEARTS, YOUNG MISTRESS.

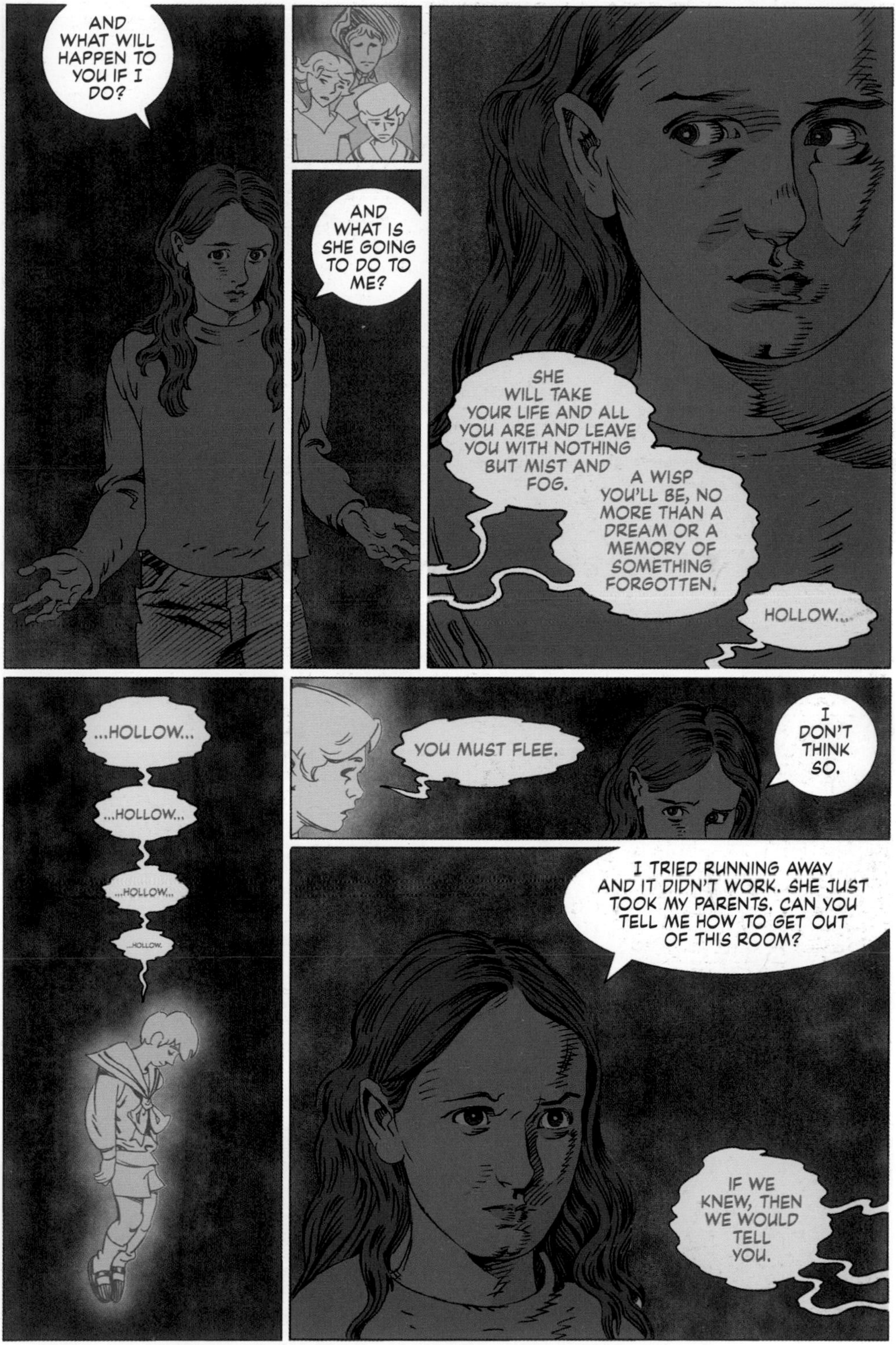
AND WHAT WILL HAPPEN TO YOU IF I DO?
AND WHAT IS SHE GOING TO DO TO ME?
SHE WILL TAKE YOUR LIFE AND ALL YOU ARE AND LEAVE YOU WITH NOTHING BUT MIST AND FOG.
A WISP YOU'LL BE, NO MORE THAN A DREAM OR A MEMORY OF SOMETHING FORGOTTEN.
HOLLOW...
...HOLLOW...
...HOLLOW...
...HOLLOW...
...HOLLOW.
YOU MUST FLEE.
I DON'T THINK SO.
I TRIED RUNNING AWAY AND IT DIDN'T WORK. SHE JUST TOOK MY PARENTS. CAN YOU TELL ME HOW TO GET OUT OF THIS ROOM?
IF WE KNEW, THEN WE WOULD TELL YOU.

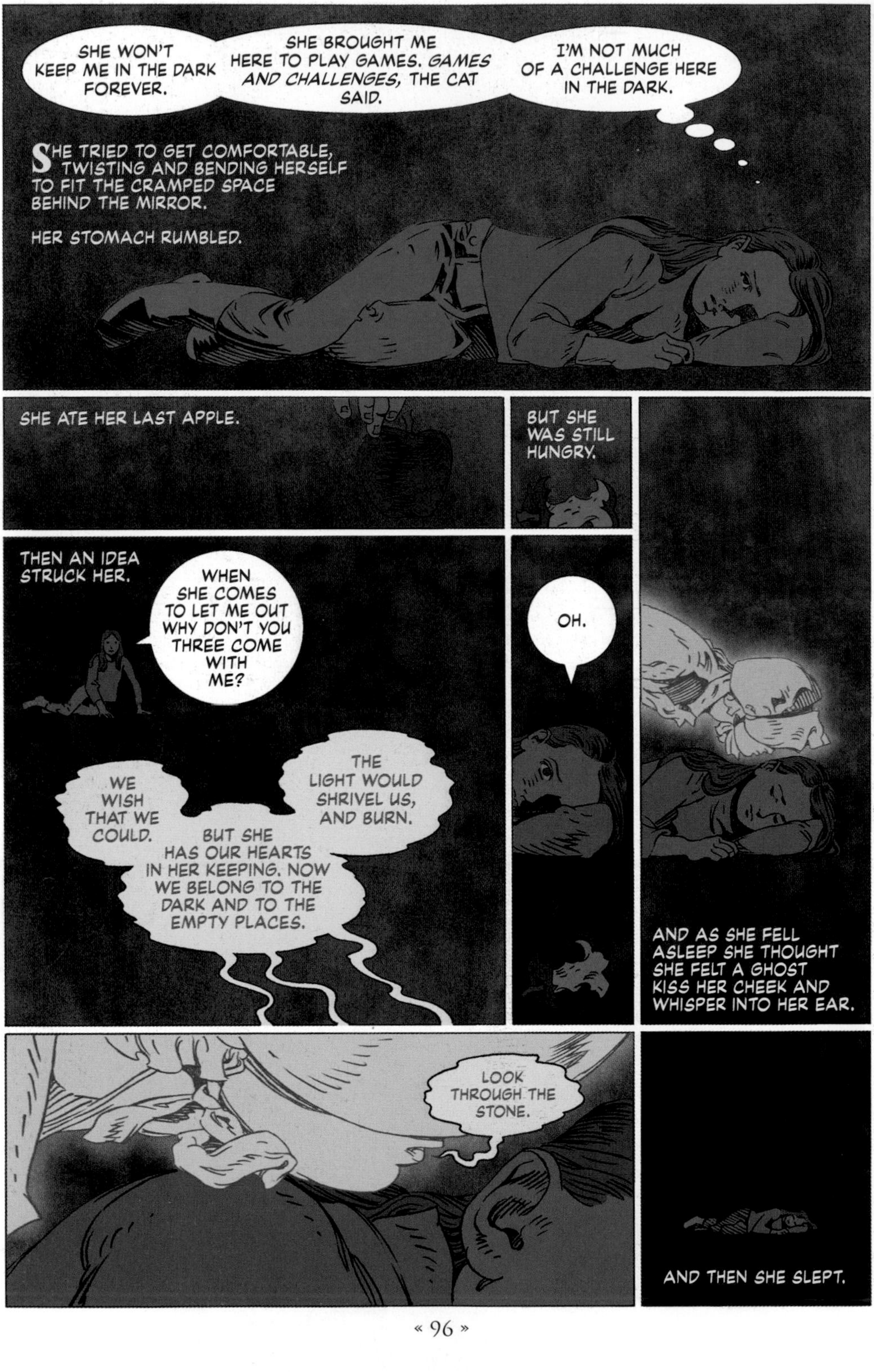
SHE WON'T KEEP ME IN THE DARK FOREVER.
SHE BROUGHT ME HERE TO PLAY GAMES. *GAMES AND CHALLENGES,* THE CAT SAID.
I'M NOT MUCH OF A CHALLENGE HERE IN THE DARK.
SHE TRIED TO GET COMFORTABLE, TWISTING AND BENDING HERSELF TO FIT THE CRAMPED SPACE BEHIND THE MIRROR.
HER STOMACH RUMBLED.
SHE ATE HER LAST APPLE.
BUT SHE WAS STILL HUNGRY.
THEN AN IDEA STRUCK HER.
WHEN SHE COMES TO LET ME OUT WHY DON'T YOU THREE COME WITH ME?
WE WISH THAT WE COULD.
THE LIGHT WOULD SHRIVEL US, AND BURN.
BUT SHE HAS OUR HEARTS IN HER KEEPING. NOW WE BELONG TO THE DARK AND TO THE EMPTY PLACES.
OH.
AND AS SHE FELL ASLEEP SHE THOUGHT SHE FELT A GHOST KISS HER CHEEK AND WHISPER INTO HER EAR.
LOOK THROUGH THE STONE.
AND THEN SHE SLEPT.

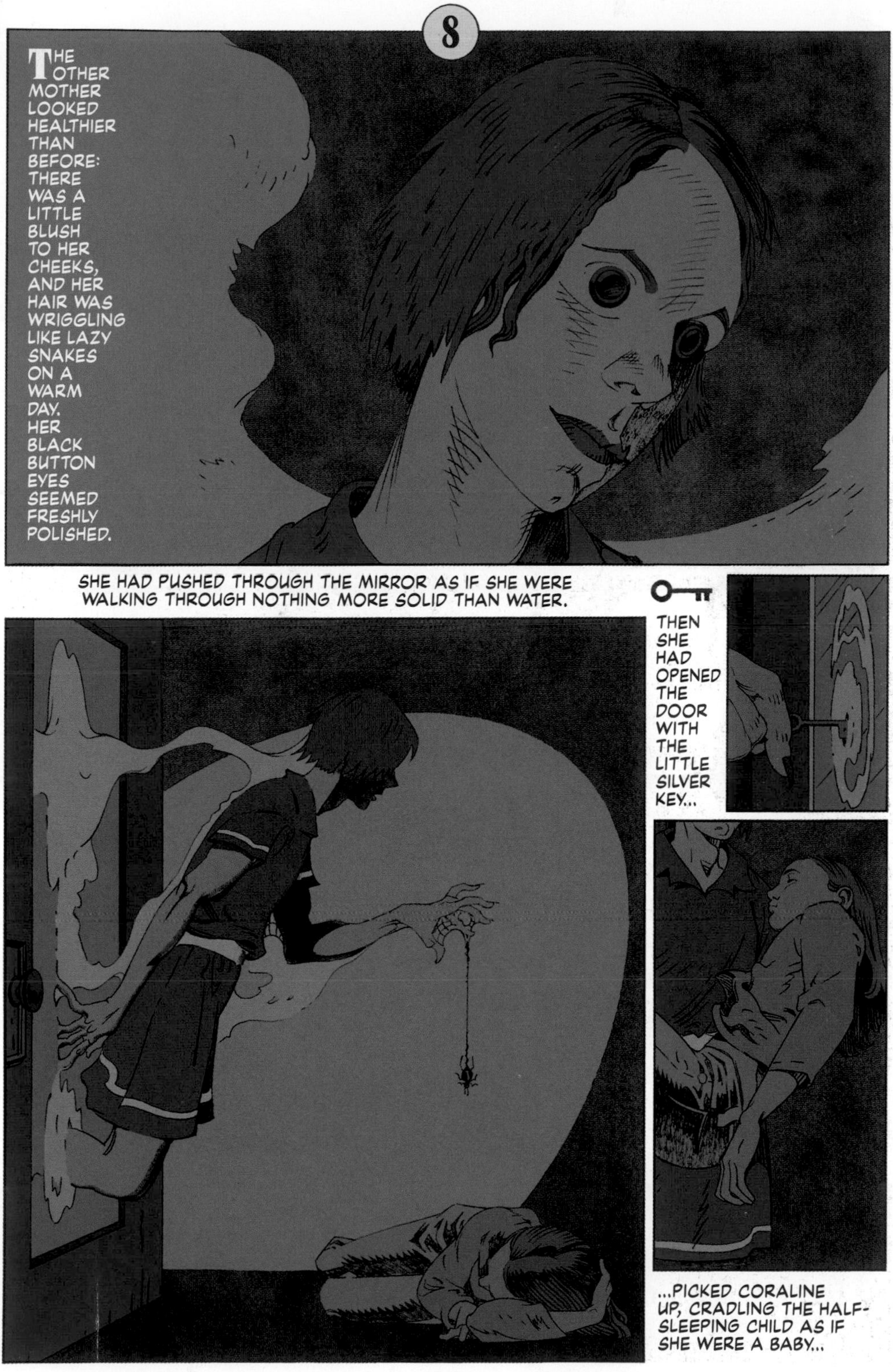
8
THE OTHER MOTHER LOOKED HEALTHIER THAN BEFORE: THERE WAS A LITTLE BLUSH TO HER CHEEKS, AND HER HAIR WAS WRIGGLING LIKE LAZY SNAKES ON A WARM DAY. HER BLACK BUTTON EYES SEEMED FRESHLY POLISHED.
SHE HAD PUSHED THROUGH THE MIRROR AS IF SHE WERE WALKING THROUGH NOTHING MORE SOLID THAN WATER.
THEN SHE HAD OPENED THE DOOR WITH THE LITTLE SILVER KEY...
...PICKED CORALINE UP, CRADLING THE HALF-SLEEPING CHILD AS IF SHE WERE A BABY...

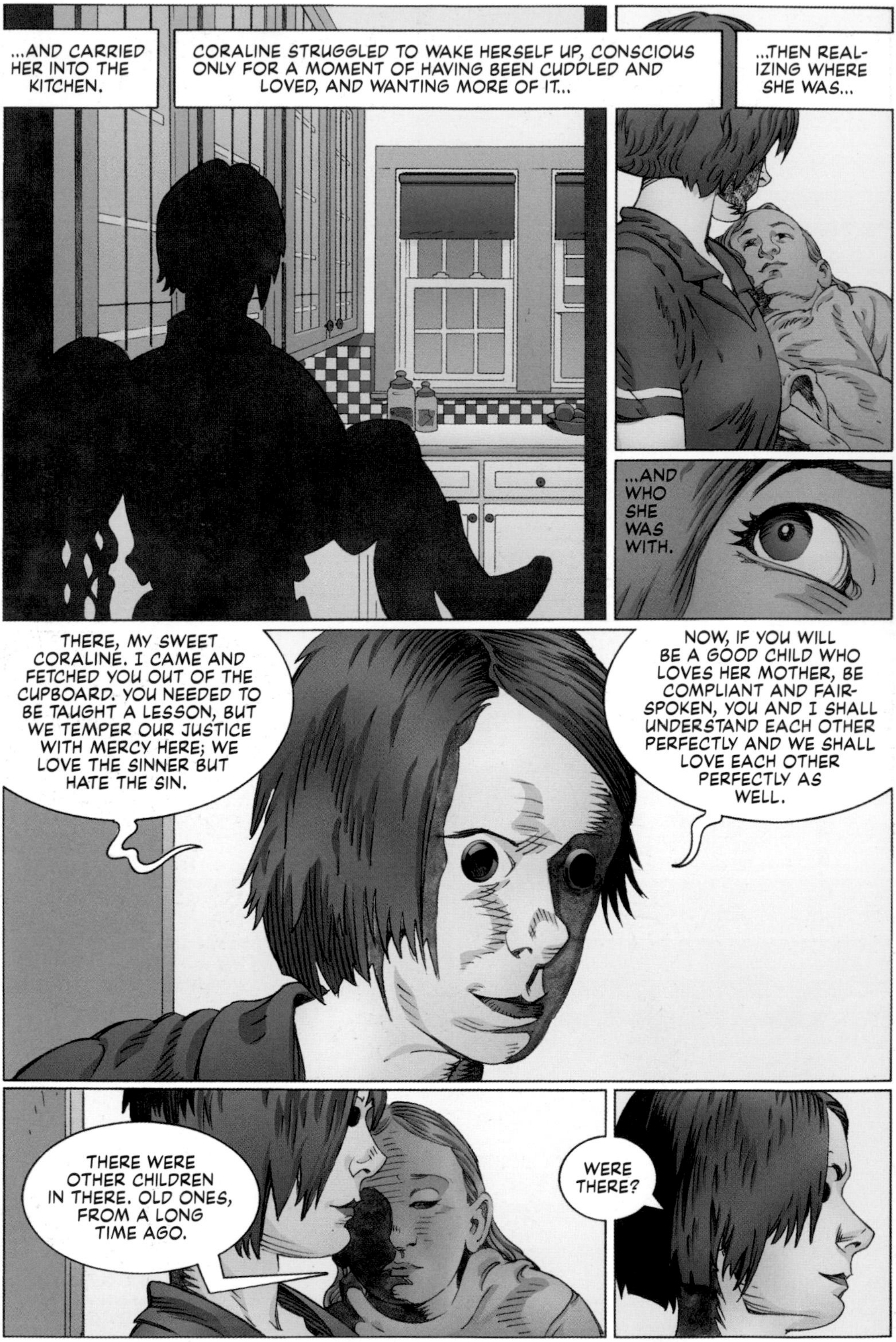
...AND CARRIED HER INTO THE KITCHEN.
CORALINE STRUGGLED TO WAKE HERSELF UP, CONSCIOUS ONLY FOR A MOMENT OF HAVING BEEN CUDDLED AND LOVED, AND WANTING MORE OF IT...
...THEN REALIZING WHERE SHE WAS...
...AND WHO SHE WAS WITH.
THERE, MY SWEET CORALINE. I CAME AND FETCHED YOU OUT OF THE CUPBOARD. YOU NEEDED TO BE TAUGHT A LESSON, BUT WE TEMPER OUR JUSTICE WITH MERCY HERE; WE LOVE THE SINNER BUT HATE THE SIN.
NOW, IF YOU WILL BE A GOOD CHILD WHO LOVES HER MOTHER, BE COMPLIANT AND FAIR-SPOKEN, YOU AND I SHALL UNDERSTAND EACH OTHER PERFECTLY AND WE SHALL LOVE EACH OTHER PERFECTLY AS WELL.
THERE WERE OTHER CHILDREN IN THERE. OLD ONES, FROM A LONG TIME AGO.
WERE THERE?

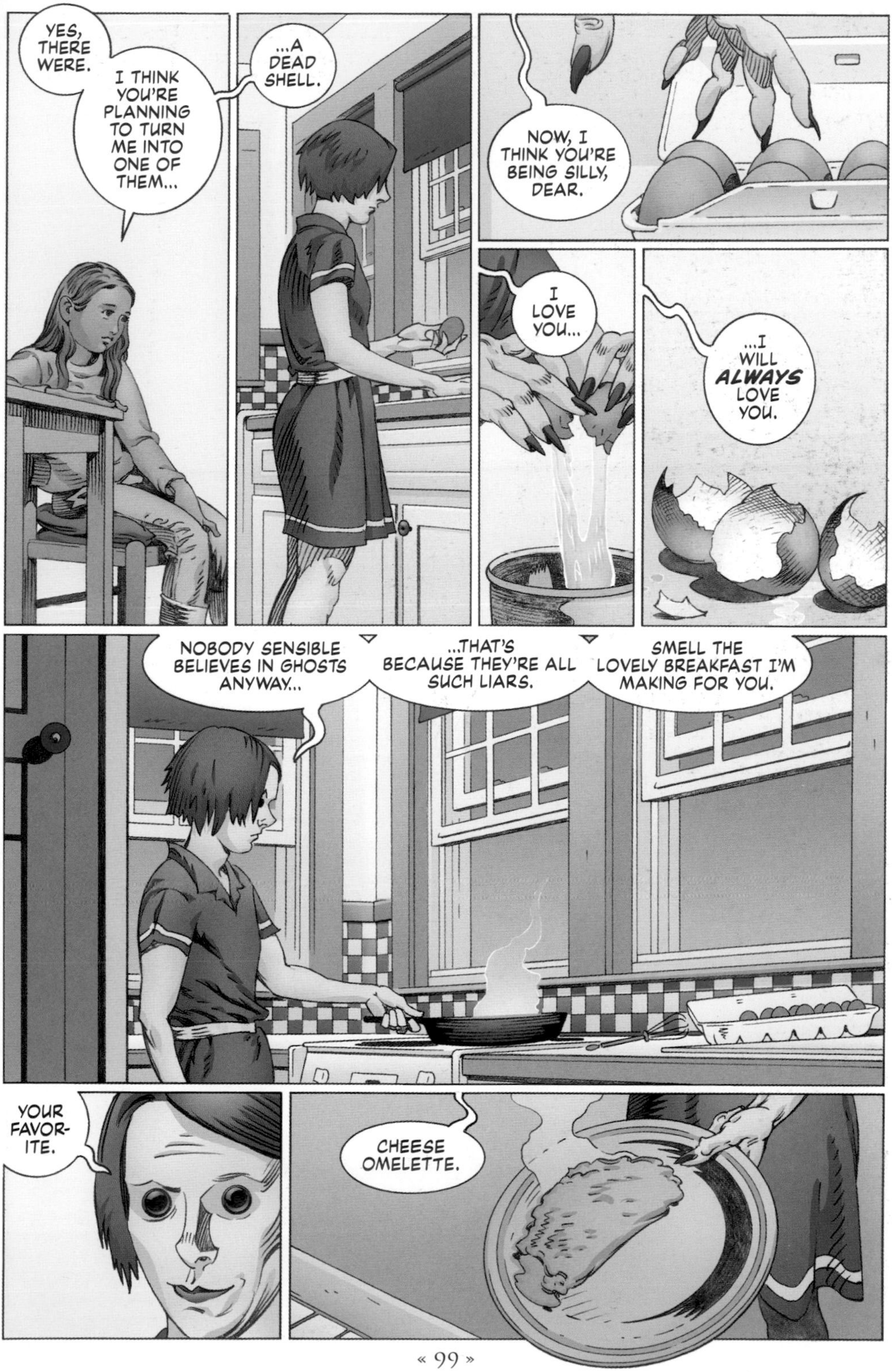
YES, THERE WERE.
I THINK YOU'RE PLANNING TO TURN ME INTO ONE OF THEM...
...A DEAD SHELL.
NOW, I THINK YOU'RE BEING SILLY, DEAR.
I LOVE YOU...
...I WILL ALWAYS LOVE YOU.
NOBODY SENSIBLE BELIEVES IN GHOSTS ANYWAY...
...THAT'S BECAUSE THEY'RE ALL SUCH LIARS.
SMELL THE LOVELY BREAKFAST I'M MAKING FOR YOU.
YOUR FAVOR-ITE.
CHEESE OMELETTE.

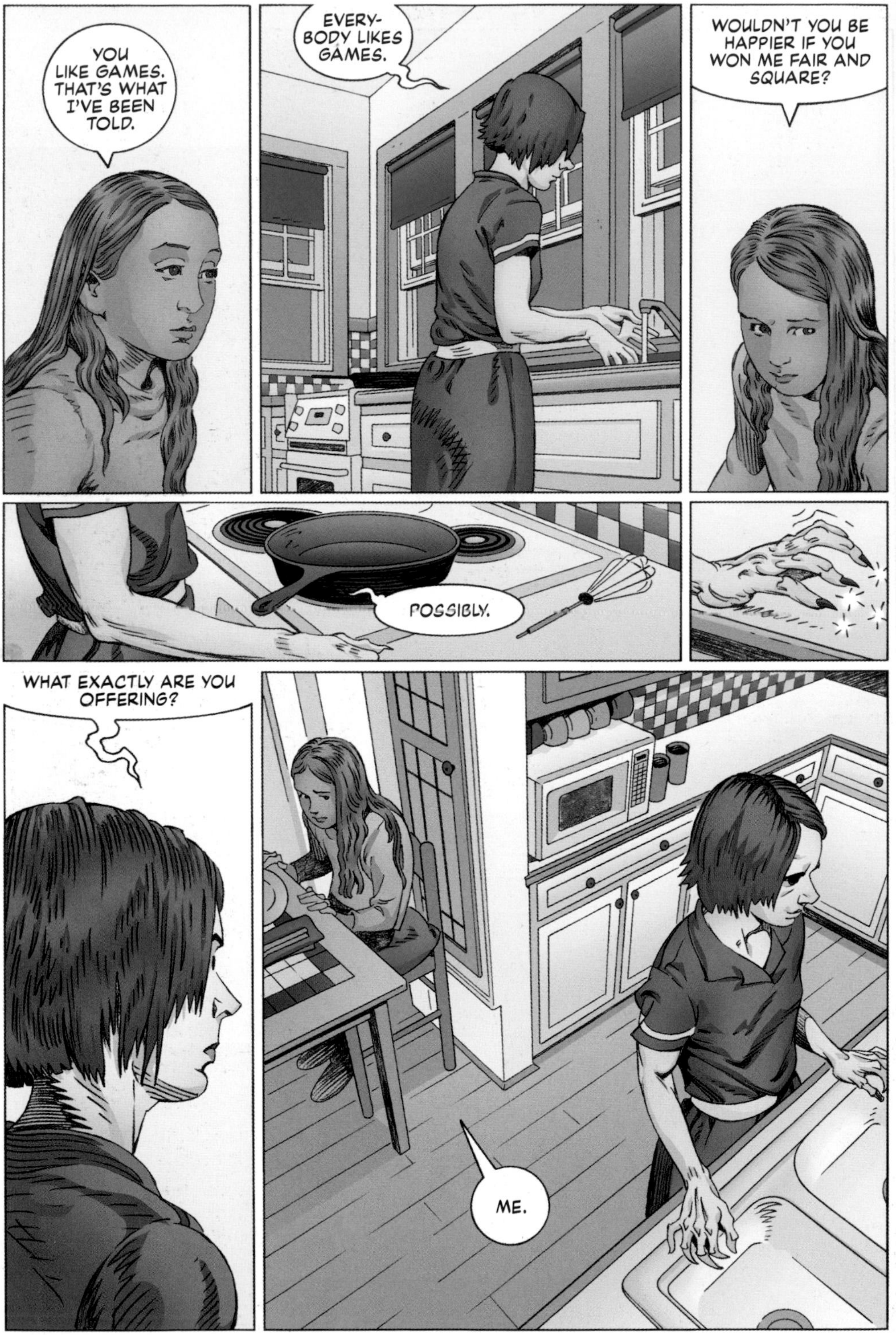
YOU LIKE GAMES. THAT'S WHAT I'VE BEEN TOLD.
EVERY-BODY LIKES GAMES.
WOULDN'T YOU BE HAPPIER IF YOU WON ME FAIR AND SQUARE?
POSSIBLY.
WHAT EXACTLY ARE YOU OFFERING?
ME.

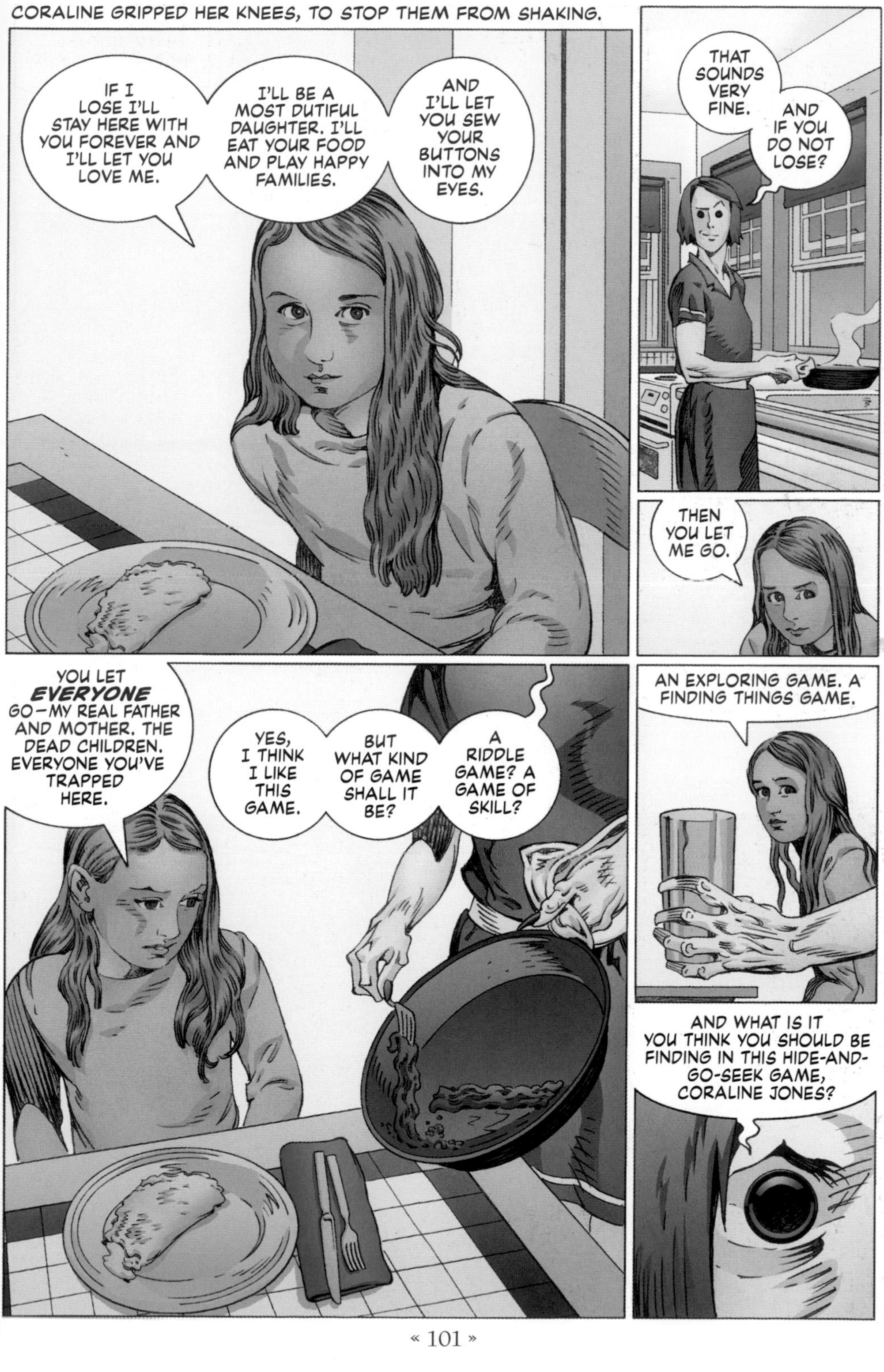
CORALINE GRIPPED HER KNEES, TO STOP THEM FROM SHAKING.
IF I LOSE I'LL STAY HERE WITH YOU FOREVER AND I'LL LET YOU LOVE ME.
I'LL BE A MOST DUTIFUL DAUGHTER. I'LL EAT YOUR FOOD AND PLAY HAPPY FAMILIES.
AND I'LL LET YOU SEW YOUR BUTTONS INTO MY EYES.
THAT SOUNDS VERY FINE.
AND IF YOU DO NOT LOSE?
THEN YOU LET ME GO.
YOU LET *EVERYONE* GO—MY REAL FATHER AND MOTHER. THE DEAD CHILDREN. EVERYONE YOU'VE TRAPPED HERE.
YES, I THINK I LIKE THIS GAME.
BUT WHAT KIND OF GAME SHALL IT BE?
A RIDDLE GAME? A GAME OF SKILL?
AN EXPLORING GAME. A FINDING THINGS GAME.
AND WHAT IS IT YOU THINK YOU SHOULD BE FINDING IN THIS HIDE-AND-GO-SEEK GAME, CORALINE JONES?

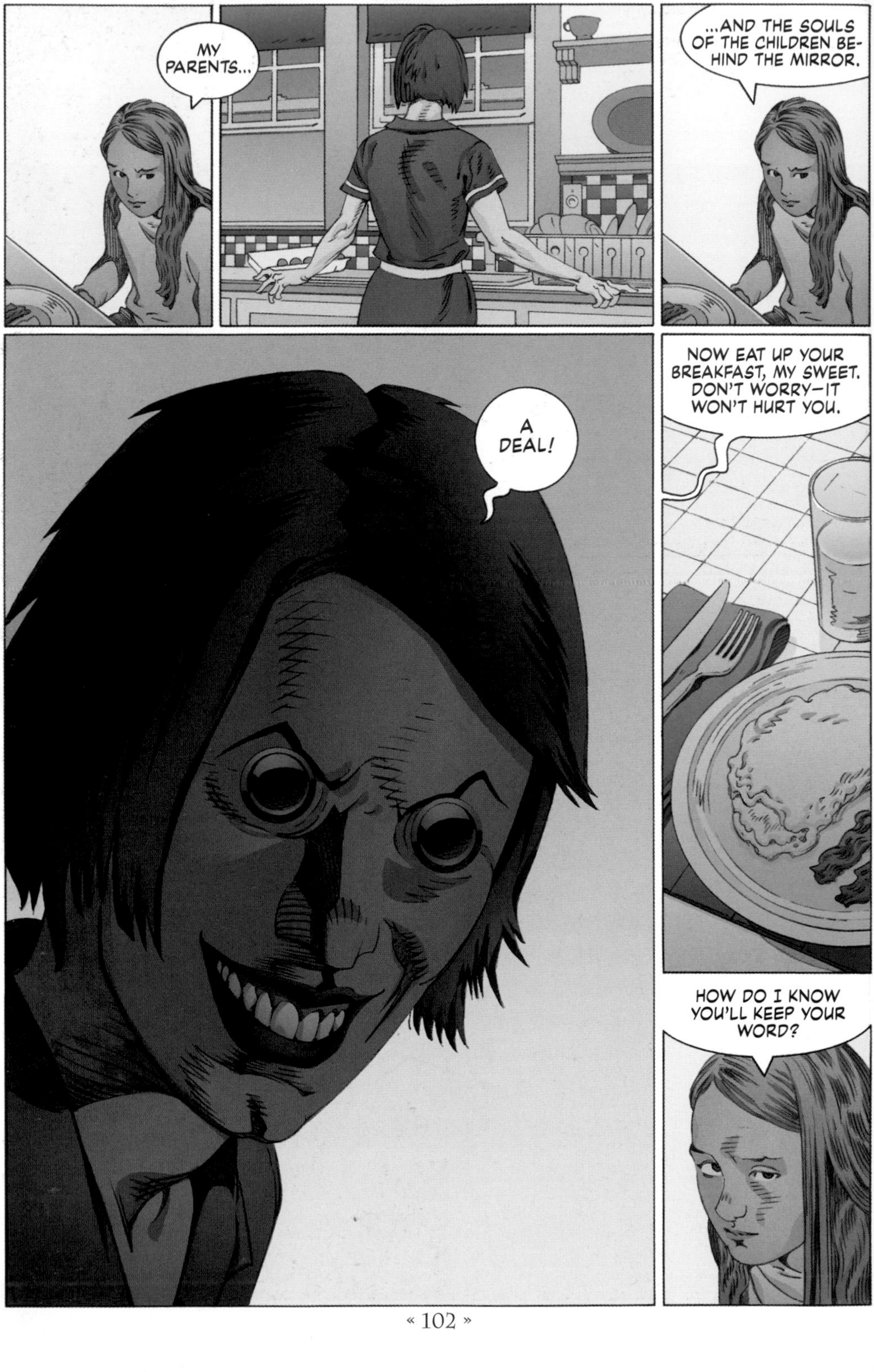
MY PARENTS...
...AND THE SOULS OF THE CHILDREN BEHIND THE MIRROR.
A DEAL!
NOW EAT UP YOUR BREAKFAST, MY SWEET. DON'T WORRY—IT WON'T HURT YOU.
HOW DO I KNOW YOU'LL KEEP YOUR WORD?

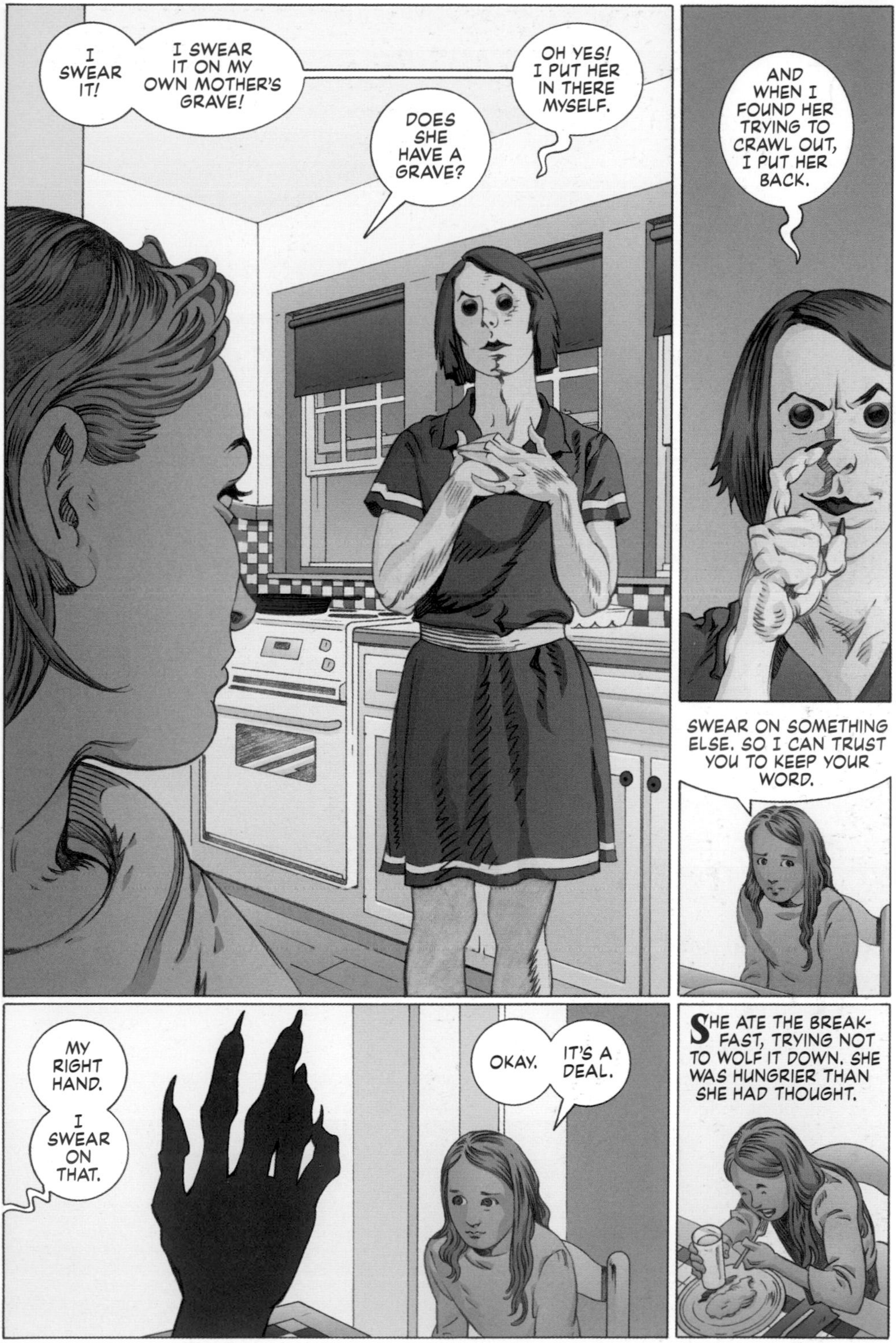
I SWEAR IT!
I SWEAR IT ON MY OWN MOTHER'S GRAVE!
DOES SHE HAVE A GRAVE?
OH YES! I PUT HER IN THERE MYSELF.
AND WHEN I FOUND HER TRYING TO CRAWL OUT, I PUT HER BACK.
SWEAR ON SOMETHING ELSE. SO I CAN TRUST YOU TO KEEP YOUR WORD.
MY RIGHT HAND.
I SWEAR ON THAT.
OKAY.
IT'S A DEAL.
SHE ATE THE BREAKFAST, TRYING NOT TO WOLF IT DOWN. SHE WAS HUNGRIER THAN SHE HAD THOUGHT.

AS SHE ATE, HER OTHER MOTHER STARED AT HER. CORALINE THOUGHT SHE LOOKED HUNGRY, TOO.

WHERE SHOULD I START LOOKING?

WHERE YOU WISH.

CORALINE THOUGHT HARD. THERE WAS NO POINT IN EXPLORING THE GARDEN AND THE GROUNDS: THEY DIDN'T EXIST; THEY WEREN'T REAL.

ALL THAT WAS REAL WAS THE HOUSE ITSELF.

SHE LOOKED AROUND THE KITCHEN.

SHE OPENED THE OVEN...

...PEERED INTO THE FREEZER...

WARNING

...POKED INTO THE SALAD COMPARTMENT.

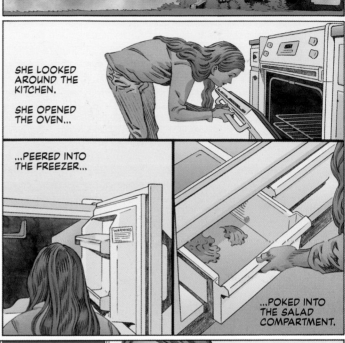

THE OTHER MOTHER FOLLOWED HER ABOUT, LOOKING AT CORALINE WITH A SMIRK ALWAYS HOVERING AT THE EDGE OF HER LIPS.

HOW BIG ARE SOULS ANYWAY?

MMM.

TAP TAP TAP TAP TAP

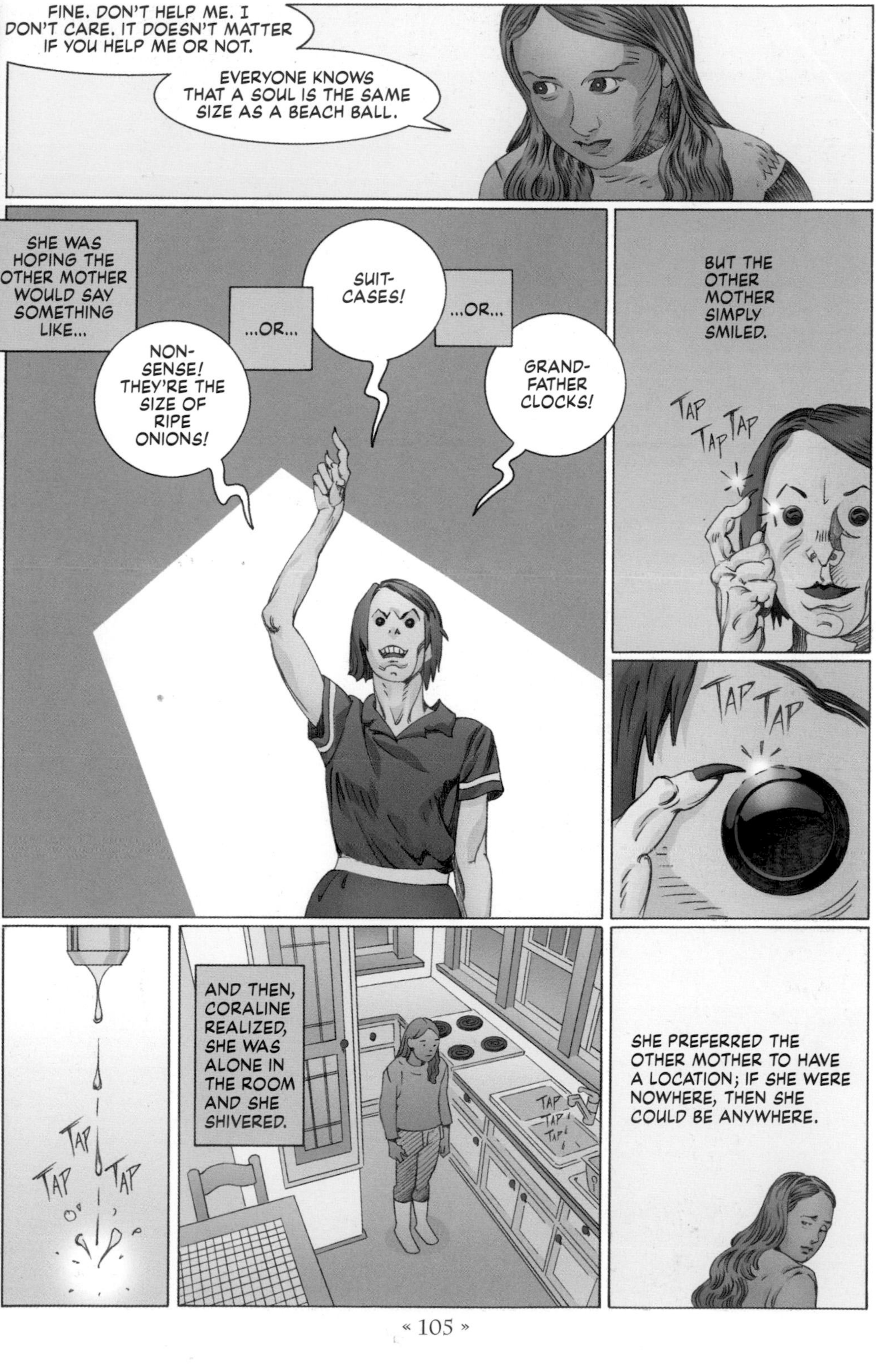
FINE. DON'T HELP ME. I DON'T CARE. IT DOESN'T MATTER IF YOU HELP ME OR NOT.
EVERYONE KNOWS THAT A SOUL IS THE SAME SIZE AS A BEACH BALL.
SHE WAS HOPING THE OTHER MOTHER WOULD SAY SOMETHING LIKE...
NON-SENSE! THEY'RE THE SIZE OF RIPE ONIONS!
...OR...
SUIT-CASES!
...OR...
GRAND-FATHER CLOCKS!
BUT THE OTHER MOTHER SIMPLY SMILED.
TAP TAP TAP
TAP TAP
TAP TAP TAP
AND THEN, CORALINE REALIZED, SHE WAS ALONE IN THE ROOM AND SHE SHIVERED.
TAP TAP TAP
SHE PREFERRED THE OTHER MOTHER TO HAVE A LOCATION; IF SHE WERE NOWHERE, THEN SHE COULD BE ANYWHERE.

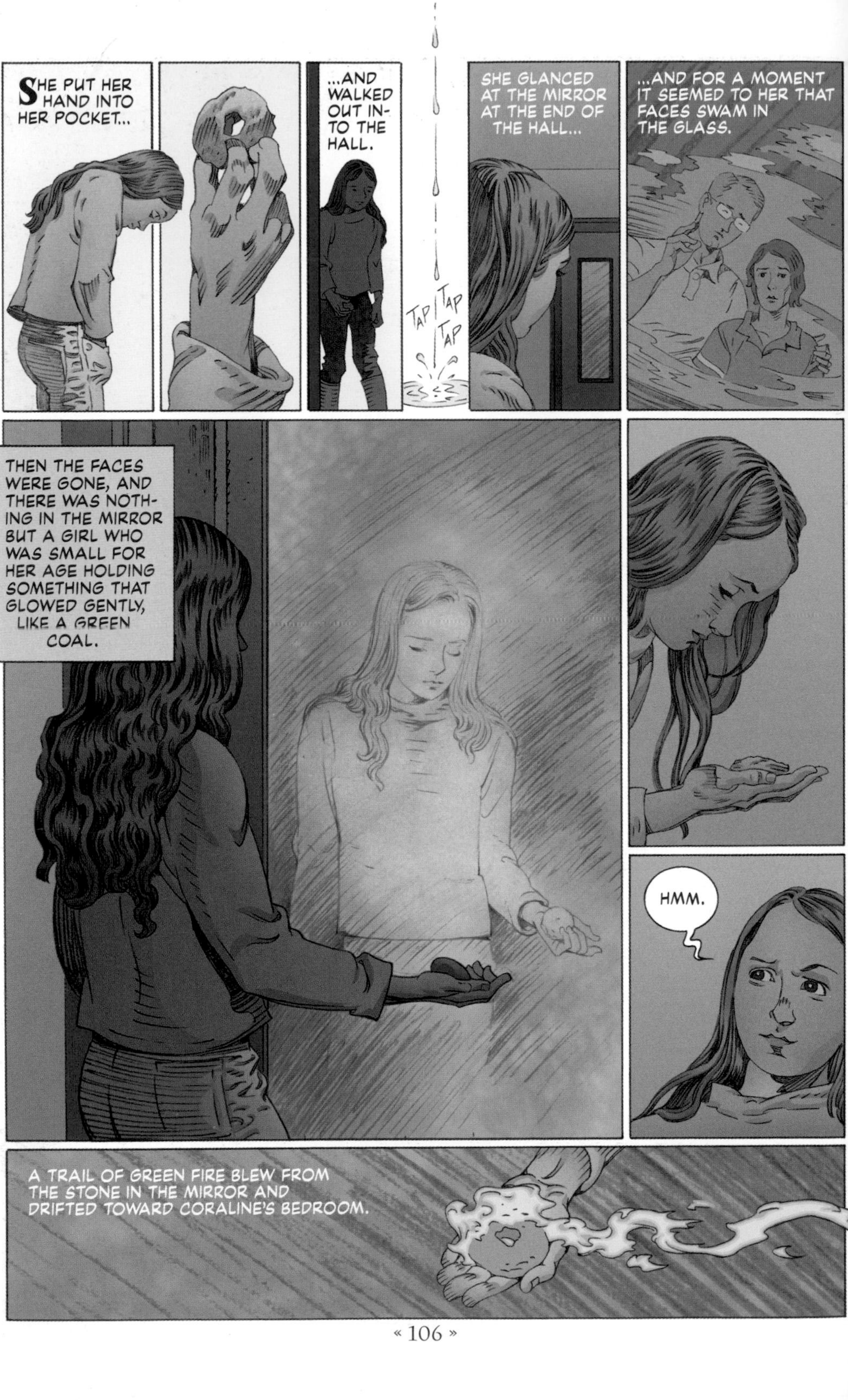
SHE PUT HER HAND INTO HER POCKET...
...AND WALKED OUT IN-TO THE HALL.
TAP TAP TAP
SHE GLANCED AT THE MIRROR AT THE END OF THE HALL...
...AND FOR A MOMENT IT SEEMED TO HER THAT FACES SWAM IN THE GLASS.
THEN THE FACES WERE GONE, AND THERE WAS NOTHING IN THE MIRROR BUT A GIRL WHO WAS SMALL FOR HER AGE HOLDING SOMETHING THAT GLOWED GENTLY, LIKE A GREEN COAL.
HMM.
A TRAIL OF GREEN FIRE BLEW FROM THE STONE IN THE MIRROR AND DRIFTED TOWARD CORALINE'S BEDROOM.

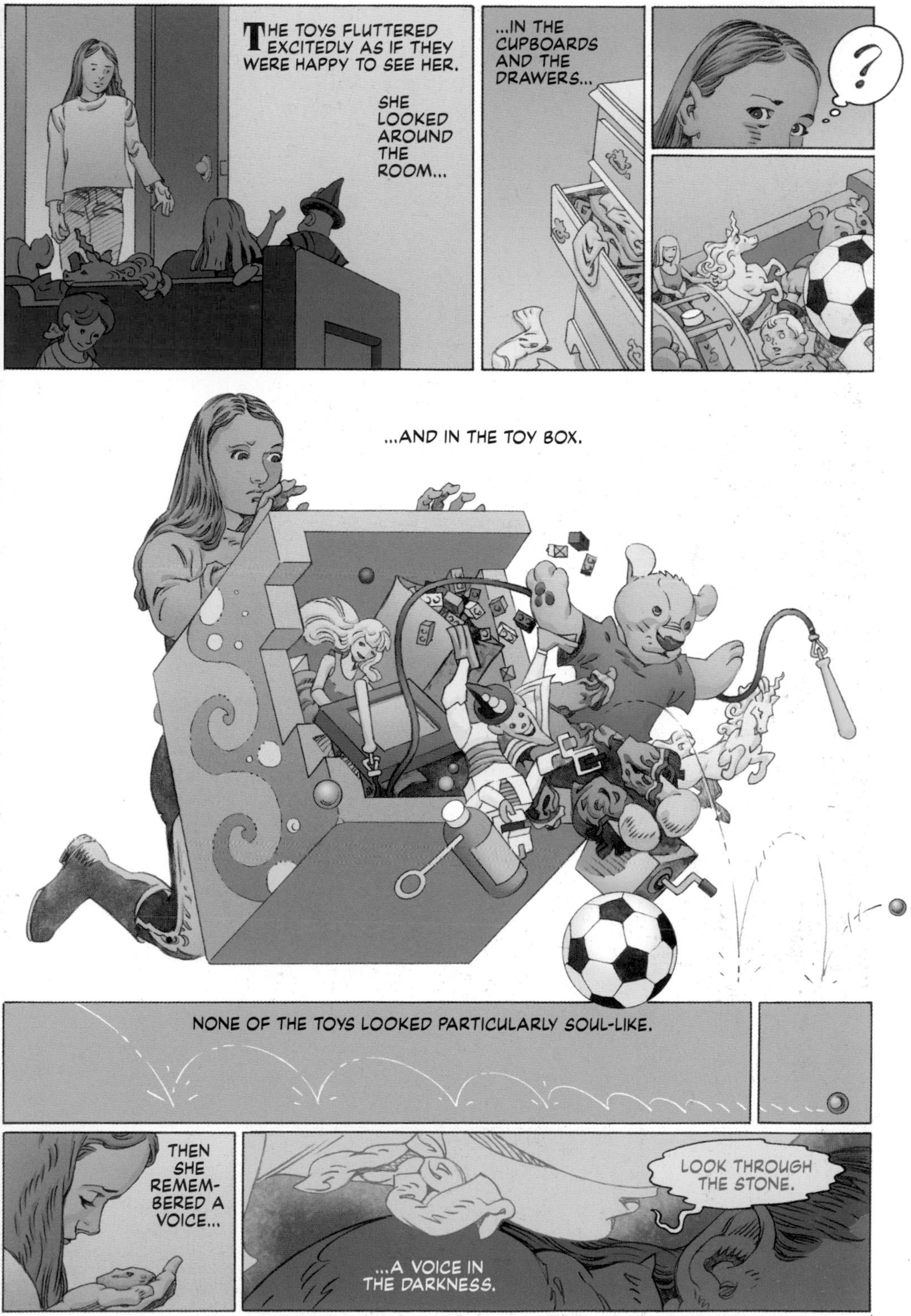
THE TOYS FLUTTERED EXCITEDLY AS IF THEY WERE HAPPY TO SEE HER.
SHE LOOKED AROUND THE ROOM...
...IN THE CUPBOARDS AND THE DRAWERS...
?
...AND IN THE TOY BOX.
NONE OF THE TOYS LOOKED PARTICULARLY SOUL-LIKE.
THEN SHE REMEM-BERED A VOICE...
LOOK THROUGH THE STONE.
...A VOICE IN THE DARKNESS.

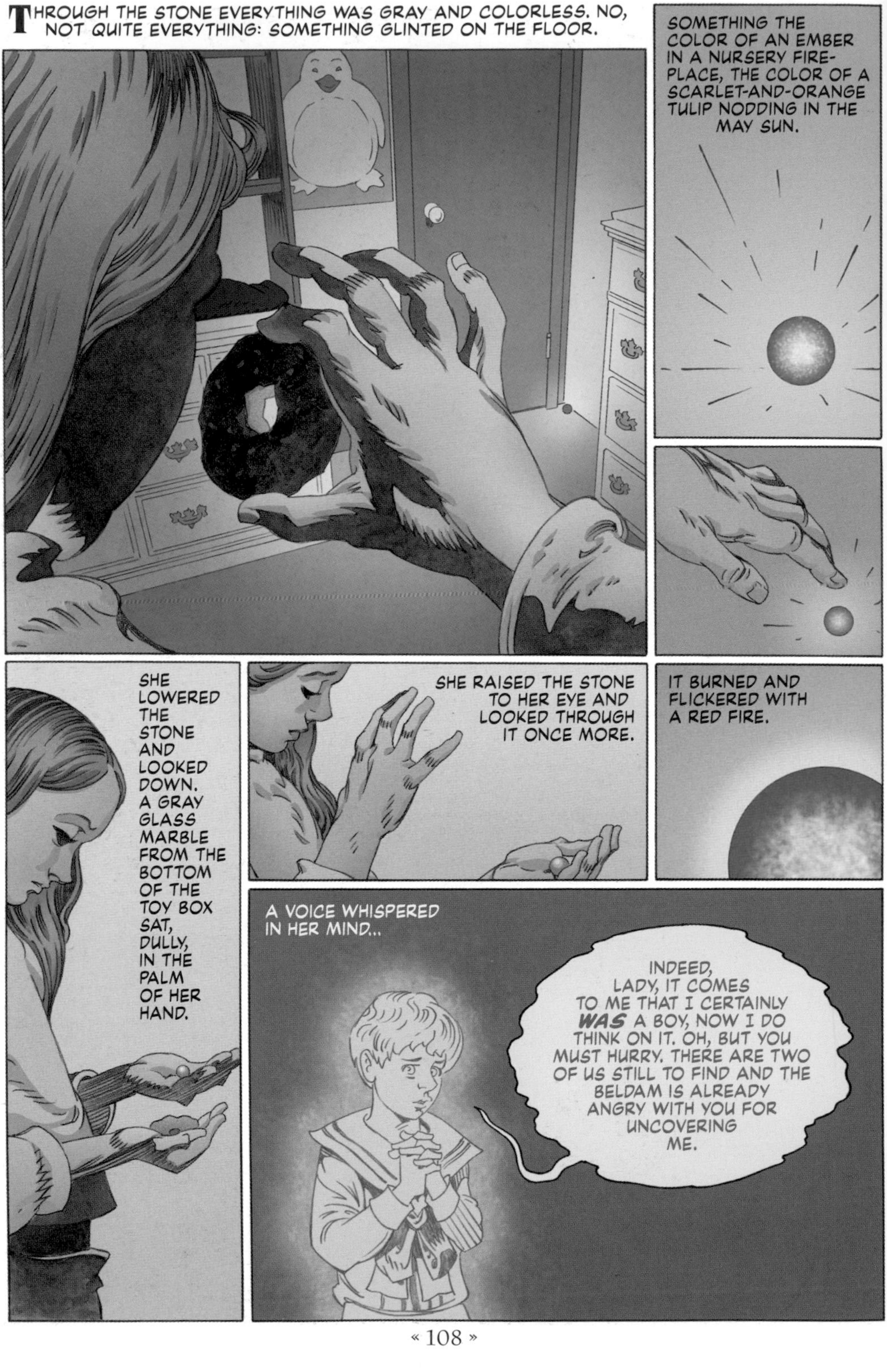
THROUGH THE STONE EVERYTHING WAS GRAY AND COLORLESS. NO, NOT QUITE EVERYTHING: SOMETHING GLINTED ON THE FLOOR.
SOMETHING THE COLOR OF AN EMBER IN A NURSERY FIRE-PLACE, THE COLOR OF A SCARLET-AND-ORANGE TULIP NODDING IN THE MAY SUN.
SHE LOWERED THE STONE AND LOOKED DOWN. A GRAY GLASS MARBLE FROM THE BOTTOM OF THE TOY BOX SAT, DULLY, IN THE PALM OF HER HAND.
SHE RAISED THE STONE TO HER EYE AND LOOKED THROUGH IT ONCE MORE.
IT BURNED AND FLICKERED WITH A RED FIRE.
A VOICE WHISPERED IN HER MIND...
INDEED, LADY, IT COMES TO ME THAT I CERTAINLY WAS A BOY, NOW I DO THINK ON IT. OH, BUT YOU MUST HURRY. THERE ARE TWO OF US STILL TO FIND AND THE BELDAM IS ALREADY ANGRY WITH YOU FOR UNCOVERING ME.

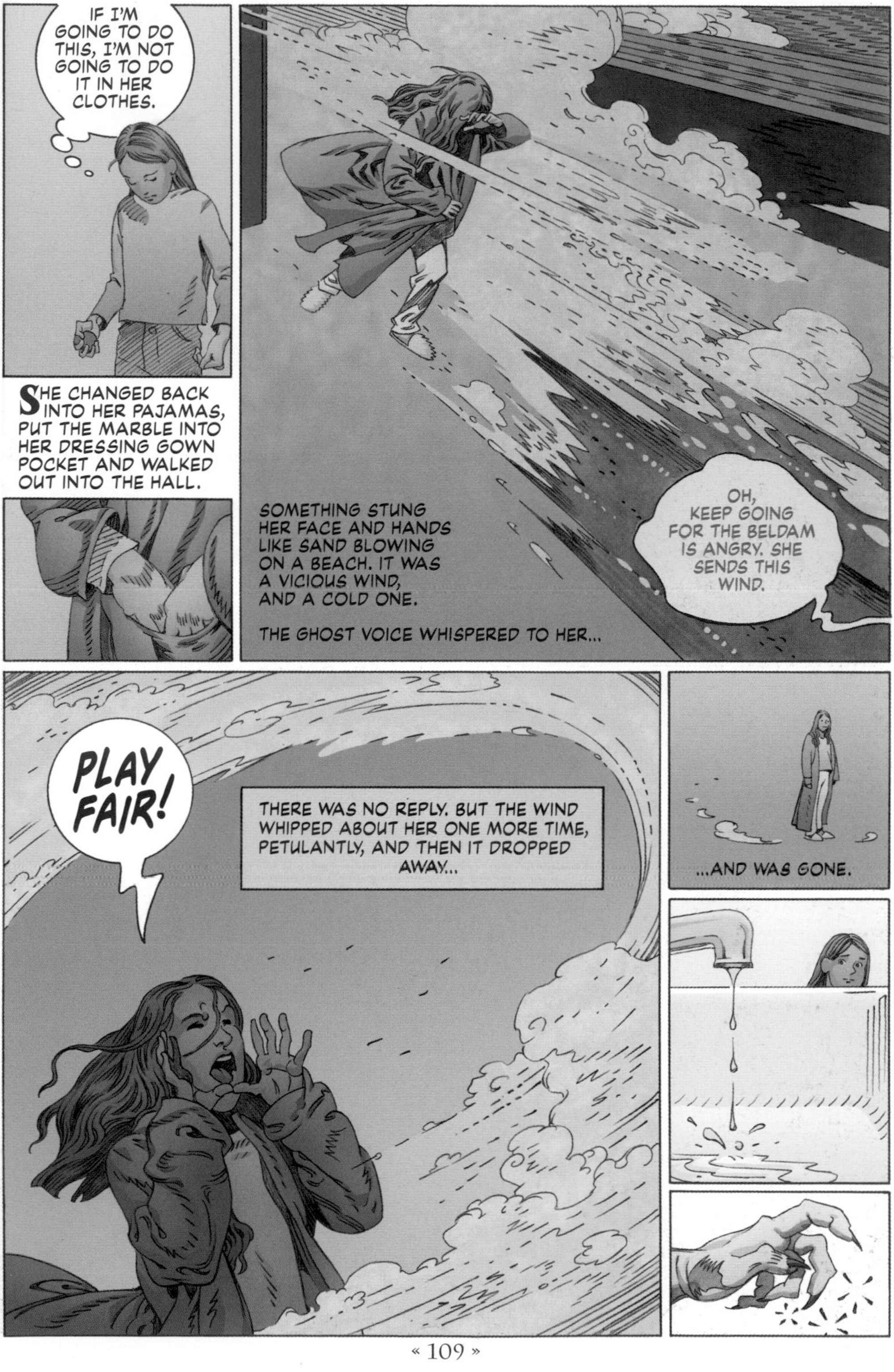
IF I'M GOING TO DO THIS, I'M NOT GOING TO DO IT IN HER CLOTHES.
SHE CHANGED BACK INTO HER PAJAMAS, PUT THE MARBLE INTO HER DRESSING GOWN POCKET AND WALKED OUT INTO THE HALL.
SOMETHING STUNG HER FACE AND HANDS LIKE SAND BLOWING ON A BEACH. IT WAS A VICIOUS WIND, AND A COLD ONE.
THE GHOST VOICE WHISPERED TO HER...
OH, KEEP GOING FOR THE BELDAM IS ANGRY. SHE SENDS THIS WIND.
PLAY FAIR!
THERE WAS NO REPLY. BUT THE WIND WHIPPED ABOUT HER ONE MORE TIME, PETULANTLY, AND THEN IT DROPPED AWAY...
...AND WAS GONE.

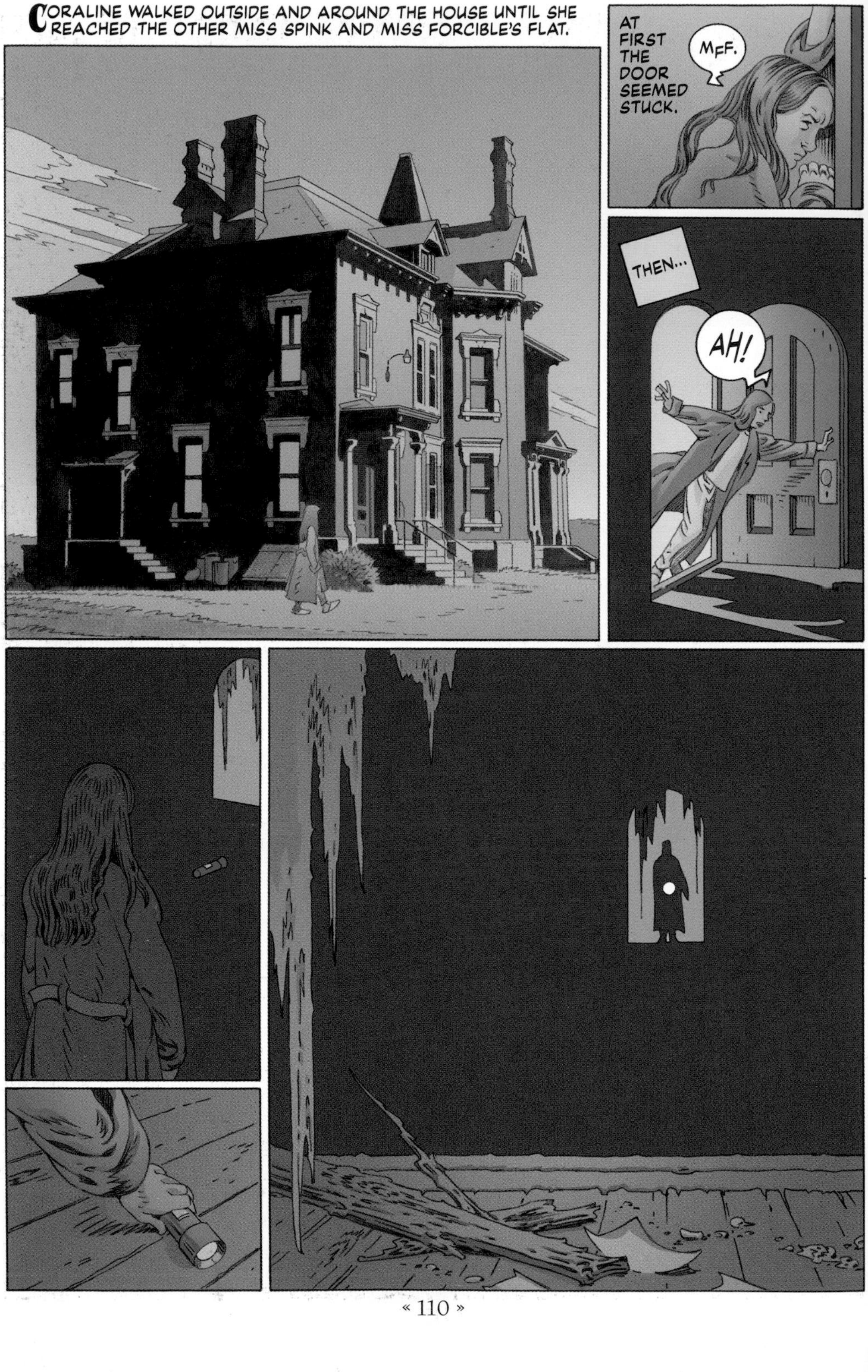
CORALINE WALKED OUTSIDE AND AROUND THE HOUSE UNTIL SHE REACHED THE OTHER MISS SPINK AND MISS FORCIBLE'S FLAT.
AT FIRST THE DOOR SEEMED STUCK.
MFF.
THEN...
AH!

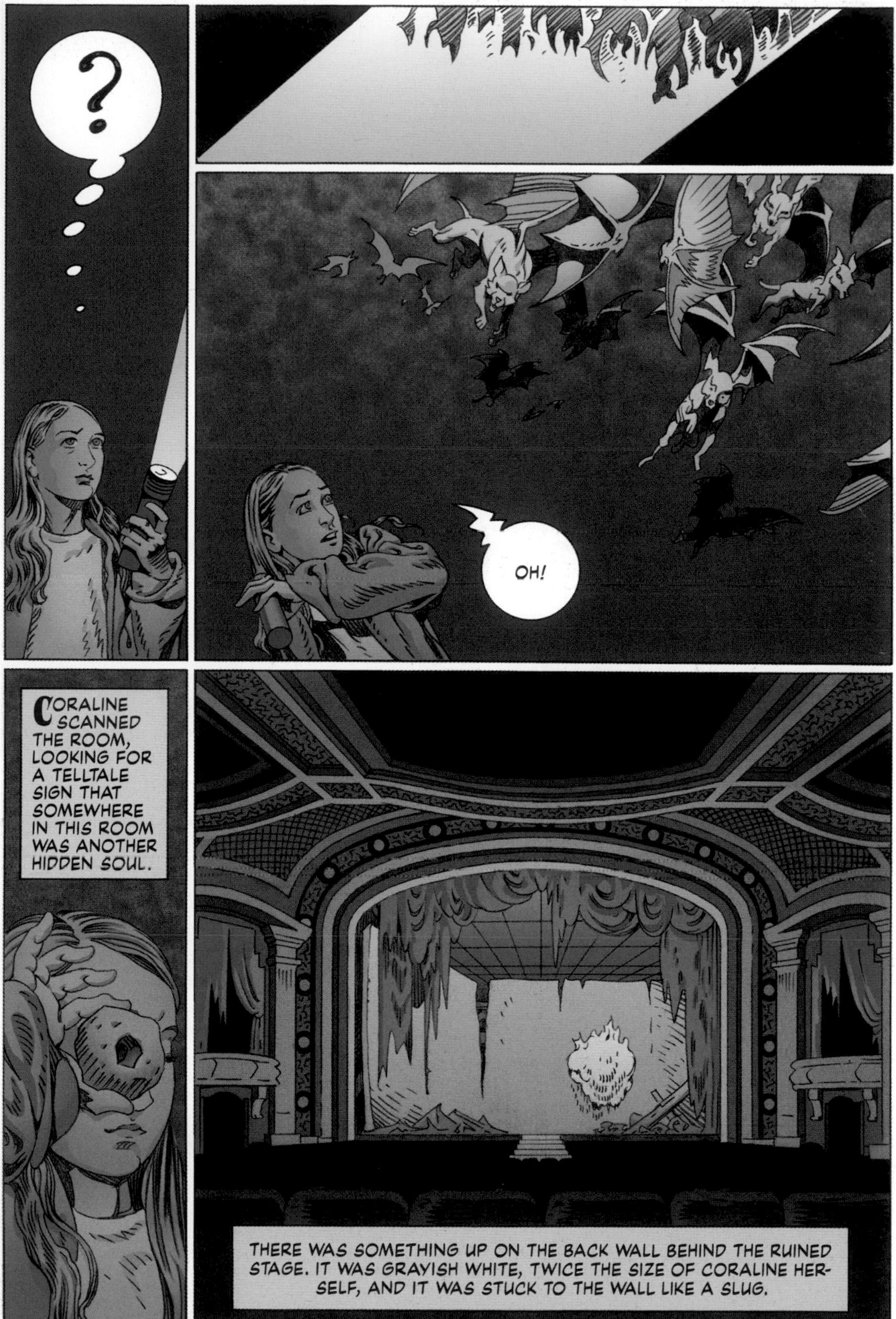
?
OH!
CORALINE SCANNED THE ROOM, LOOKING FOR A TELLTALE SIGN THAT SOMEWHERE IN THIS ROOM WAS ANOTHER HIDDEN SOUL.
THERE WAS SOMETHING UP ON THE BACK WALL BEHIND THE RUINED STAGE. IT WAS GRAYISH WHITE, TWICE THE SIZE OF CORALINE HER-SELF, AND IT WAS STUCK TO THE WALL LIKE A SLUG.

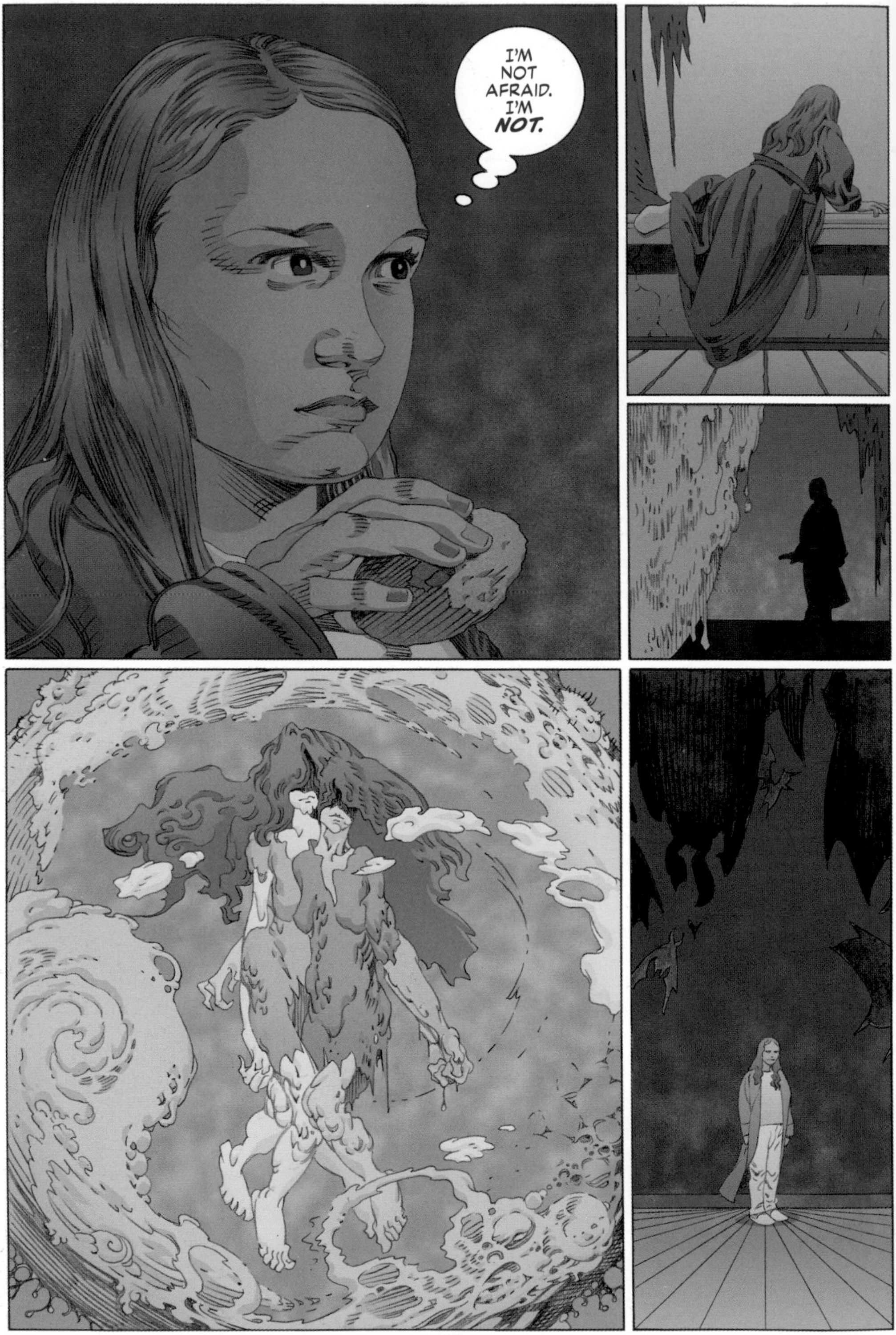
I'M NOT AFRAID. I'M NOT.

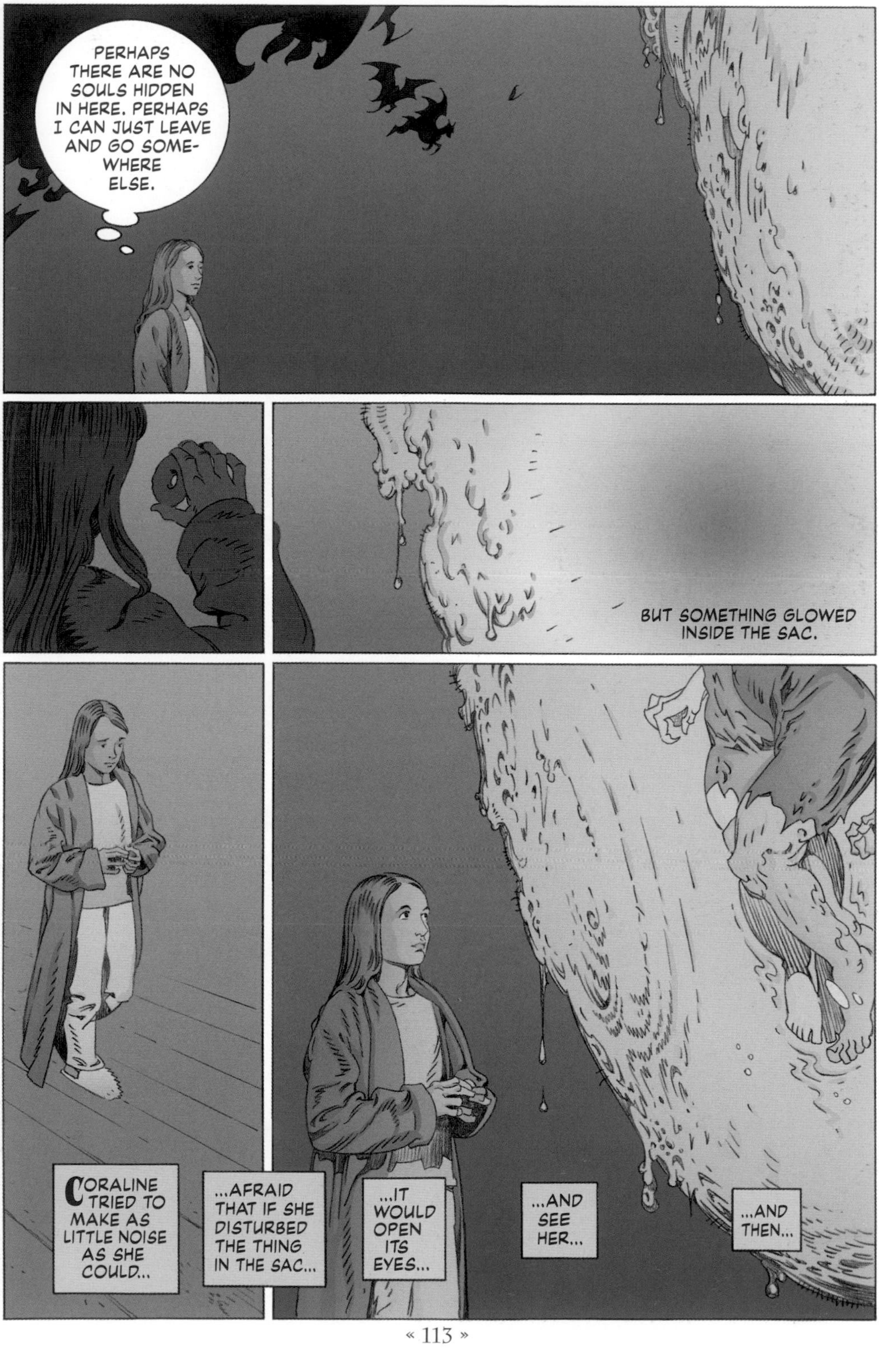
PERHAPS THERE ARE NO SOULS HIDDEN IN HERE. PERHAPS I CAN JUST LEAVE AND GO SOMEWHERE ELSE.
BUT SOMETHING GLOWED INSIDE THE SAC.
CORALINE TRIED TO MAKE AS LITTLE NOISE AS SHE COULD...
...AFRAID THAT IF SHE DISTURBED THE THING IN THE SAC...
...IT WOULD OPEN ITS EYES...
...AND SEE HER...
...AND THEN...

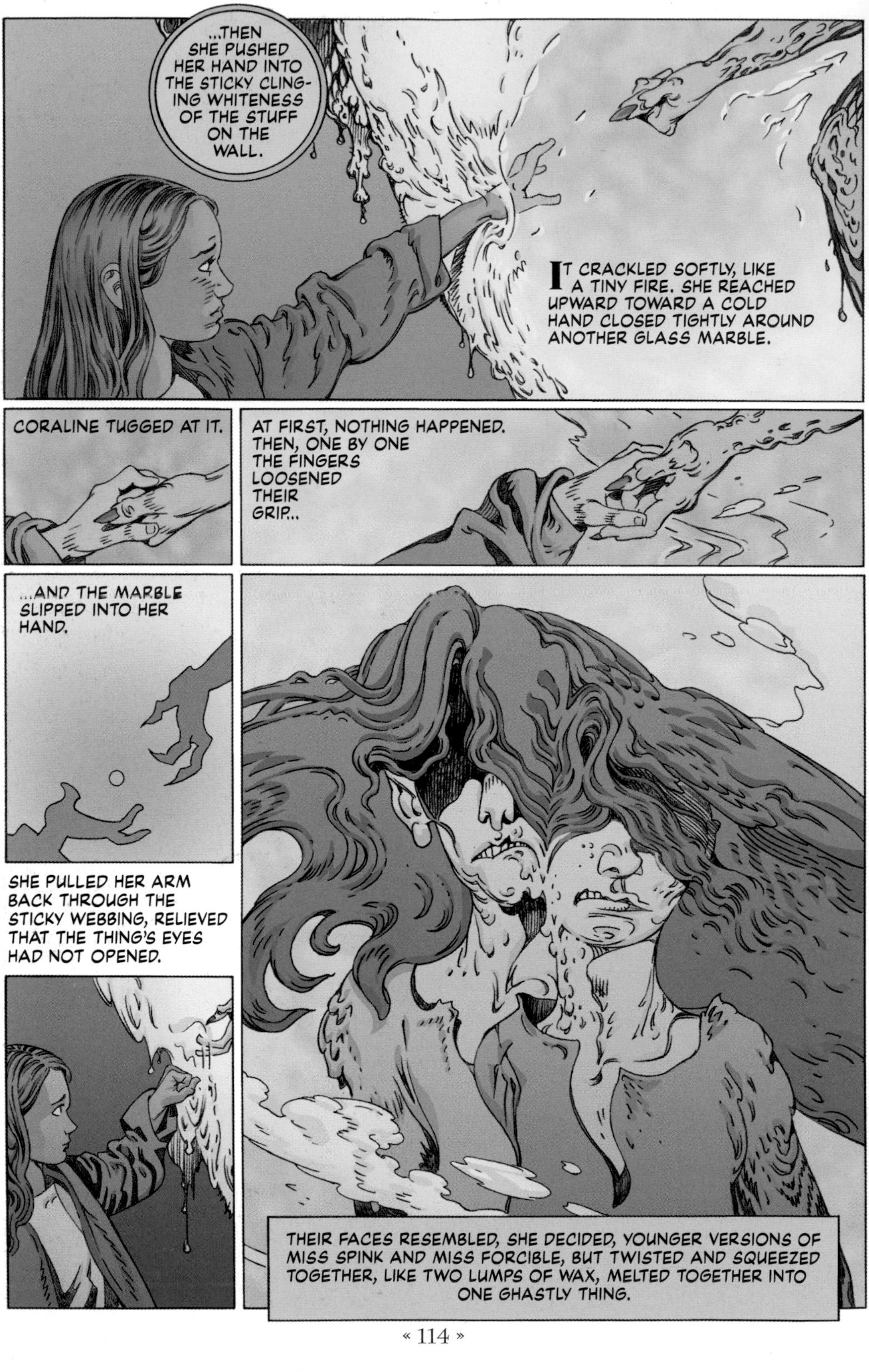
...THEN SHE PUSHED HER HAND INTO THE STICKY CLING-ING WHITENESS OF THE STUFF ON THE WALL.
IT CRACKLED SOFTLY, LIKE A TINY FIRE. SHE REACHED UPWARD TOWARD A COLD HAND CLOSED TIGHTLY AROUND ANOTHER GLASS MARBLE.
CORALINE TUGGED AT IT.
AT FIRST, NOTHING HAPPENED. THEN, ONE BY ONE THE FINGERS LOOSENED THEIR GRIP...
...AND THE MARBLE SLIPPED INTO HER HAND.
SHE PULLED HER ARM BACK THROUGH THE STICKY WEBBING, RELIEVED THAT THE THING'S EYES HAD NOT OPENED.
THEIR FACES RESEMBLED, SHE DECIDED, YOUNGER VERSIONS OF MISS SPINK AND MISS FORCIBLE, BUT TWISTED AND SQUEEZED TOGETHER, LIKE TWO LUMPS OF WAX, MELTED TOGETHER INTO ONE GHASTLY THING.

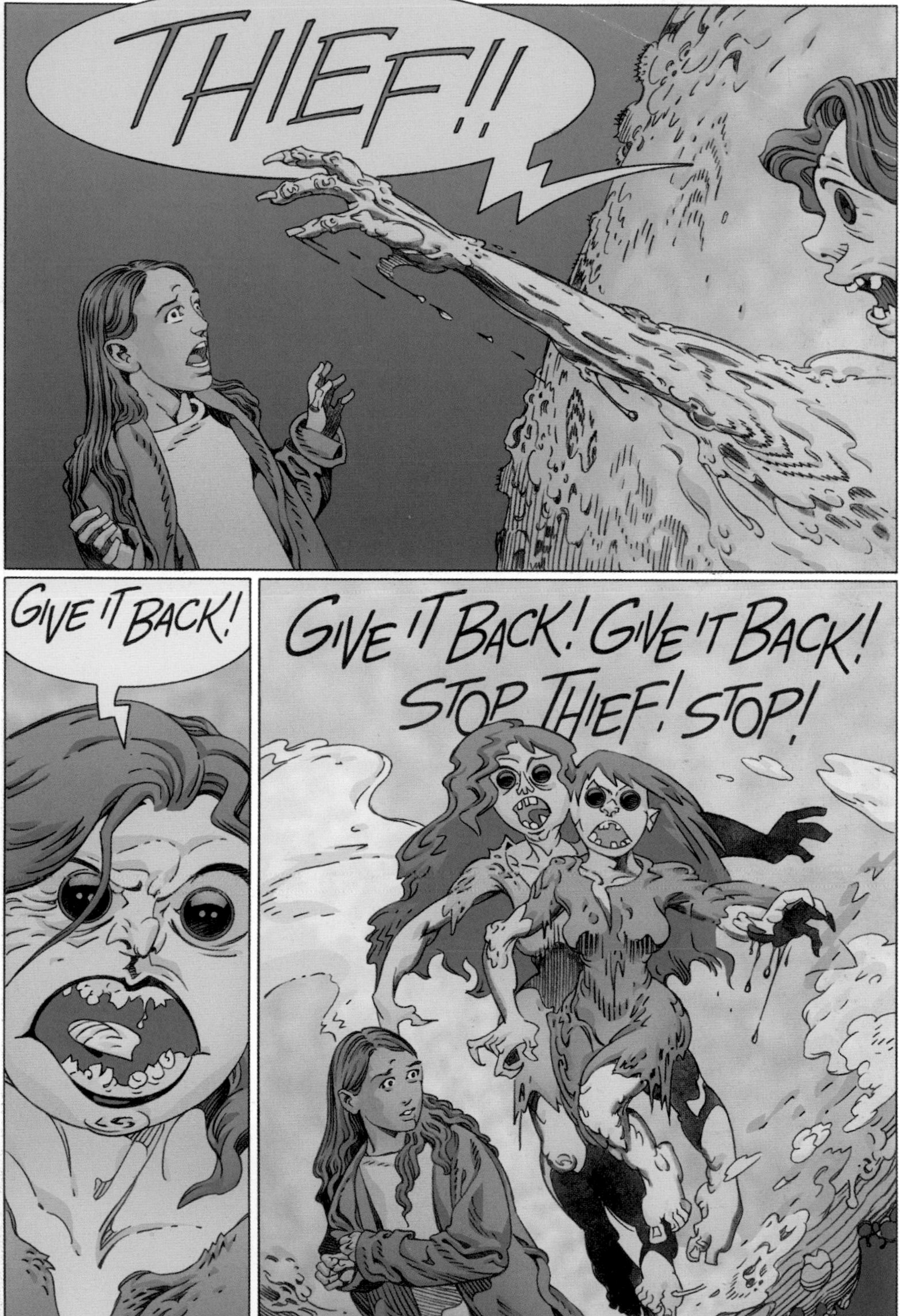
THIEF!!
GIVE IT BACK!
GIVE IT BACK! GIVE IT BACK! STOP THIEF! STOP!

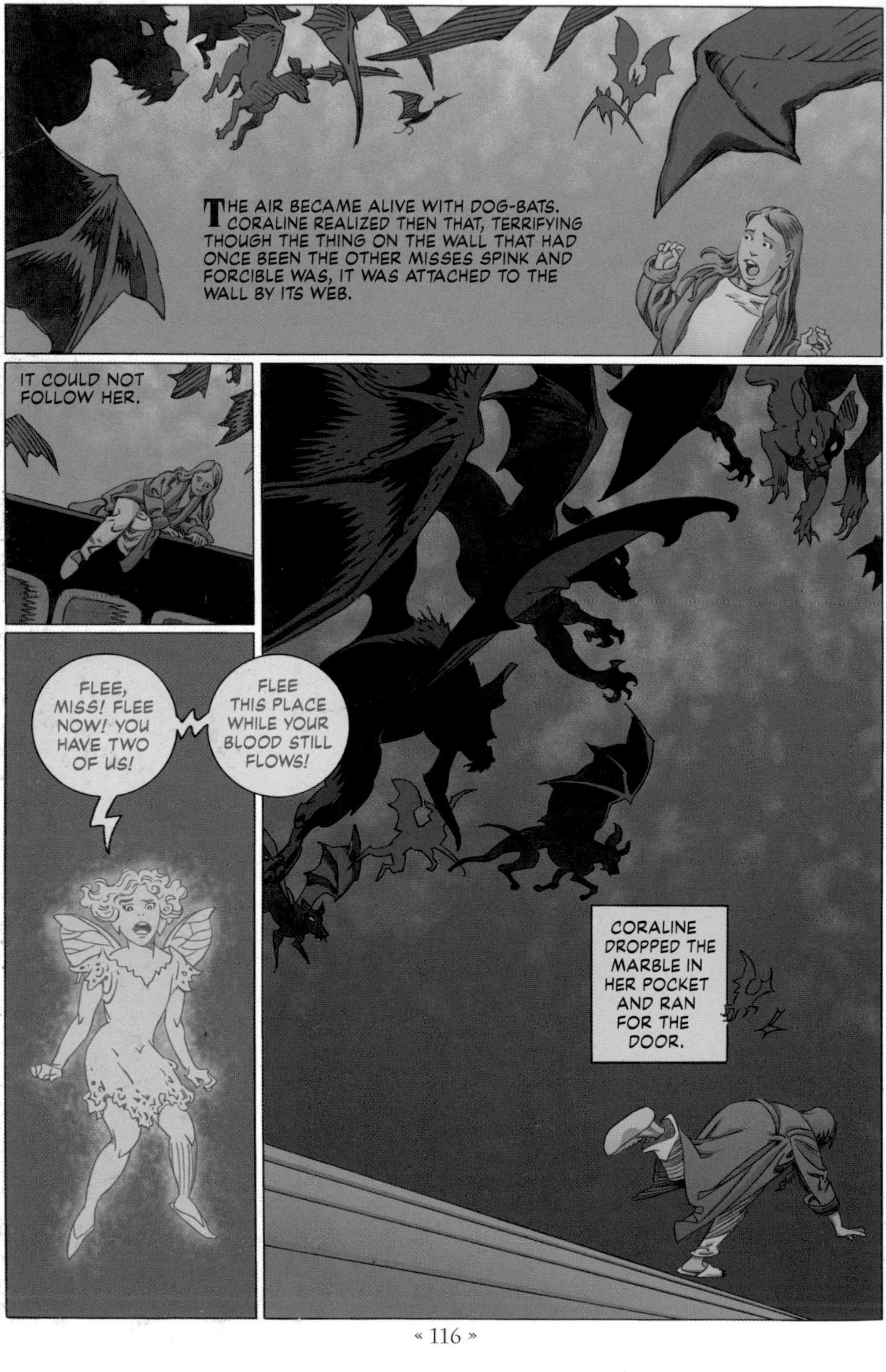
THE AIR BECAME ALIVE WITH DOG-BATS. CORALINE REALIZED THEN THAT, TERRIFYING THOUGH THE THING ON THE WALL THAT HAD ONCE BEEN THE OTHER MISSES SPINK AND FORCIBLE WAS, IT WAS ATTACHED TO THE WALL BY ITS WEB.
IT COULD NOT FOLLOW HER.
FLEE, MISS! FLEE NOW! YOU HAVE TWO OF US!
FLEE THIS PLACE WHILE YOUR BLOOD STILL FLOWS!
CORALINE DROPPED THE MARBLE IN HER POCKET AND RAN FOR THE DOOR.

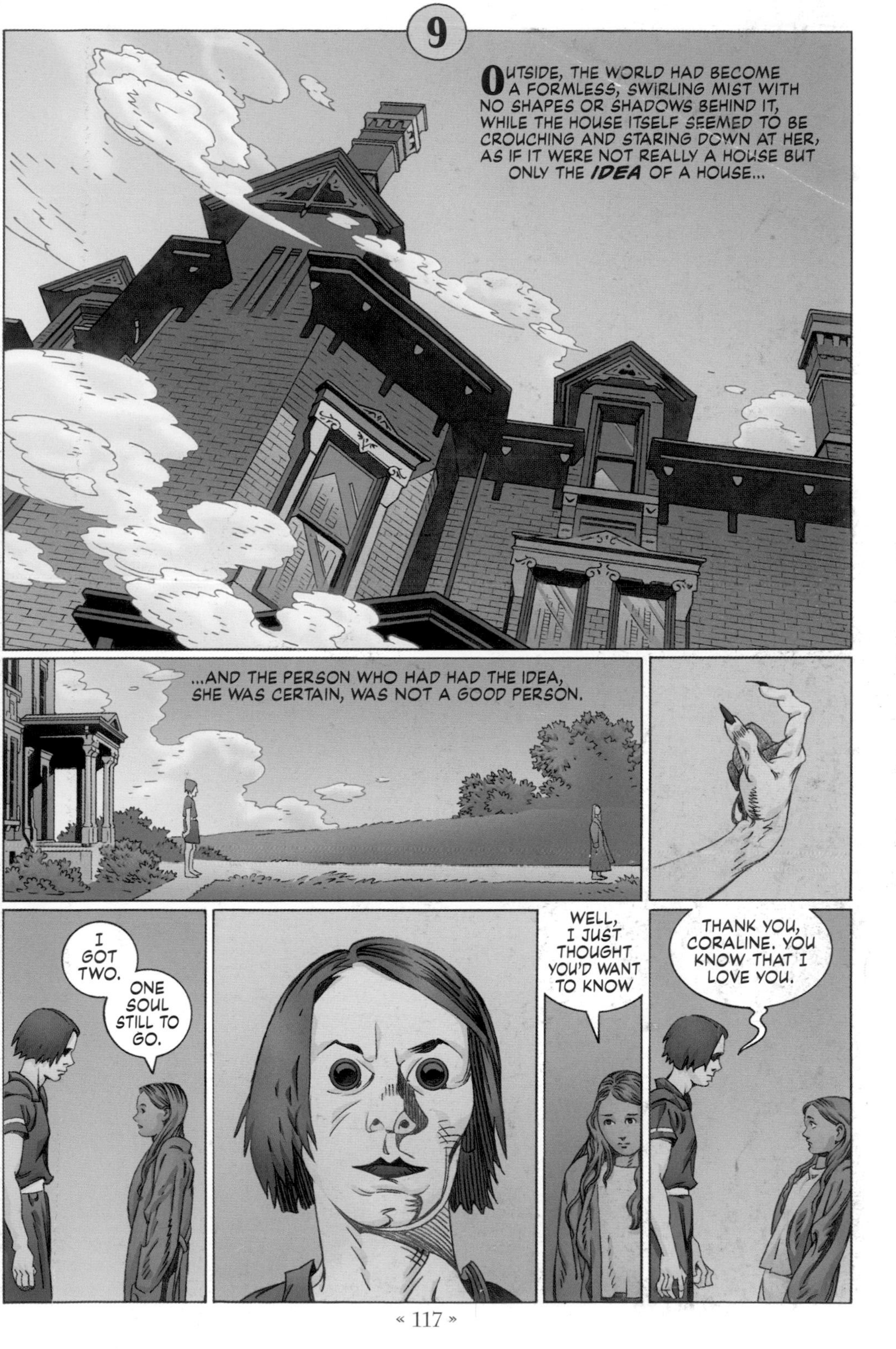
9
OUTSIDE, THE WORLD HAD BECOME A FORMLESS, SWIRLING MIST WITH NO SHAPES OR SHADOWS BEHIND IT, WHILE THE HOUSE ITSELF SEEMED TO BE CROUCHING AND STARING DOWN AT HER, AS IF IT WERE NOT REALLY A HOUSE BUT ONLY THE *IDEA* OF A HOUSE...
...AND THE PERSON WHO HAD HAD THE IDEA, SHE WAS CERTAIN, WAS NOT A GOOD PERSON.
I GOT TWO.
ONE SOUL STILL TO GO.
WELL, I JUST THOUGHT YOU'D WANT TO KNOW
THANK YOU, CORALINE. YOU KNOW THAT I LOVE YOU.

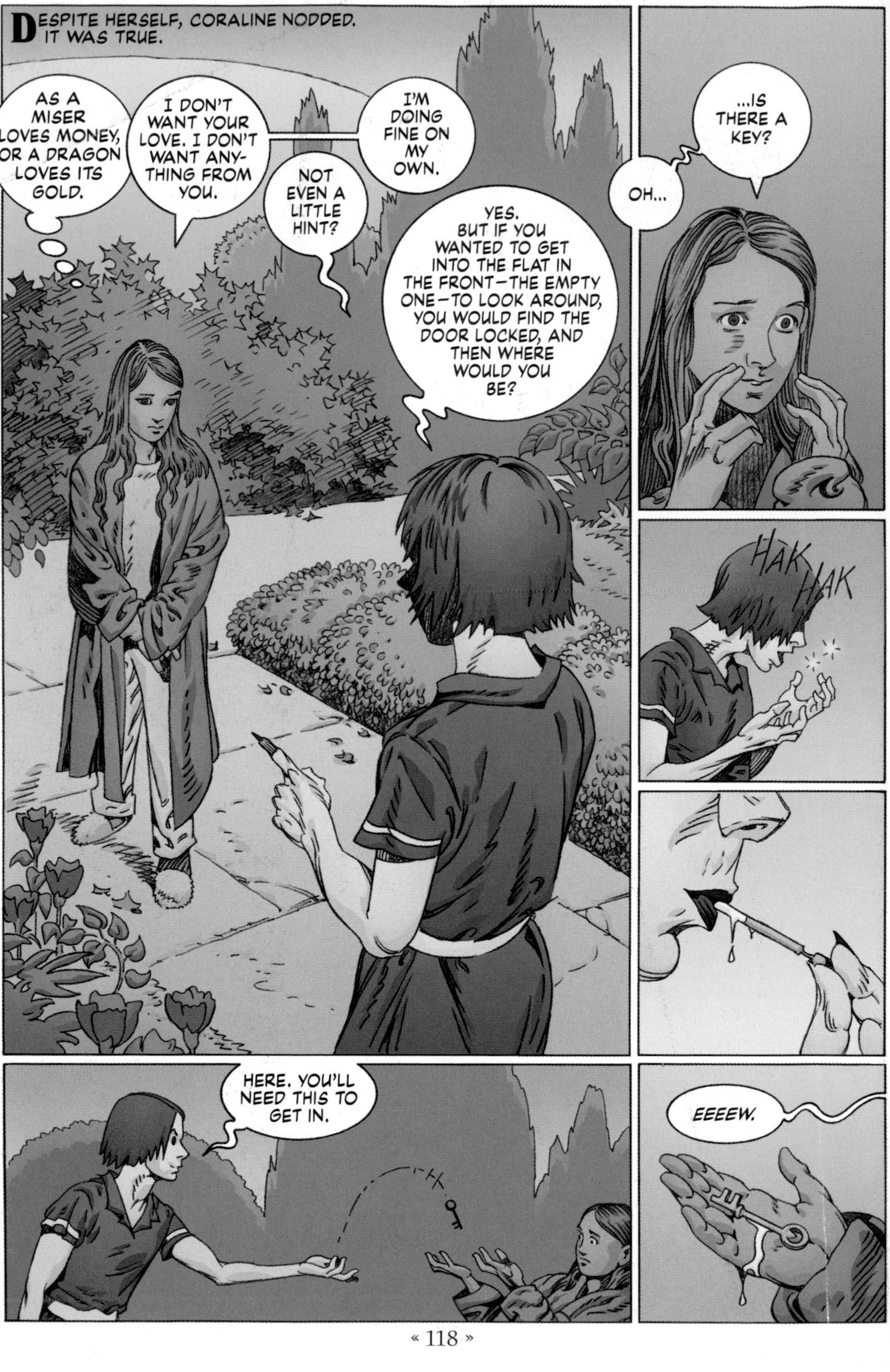
DESPITE HERSELF, CORALINE NODDED. IT WAS TRUE.
AS A MISER LOVES MONEY, OR A DRAGON LOVES ITS GOLD.
I DON'T WANT YOUR LOVE. I DON'T WANT ANYTHING FROM YOU.
I'M DOING FINE ON MY OWN.
NOT EVEN A LITTLE HINT?
YES. BUT IF YOU WANTED TO GET INTO THE FLAT IN THE FRONT—THE EMPTY ONE—TO LOOK AROUND, YOU WOULD FIND THE DOOR LOCKED, AND THEN WHERE WOULD YOU BE?
OH...
...IS THERE A KEY?
HAK HAK
HERE. YOU'LL NEED THIS TO GET IN.
EEEEW.

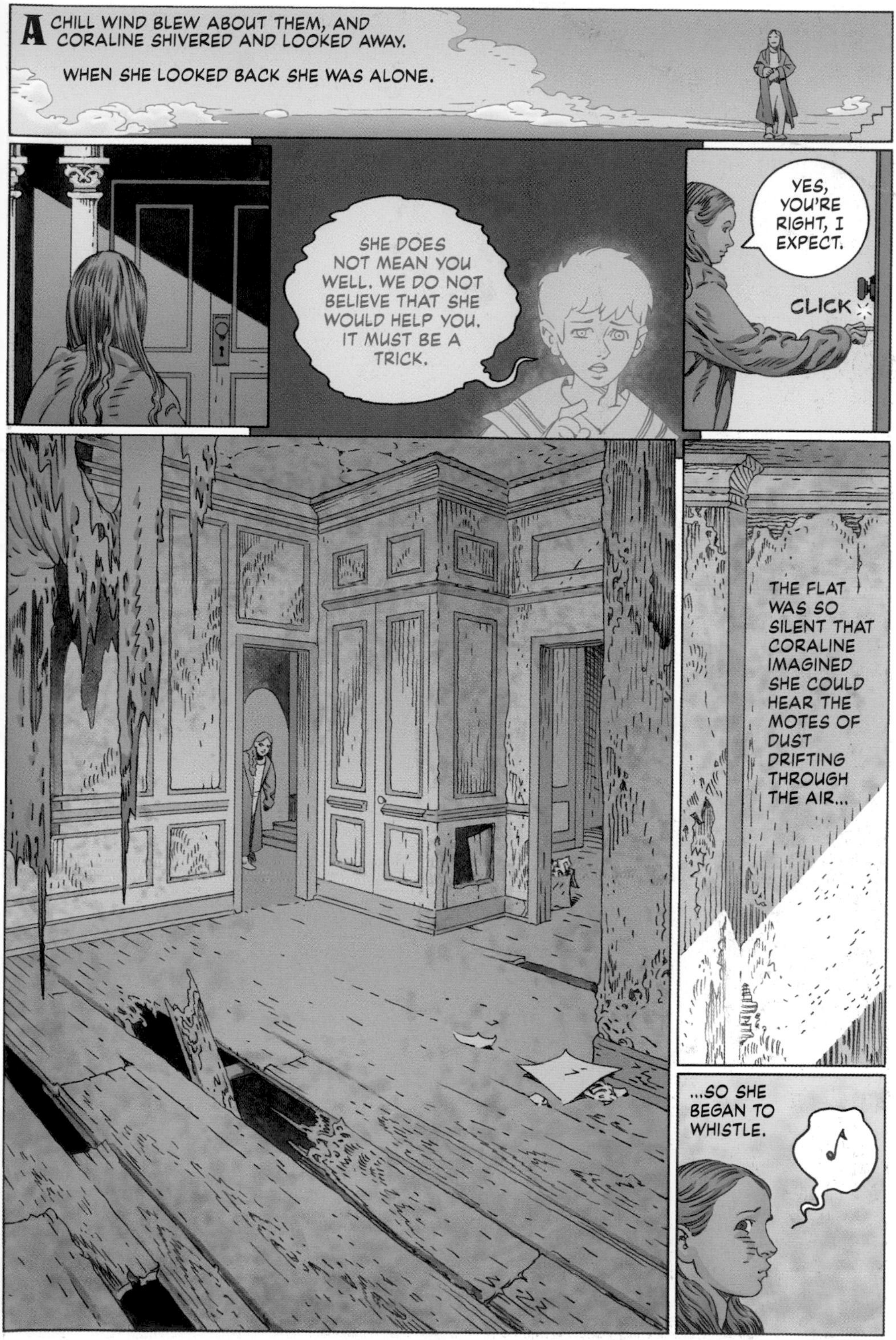
A CHILL WIND BLEW ABOUT THEM, AND CORALINE SHIVERED AND LOOKED AWAY.
WHEN SHE LOOKED BACK SHE WAS ALONE.
SHE DOES NOT MEAN YOU WELL. WE DO NOT BELIEVE THAT SHE WOULD HELP YOU. IT MUST BE A TRICK.
YES, YOU'RE RIGHT, I EXPECT.
CLICK
THE FLAT WAS SO SILENT THAT CORALINE IMAGINED SHE COULD HEAR THE MOTES OF DUST DRIFTING THROUGH THE AIR...
...SO SHE BEGAN TO WHISTLE.
♪

SHE WALKED THROUGH THE EMPTY KITCHEN...

...PAST THE EMPTY BATHROOM. IN THE TUB WAS A DEAD SPIDER THE SIZE OF A SMALL CAT.

THEN, WALKING THROUGH AN EMPTY BEDROOM, SHE SAW SOMETHING...

A TRAP-DOOR?!

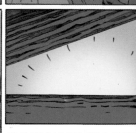

UP THROUGH THE HOLE CAME THE SMELL OF DAMP CLAY, AND SOMETHING ELSE.

SOUR VINEGAR.

CORALINE LOOKED AT THE CELLAR THROUGH THE STONE WITH THE HOLE IN IT BUT SAW NOTHING.

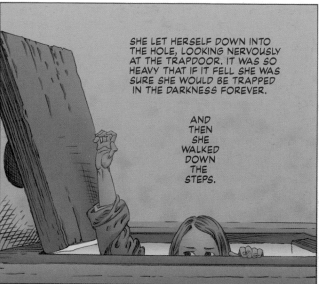

SHE LET HERSELF DOWN INTO THE HOLE, LOOKING NERVOUSLY AT THE TRAPDOOR. IT WAS SO HEAVY THAT IF IT FELL SHE WAS SURE SHE WOULD BE TRAPPED IN THE DARKNESS FOREVER.

AND THEN SHE WALKED DOWN THE STEPS.

THE BAD SMELL WAS WORSE NOW.

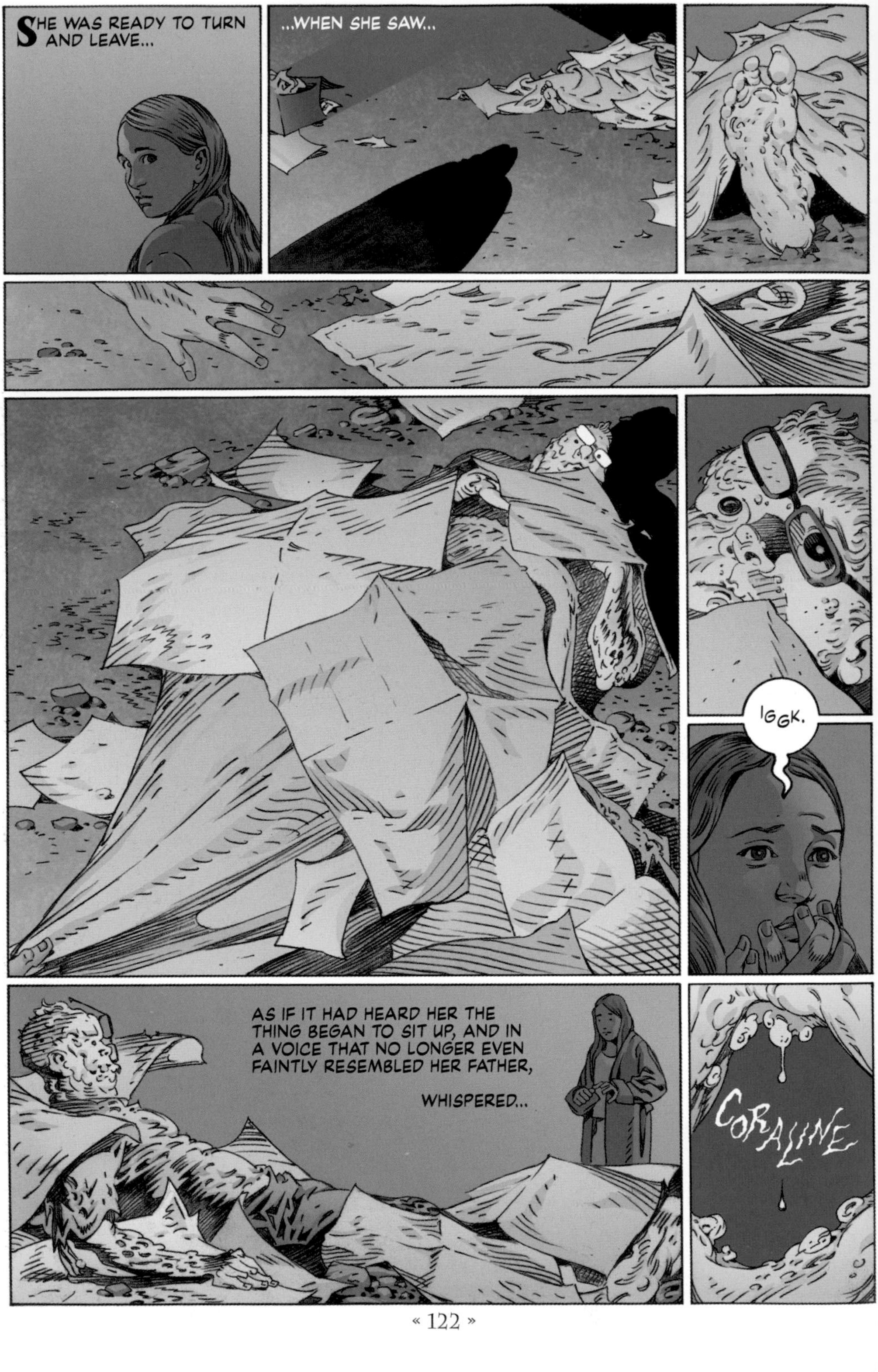
SHE WAS READY TO TURN AND LEAVE...
...WHEN SHE SAW...
IGGK.
AS IF IT HAD HEARD HER THE THING BEGAN TO SIT UP, AND IN A VOICE THAT NO LONGER EVEN FAINTLY RESEMBLED HER FATHER,
WHISPERED...
CORALINE

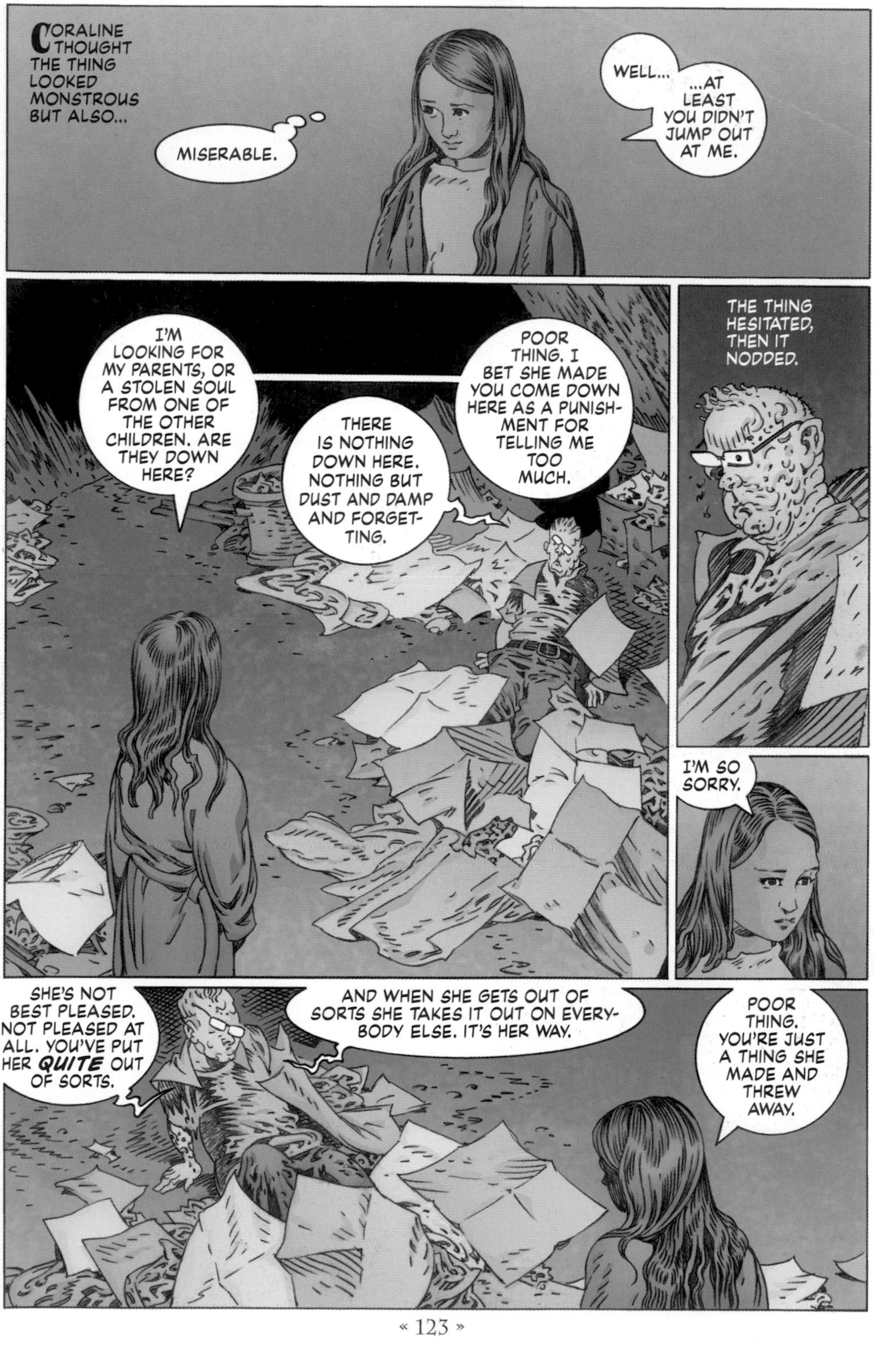
CORALINE THOUGHT THE THING LOOKED MONSTROUS BUT ALSO...
MISERABLE.
WELL...
...AT LEAST YOU DIDN'T JUMP OUT AT ME.
I'M LOOKING FOR MY PARENTS, OR A STOLEN SOUL FROM ONE OF THE OTHER CHILDREN. ARE THEY DOWN HERE?
THERE IS NOTHING DOWN HERE. NOTHING BUT DUST AND DAMP AND FORGET-TING.
POOR THING. I BET SHE MADE YOU COME DOWN HERE AS A PUNISH-MENT FOR TELLING ME TOO MUCH.
THE THING HESITATED, THEN IT NODDED.
I'M SO SORRY.
SHE'S NOT BEST PLEASED. NOT PLEASED AT ALL. YOU'VE PUT HER *QUITE* OUT OF SORTS.
AND WHEN SHE GETS OUT OF SORTS SHE TAKES IT OUT ON EVERY-BODY ELSE. IT'S HER WAY.
POOR THING. YOU'RE JUST A THING SHE MADE AND THREW AWAY.

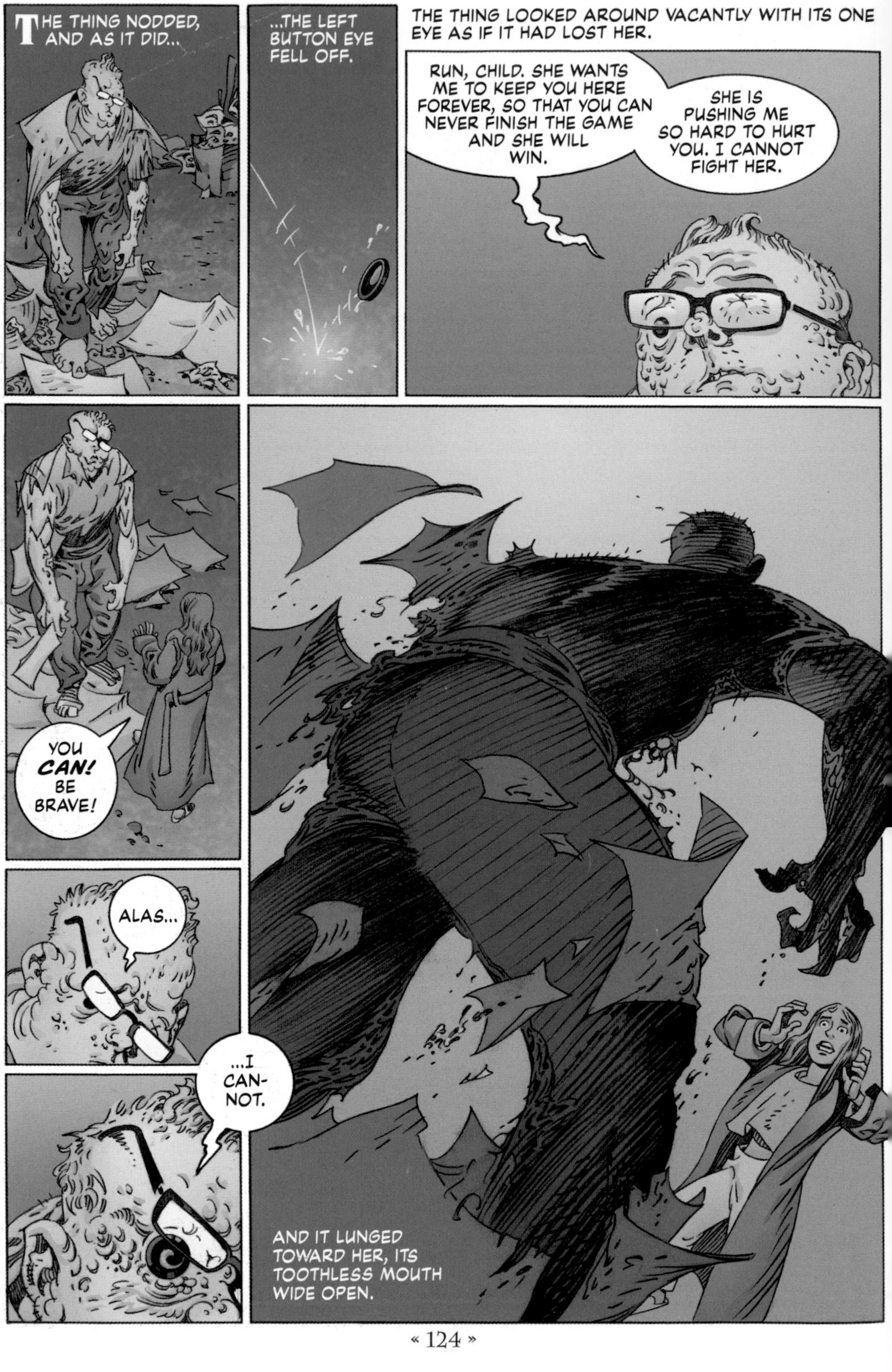
THE THING NODDED, AND AS IT DID...
...THE LEFT BUTTON EYE FELL OFF.
THE THING LOOKED AROUND VACANTLY WITH ITS ONE EYE AS IF IT HAD LOST HER.
RUN, CHILD. SHE WANTS ME TO KEEP YOU HERE FOREVER, SO THAT YOU CAN NEVER FINISH THE GAME AND SHE WILL WIN.
SHE IS PUSHING ME SO HARD TO HURT YOU. I CANNOT FIGHT HER.
YOU CAN! BE BRAVE!
ALAS...
...I CAN-NOT.
AND IT LUNGED TOWARD HER, ITS TOOTHLESS MOUTH WIDE OPEN.

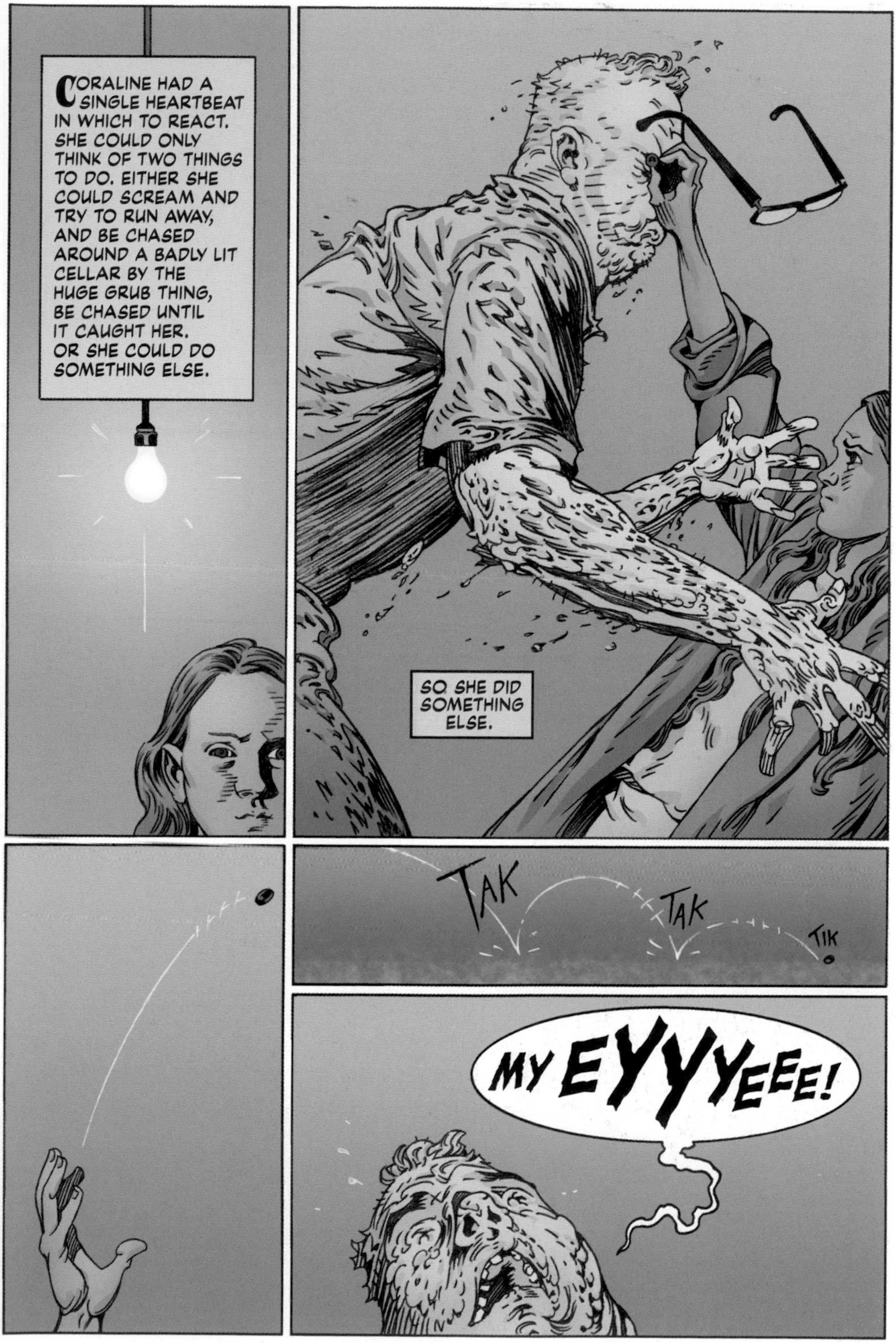
CORALINE HAD A SINGLE HEARTBEAT IN WHICH TO REACT. SHE COULD ONLY THINK OF TWO THINGS TO DO. EITHER SHE COULD SCREAM AND TRY TO RUN AWAY, AND BE CHASED AROUND A BADLY LIT CELLAR BY THE HUGE GRUB THING, BE CHASED UNTIL IT CAUGHT HER. OR SHE COULD DO SOMETHING ELSE.
SO SHE DID SOMETHING ELSE.
TAK
TAK
TIK
MY EYYYEEEE!

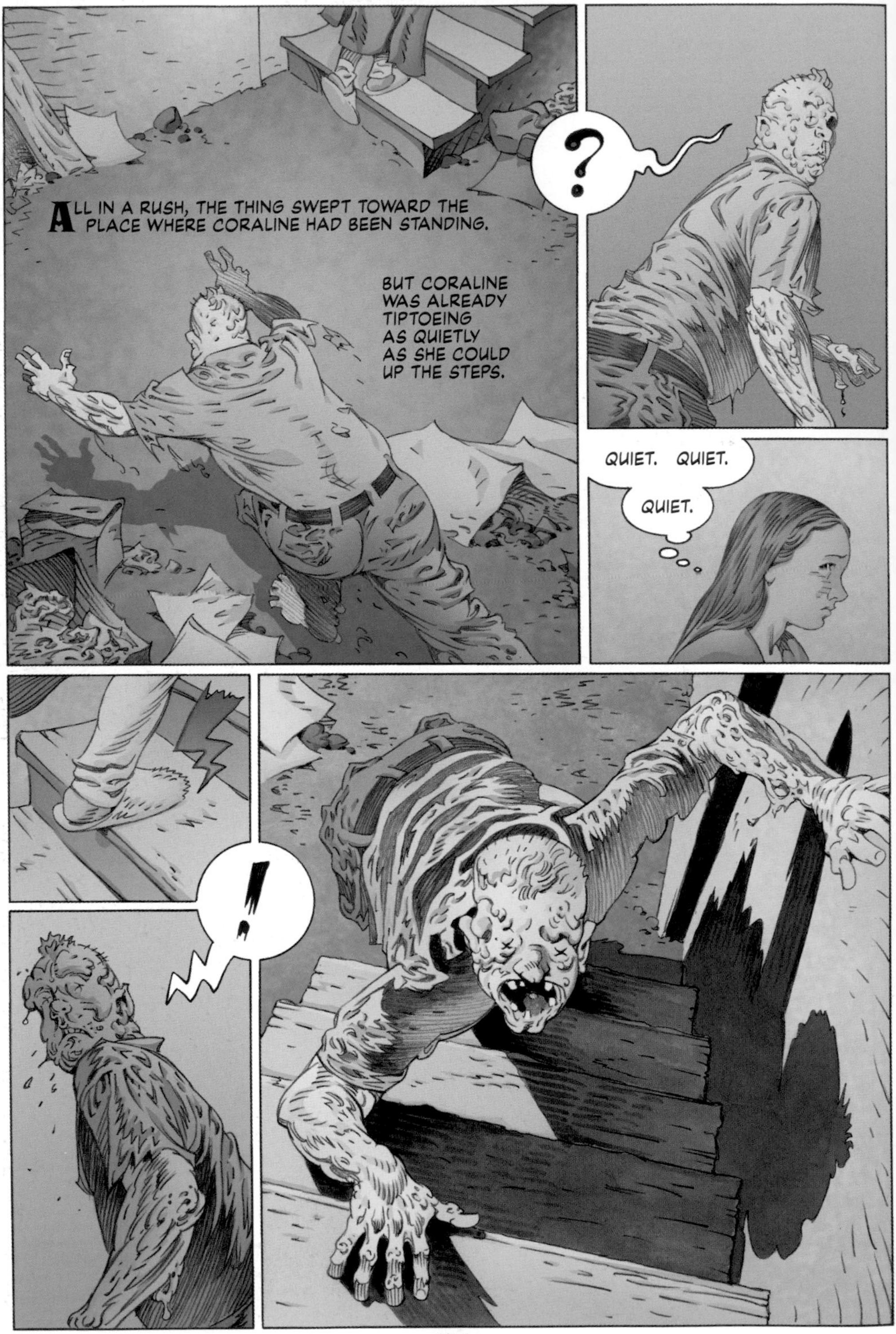

ALL IN A RUSH, THE THING SWEPT TOWARD THE PLACE WHERE CORALINE HAD BEEN STANDING.
BUT CORALINE WAS ALREADY TIPTOEING AS QUIETLY AS SHE COULD UP THE STEPS.
?
QUIET. QUIET.
QUIET.
!

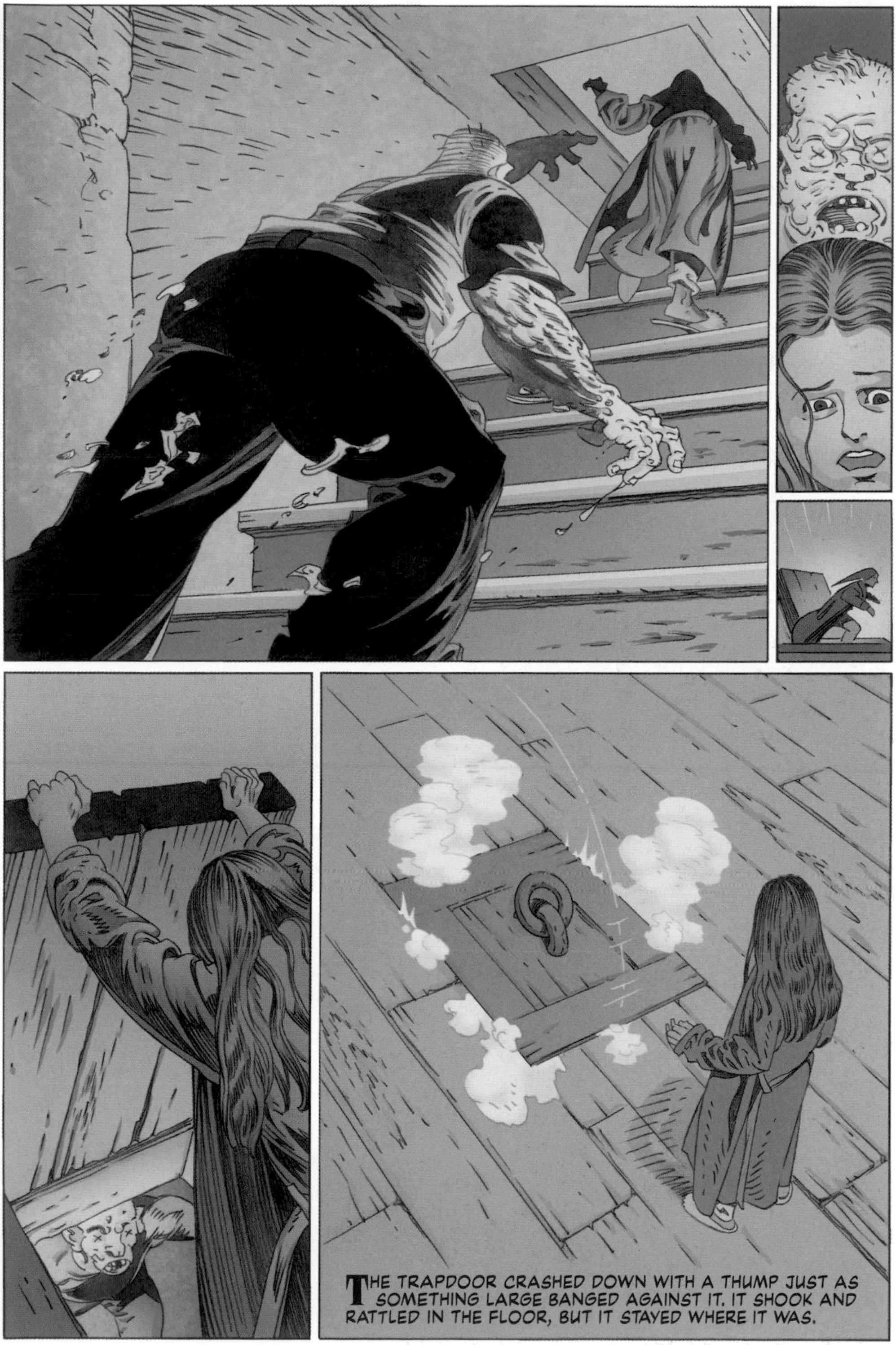
THE TRAPDOOR CRASHED DOWN WITH A THUMP JUST AS SOMETHING LARGE BANGED AGAINST IT. IT SHOOK AND RATTLED IN THE FLOOR, BUT IT STAYED WHERE IT WAS.

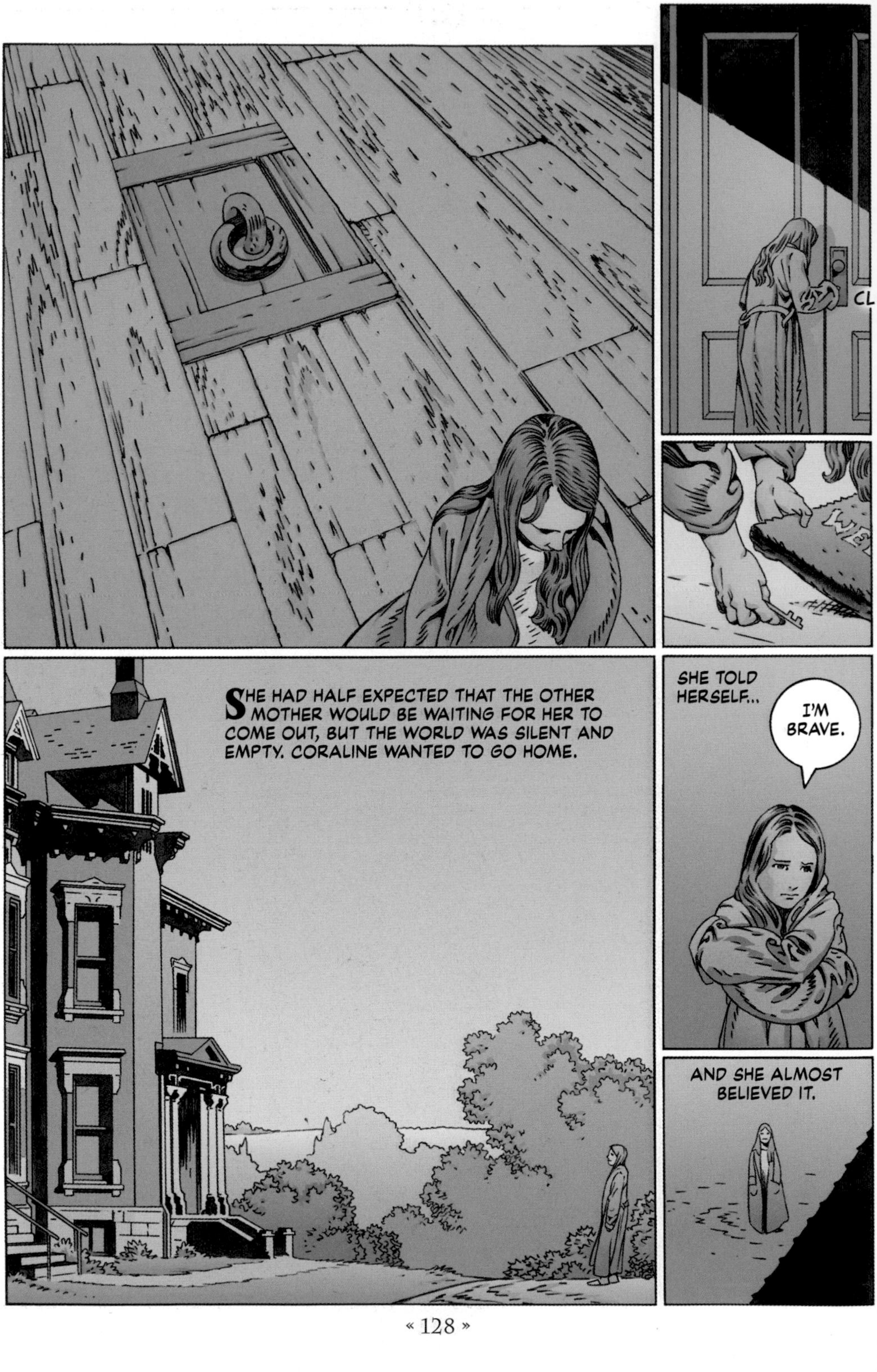
CL
SHE HAD HALF EXPECTED THAT THE OTHER MOTHER WOULD BE WAITING FOR HER TO COME OUT, BUT THE WORLD WAS SILENT AND EMPTY. CORALINE WANTED TO GO HOME.
SHE TOLD HERSELF...
I'M BRAVE.
AND SHE ALMOST BELIEVED IT.

10

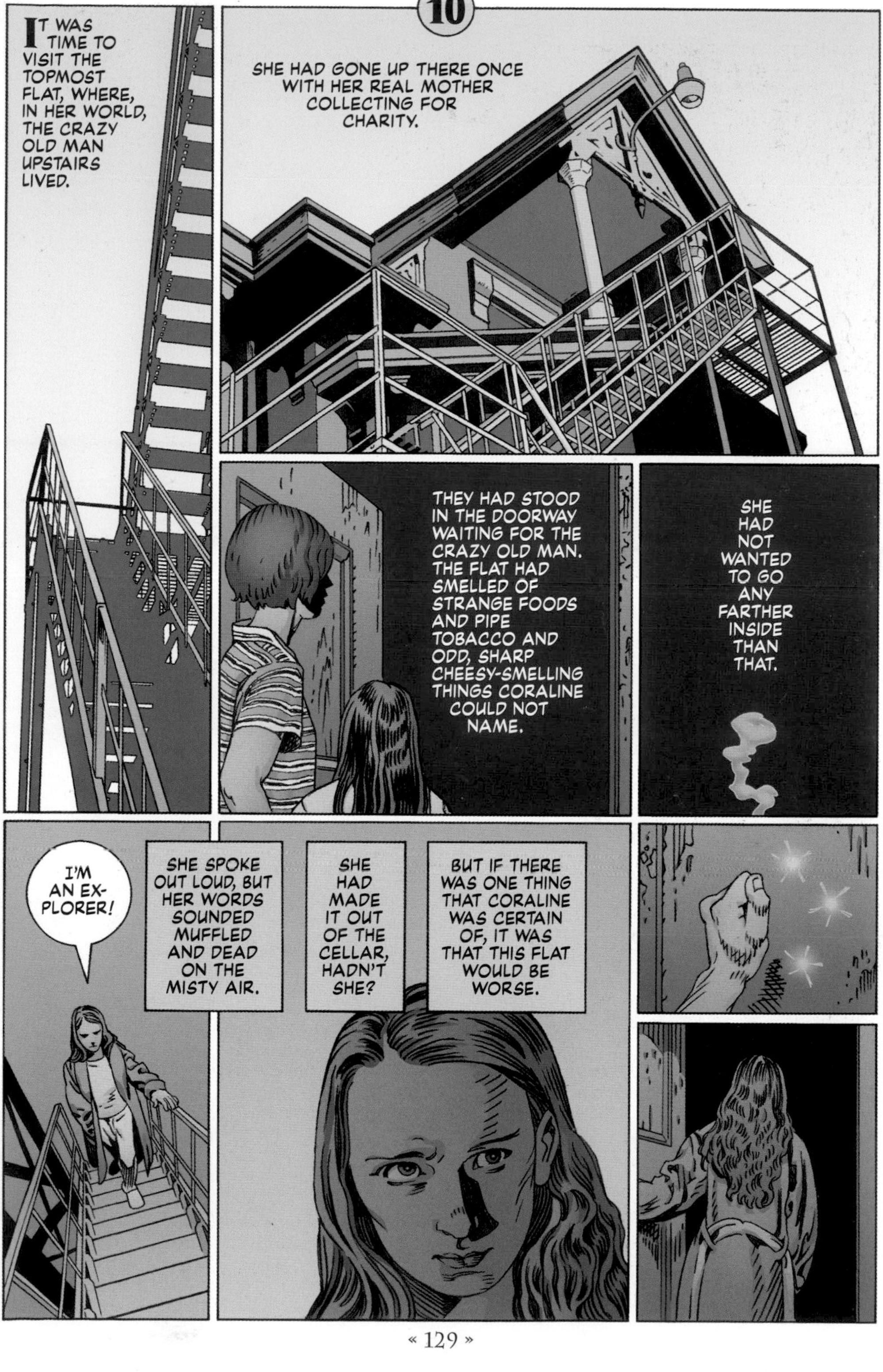
IT WAS TIME TO VISIT THE TOPMOST FLAT, WHERE, IN HER WORLD, THE CRAZY OLD MAN UPSTAIRS LIVED.
SHE HAD GONE UP THERE ONCE WITH HER REAL MOTHER COLLECTING FOR CHARITY.
THEY HAD STOOD IN THE DOORWAY WAITING FOR THE CRAZY OLD MAN. THE FLAT HAD SMELLED OF STRANGE FOODS AND PIPE TOBACCO AND ODD, SHARP CHEESY-SMELLING THINGS CORALINE COULD NOT NAME.
SHE HAD NOT WANTED TO GO ANY FARTHER INSIDE THAN THAT.
I'M AN EXPLORER!
SHE SPOKE OUT LOUD, BUT HER WORDS SOUNDED MUFFLED AND DEAD ON THE MISTY AIR.
SHE HAD MADE IT OUT OF THE CELLAR, HADN'T SHE?
BUT IF THERE WAS ONE THING THAT CORALINE WAS CERTAIN OF, IT WAS THAT THIS FLAT WOULD BE WORSE.

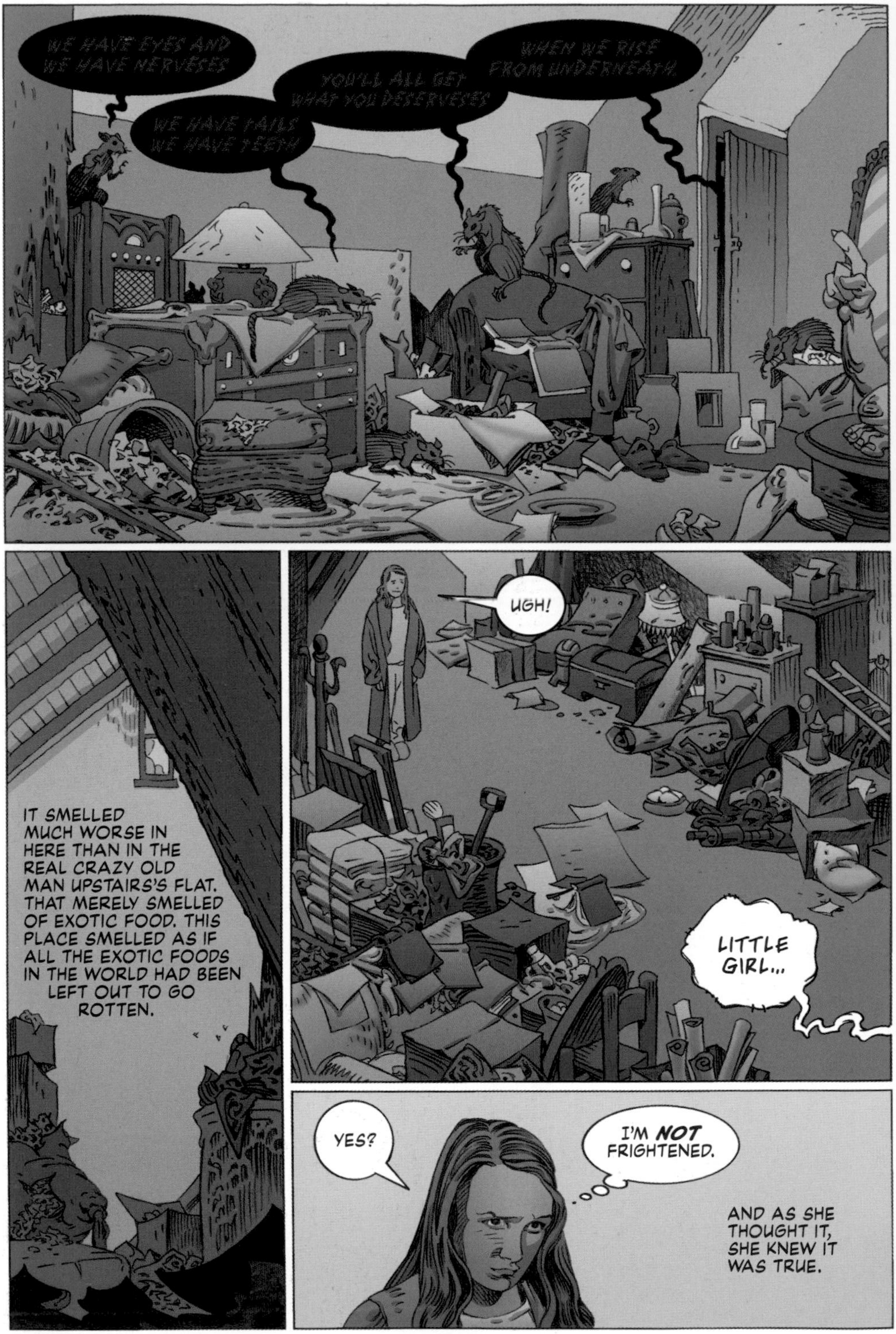
WE HAVE EYES AND WE HAVE NERVESES
WE HAVE TAILS WE HAVE TEETH
YOU'LL ALL GET WHAT YOU DESERVESES
WHEN WE RISE FROM UNDERNEATH.
IT SMELLED MUCH WORSE IN HERE THAN IN THE REAL CRAZY OLD MAN UPSTAIRS'S FLAT. THAT MERELY SMELLED OF EXOTIC FOOD. THIS PLACE SMELLED AS IF ALL THE EXOTIC FOODS IN THE WORLD HAD BEEN LEFT OUT TO GO ROTTEN.
UGH!
LITTLE GIRL...
YES?
I'M NOT FRIGHTENED.
AND AS SHE THOUGHT IT, SHE KNEW IT WAS TRUE.

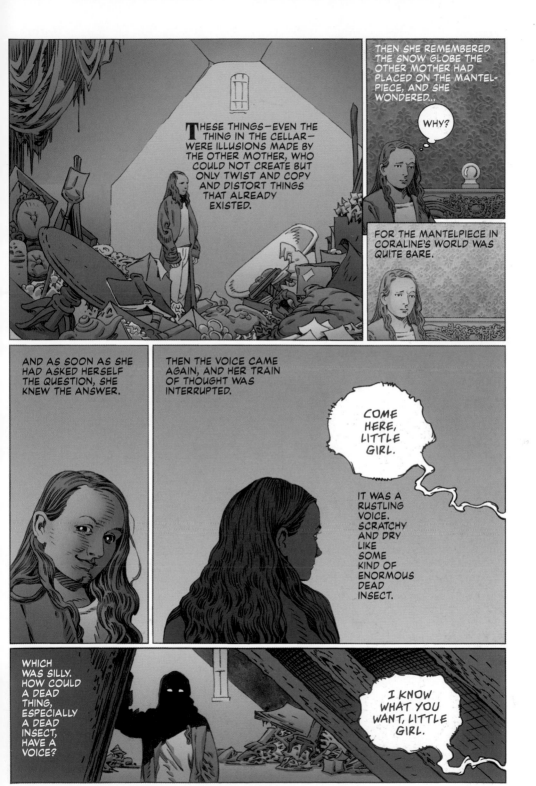

THEN SHE REMEMBERED THE SNOW GLOBE THE OTHER MOTHER HAD PLACED ON THE MANTELPIECE, AND SHE WONDERED...

WHY?

THESE THINGS—EVEN THE THING IN THE CELLAR—WERE ILLUSIONS MADE BY THE OTHER MOTHER, WHO COULD NOT CREATE BUT ONLY TWIST AND COPY AND DISTORT THINGS THAT ALREADY EXISTED.

FOR THE MANTELPIECE IN CORALINE'S WORLD WAS QUITE BARE.

AND AS SOON AS SHE HAD ASKED HERSELF THE QUESTION, SHE KNEW THE ANSWER.

THEN THE VOICE CAME AGAIN, AND HER TRAIN OF THOUGHT WAS INTERRUPTED.

COME HERE, LITTLE GIRL.

IT WAS A RUSTLING VOICE. SCRATCHY AND DRY LIKE SOME KIND OF ENORMOUS DEAD INSECT.

WHICH WAS SILLY. HOW COULD A DEAD THING, ESPECIALLY A DEAD INSECT, HAVE A VOICE?

I KNOW WHAT YOU WANT, LITTLE GIRL.

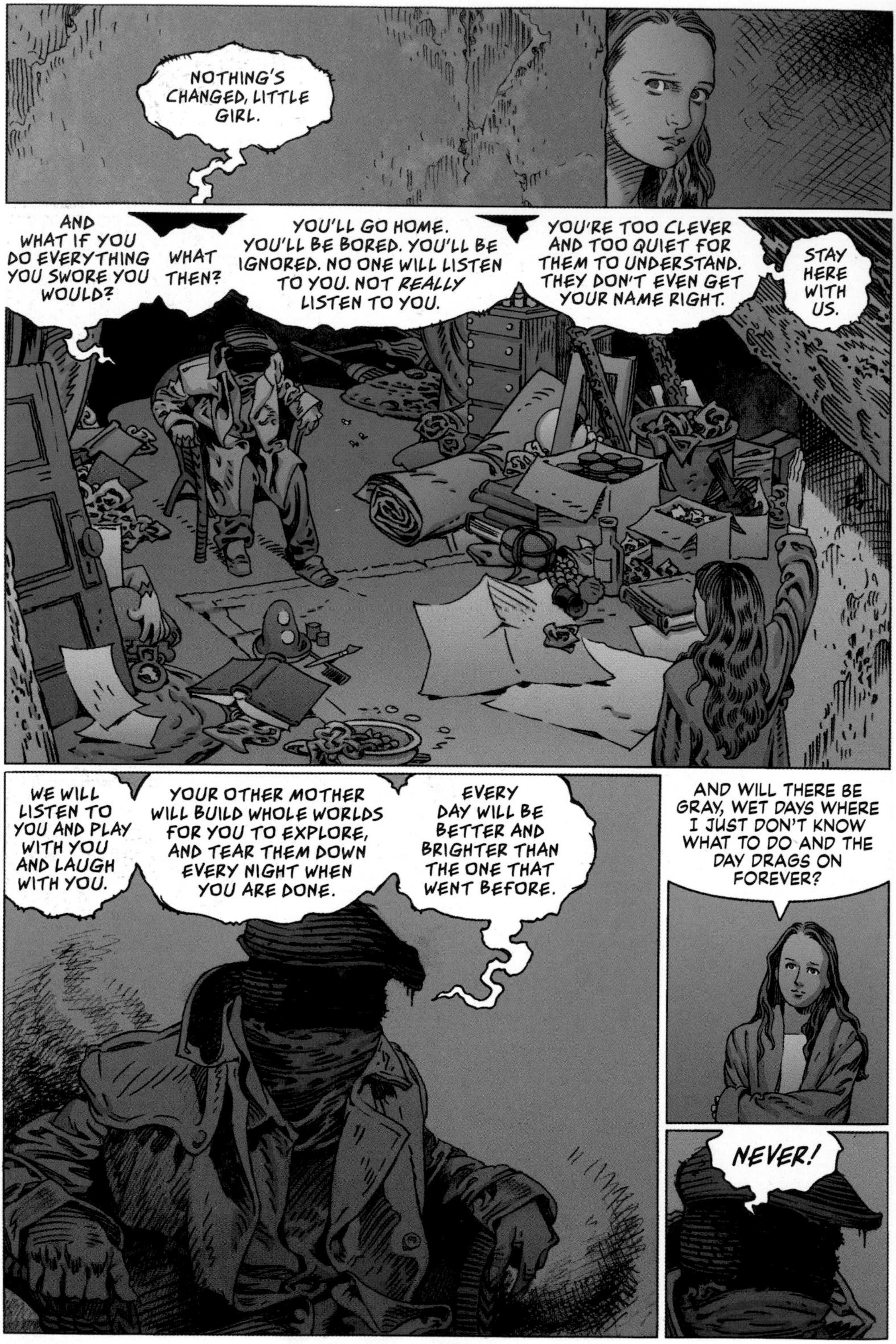
NOTHING'S CHANGED, LITTLE GIRL.
AND WHAT IF YOU DO EVERYTHING YOU SWORE YOU WOULD?
WHAT THEN?
YOU'LL GO HOME. YOU'LL BE BORED. YOU'LL BE IGNORED. NO ONE WILL LISTEN TO YOU. NOT *REALLY* LISTEN TO YOU.
YOU'RE TOO CLEVER AND TOO QUIET FOR THEM TO UNDERSTAND. THEY DON'T EVEN GET YOUR NAME RIGHT.
STAY HERE WITH US.
WE WILL LISTEN TO YOU AND PLAY WITH YOU AND LAUGH WITH YOU.
YOUR OTHER MOTHER WILL BUILD WHOLE WORLDS FOR YOU TO EXPLORE, AND TEAR THEM DOWN EVERY NIGHT WHEN YOU ARE DONE.
EVERY DAY WILL BE BETTER AND BRIGHTER THAN THE ONE THAT WENT BEFORE.
AND WILL THERE BE GRAY, WET DAYS WHERE I JUST DON'T KNOW WHAT TO DO AND THE DAY DRAGS ON FOREVER?
NEVER!

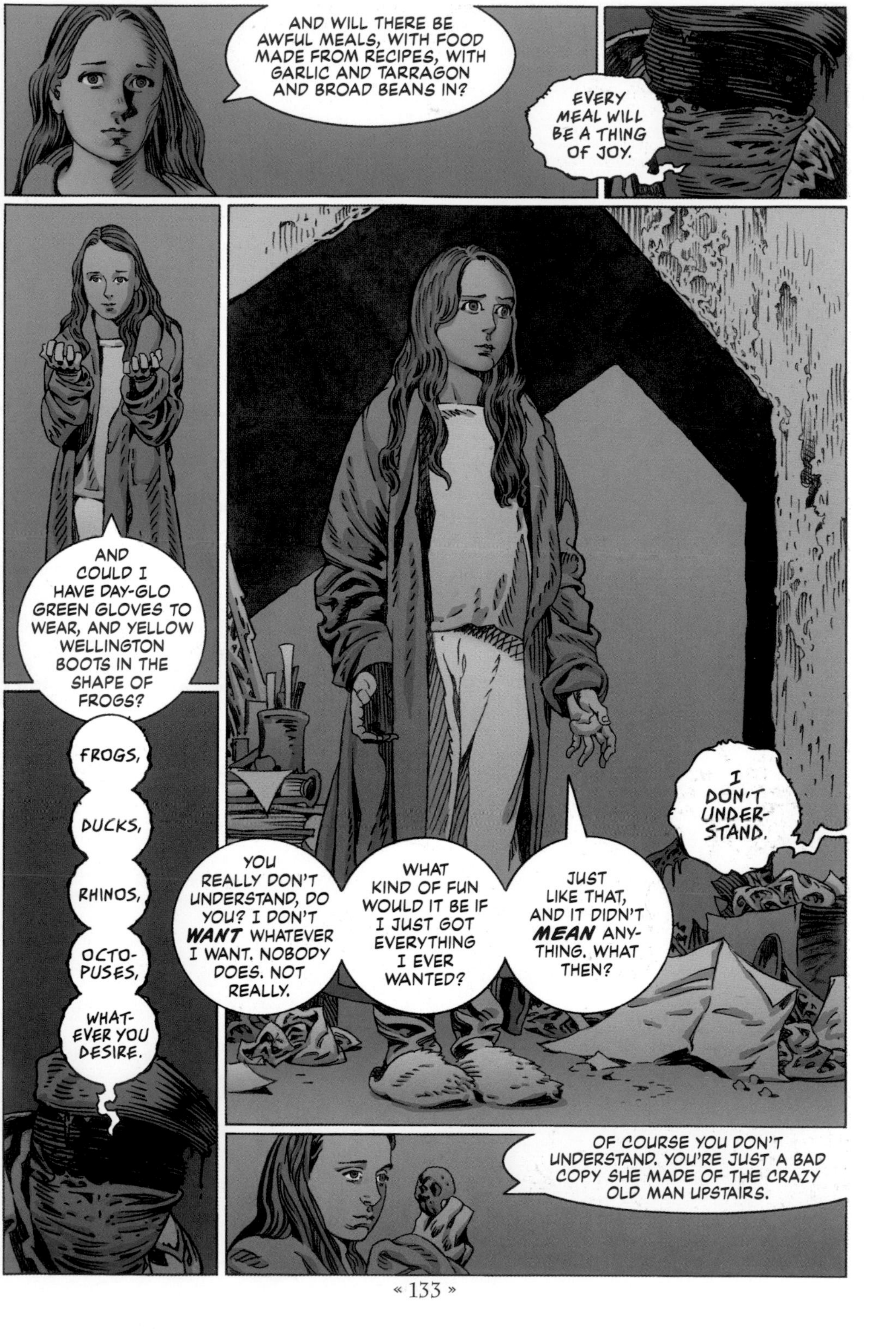
AND WILL THERE BE AWFUL MEALS, WITH FOOD MADE FROM RECIPES, WITH GARLIC AND TARRAGON AND BROAD BEANS IN?
EVERY MEAL WILL BE A THING OF JOY.
AND COULD I HAVE DAY-GLO GREEN GLOVES TO WEAR, AND YELLOW WELLINGTON BOOTS IN THE SHAPE OF FROGS?
FROGS,
DUCKS,
RHINOS,
OCTO-PUSES,
WHAT-EVER YOU DESIRE.
YOU REALLY DON'T UNDERSTAND, DO YOU? I DON'T **WANT** WHATEVER I WANT. NOBODY DOES. NOT REALLY.
WHAT KIND OF FUN WOULD IT BE IF I JUST GOT EVERYTHING I EVER WANTED?
JUST LIKE THAT, AND IT DIDN'T **MEAN** ANY-THING. WHAT THEN?
I DON'T UNDER-STAND.
OF COURSE YOU DON'T UNDERSTAND. YOU'RE JUST A BAD COPY SHE MADE OF THE CRAZY OLD MAN UPSTAIRS.

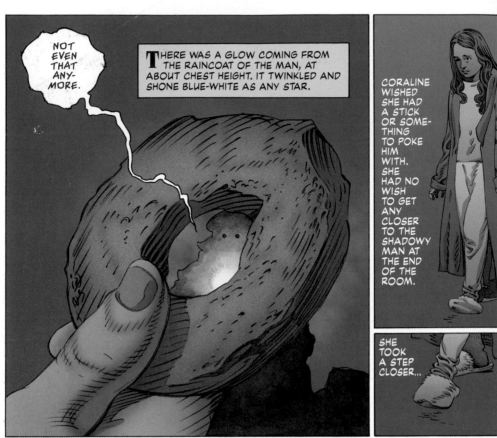

NOT EVEN THAT ANYMORE.

THERE WAS A GLOW COMING FROM THE RAINCOAT OF THE MAN, AT ABOUT CHEST HEIGHT. IT TWINKLED AND SHONE BLUE-WHITE AS ANY STAR.

CORALINE WISHED SHE HAD A STICK OR SOMETHING TO POKE HIM WITH. SHE HAD NO WISH TO GET ANY CLOSER TO THE SHADOWY MAN AT THE END OF THE ROOM.

SHE TOOK A STEP CLOSER...

...AND HE FELL APART.

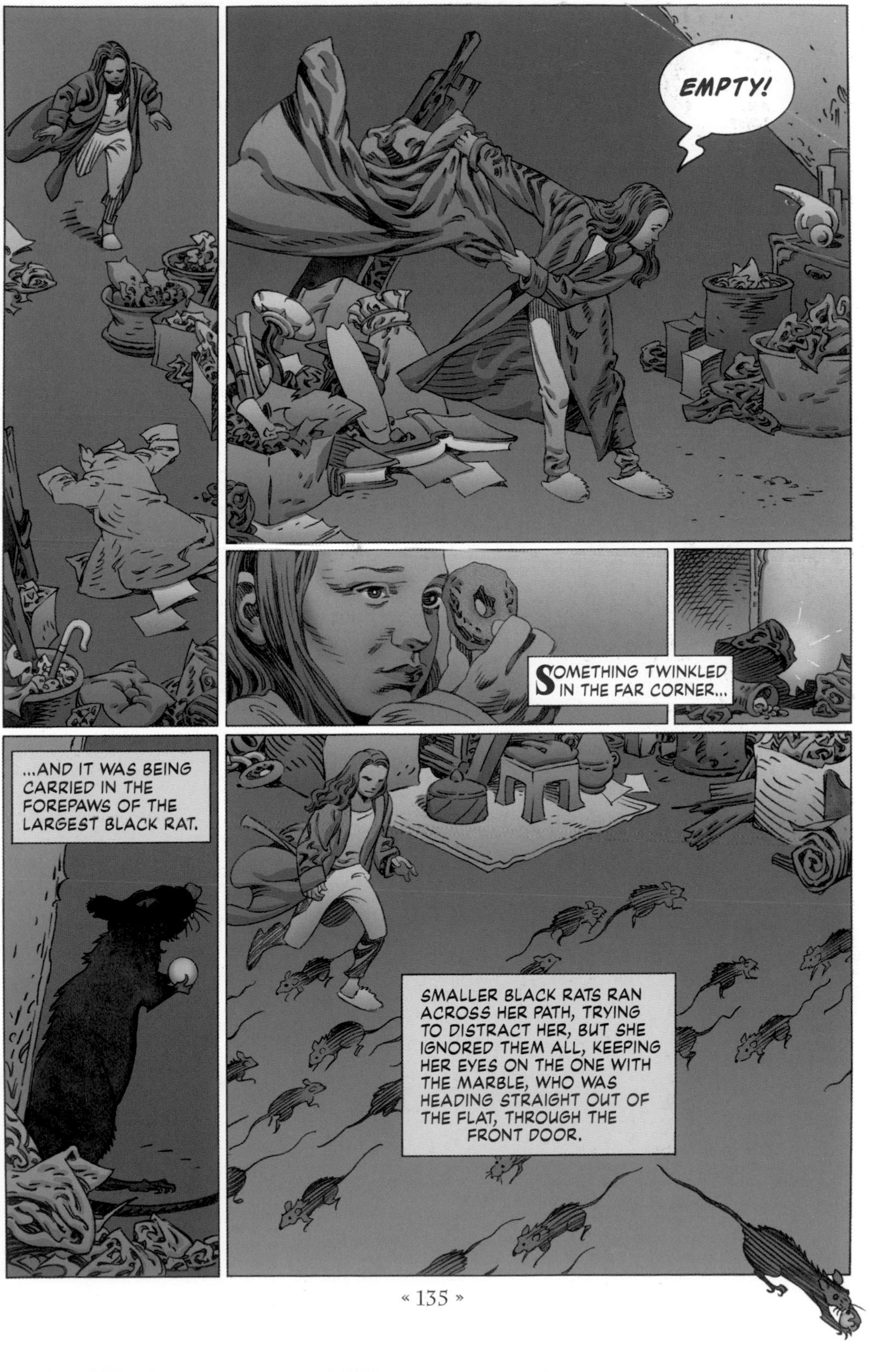
EMPTY!
SOMETHING TWINKLED IN THE FAR CORNER...
...AND IT WAS BEING CARRIED IN THE FOREPAWS OF THE LARGEST BLACK RAT.
SMALLER BLACK RATS RAN ACROSS HER PATH, TRYING TO DISTRACT HER, BUT SHE IGNORED THEM ALL, KEEPING HER EYES ON THE ONE WITH THE MARBLE, WHO WAS HEADING STRAIGHT OUT OF THE FLAT, THROUGH THE FRONT DOOR.

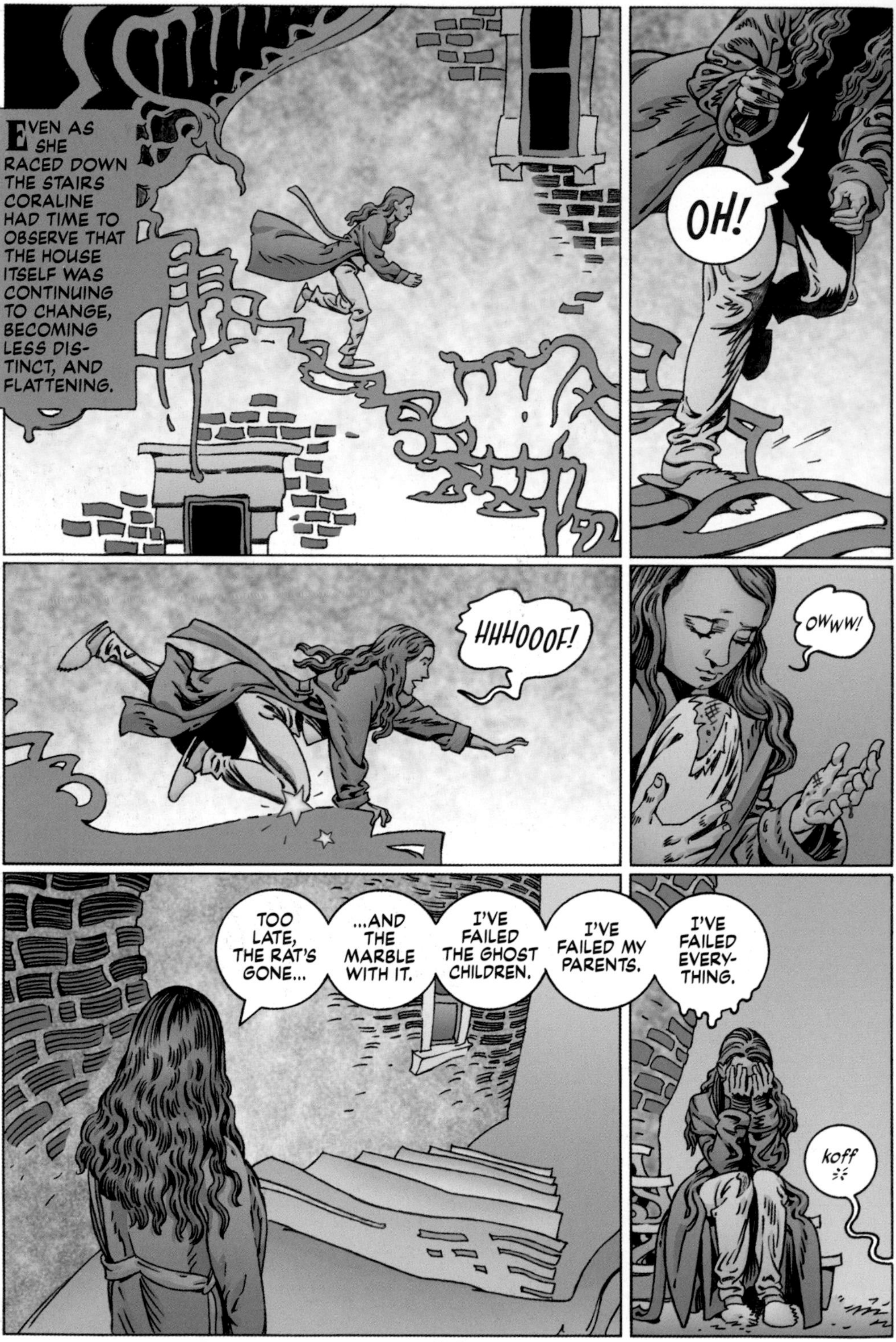
EVEN AS SHE RACED DOWN THE STAIRS CORALINE HAD TIME TO OBSERVE THAT THE HOUSE ITSELF WAS CONTINUING TO CHANGE, BECOMING LESS DISTINCT, AND FLATTENING.
OH!
HHHOOOF!
OWWW!
TOO LATE, THE RAT'S GONE...
...AND THE MARBLE WITH IT.
I'VE FAILED THE GHOST CHILDREN.
I'VE FAILED MY PARENTS.
I'VE FAILED EVERYTHING.
koff

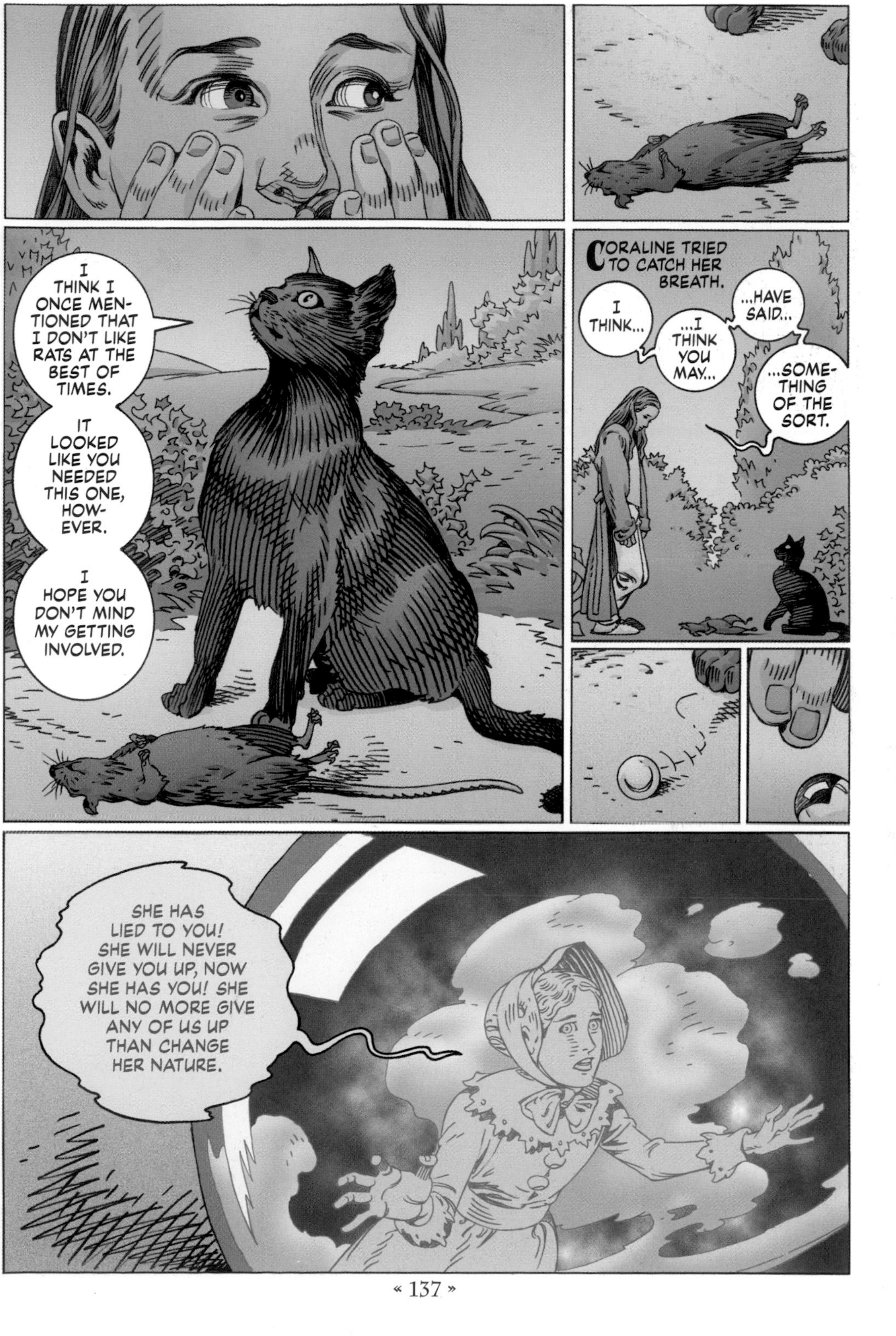
I THINK I ONCE MENTIONED THAT I DON'T LIKE RATS AT THE BEST OF TIMES.
IT LOOKED LIKE YOU NEEDED THIS ONE, HOWEVER.
I HOPE YOU DON'T MIND MY GETTING INVOLVED.
CORALINE TRIED TO CATCH HER BREATH.
I THINK...
...I THINK YOU MAY...
...HAVE SAID...
...SOMETHING OF THE SORT.
SHE HAS LIED TO YOU! SHE WILL NEVER GIVE YOU UP, NOW SHE HAS YOU! SHE WILL NO MORE GIVE ANY OF US UP THAN CHANGE HER NATURE.

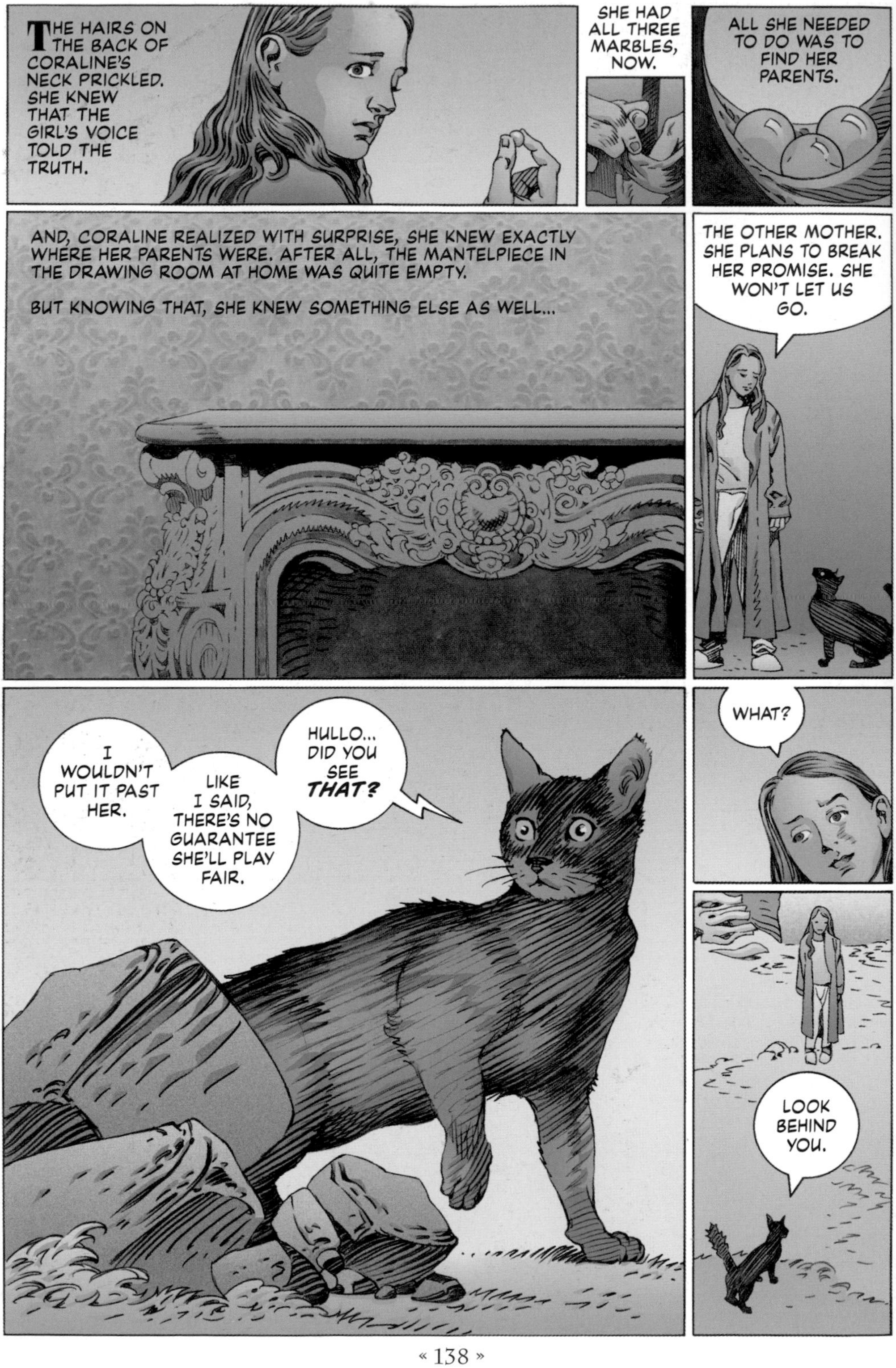
THE HAIRS ON THE BACK OF CORALINE'S NECK PRICKLED. SHE KNEW THAT THE GIRL'S VOICE TOLD THE TRUTH.
SHE HAD ALL THREE MARBLES, NOW.
ALL SHE NEEDED TO DO WAS TO FIND HER PARENTS.
AND, CORALINE REALIZED WITH SURPRISE, SHE KNEW EXACTLY WHERE HER PARENTS WERE. AFTER ALL, THE MANTELPIECE IN THE DRAWING ROOM AT HOME WAS QUITE EMPTY.
BUT KNOWING THAT, SHE KNEW SOMETHING ELSE AS WELL...
THE OTHER MOTHER. SHE PLANS TO BREAK HER PROMISE. SHE WON'T LET US GO.
I WOULDN'T PUT IT PAST HER.
LIKE I SAID, THERE'S NO GUARANTEE SHE'LL PLAY FAIR.
HULLO... DID YOU SEE THAT?
WHAT?
LOOK BEHIND YOU.

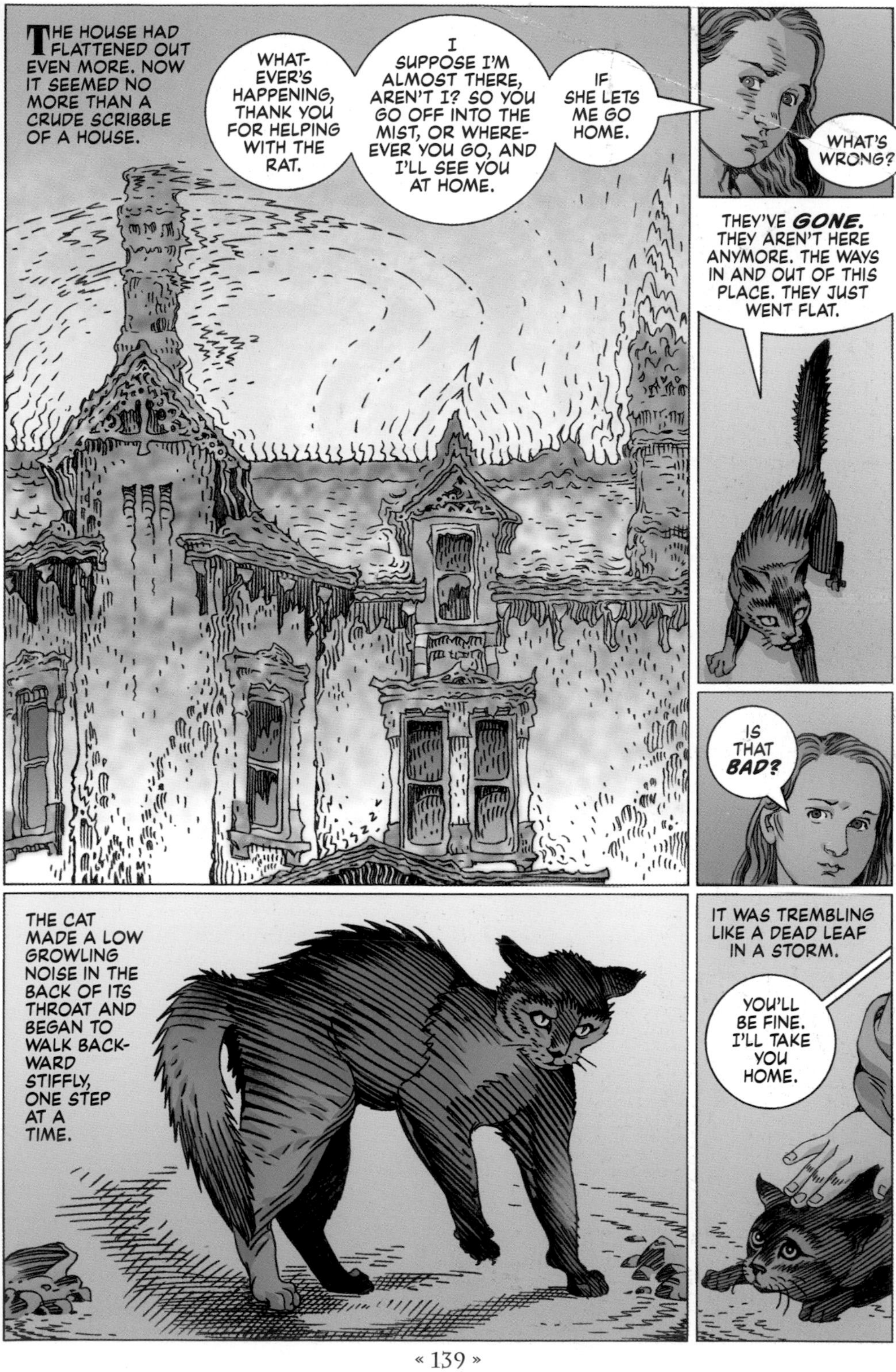

THE HOUSE HAD FLATTENED OUT EVEN MORE. NOW IT SEEMED NO MORE THAN A CRUDE SCRIBBLE OF A HOUSE.
WHAT-EVER'S HAPPENING, THANK YOU FOR HELPING WITH THE RAT.
I SUPPOSE I'M ALMOST THERE, AREN'T I? SO YOU GO OFF INTO THE MIST, OR WHERE-EVER YOU GO, AND I'LL SEE YOU AT HOME.
IF SHE LETS ME GO HOME.
WHAT'S WRONG?
THEY'VE **GONE.** THEY AREN'T HERE ANYMORE. THE WAYS IN AND OUT OF THIS PLACE. THEY JUST WENT FLAT.
IS THAT **BAD?**
THE CAT MADE A LOW GROWLING NOISE IN THE BACK OF ITS THROAT AND BEGAN TO WALK BACK-WARD STIFFLY, ONE STEP AT A TIME.
IT WAS TREMBLING LIKE A DEAD LEAF IN A STORM.
YOU'LL BE FINE. I'LL TAKE YOU HOME.

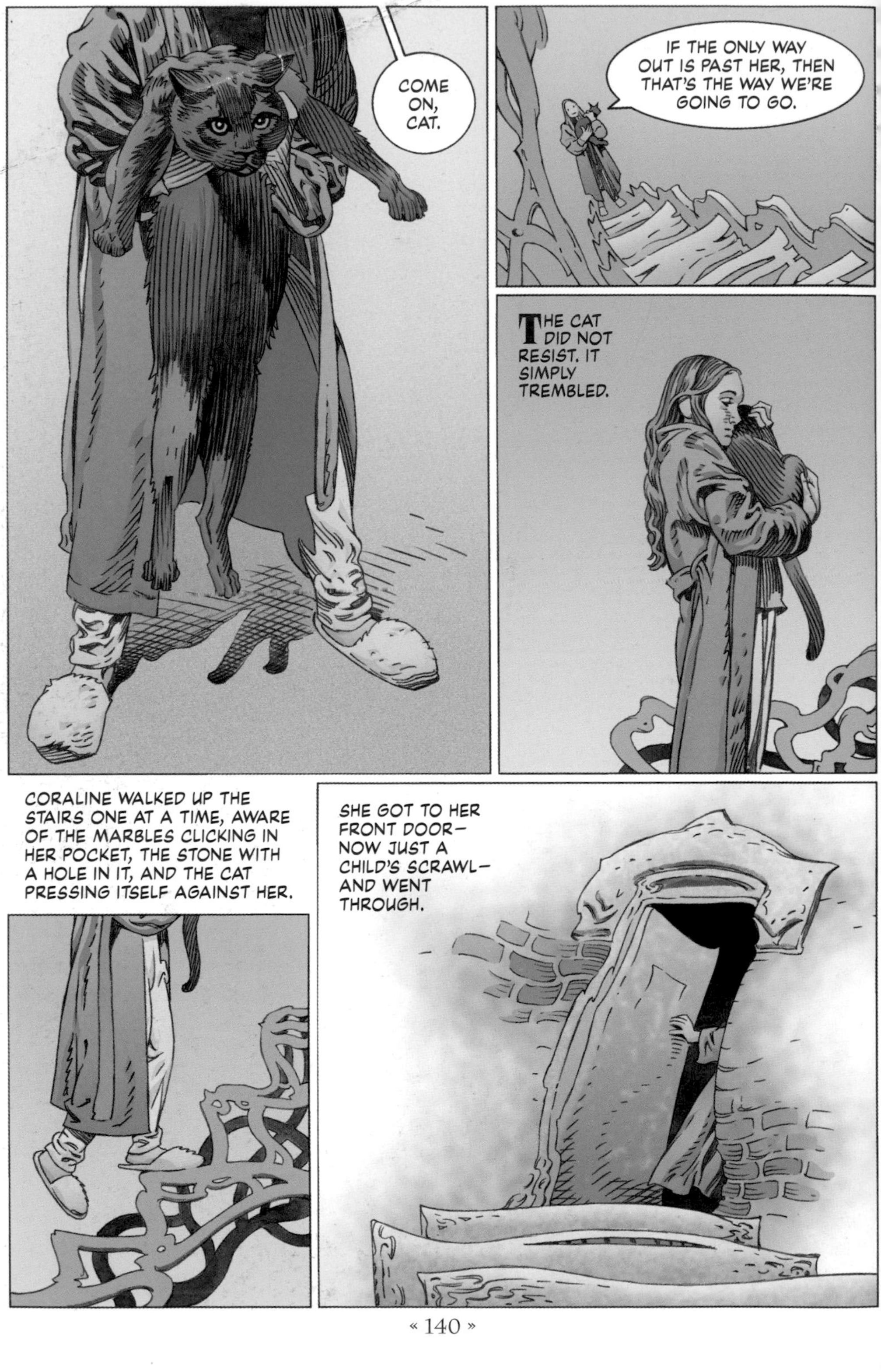
COME ON, CAT.
IF THE ONLY WAY OUT IS PAST HER, THEN THAT'S THE WAY WE'RE GOING TO GO.
THE CAT DID NOT RESIST. IT SIMPLY TREMBLED.
CORALINE WALKED UP THE STAIRS ONE AT A TIME, AWARE OF THE MARBLES CLICKING IN HER POCKET, THE STONE WITH A HOLE IN IT, AND THE CAT PRESSING ITSELF AGAINST HER.
SHE GOT TO HER FRONT DOOR— NOW JUST A CHILD'S SCRAWL— AND WENT THROUGH.

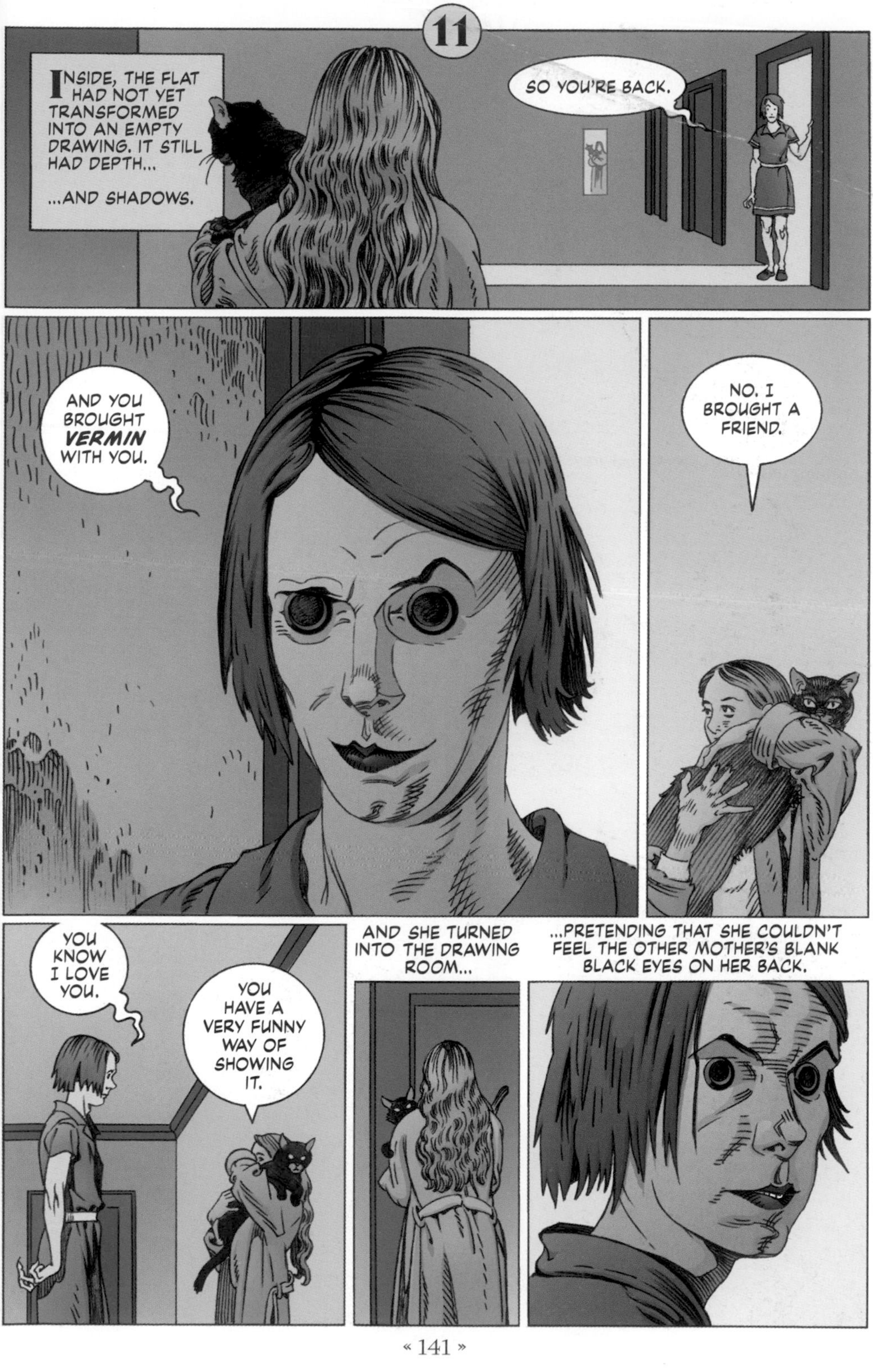
11
INSIDE, THE FLAT HAD NOT YET TRANSFORMED INTO AN EMPTY DRAWING. IT STILL HAD DEPTH...
...AND SHADOWS.
SO YOU'RE BACK.
AND YOU BROUGHT **VERMIN** WITH YOU.
NO. I BROUGHT A FRIEND.
YOU KNOW I LOVE YOU.
YOU HAVE A VERY FUNNY WAY OF SHOWING IT.
AND SHE TURNED INTO THE DRAWING ROOM...
...PRETENDING THAT SHE COULDN'T FEEL THE OTHER MOTHER'S BLANK BLACK EYES ON HER BACK.

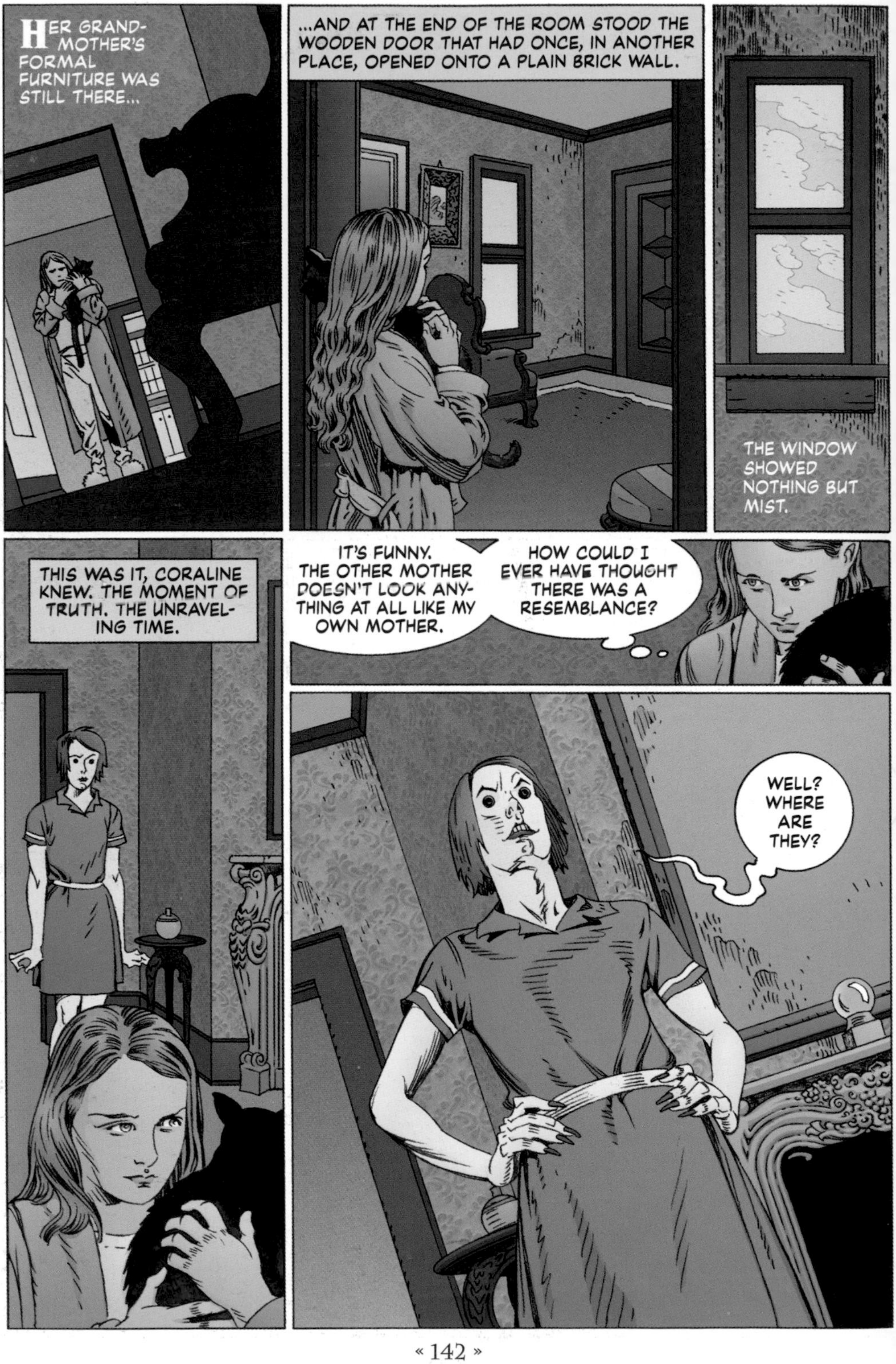
HER GRAND-MOTHER'S FORMAL FURNITURE WAS STILL THERE...
...AND AT THE END OF THE ROOM STOOD THE WOODEN DOOR THAT HAD ONCE, IN ANOTHER PLACE, OPENED ONTO A PLAIN BRICK WALL.
THE WINDOW SHOWED NOTHING BUT MIST.
THIS WAS IT, CORALINE KNEW. THE MOMENT OF TRUTH. THE UNRAVELING TIME.
IT'S FUNNY. THE OTHER MOTHER DOESN'T LOOK ANYTHING AT ALL LIKE MY OWN MOTHER.
HOW COULD I EVER HAVE THOUGHT THERE WAS A RESEMBLANCE?
WELL? WHERE ARE THEY?

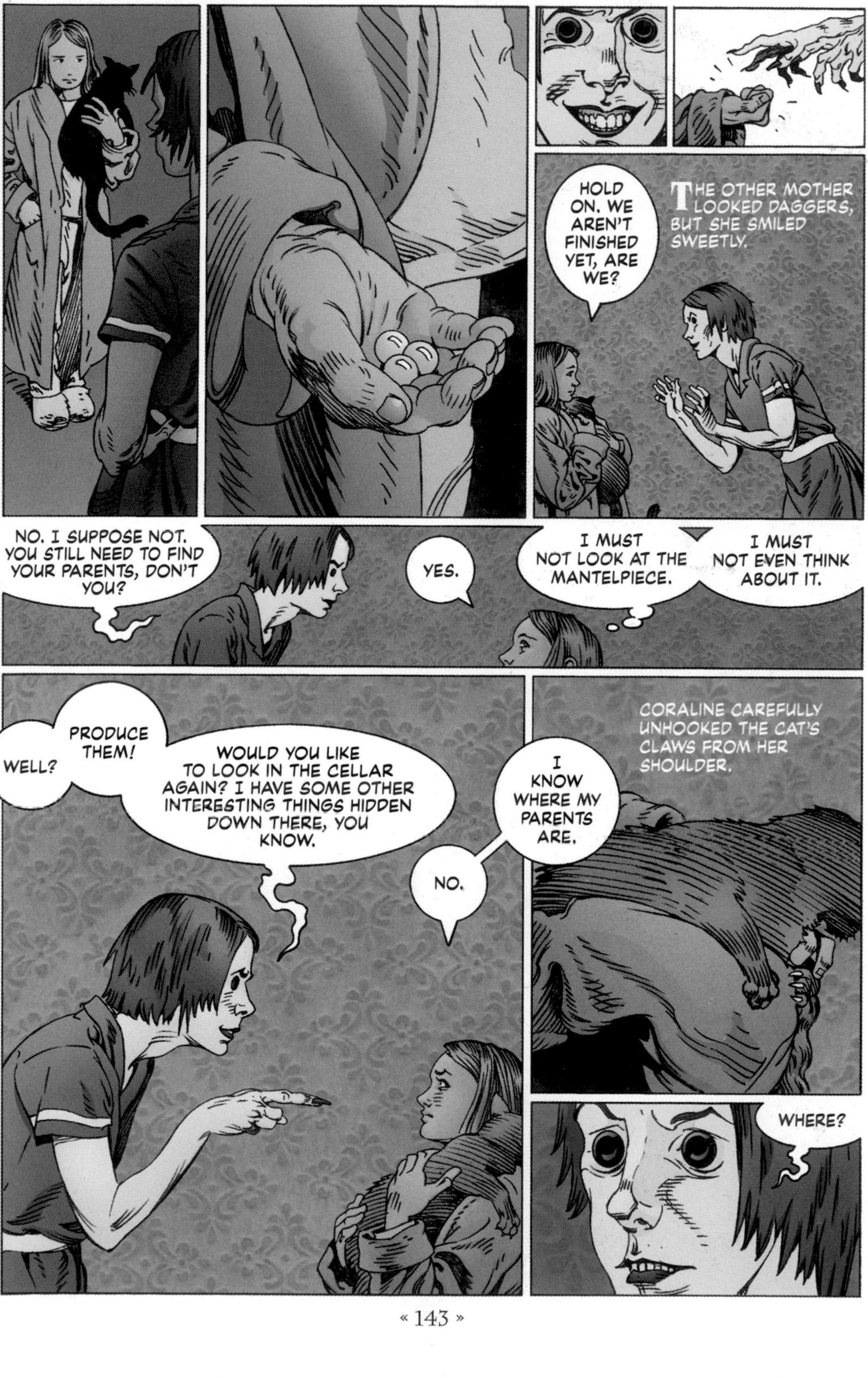
HOLD ON. WE AREN'T FINISHED YET, ARE WE?
THE OTHER MOTHER LOOKED DAGGERS, BUT SHE SMILED SWEETLY.
NO. I SUPPOSE NOT. YOU STILL NEED TO FIND YOUR PARENTS, DON'T YOU?
YES.
I MUST NOT LOOK AT THE MANTELPIECE.
I MUST NOT EVEN THINK ABOUT IT.
WELL?
PRODUCE THEM!
WOULD YOU LIKE TO LOOK IN THE CELLAR AGAIN? I HAVE SOME OTHER INTERESTING THINGS HIDDEN DOWN THERE, YOU KNOW.
NO.
I KNOW WHERE MY PARENTS ARE.
CORALINE CAREFULLY UNHOOKED THE CAT'S CLAWS FROM HER SHOULDER.
WHERE?

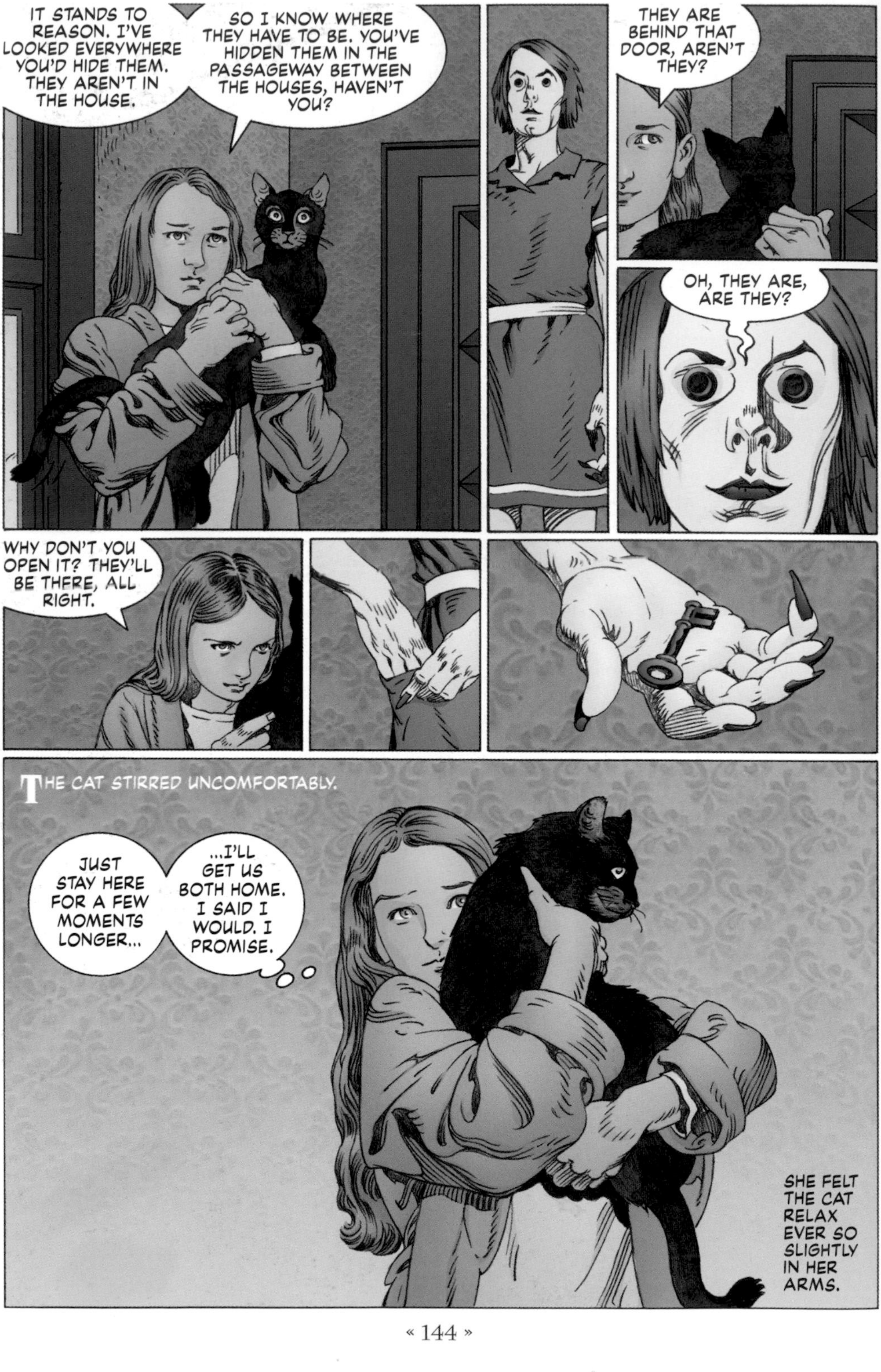
IT STANDS TO REASON. I'VE LOOKED EVERYWHERE YOU'D HIDE THEM. THEY AREN'T IN THE HOUSE.
SO I KNOW WHERE THEY HAVE TO BE. YOU'VE HIDDEN THEM IN THE PASSAGEWAY BETWEEN THE HOUSES, HAVEN'T YOU?
THEY ARE BEHIND THAT DOOR, AREN'T THEY?
OH, THEY ARE, ARE THEY?
WHY DON'T YOU OPEN IT? THEY'LL BE THERE, ALL RIGHT.
THE CAT STIRRED UNCOMFORTABLY.
JUST STAY HERE FOR A FEW MOMENTS LONGER...
...I'LL GET US BOTH HOME. I SAID I WOULD. I PROMISE.
SHE FELT THE CAT RELAX EVER SO SLIGHTLY IN HER ARMS.

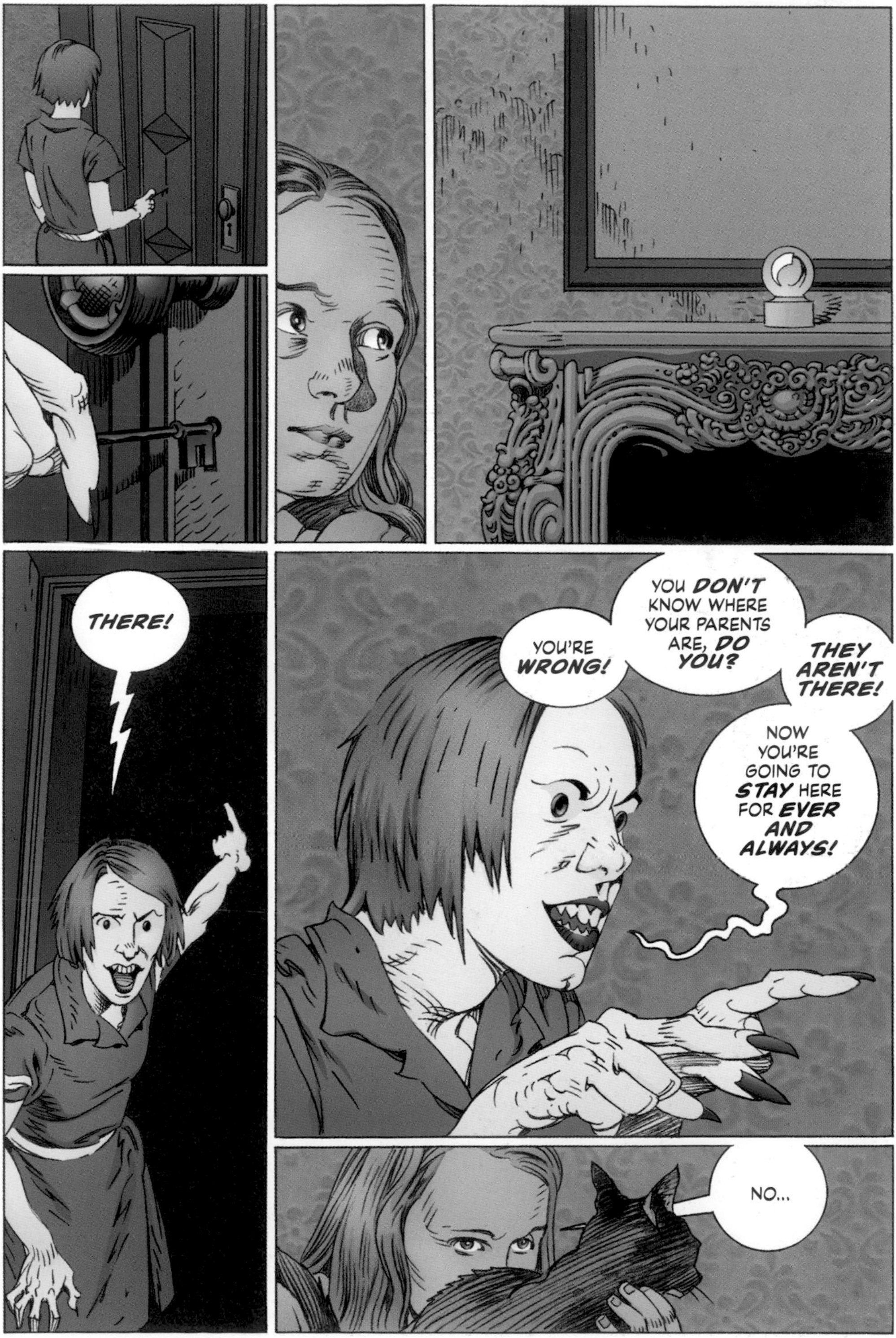
THERE!
YOU'RE WRONG!
YOU DON'T KNOW WHERE YOUR PARENTS ARE, DO YOU?
THEY AREN'T THERE!
NOW YOU'RE GOING TO STAY HERE FOR EVER AND ALWAYS!
NO...

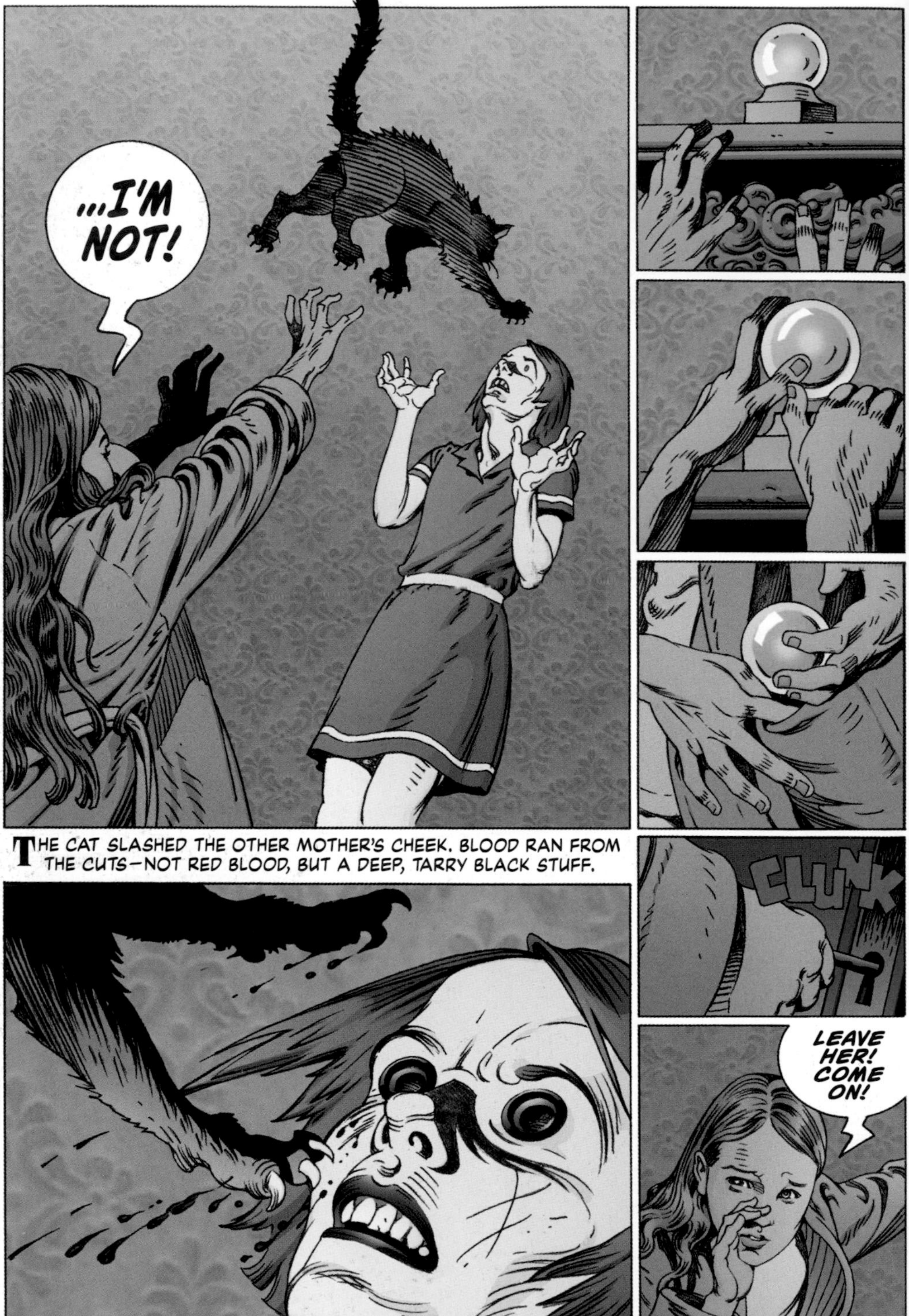
...I'M NOT!
THE CAT SLASHED THE OTHER MOTHER'S CHEEK. BLOOD RAN FROM THE CUTS—NOT RED BLOOD, BUT A DEEP, TARRY BLACK STUFF.
CLUNK
LEAVE HER! COME ON!

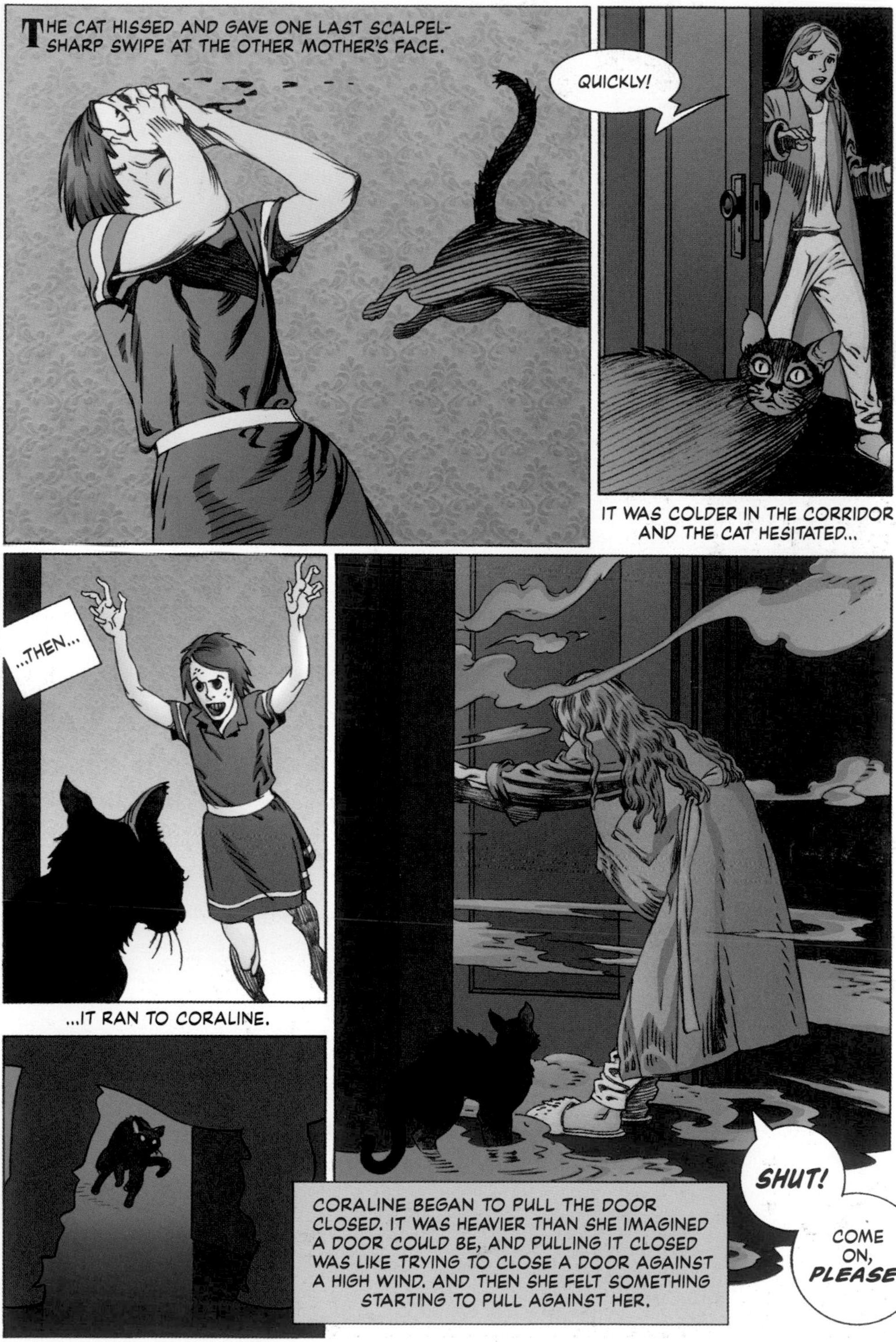
THE CAT HISSED AND GAVE ONE LAST SCALPEL-SHARP SWIPE AT THE OTHER MOTHER'S FACE.
QUICKLY!
IT WAS COLDER IN THE CORRIDOR AND THE CAT HESITATED...
...THEN...
...IT RAN TO CORALINE.
CORALINE BEGAN TO PULL THE DOOR CLOSED. IT WAS HEAVIER THAN SHE IMAGINED A DOOR COULD BE, AND PULLING IT CLOSED WAS LIKE TRYING TO CLOSE A DOOR AGAINST A HIGH WIND. AND THEN SHE FELT SOMETHING STARTING TO PULL AGAINST HER.
SHUT!
COME ON, *PLEASE!*

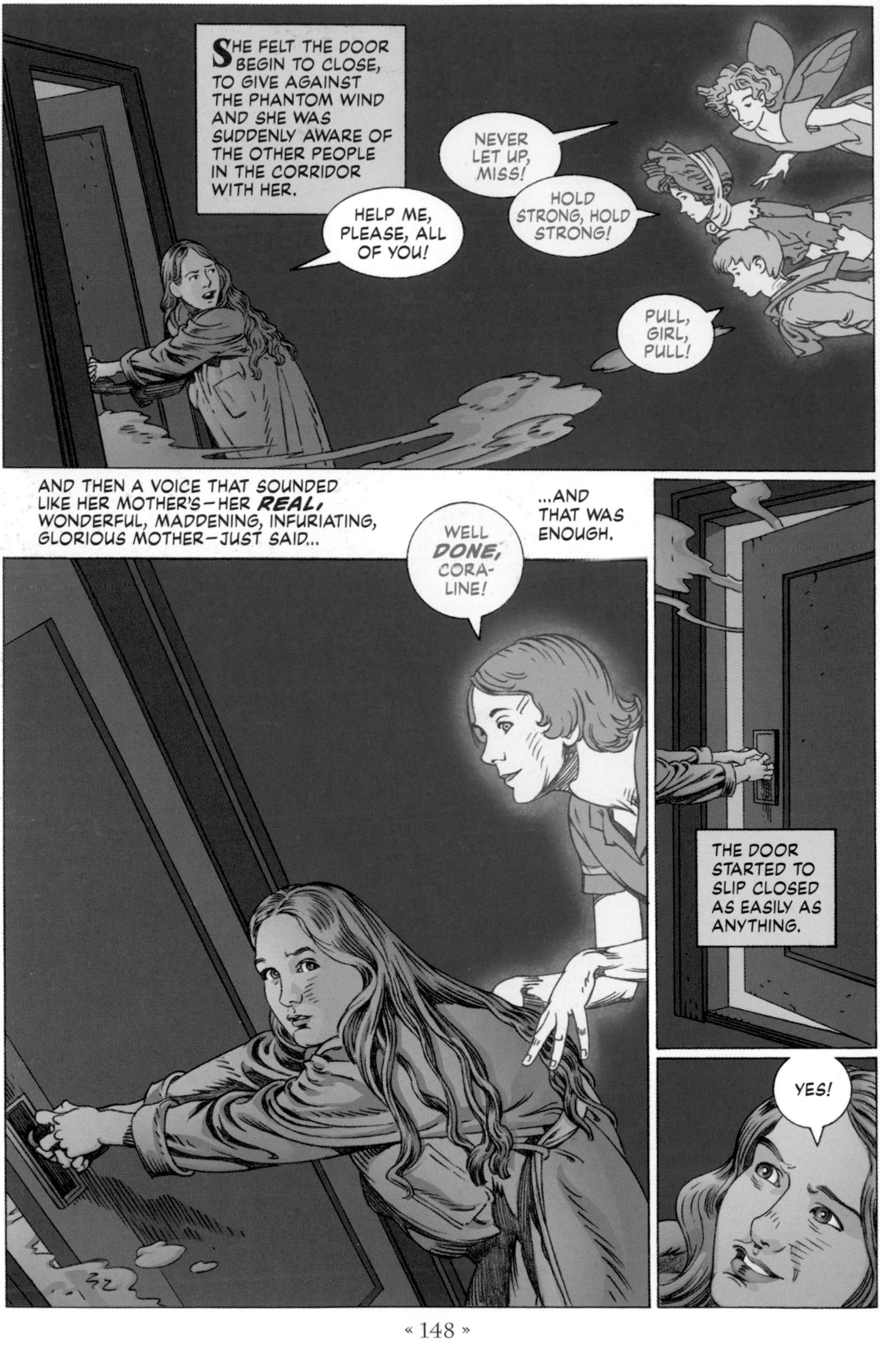
SHE FELT THE DOOR BEGIN TO CLOSE, TO GIVE AGAINST THE PHANTOM WIND AND SHE WAS SUDDENLY AWARE OF THE OTHER PEOPLE IN THE CORRIDOR WITH HER.
HELP ME, PLEASE, ALL OF YOU!
NEVER LET UP, MISS!
HOLD STRONG, HOLD STRONG!
PULL, GIRL, PULL!
AND THEN A VOICE THAT SOUNDED LIKE HER MOTHER'S—HER REAL, WONDERFUL, MADDENING, INFURIATING, GLORIOUS MOTHER—JUST SAID...
WELL DONE, CORA-LINE!
...AND THAT WAS ENOUGH.
THE DOOR STARTED TO SLIP CLOSED AS EASILY AS ANYTHING.
YES!

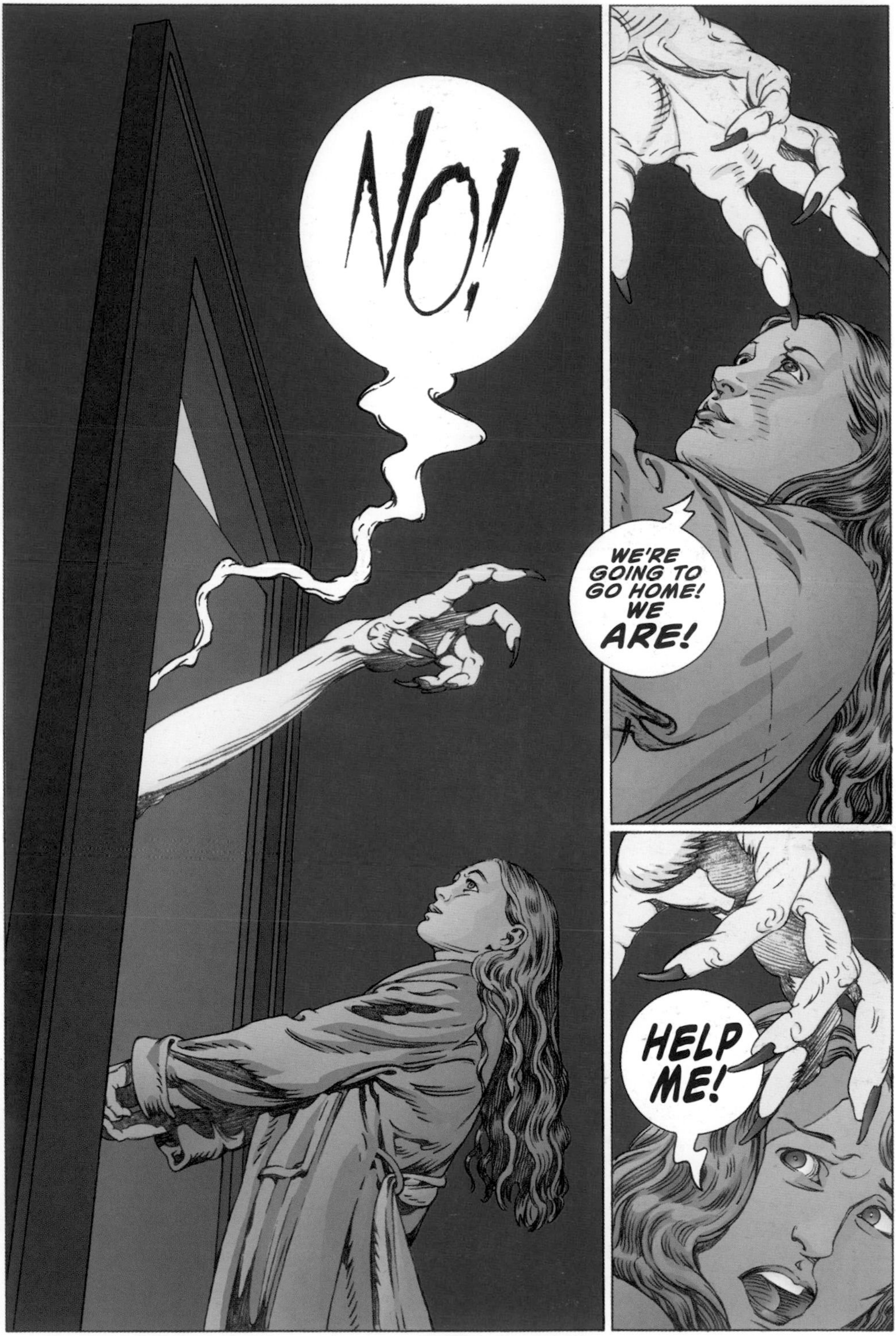
NO!
WE'RE GOING TO GO HOME! WE ARE!
HELP ME!

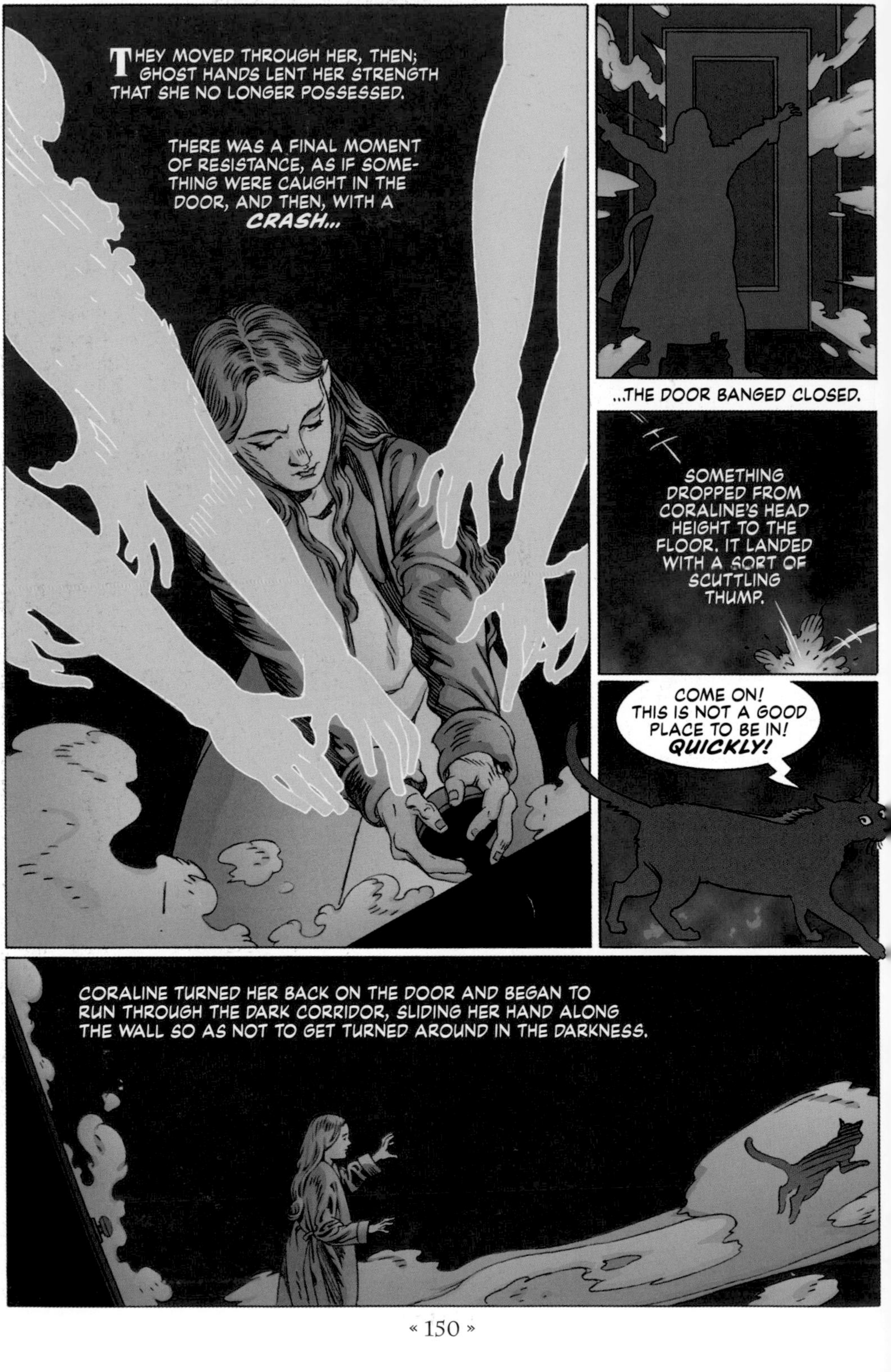
THEY MOVED THROUGH HER, THEN; GHOST HANDS LENT HER STRENGTH THAT SHE NO LONGER POSSESSED.
THERE WAS A FINAL MOMENT OF RESISTANCE, AS IF SOME-THING WERE CAUGHT IN THE DOOR, AND THEN, WITH A *CRASH*...
...THE DOOR BANGED CLOSED.
SOMETHING DROPPED FROM CORALINE'S HEAD HEIGHT TO THE FLOOR. IT LANDED WITH A SORT OF SCUTTLING THUMP.
COME ON! THIS IS NOT A GOOD PLACE TO BE IN! *QUICKLY!*
CORALINE TURNED HER BACK ON THE DOOR AND BEGAN TO RUN THROUGH THE DARK CORRIDOR, SLIDING HER HAND ALONG THE WALL SO AS NOT TO GET TURNED AROUND IN THE DARKNESS.

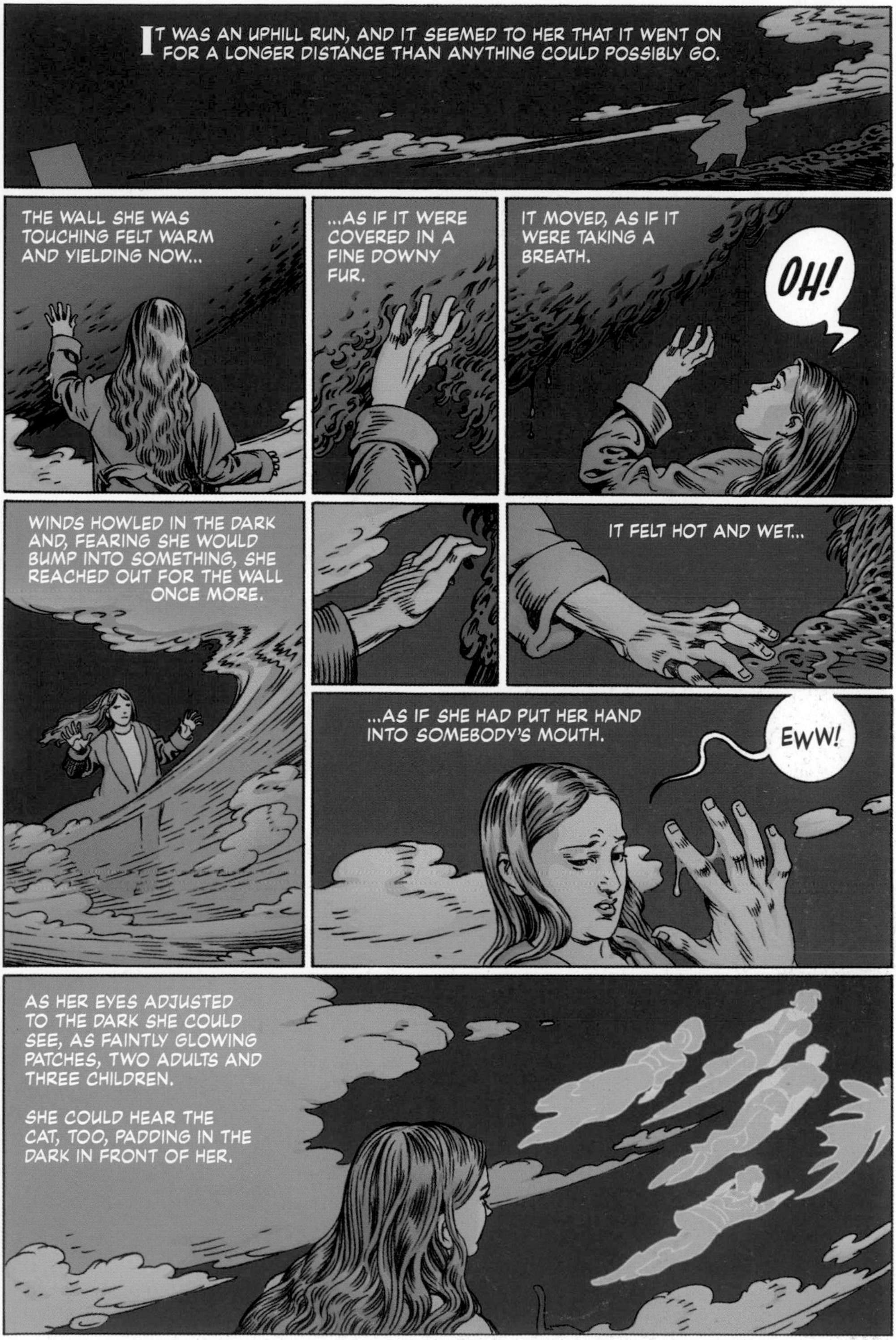
IT WAS AN UPHILL RUN, AND IT SEEMED TO HER THAT IT WENT ON FOR A LONGER DISTANCE THAN ANYTHING COULD POSSIBLY GO.
THE WALL SHE WAS TOUCHING FELT WARM AND YIELDING NOW...
...AS IF IT WERE COVERED IN A FINE DOWNY FUR.
IT MOVED, AS IF IT WERE TAKING A BREATH.
OH!
WINDS HOWLED IN THE DARK AND, FEARING SHE WOULD BUMP INTO SOMETHING, SHE REACHED OUT FOR THE WALL ONCE MORE.
IT FELT HOT AND WET...
...AS IF SHE HAD PUT HER HAND INTO SOMEBODY'S MOUTH.
EWW!
AS HER EYES ADJUSTED TO THE DARK SHE COULD SEE, AS FAINTLY GLOWING PATCHES, TWO ADULTS AND THREE CHILDREN.
SHE COULD HEAR THE CAT, TOO, PADDING IN THE DARK IN FRONT OF HER.

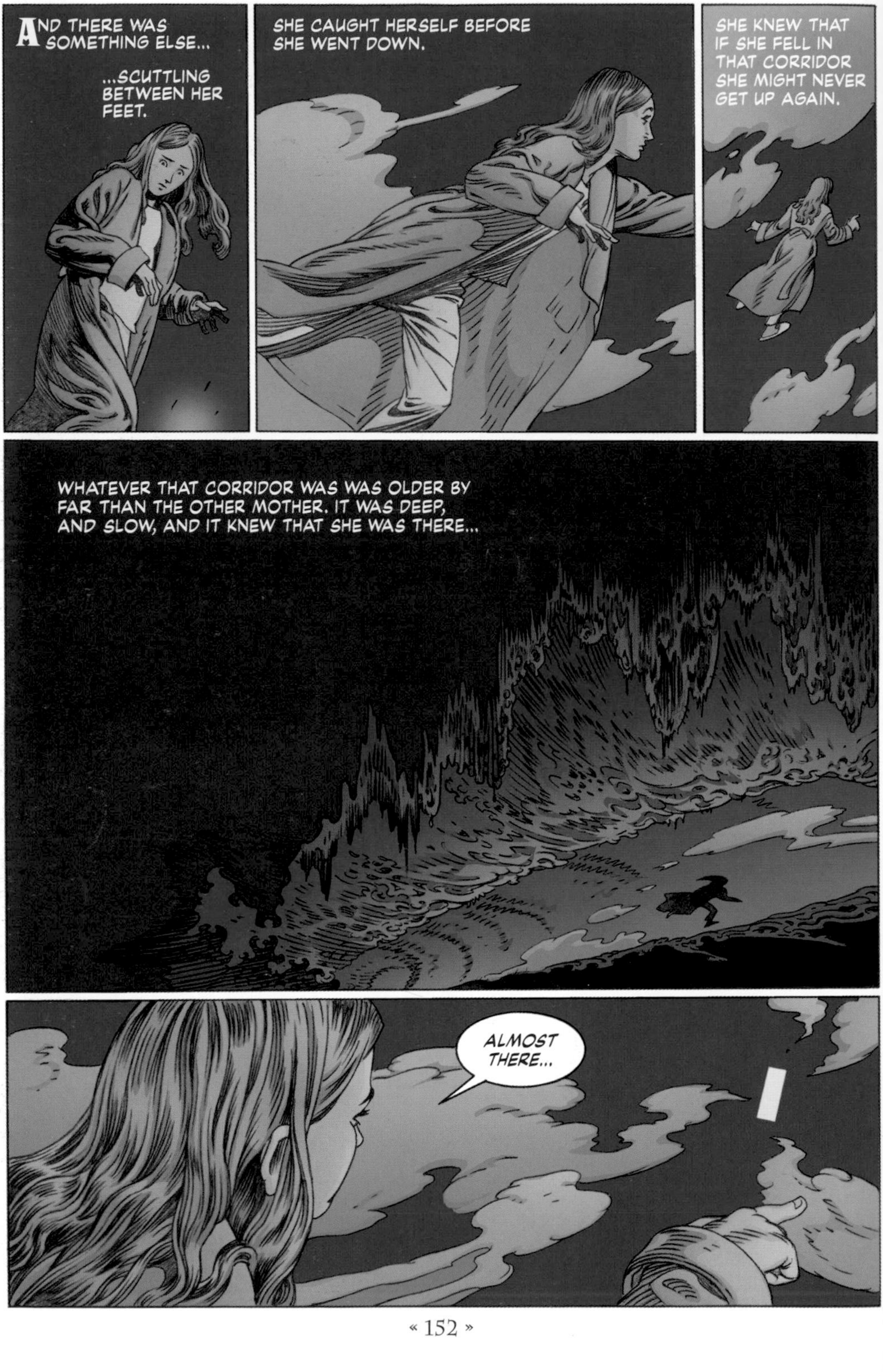
AND THERE WAS SOMETHING ELSE...
...SCUTTLING BETWEEN HER FEET.
SHE CAUGHT HERSELF BEFORE SHE WENT DOWN.
SHE KNEW THAT IF SHE FELL IN THAT CORRIDOR SHE MIGHT NEVER GET UP AGAIN.
WHATEVER THAT CORRIDOR WAS WAS OLDER BY FAR THAN THE OTHER MOTHER. IT WAS DEEP, AND SLOW, AND IT KNEW THAT SHE WAS THERE...
ALMOST THERE...

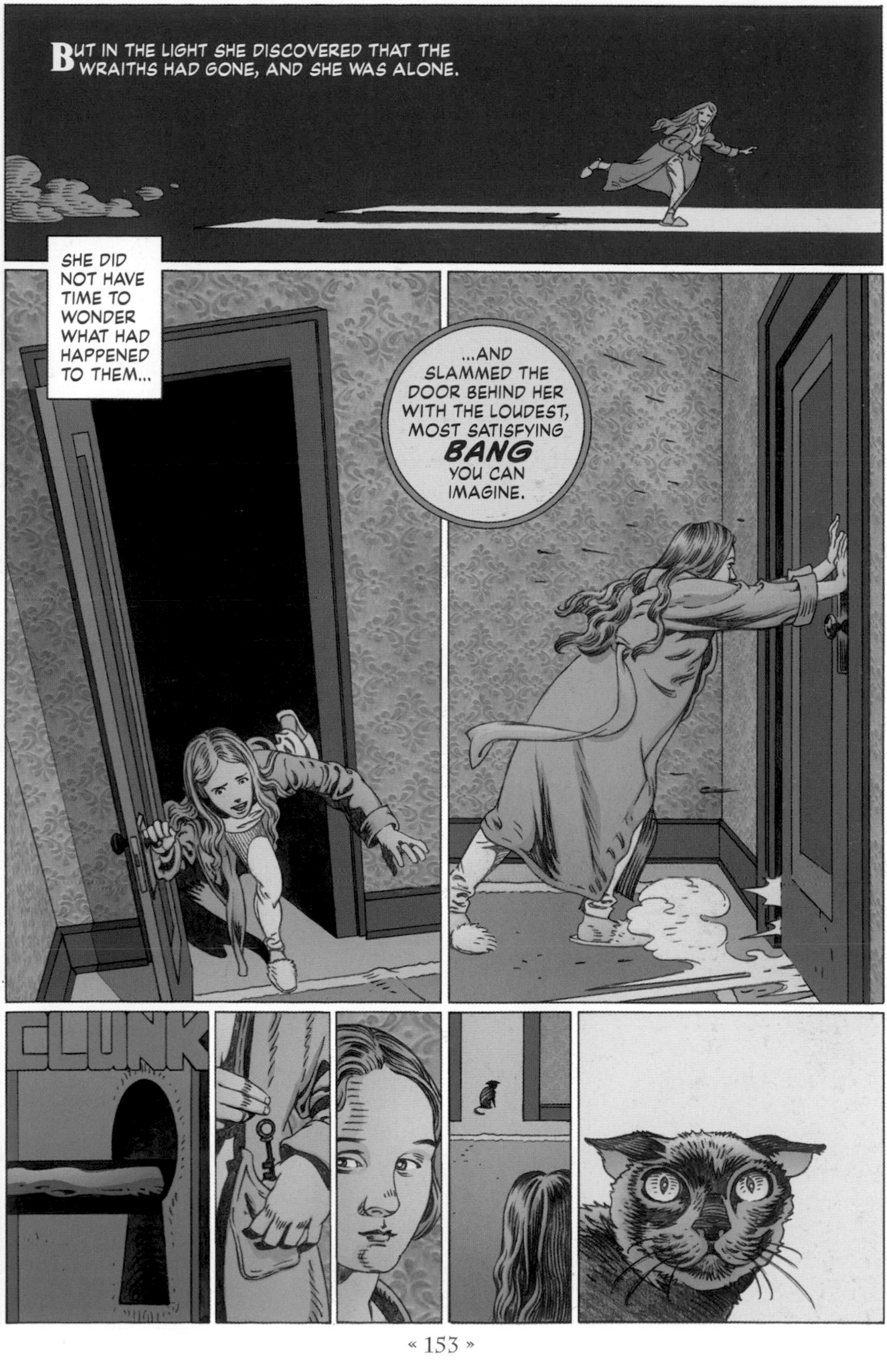
But in the light she discovered that the wraiths had gone, and she was alone.
She did not have time to wonder what had happened to them...
...and slammed the door behind her with the loudest, most satisfying BANG you can imagine.
CLUNK

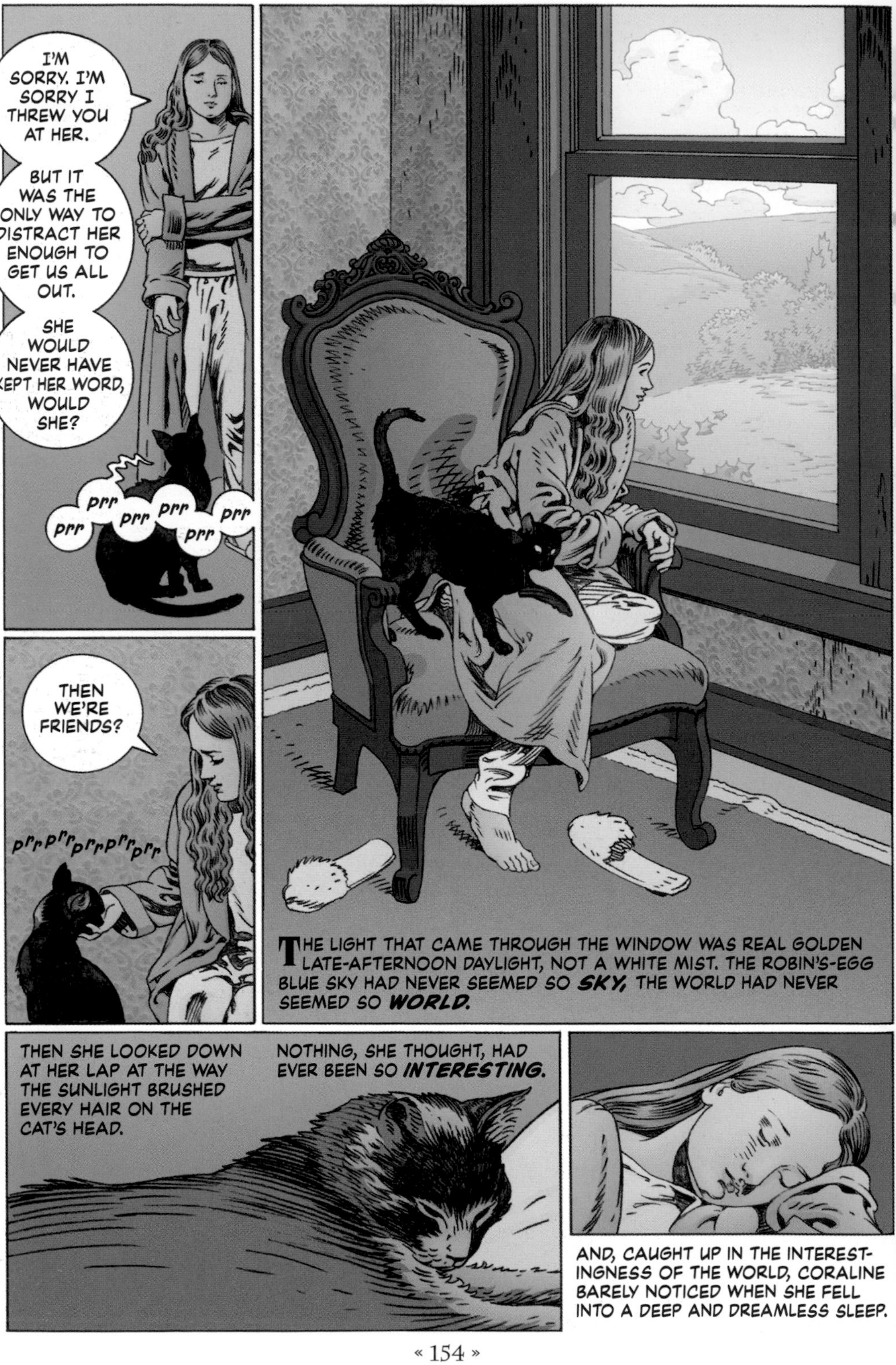
I'M SORRY. I'M SORRY I THREW YOU AT HER.
BUT IT WAS THE ONLY WAY TO DISTRACT HER ENOUGH TO GET US ALL OUT.
SHE WOULD NEVER HAVE KEPT HER WORD, WOULD SHE?
prr prr prr prr prr prr
THEN WE'RE FRIENDS?
prrprrprrprrprr
THE LIGHT THAT CAME THROUGH THE WINDOW WAS REAL GOLDEN LATE-AFTERNOON DAYLIGHT, NOT A WHITE MIST. THE ROBIN'S-EGG BLUE SKY HAD NEVER SEEMED SO SKY, THE WORLD HAD NEVER SEEMED SO WORLD.
THEN SHE LOOKED DOWN AT HER LAP AT THE WAY THE SUNLIGHT BRUSHED EVERY HAIR ON THE CAT'S HEAD.
NOTHING, SHE THOUGHT, HAD EVER BEEN SO INTERESTING.
AND, CAUGHT UP IN THE INTEREST-INGNESS OF THE WORLD, CORALINE BARELY NOTICED WHEN SHE FELL INTO A DEEP AND DREAMLESS SLEEP.

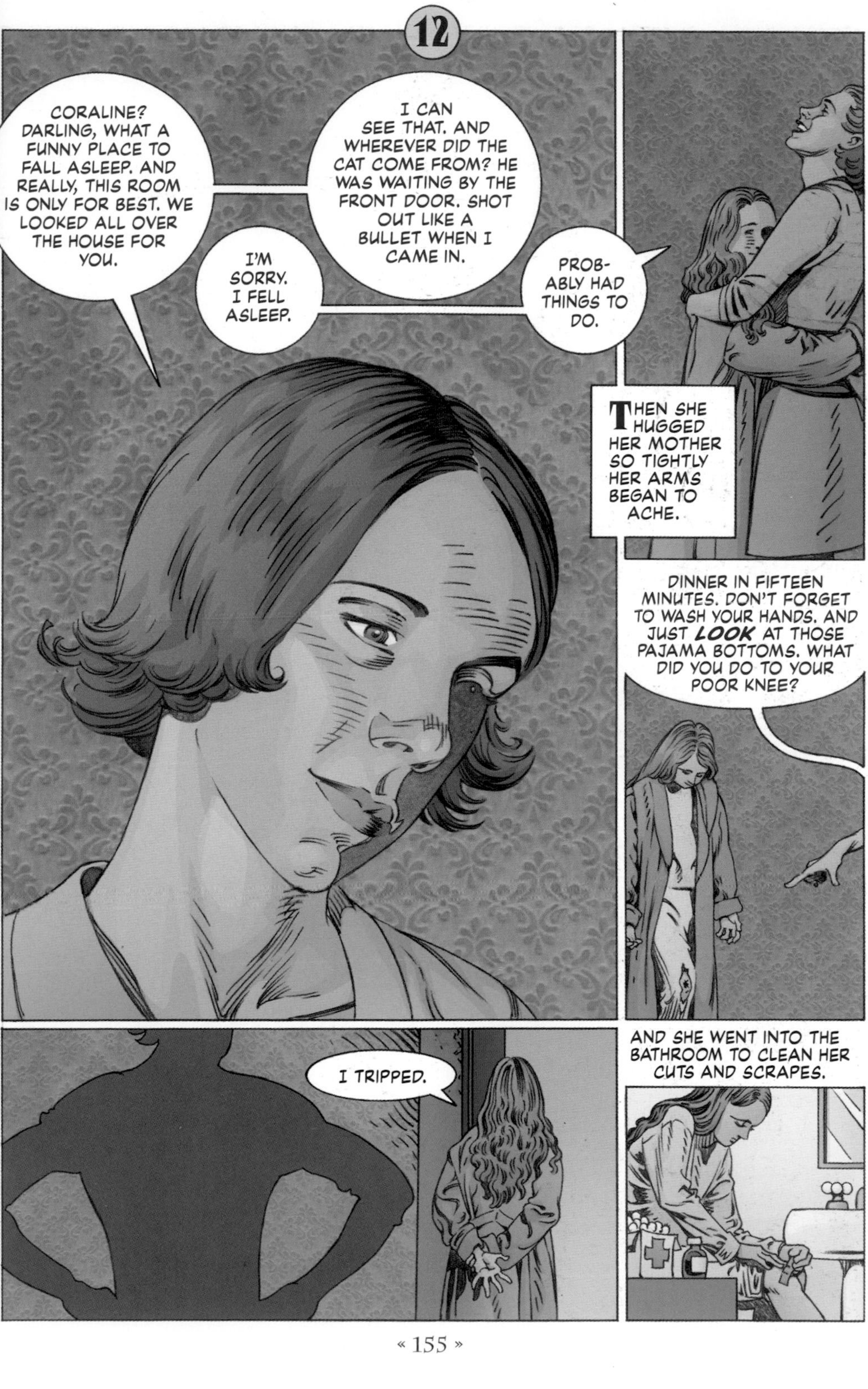
12
CORALINE? DARLING, WHAT A FUNNY PLACE TO FALL ASLEEP. AND REALLY, THIS ROOM IS ONLY FOR BEST. WE LOOKED ALL OVER THE HOUSE FOR YOU.
I'M SORRY. I FELL ASLEEP.
I CAN SEE THAT. AND WHEREVER DID THE CAT COME FROM? HE WAS WAITING BY THE FRONT DOOR. SHOT OUT LIKE A BULLET WHEN I CAME IN.
PROB-ABLY HAD THINGS TO DO.
THEN SHE HUGGED HER MOTHER SO TIGHTLY HER ARMS BEGAN TO ACHE.
DINNER IN FIFTEEN MINUTES. DON'T FORGET TO WASH YOUR HANDS. AND JUST **LOOK** AT THOSE PAJAMA BOTTOMS. WHAT DID YOU DO TO YOUR POOR KNEE?
I TRIPPED.
AND SHE WENT INTO THE BATHROOM TO CLEAN HER CUTS AND SCRAPES.

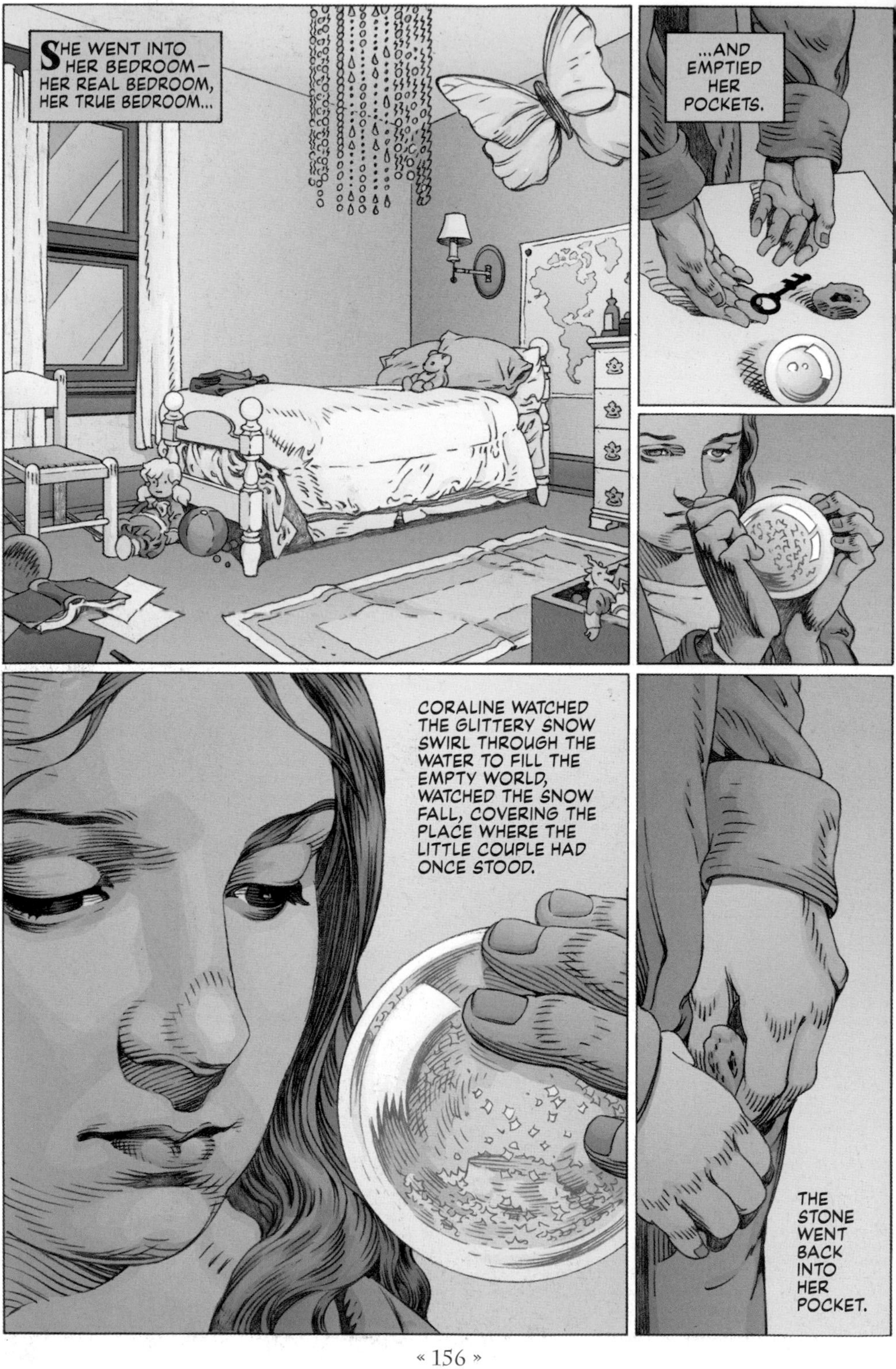
SHE WENT INTO HER BEDROOM— HER REAL BEDROOM, HER TRUE BEDROOM...
...AND EMPTIED HER POCKETS.
CORALINE WATCHED THE GLITTERY SNOW SWIRL THROUGH THE WATER TO FILL THE EMPTY WORLD, WATCHED THE SNOW FALL, COVERING THE PLACE WHERE THE LITTLE COUPLE HAD ONCE STOOD.
THE STONE WENT BACK INTO HER POCKET.

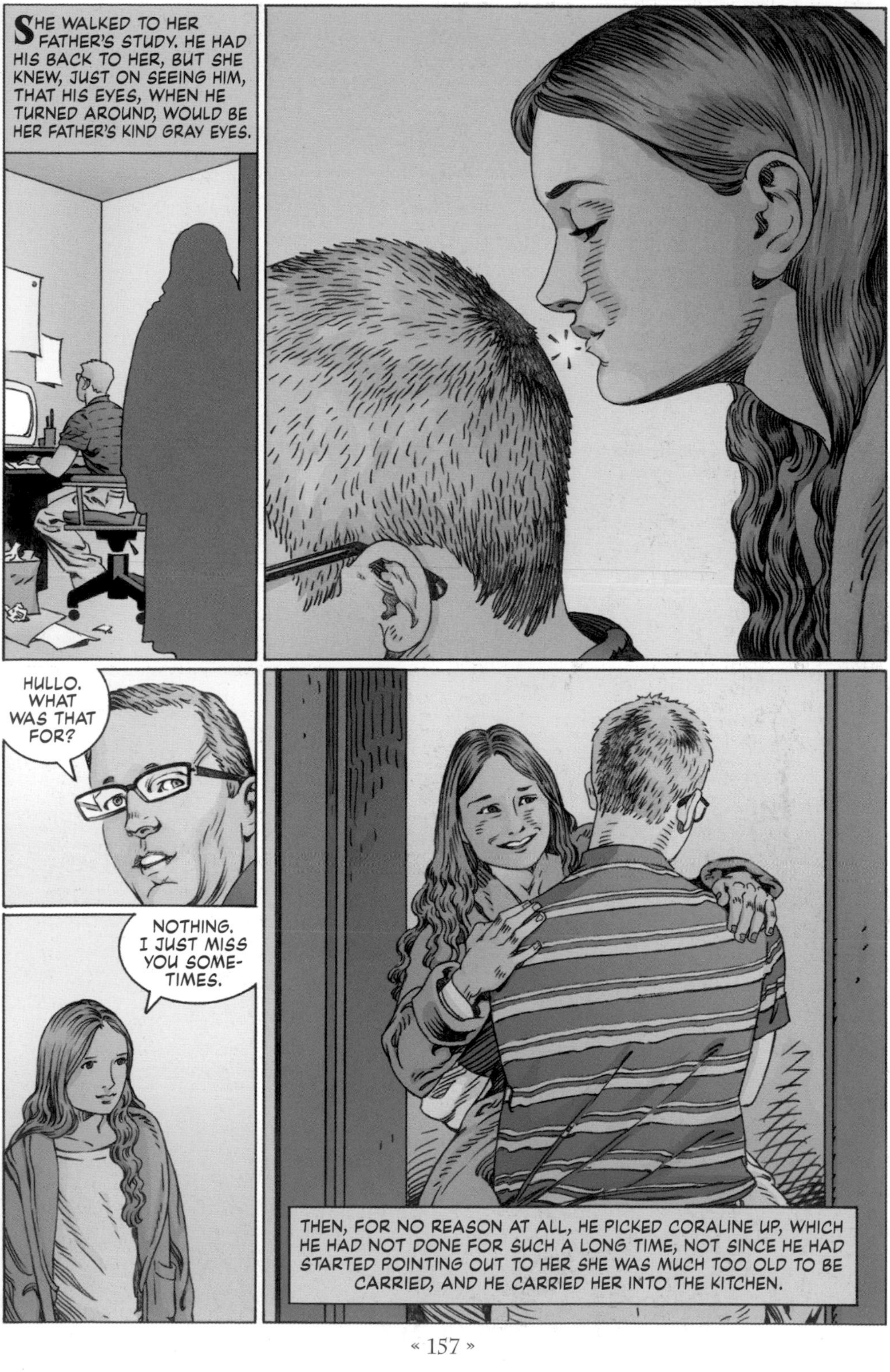
SHE WALKED TO HER FATHER'S STUDY. HE HAD HIS BACK TO HER, BUT SHE KNEW, JUST ON SEEING HIM, THAT HIS EYES, WHEN HE TURNED AROUND, WOULD BE HER FATHER'S KIND GRAY EYES.
HULLO. WHAT WAS THAT FOR?
NOTHING. I JUST MISS YOU SOMETIMES.
THEN, FOR NO REASON AT ALL, HE PICKED CORALINE UP, WHICH HE HAD NOT DONE FOR SUCH A LONG TIME, NOT SINCE HE HAD STARTED POINTING OUT TO HER SHE WAS MUCH TOO OLD TO BE CARRIED, AND HE CARRIED HER INTO THE KITCHEN.

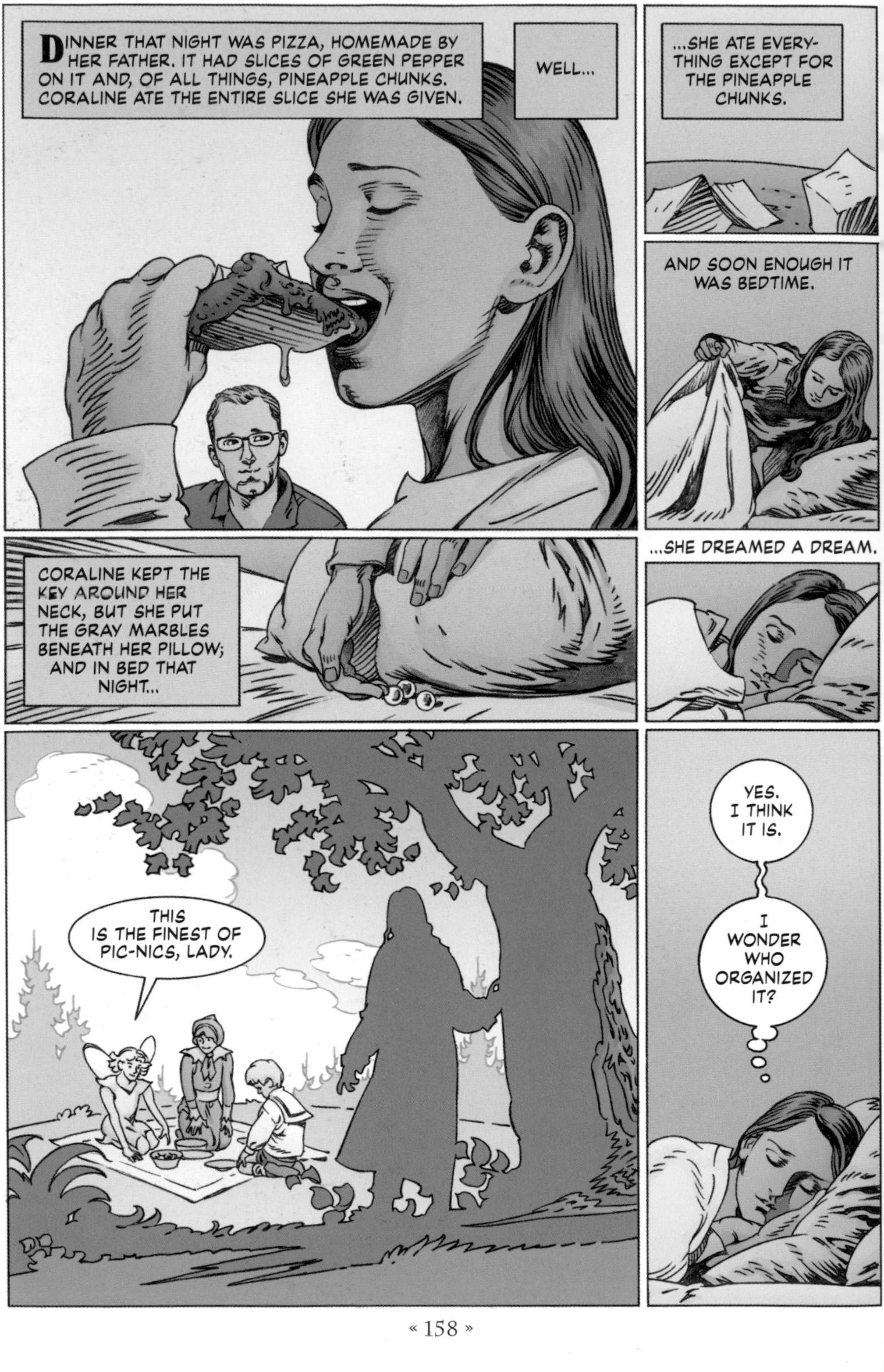
DINNER THAT NIGHT WAS PIZZA, HOMEMADE BY HER FATHER. IT HAD SLICES OF GREEN PEPPER ON IT AND, OF ALL THINGS, PINEAPPLE CHUNKS. CORALINE ATE THE ENTIRE SLICE SHE WAS GIVEN.
WELL...
...SHE ATE EVERYTHING EXCEPT FOR THE PINEAPPLE CHUNKS.
AND SOON ENOUGH IT WAS BEDTIME.
CORALINE KEPT THE KEY AROUND HER NECK, BUT SHE PUT THE GRAY MARBLES BENEATH HER PILLOW; AND IN BED THAT NIGHT...
...SHE DREAMED A DREAM.
THIS IS THE FINEST OF PIC-NICS, LADY.
YES. I THINK IT IS.
I WONDER WHO ORGANIZED IT?

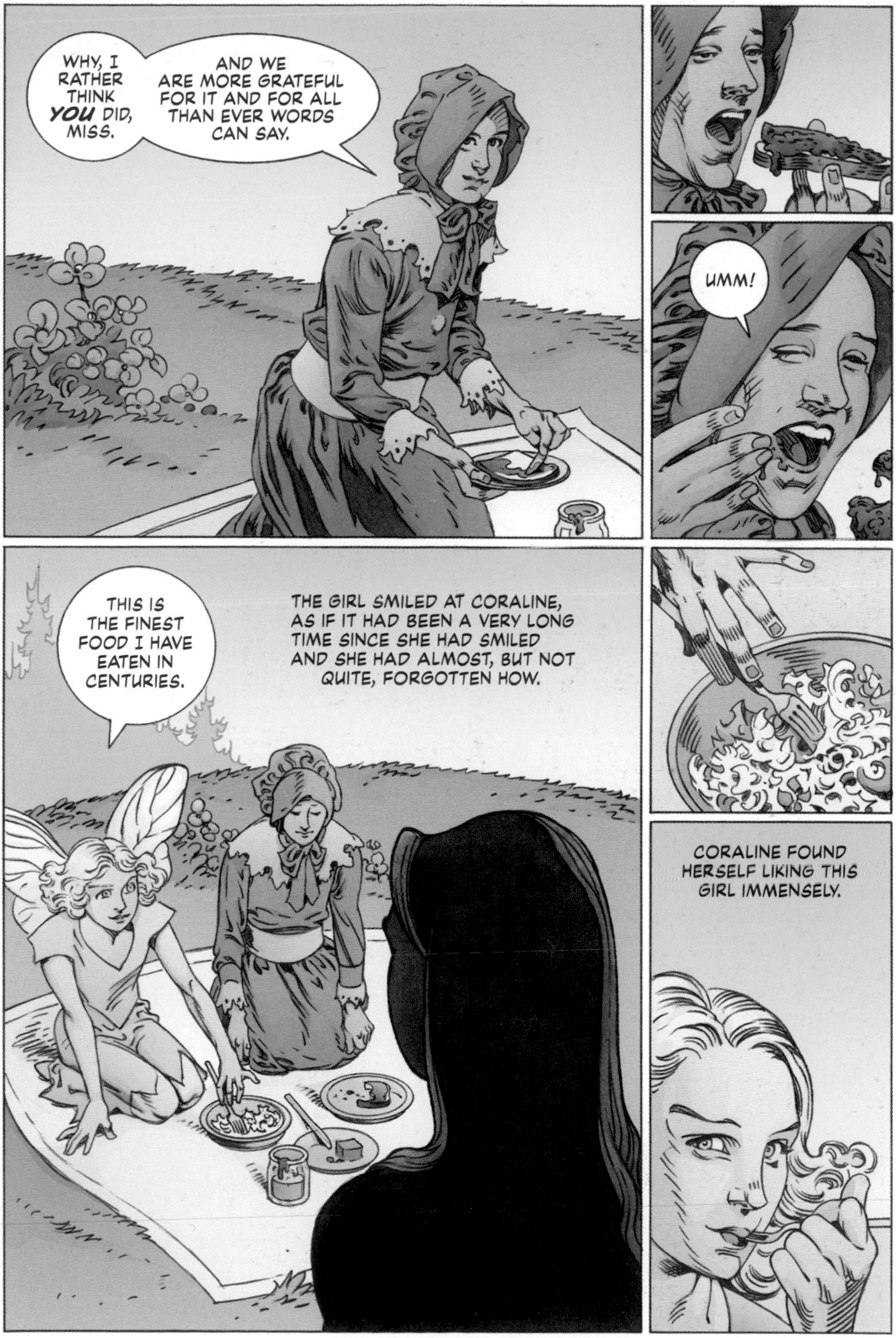
WHY, I RATHER THINK **YOU** DID, MISS.
AND WE ARE MORE GRATEFUL FOR IT AND FOR ALL THAN EVER WORDS CAN SAY.
UMM!
THIS IS THE FINEST FOOD I HAVE EATEN IN CENTURIES.
THE GIRL SMILED AT CORALINE, AS IF IT HAD BEEN A VERY LONG TIME SINCE SHE HAD SMILED AND SHE HAD ALMOST, BUT NOT QUITE, FORGOTTEN HOW.
CORALINE FOUND HERSELF LIKING THIS GIRL IMMENSELY.

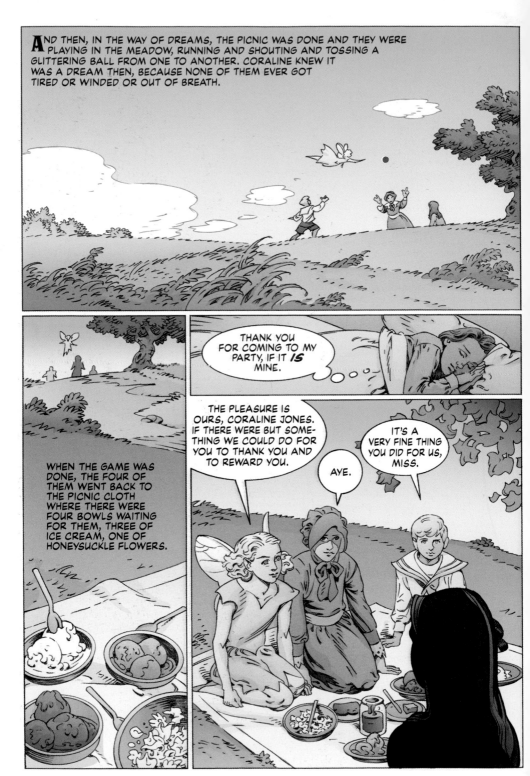

AND THEN, IN THE WAY OF DREAMS, THE PICNIC WAS DONE AND THEY WERE PLAYING IN THE MEADOW, RUNNING AND SHOUTING AND TOSSING A GLITTERING BALL FROM ONE TO ANOTHER. CORALINE KNEW IT WAS A DREAM THEN, BECAUSE NONE OF THEM EVER GOT TIRED OR WINDED OR OUT OF BREATH.

WHEN THE GAME WAS DONE, THE FOUR OF THEM WENT BACK TO THE PICNIC CLOTH WHERE THERE WERE FOUR BOWLS WAITING FOR THEM, THREE OF ICE CREAM, ONE OF HONEYSUCKLE FLOWERS.

THANK YOU FOR COMING TO MY PARTY, IF IT *IS* MINE.

THE PLEASURE IS OURS, CORALINE JONES. IF THERE WERE BUT SOMETHING WE COULD DO FOR YOU TO THANK YOU AND TO REWARD YOU.

AYE.

IT'S A VERY FINE THING YOU DID FOR US, MISS.

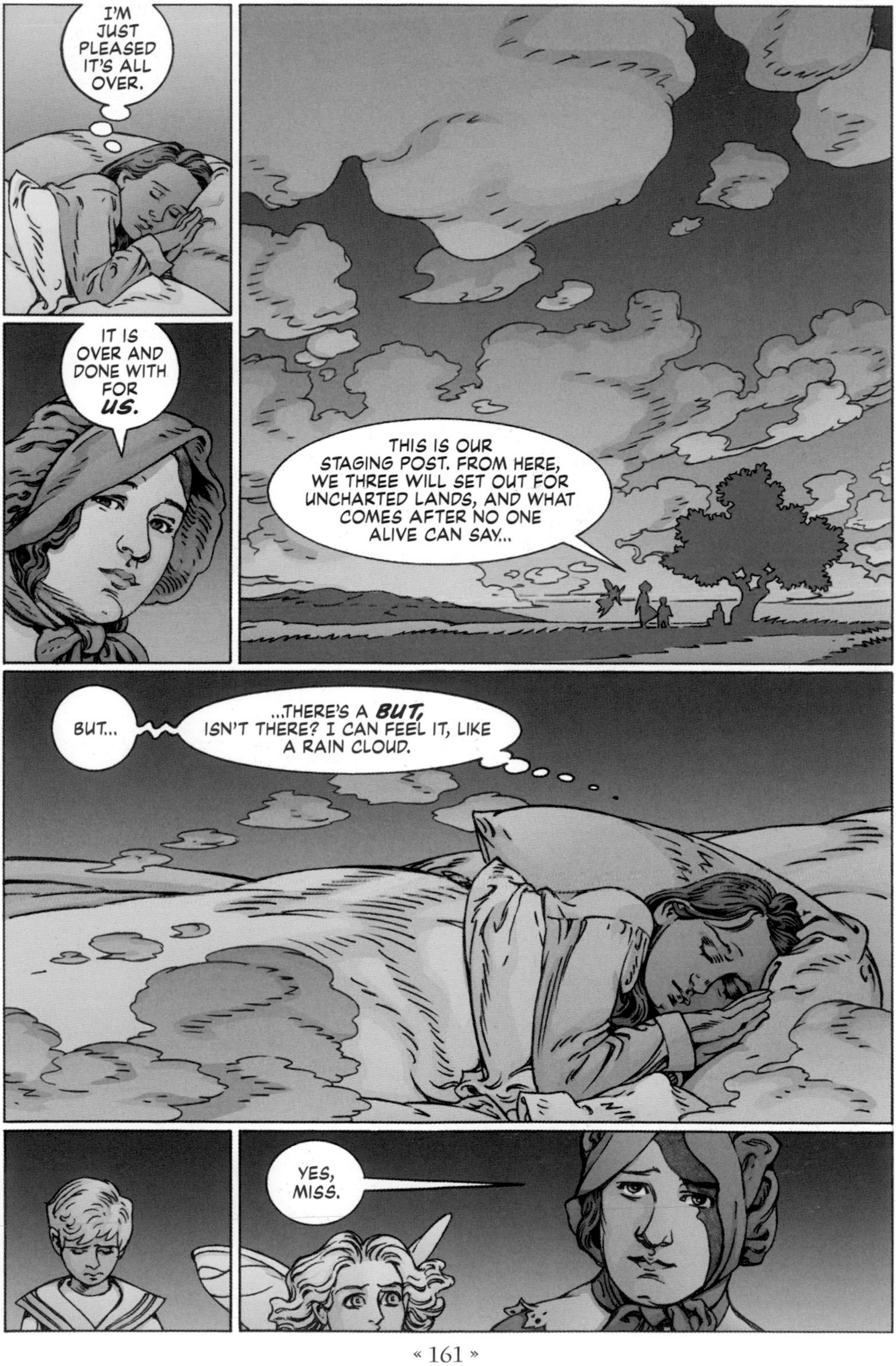
I'M JUST PLEASED IT'S ALL OVER.
IT IS OVER AND DONE WITH FOR US.
THIS IS OUR STAGING POST. FROM HERE, WE THREE WILL SET OUT FOR UNCHARTED LANDS, AND WHAT COMES AFTER NO ONE ALIVE CAN SAY...
BUT...
...THERE'S A BUT, ISN'T THERE? I CAN FEEL IT, LIKE A RAIN CLOUD.
YES, MISS.

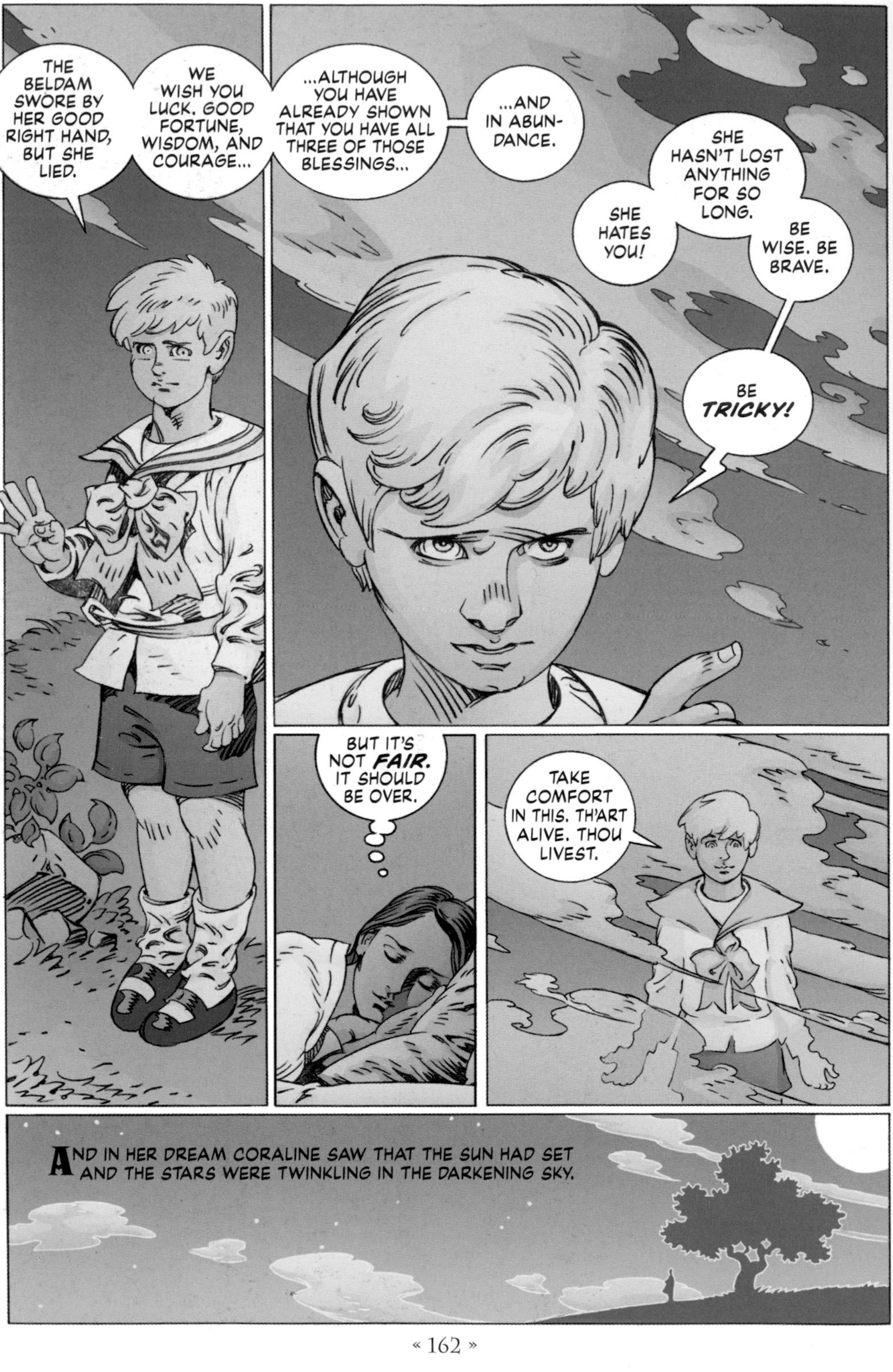
THE BELDAM SWORE BY HER GOOD RIGHT HAND, BUT SHE LIED.
WE WISH YOU LUCK. GOOD FORTUNE, WISDOM, AND COURAGE...
...ALTHOUGH YOU HAVE ALREADY SHOWN THAT YOU HAVE ALL THREE OF THOSE BLESSINGS...
...AND IN ABUNDANCE.
SHE HATES YOU!
SHE HASN'T LOST ANYTHING FOR SO LONG.
BE WISE. BE BRAVE.
BE TRICKY!
BUT IT'S NOT FAIR. IT SHOULD BE OVER.
TAKE COMFORT IN THIS. TH'ART ALIVE. THOU LIVEST.
AND IN HER DREAM CORALINE SAW THAT THE SUN HAD SET AND THE STARS WERE TWINKLING IN THE DARKENING SKY.

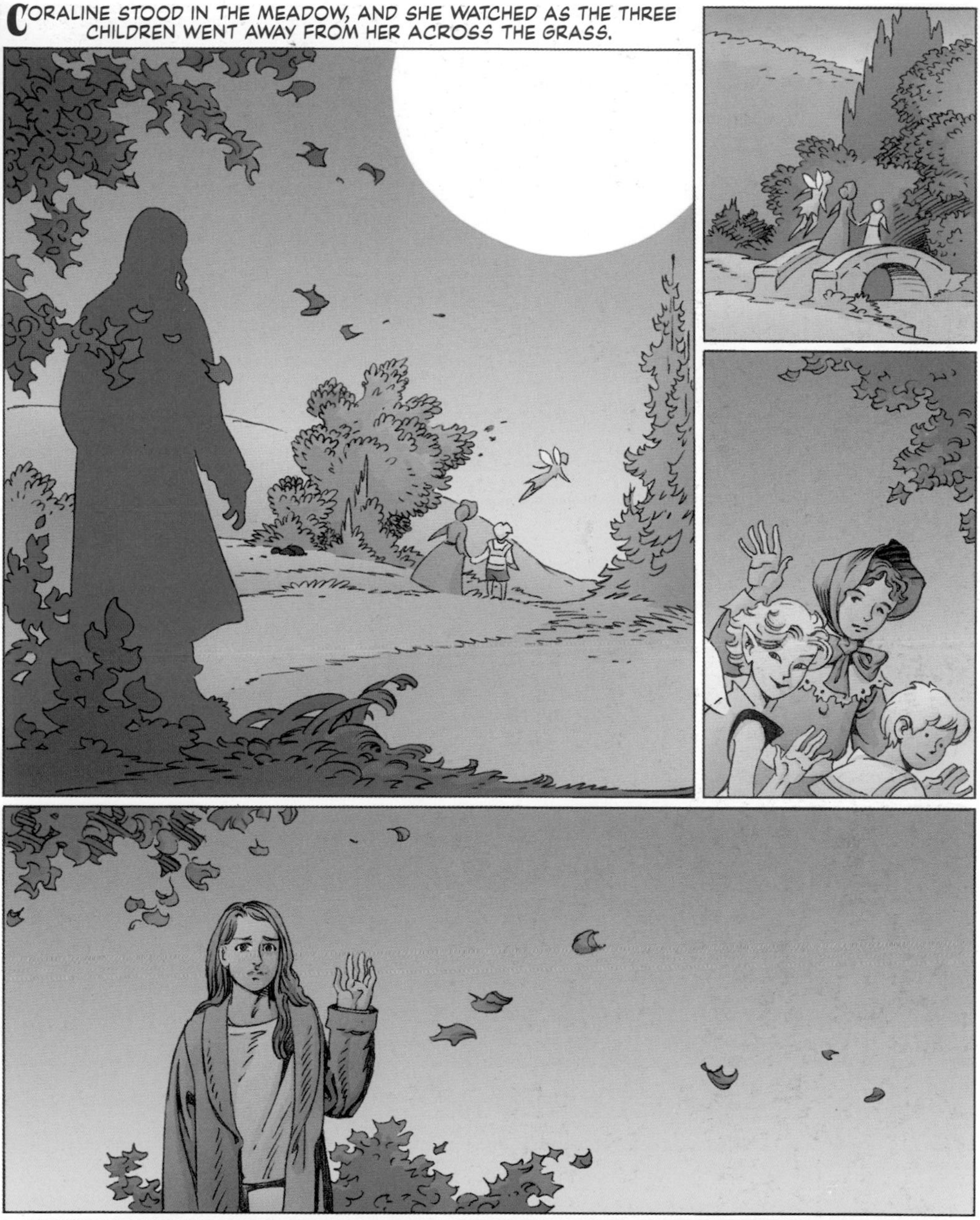
CORALINE STOOD IN THE MEADOW, AND SHE WATCHED AS THE THREE CHILDREN WENT AWAY FROM HER ACROSS THE GRASS.
AND WHAT CAME AFTER WAS DARKNESS.

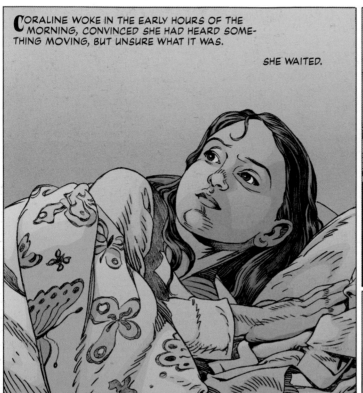

CORALINE WOKE IN THE EARLY HOURS OF THE MORNING, CONVINCED SHE HAD HEARD SOMETHING MOVING, BUT UNSURE WHAT IT WAS.

SHE WAITED.

SOMETHING MADE A RUSTLING NOISE OUTSIDE HER BEDROOM DOOR.

IS IT A RAT?

GO AWAY!

GO AWAY OR YOU'LL BE SORRY!

THERE WAS A PAUSE. THEN THE WHATEVER IT WAS SCUTTLED AWAY DOWN THE HALL.

THERE WAS SOMETHING ODD AND IRREGULAR ABOUT ITS FOOTSTEPS, IF THEY *WERE* FOOTSTEPS. CORALINE FOUND HERSELF WONDERING IF IT WAS PERHAPS A RAT WITH AN EXTRA LEG.

IT ISN'T OVER YET, IS IT?

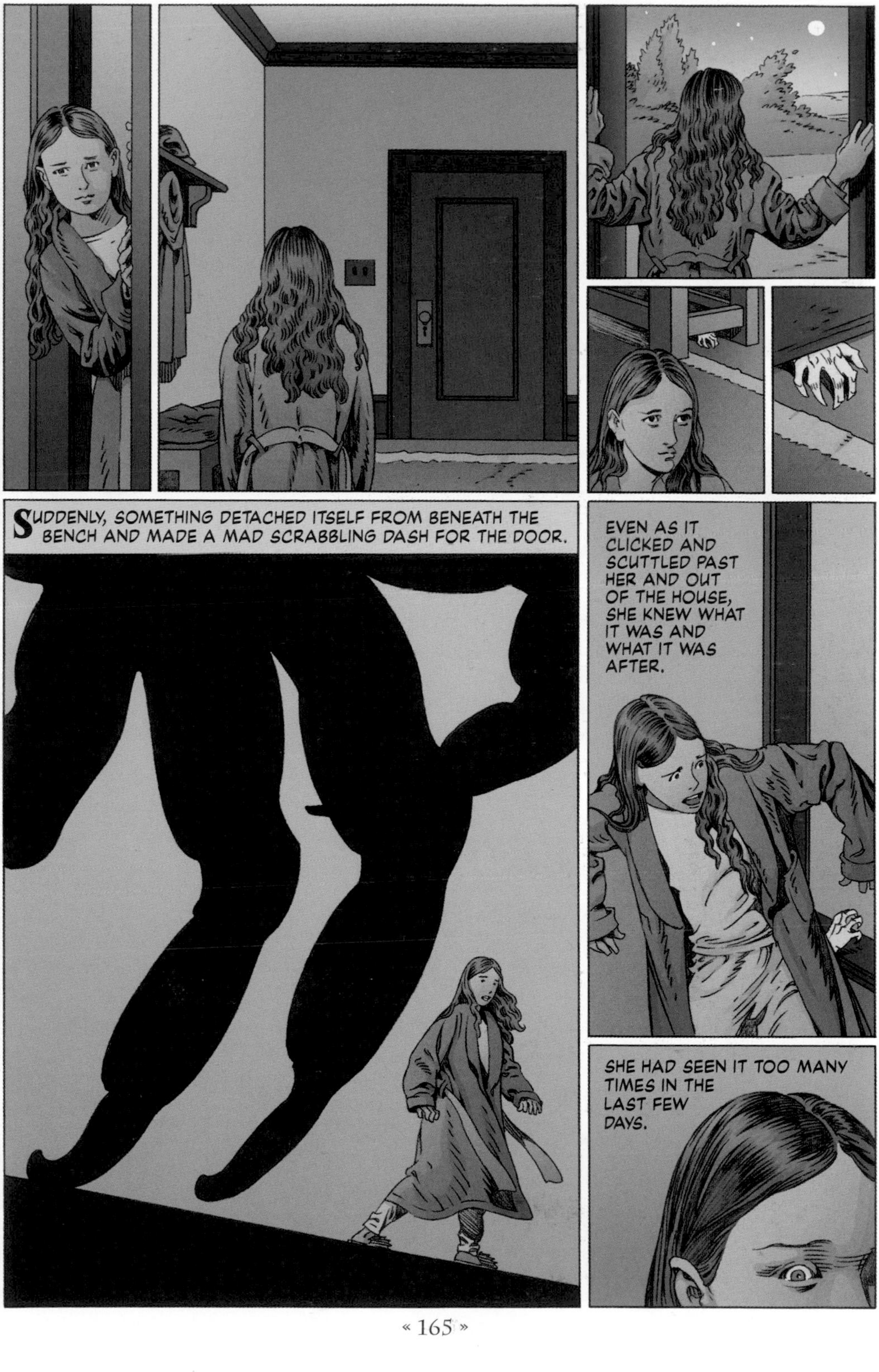
SUDDENLY, SOMETHING DETACHED ITSELF FROM BENEATH THE BENCH AND MADE A MAD SCRABBLING DASH FOR THE DOOR.
EVEN AS IT CLICKED AND SCUTTLED PAST HER AND OUT OF THE HOUSE, SHE KNEW WHAT IT WAS AND WHAT IT WAS AFTER.
SHE HAD SEEN IT TOO MANY TIMES IN THE LAST FEW DAYS.

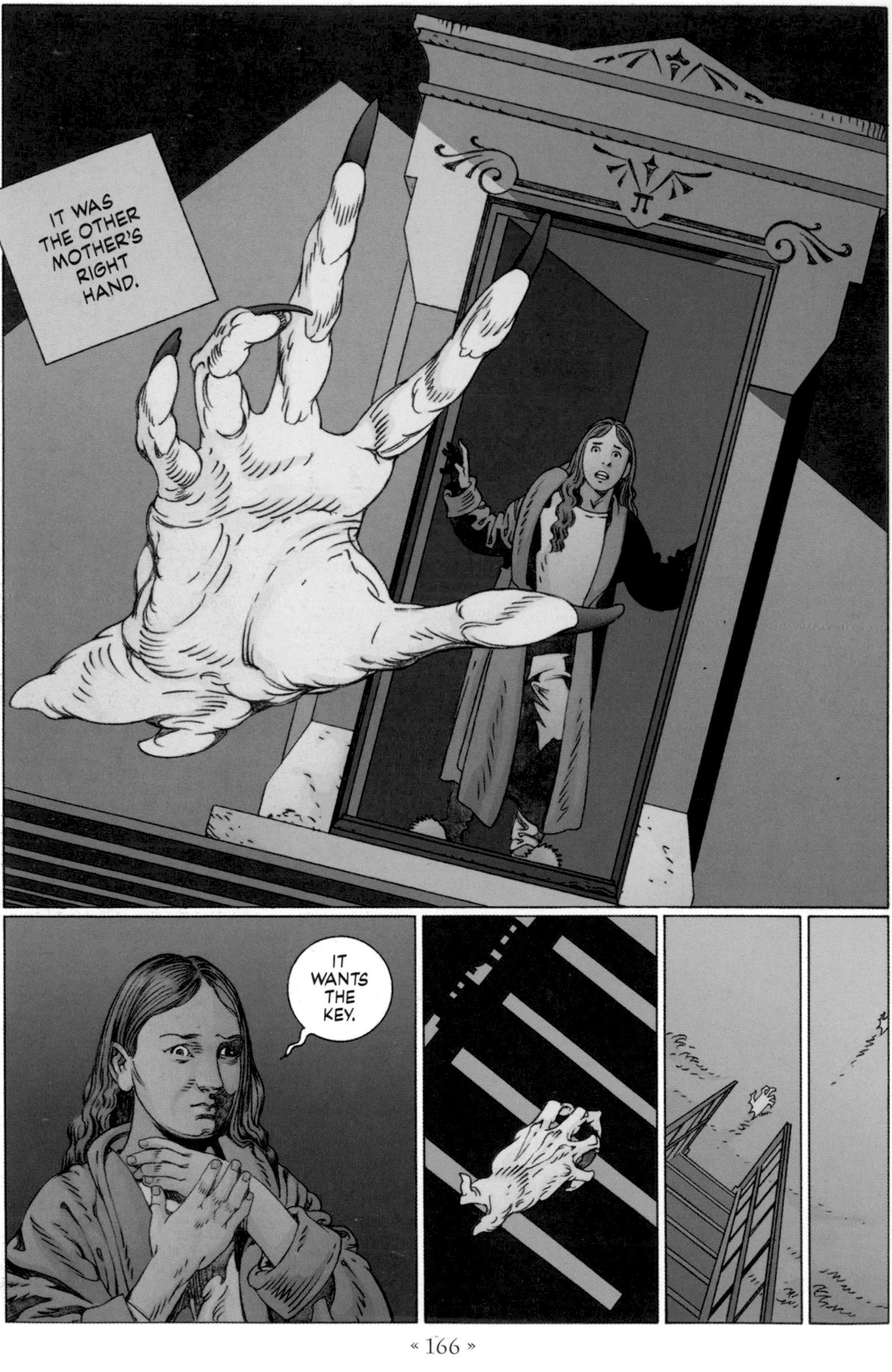
IT WAS THE OTHER MOTHER'S RIGHT HAND.
IT WANTS THE KEY.

13

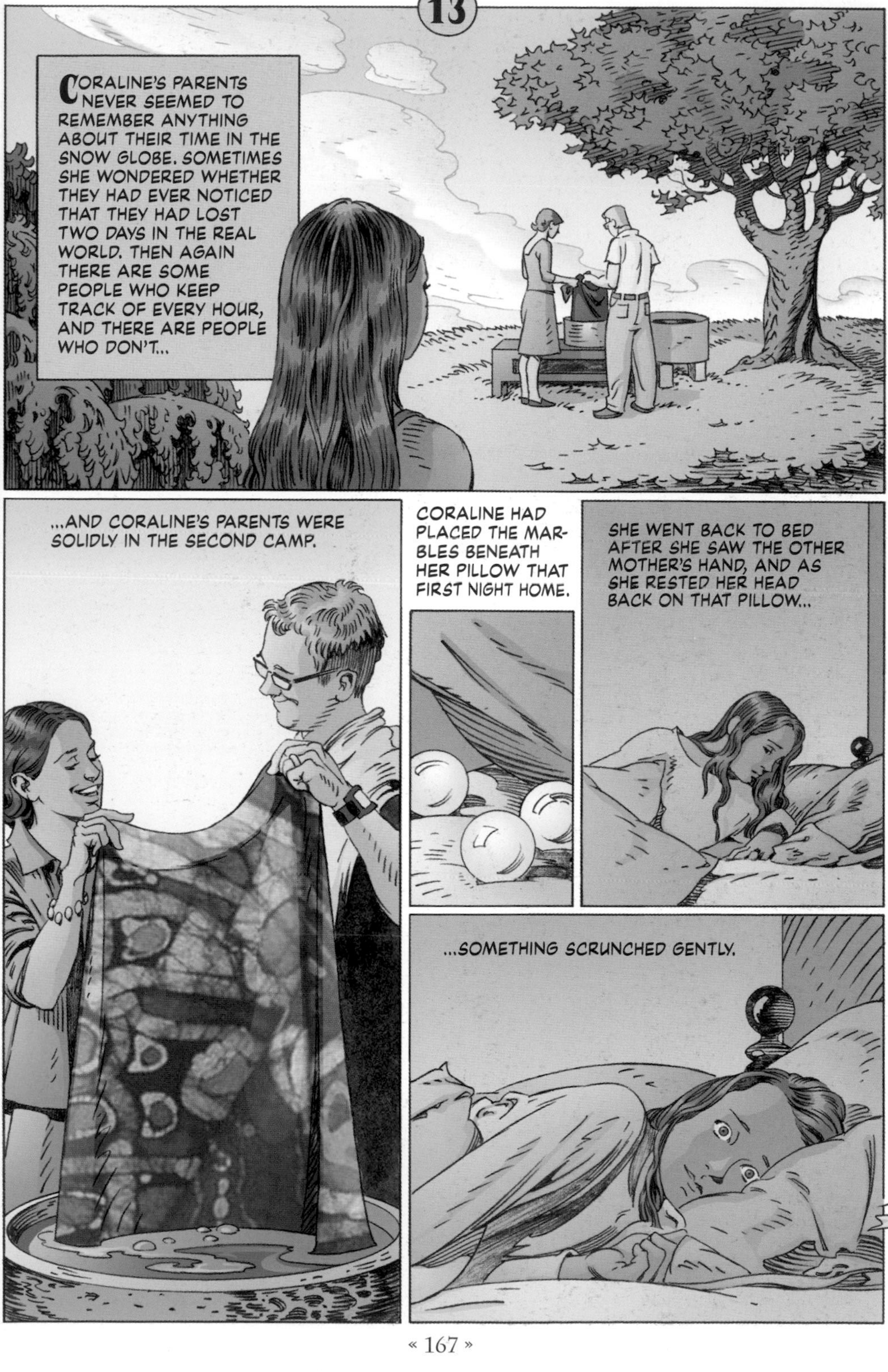
CORALINE'S PARENTS NEVER SEEMED TO REMEMBER ANYTHING ABOUT THEIR TIME IN THE SNOW GLOBE. SOMETIMES SHE WONDERED WHETHER THEY HAD EVER NOTICED THAT THEY HAD LOST TWO DAYS IN THE REAL WORLD. THEN AGAIN THERE ARE SOME PEOPLE WHO KEEP TRACK OF EVERY HOUR, AND THERE ARE PEOPLE WHO DON'T...
...AND CORALINE'S PARENTS WERE SOLIDLY IN THE SECOND CAMP.
CORALINE HAD PLACED THE MARBLES BENEATH HER PILLOW THAT FIRST NIGHT HOME.
SHE WENT BACK TO BED AFTER SHE SAW THE OTHER MOTHER'S HAND, AND AS SHE RESTED HER HEAD BACK ON THAT PILLOW...
...SOMETHING SCRUNCHED GENTLY.

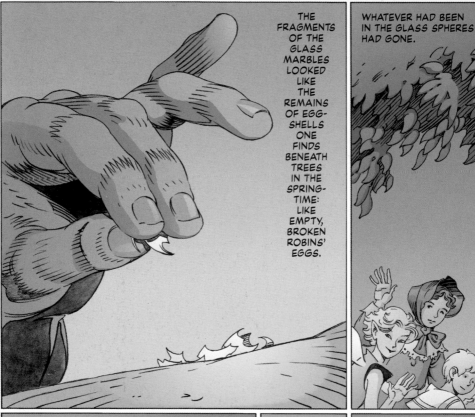

THE FRAGMENTS OF THE GLASS MARBLES LOOKED LIKE THE REMAINS OF EGG-SHELLS ONE FINDS BENEATH TREES IN THE SPRING-TIME: LIKE EMPTY, BROKEN ROBINS' EGGS.

WHATEVER HAD BEEN IN THE GLASS SPHERES HAD GONE.

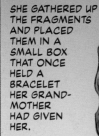

SHE GATHERED UP THE FRAGMENTS AND PLACED THEM IN A SMALL BOX THAT ONCE HELD A BRACELET HER GRAND-MOTHER HAD GIVEN HER.

THE BRACELET WAS LONG LOST...

...BUT THE BOX REMAINED.

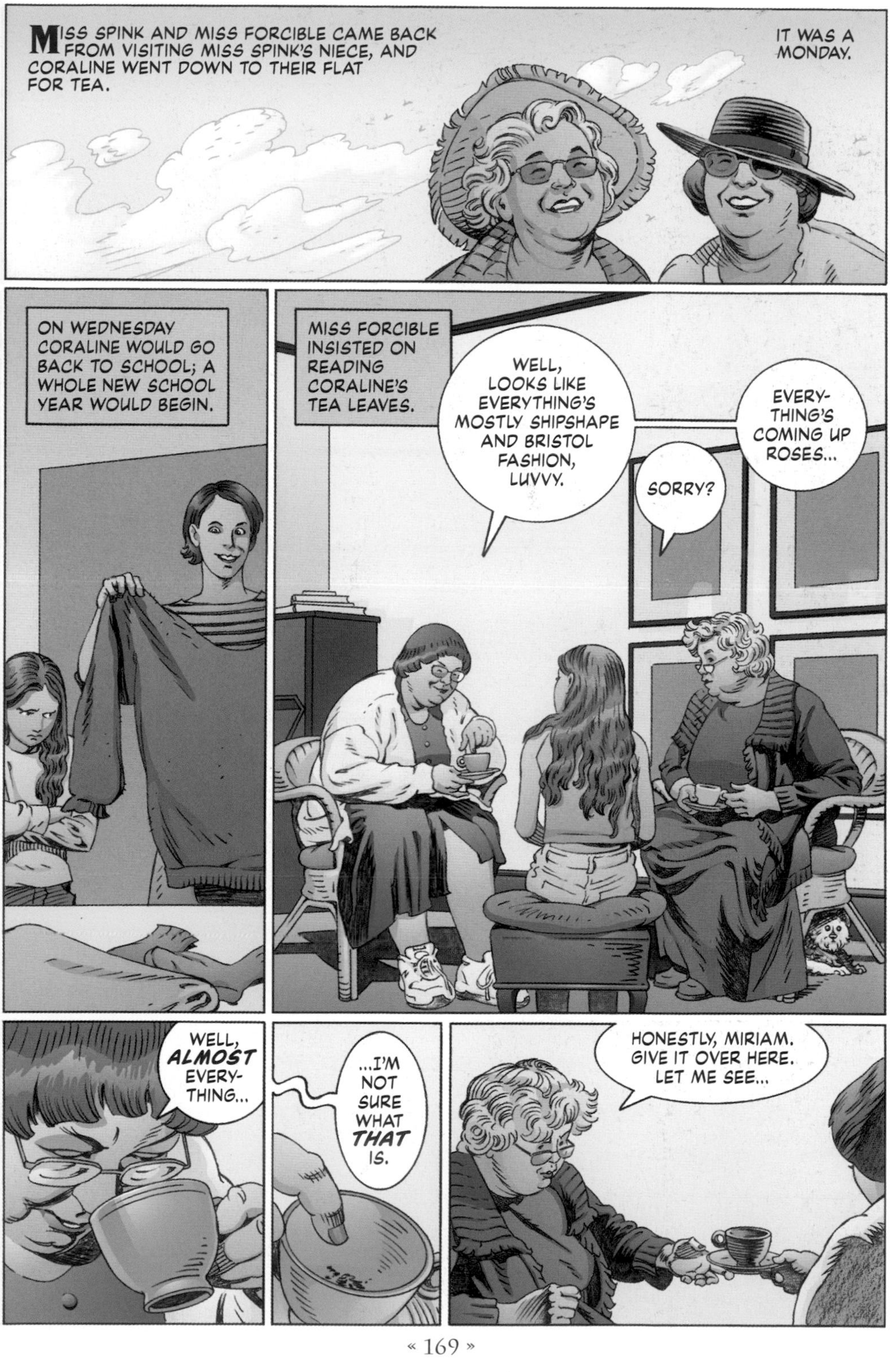
MISS SPINK AND MISS FORCIBLE CAME BACK FROM VISITING MISS SPINK'S NIECE, AND CORALINE WENT DOWN TO THEIR FLAT FOR TEA.
IT WAS A MONDAY.
ON WEDNESDAY CORALINE WOULD GO BACK TO SCHOOL; A WHOLE NEW SCHOOL YEAR WOULD BEGIN.
MISS FORCIBLE INSISTED ON READING CORALINE'S TEA LEAVES.
WELL, LOOKS LIKE EVERYTHING'S MOSTLY SHIPSHAPE AND BRISTOL FASHION, LUVVY.
EVERY-THING'S COMING UP ROSES...
SORRY?
WELL, ALMOST EVERY-THING...
...I'M NOT SURE WHAT THAT IS.
HONESTLY, MIRIAM. GIVE IT OVER HERE. LET ME SEE...

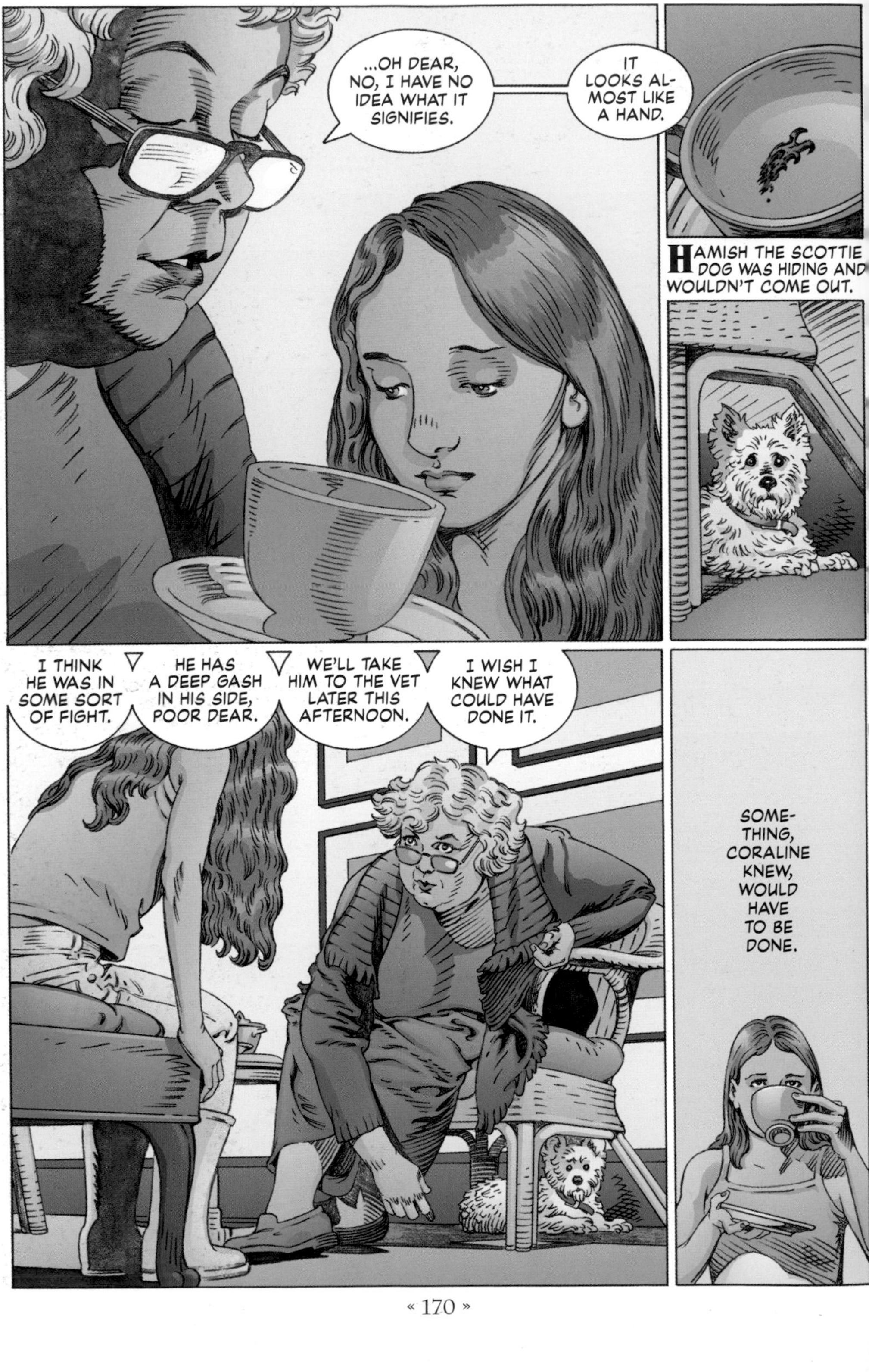
...OH DEAR, NO, I HAVE NO IDEA WHAT IT SIGNIFIES.
IT LOOKS AL- MOST LIKE A HAND.
HAMISH THE SCOTTIE DOG WAS HIDING AND WOULDN'T COME OUT.
I THINK HE WAS IN SOME SORT OF FIGHT.
HE HAS A DEEP GASH IN HIS SIDE, POOR DEAR.
WE'LL TAKE HIM TO THE VET LATER THIS AFTERNOON.
I WISH I KNEW WHAT COULD HAVE DONE IT.
SOME- THING, CORALINE KNEW, WOULD HAVE TO BE DONE.

THAT FINAL WEEK OF THE HOLIDAYS THE WEATHER WAS MAGNIFICENT, AS IF THE SUMMER ITSELF WERE TRYING TO MAKE UP FOR THE RECENT MISERABLE WEATHER BY GIVING THEM SOME BRIGHT AND GLORIOUS DAYS BEFORE IT ENDED.

HEY!

HI! YOU!

CAROLINE!

IT'S *CORALINE.*

HOW ARE THE MICE?

SOMETHING HAS **FRIGHTENED** THEM. I THINK MAYBE THERE IS A **WEASEL** IN THE HOUSE.

WE SHOULD PUT A TRAP DOWN FOR IT WITH A LITTLE MEAT OR HAMBURGER, AND WHEN THE CREATURE COMES TO FEAST, THEN...

...BAM!

I DON'T THINK IT WANTS **MEAT.**

SHE TOUCHED THE BLACK KEY THAT HUNG AROUND HER NECK...

...THEN SHE WENT INSIDE.

SHE BATHED HERSELF BUT KEPT THE KEY AROUND HER NECK. SHE NEVER TOOK IT OFF ANYMORE.

THAT NIGHT SOMETHING SCRATCHED AT HER WINDOW AFTER SHE WENT TO BED.

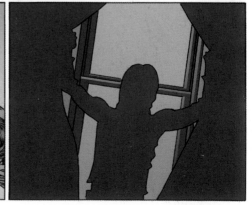

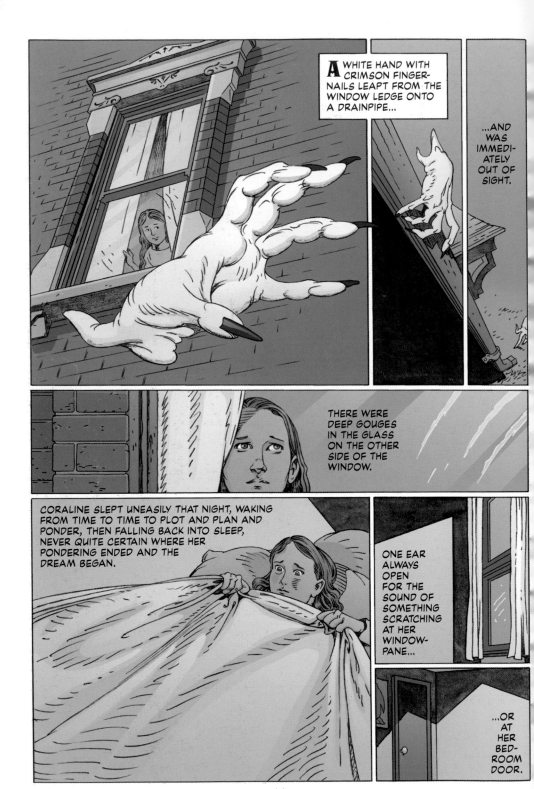

A WHITE HAND WITH CRIMSON FINGER-NAILS LEAPT FROM THE WINDOW LEDGE ONTO A DRAINPIPE...

...AND WAS IMMEDIATELY OUT OF SIGHT.

THERE WERE DEEP GOUGES IN THE GLASS ON THE OTHER SIDE OF THE WINDOW.

CORALINE SLEPT UNEASILY THAT NIGHT, WAKING FROM TIME TO TIME TO PLOT AND PLAN AND PONDER, THEN FALLING BACK INTO SLEEP, NEVER QUITE CERTAIN WHERE HER PONDERING ENDED AND THE DREAM BEGAN.

ONE EAR ALWAYS OPEN FOR THE SOUND OF SOMETHING SCRATCHING AT HER WINDOW-PANE...

...OR AT HER BED-ROOM DOOR.

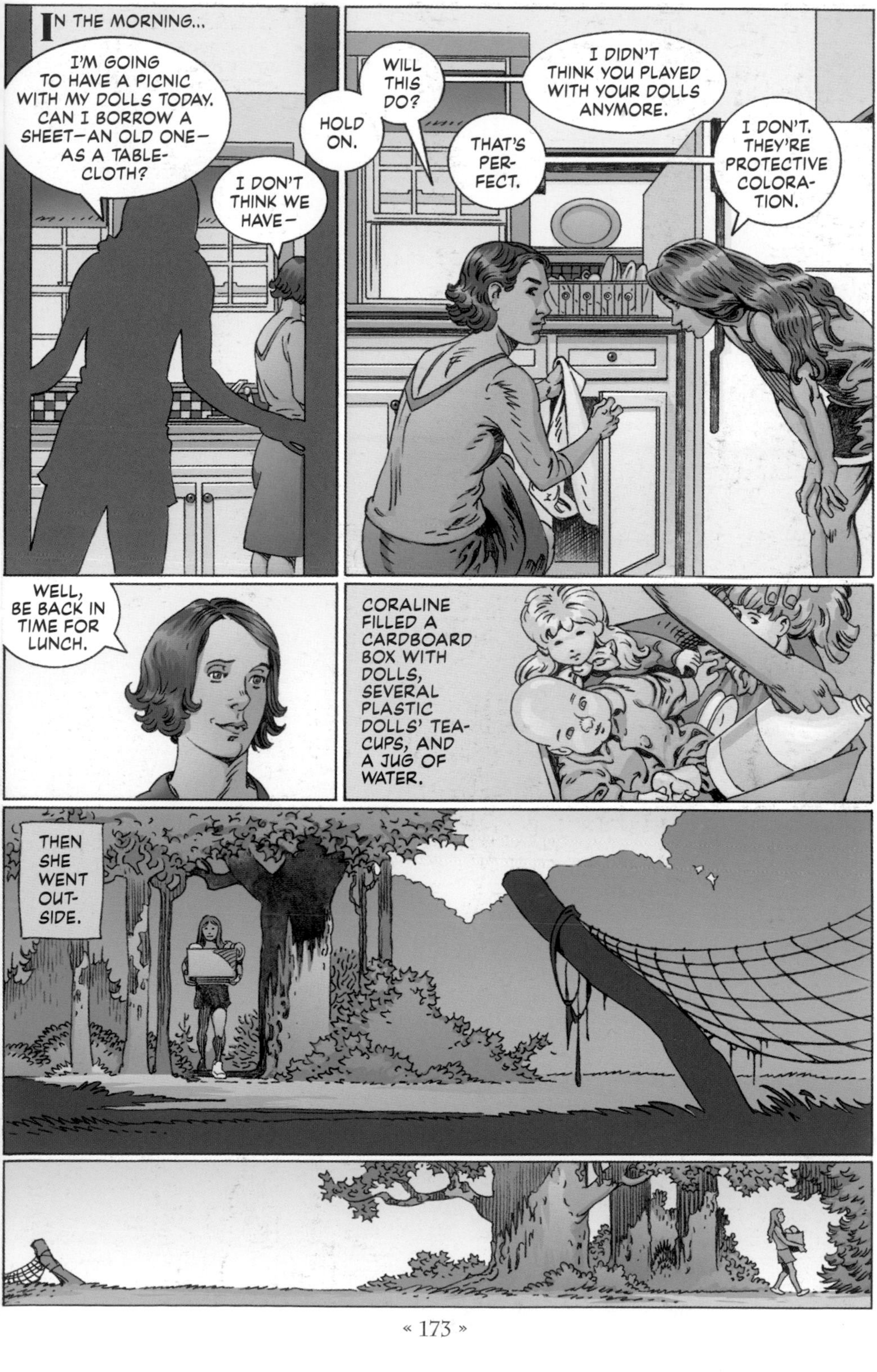
IN THE MORNING...
I'M GOING TO HAVE A PICNIC WITH MY DOLLS TODAY. CAN I BORROW A SHEET—AN OLD ONE—AS A TABLE-CLOTH?
I DON'T THINK WE HAVE—
HOLD ON.
WILL THIS DO?
THAT'S PER-FECT.
I DIDN'T THINK YOU PLAYED WITH YOUR DOLLS ANYMORE.
I DON'T. THEY'RE PROTECTIVE COLORA-TION.
WELL, BE BACK IN TIME FOR LUNCH.
CORALINE FILLED A CARDBOARD BOX WITH DOLLS, SEVERAL PLASTIC DOLLS' TEA-CUPS, AND A JUG OF WATER.
THEN SHE WENT OUT-SIDE.

THE PLANKS COVERING THE WELL WERE ASTONISHINGLY HEAVY— ALMOST TOO HEAVY FOR A GIRL TO LIFT, BUT SHE MANAGED. SHE DIDN'T HAVE ANY CHOICE.

SHE CAREFULLY LAID THE TABLECLOTH ACROSS THE TOP OF THE WELL. SHE PLACED DOLL CUPS AROUND IT AND WEIGHED EACH CUP DOWN WITH WATER FROM THE JUG.

SHE PUT A DOLL IN THE GRASS BESIDE EACH CUP, MAKING IT LOOK AS MUCH LIKE A DOLLS' TEA PARTY AS SHE COULD

THEN SHE RETRACED HER STEPS.

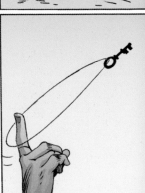

MISTER BOBO?

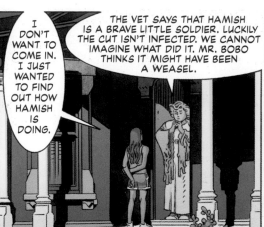

I DON'T WANT TO COME IN. I JUST WANTED TO FIND OUT HOW HAMISH IS DOING.

THE VET SAYS THAT HAMISH IS A BRAVE LITTLE SOLDIER. LUCKILY THE CUT ISN'T INFECTED. WE CANNOT IMAGINE WHAT DID IT. MR. BOBO THINKS IT MIGHT HAVE BEEN A WEASEL.

HELLO, DEAR.

THE MAN IN THE TOP FLAT, MISTER BOBO. FINE OLD CIRCUS FAMILY, I BELIEVE.

IT HAD NEVER OCCURRED TO CORALINE THAT THE CRAZY OLD MAN UPSTAIRS ACTUALLY HAD A NAME. IF SHE'D KNOWN HIS NAME WAS MR. BOBO SHE WOULD HAVE SAID IT EVERY CHANCE SHE GOT. HOW OFTEN DO YOU GET TO SAY ALOUD A NAME LIKE...

OH... MR. BOBO. RIGHT.

MR. BOBO!

WELL, I'M GOING TO GO AND PLAY WITH MY DOLLS NOW, OVER BY THE OLD TENNIS COURT, ROUND THE BACK.

THAT'S NICE, DEAR.

MAKE SURE YOU KEEP AN EYE OUT FOR THE OLD WELL.

THEY SAY IT MIGHT GO DOWN FOR HALF A MILE OR MORE.

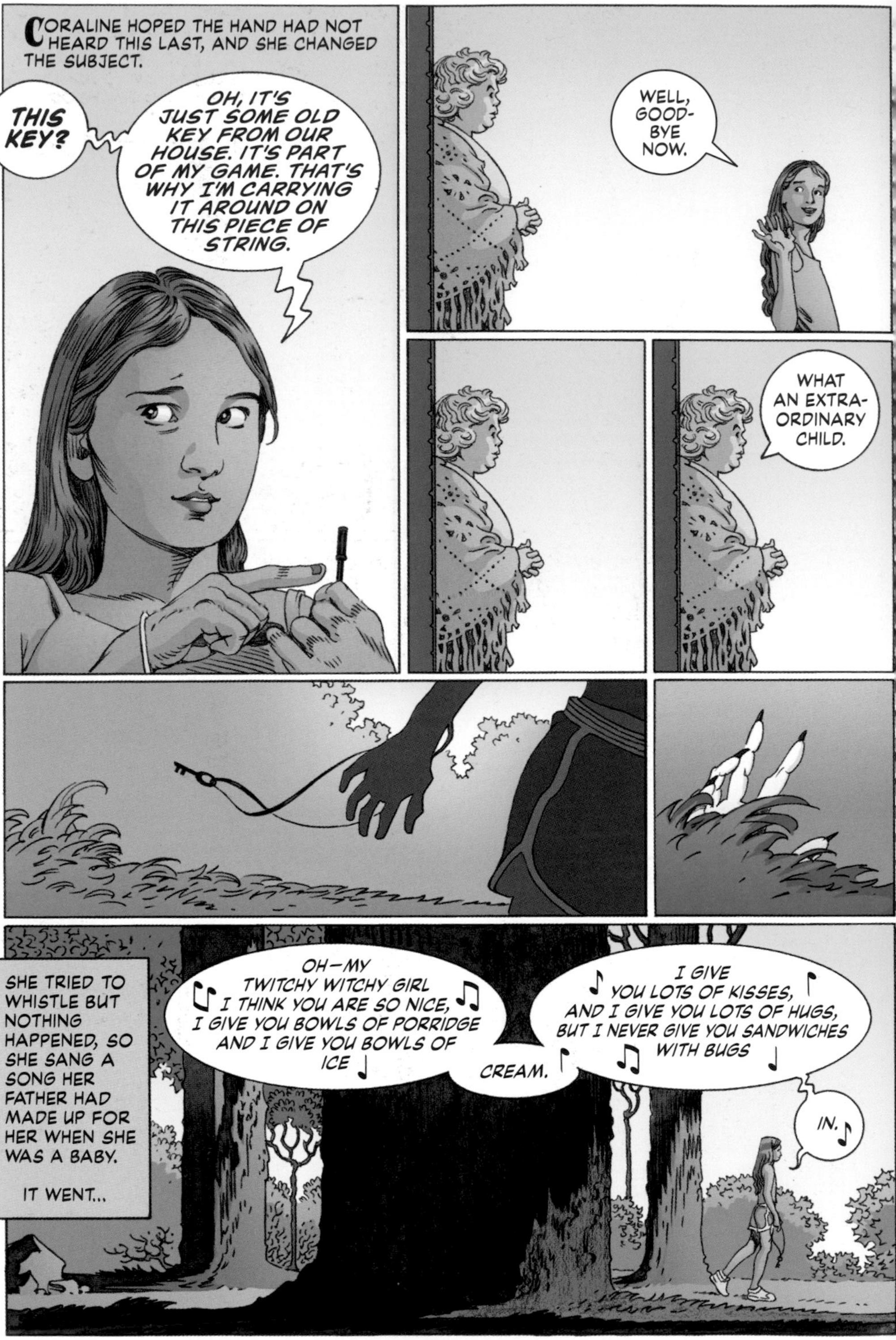
CORALINE HOPED THE HAND HAD NOT HEARD THIS LAST, AND SHE CHANGED THE SUBJECT.
THIS KEY?
OH, IT'S JUST SOME OLD KEY FROM OUR HOUSE. IT'S PART OF MY GAME. THAT'S WHY I'M CARRYING IT AROUND ON THIS PIECE OF STRING.
WELL, GOOD-BYE NOW.
WHAT AN EXTRA-ORDINARY CHILD.
SHE TRIED TO WHISTLE BUT NOTHING HAPPENED, SO SHE SANG A SONG HER FATHER HAD MADE UP FOR HER WHEN SHE WAS A BABY.
IT WENT...
OH—MY TWITCHY WITCHY GIRL I THINK YOU ARE SO NICE, I GIVE YOU BOWLS OF PORRIDGE AND I GIVE YOU BOWLS OF ICE
CREAM.
I GIVE YOU LOTS OF KISSES, AND I GIVE YOU LOTS OF HUGS, BUT I NEVER GIVE YOU SANDWICHES WITH BUGS
IN.

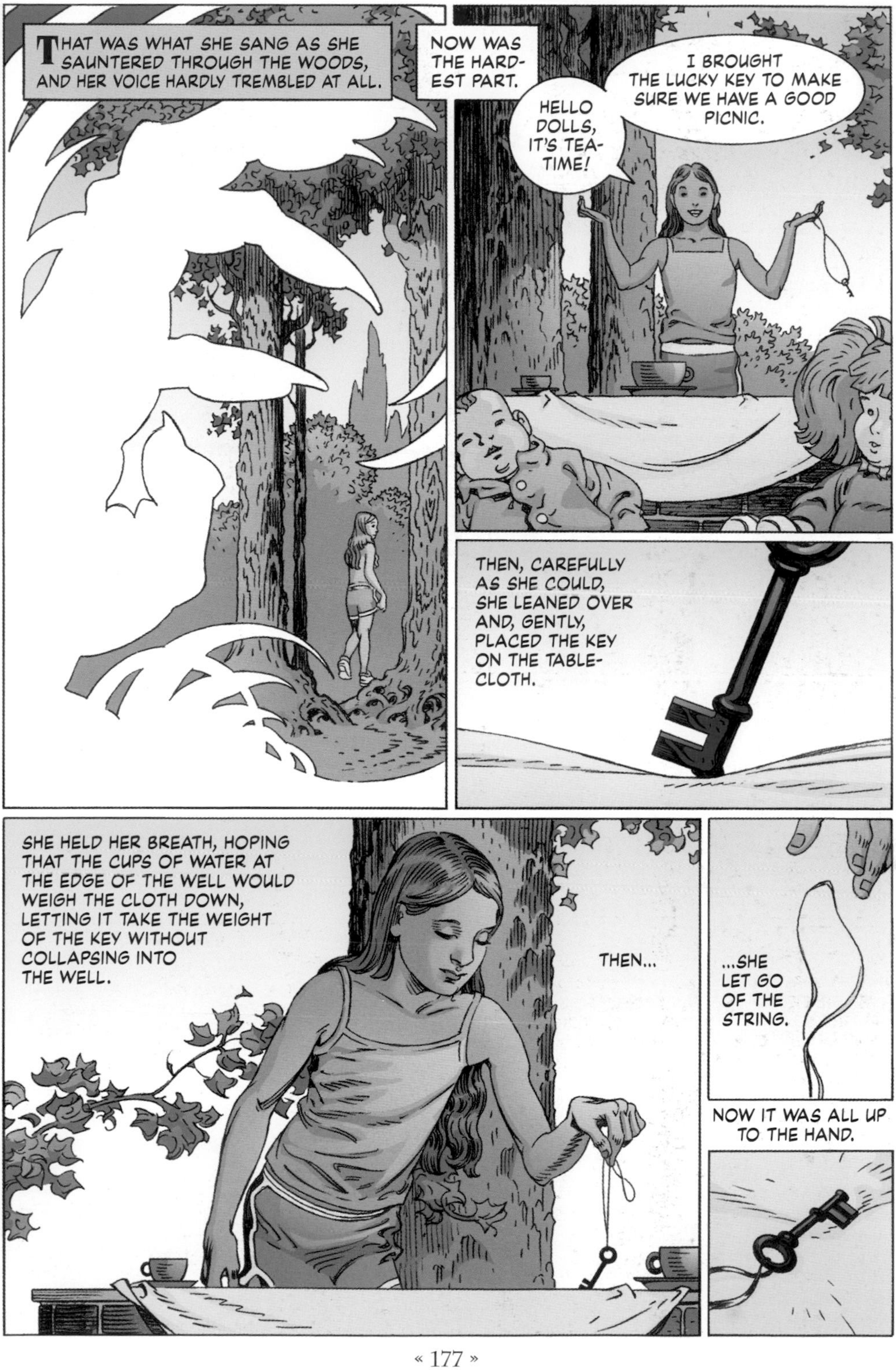
THAT WAS WHAT SHE SANG AS SHE SAUNTERED THROUGH THE WOODS, AND HER VOICE HARDLY TREMBLED AT ALL.
NOW WAS THE HARDEST PART.
HELLO DOLLS, IT'S TEA-TIME!
I BROUGHT THE LUCKY KEY TO MAKE SURE WE HAVE A GOOD PICNIC.
THEN, CAREFULLY AS SHE COULD, SHE LEANED OVER AND, GENTLY, PLACED THE KEY ON THE TABLE-CLOTH.
SHE HELD HER BREATH, HOPING THAT THE CUPS OF WATER AT THE EDGE OF THE WELL WOULD WEIGH THE CLOTH DOWN, LETTING IT TAKE THE WEIGHT OF THE KEY WITHOUT COLLAPSING INTO THE WELL.
THEN...
...SHE LET GO OF THE STRING.
NOW IT WAS ALL UP TO THE HAND.

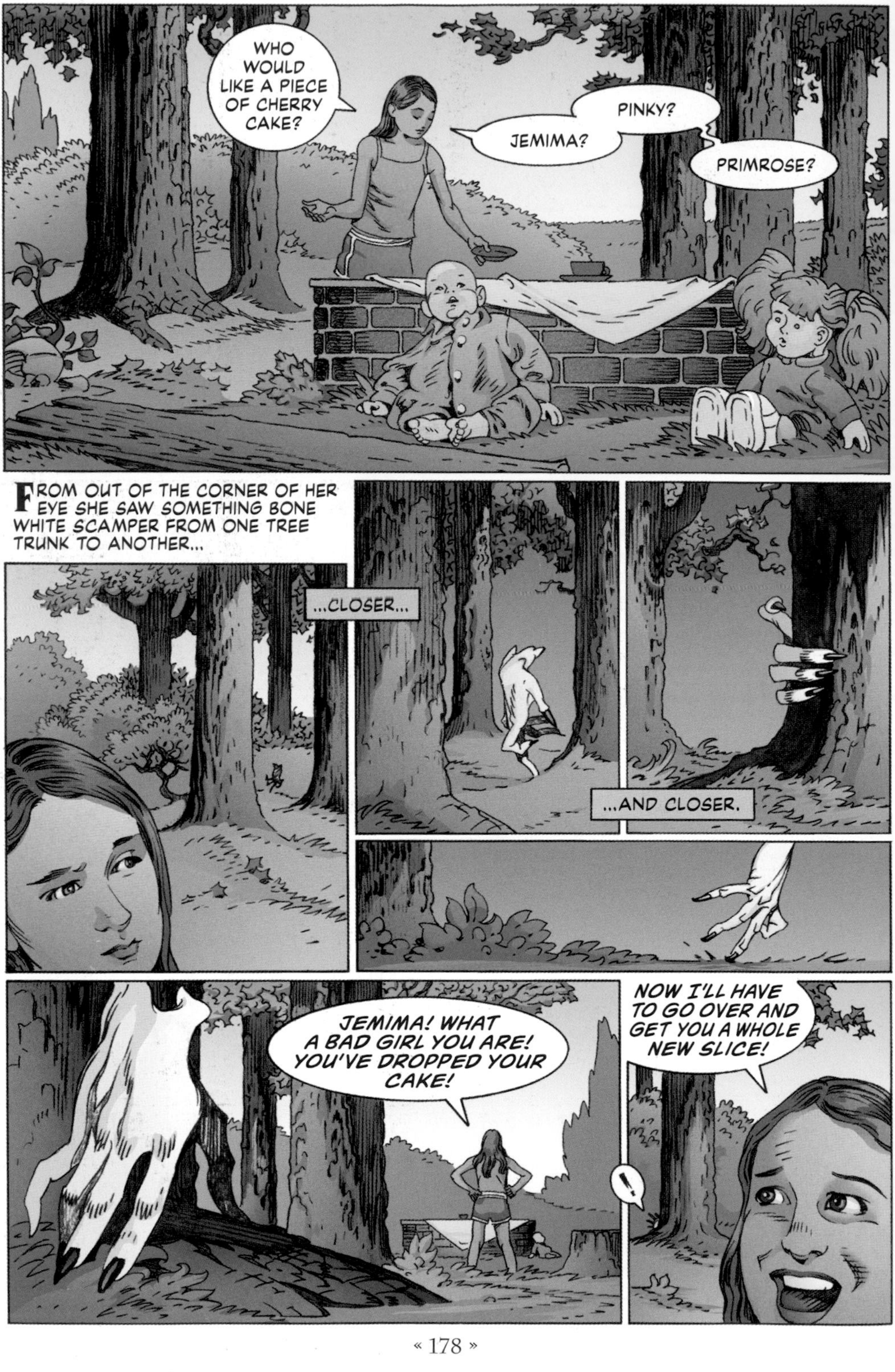
WHO WOULD LIKE A PIECE OF CHERRY CAKE?
JEMIMA?
PINKY?
PRIMROSE?
FROM OUT OF THE CORNER OF HER EYE SHE SAW SOMETHING BONE WHITE SCAMPER FROM ONE TREE TRUNK TO ANOTHER...
...CLOSER...
...AND CLOSER.
JEMIMA! WHAT A BAD GIRL YOU ARE! YOU'VE DROPPED YOUR CAKE!
NOW I'LL HAVE TO GO OVER AND GET YOU A WHOLE NEW SLICE!
!

MMM

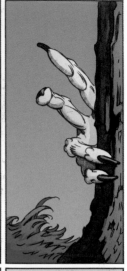

AND THEN IN A SKITTERING RUSH, IT CAME.

IT STOOD FOR A MOMENT, LIKE A CRAB TASTING THE AIR...

...AND THEN IT MADE ONE TRIUMPHANT, NAIL-CLACKING LEAP...

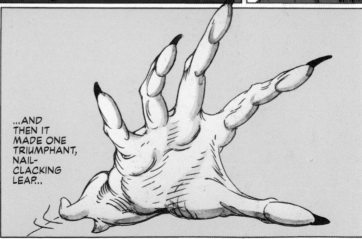

...RIGHT FOR THE CENTER OF THE TABLE-CLOTH.

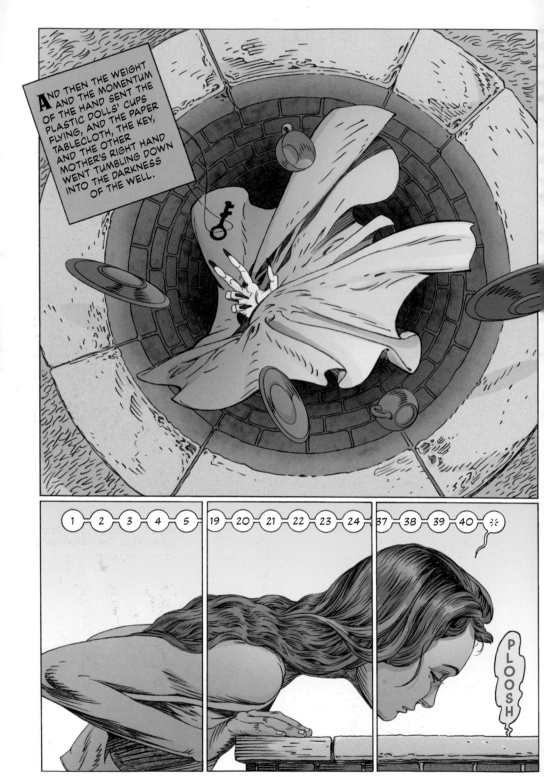

AND THEN THE WEIGHT AND THE MOMENTUM OF THE HAND SENT THE PLASTIC DOLLS' CUPS FLYING, AND THE PAPER TABLECLOTH, THE KEY, AND THE OTHER MOTHER'S RIGHT HAND WENT TUMBLING DOWN INTO THE DARKNESS OF THE WELL.

PLOOSH

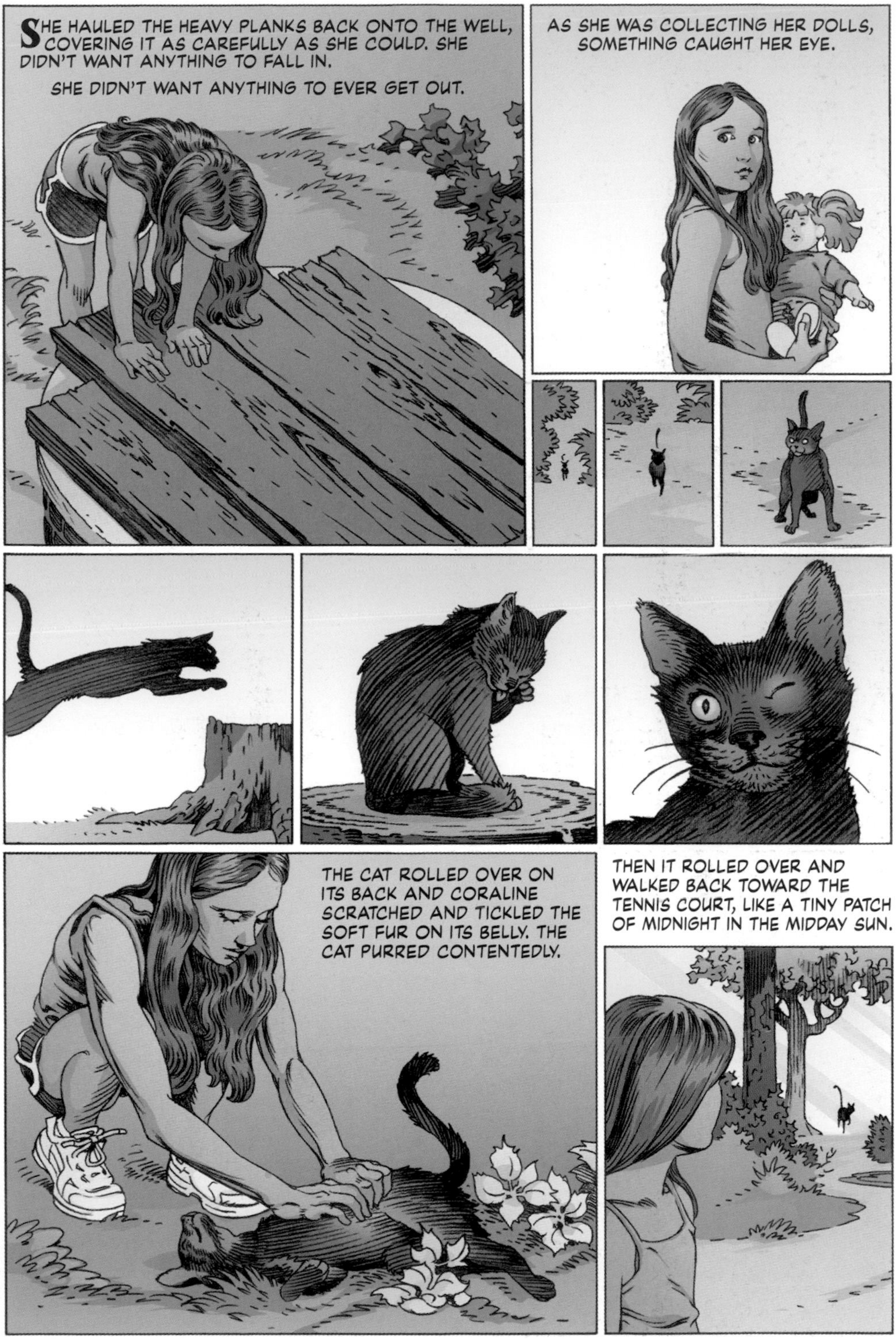
SHE HAULED THE HEAVY PLANKS BACK ONTO THE WELL, COVERING IT AS CAREFULLY AS SHE COULD. SHE DIDN'T WANT ANYTHING TO FALL IN.
SHE DIDN'T WANT ANYTHING TO EVER GET OUT.
AS SHE WAS COLLECTING HER DOLLS, SOMETHING CAUGHT HER EYE.
THE CAT ROLLED OVER ON ITS BACK AND CORALINE SCRATCHED AND TICKLED THE SOFT FUR ON ITS BELLY. THE CAT PURRED CONTENTEDLY.
THEN IT ROLLED OVER AND WALKED BACK TOWARD THE TENNIS COURT, LIKE A TINY PATCH OF MIDNIGHT IN THE MIDDAY SUN.

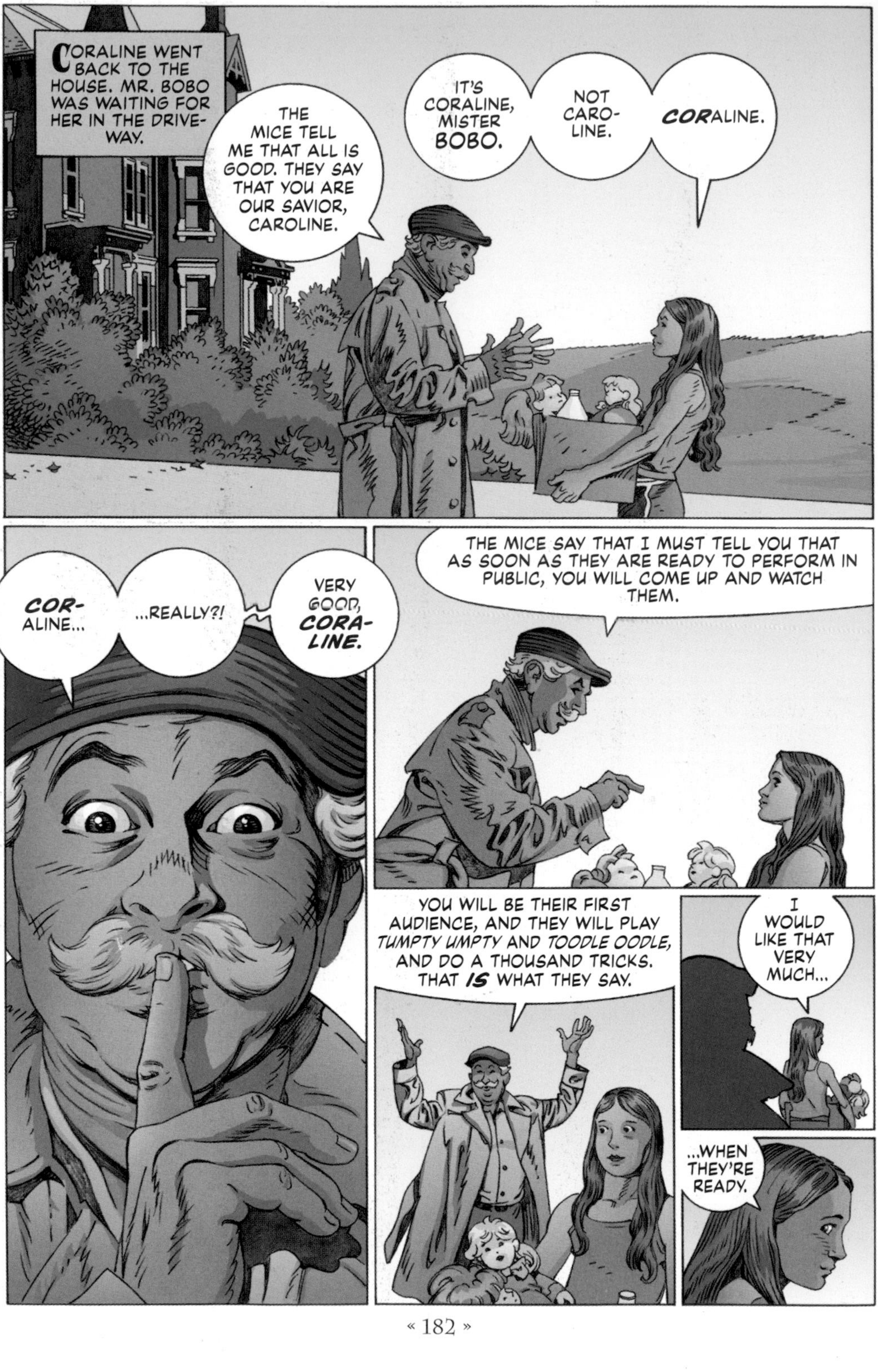
CORALINE WENT BACK TO THE HOUSE. MR. BOBO WAS WAITING FOR HER IN THE DRIVE-WAY.
THE MICE TELL ME THAT ALL IS GOOD. THEY SAY THAT YOU ARE OUR SAVIOR, CAROLINE.
IT'S CORALINE, MISTER BOBO.
NOT CARO-LINE.
CORALINE.
COR-ALINE...
...REALLY?!
VERY GOOD, CORA-LINE.
THE MICE SAY THAT I MUST TELL YOU THAT AS SOON AS THEY ARE READY TO PERFORM IN PUBLIC, YOU WILL COME UP AND WATCH THEM.
YOU WILL BE THEIR FIRST AUDIENCE, AND THEY WILL PLAY TUMPTY UMPTY AND TOODLE OODLE, AND DO A THOUSAND TRICKS. THAT IS WHAT THEY SAY.
I WOULD LIKE THAT VERY MUCH...
...WHEN THEY'RE READY.

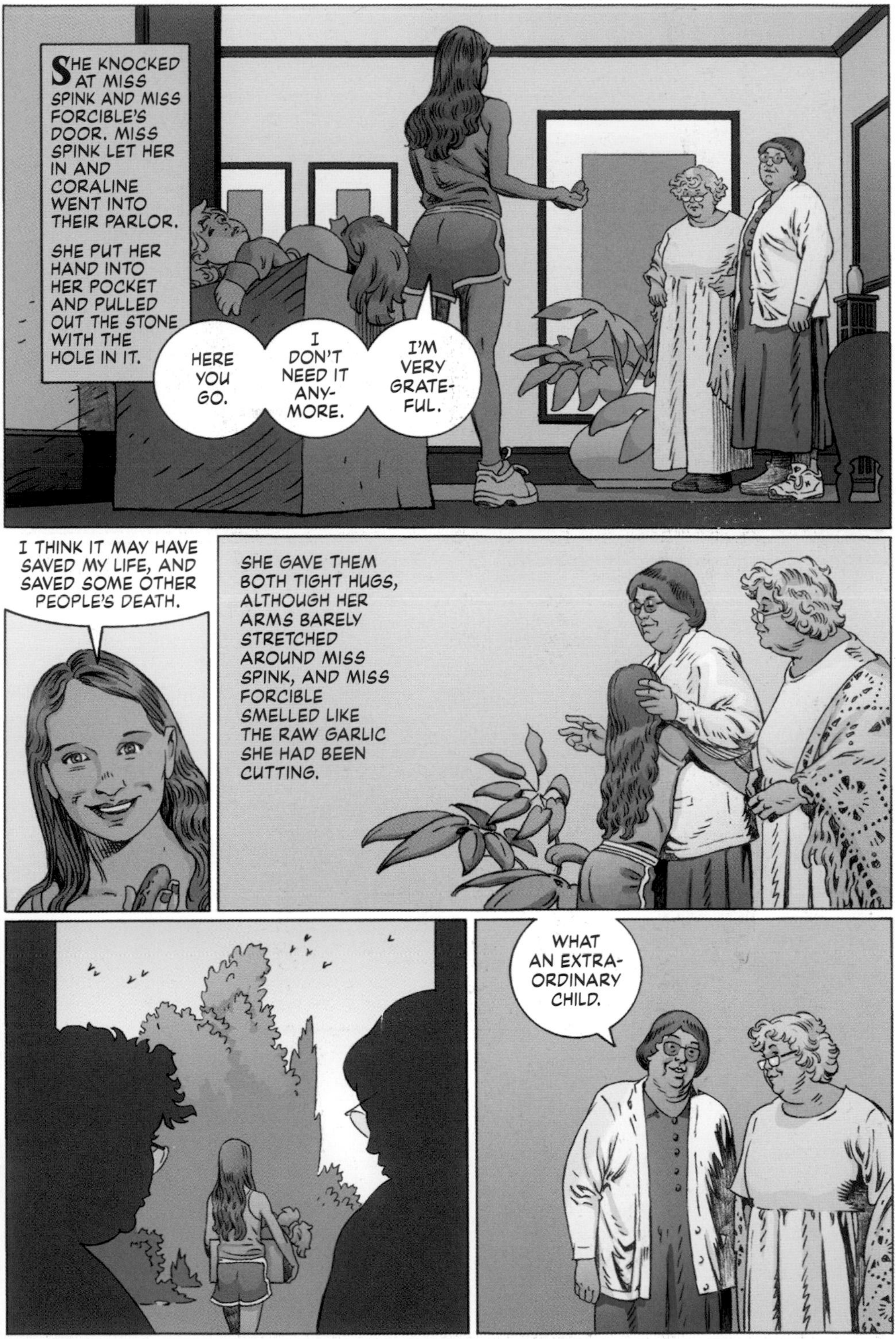
SHE KNOCKED AT MISS SPINK AND MISS FORCIBLE'S DOOR. MISS SPINK LET HER IN AND CORALINE WENT INTO THEIR PARLOR.
SHE PUT HER HAND INTO HER POCKET AND PULLED OUT THE STONE WITH THE HOLE IN IT.
HERE YOU GO.
I DON'T NEED IT ANY-MORE.
I'M VERY GRATE-FUL.
I THINK IT MAY HAVE SAVED MY LIFE, AND SAVED SOME OTHER PEOPLE'S DEATH.
SHE GAVE THEM BOTH TIGHT HUGS, ALTHOUGH HER ARMS BARELY STRETCHED AROUND MISS SPINK, AND MISS FORCIBLE SMELLED LIKE THE RAW GARLIC SHE HAD BEEN CUTTING.
WHAT AN EXTRA-ORDINARY CHILD.

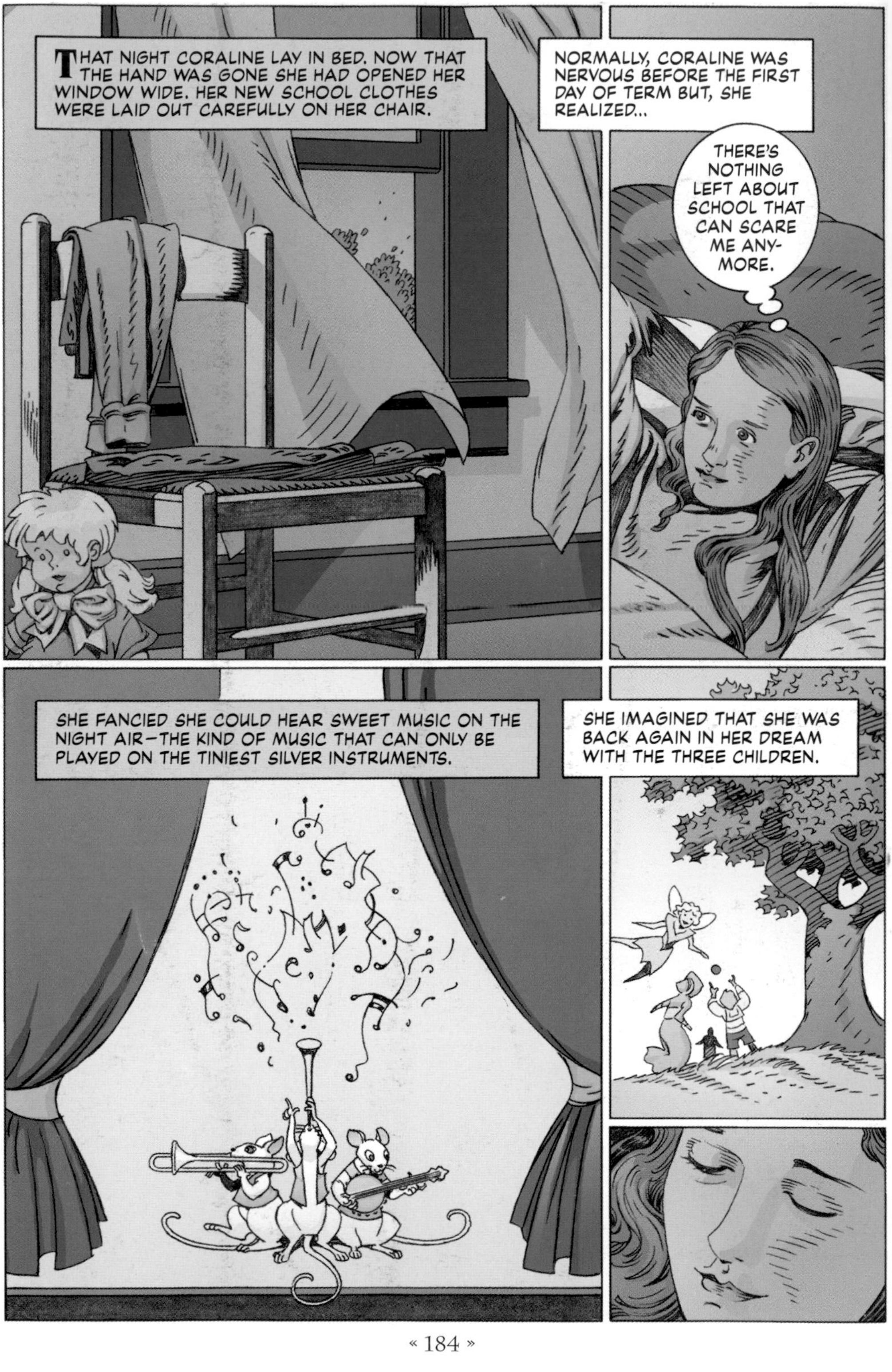
THAT NIGHT CORALINE LAY IN BED. NOW THAT THE HAND WAS GONE SHE HAD OPENED HER WINDOW WIDE. HER NEW SCHOOL CLOTHES WERE LAID OUT CAREFULLY ON HER CHAIR.
NORMALLY, CORALINE WAS NERVOUS BEFORE THE FIRST DAY OF TERM BUT, SHE REALIZED...
THERE'S NOTHING LEFT ABOUT SCHOOL THAT CAN SCARE ME ANY-MORE.
SHE FANCIED SHE COULD HEAR SWEET MUSIC ON THE NIGHT AIR—THE KIND OF MUSIC THAT CAN ONLY BE PLAYED ON THE TINIEST SILVER INSTRUMENTS.
SHE IMAGINED THAT SHE WAS BACK AGAIN IN HER DREAM WITH THE THREE CHILDREN.

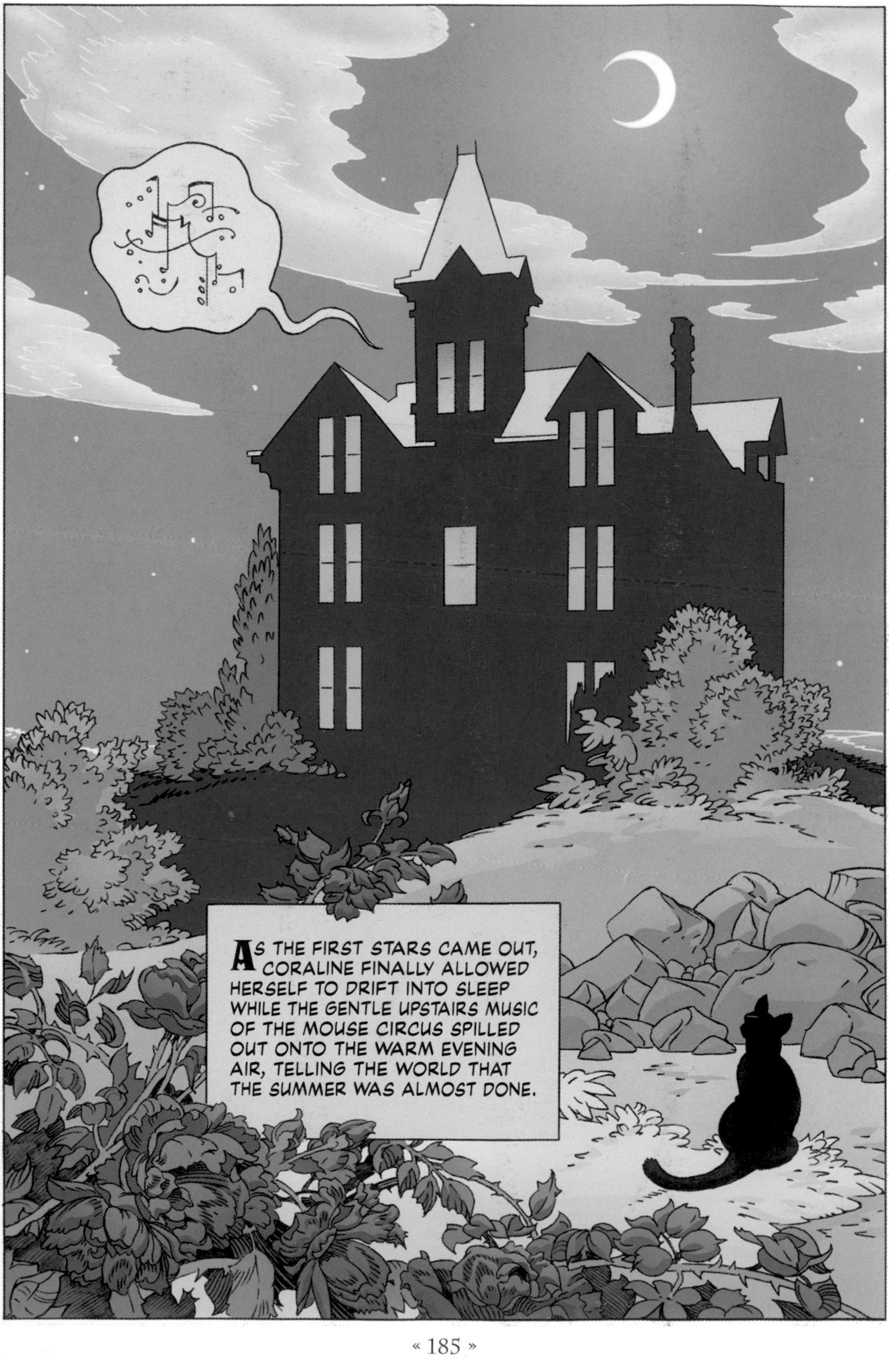
AS THE FIRST STARS CAME OUT, CORALINE FINALLY ALLOWED HERSELF TO DRIFT INTO SLEEP WHILE THE GENTLE UPSTAIRS MUSIC OF THE MOUSE CIRCUS SPILLED OUT ONTO THE WARM EVENING AIR, TELLING THE WORLD THAT THE SUMMER WAS ALMOST DONE.

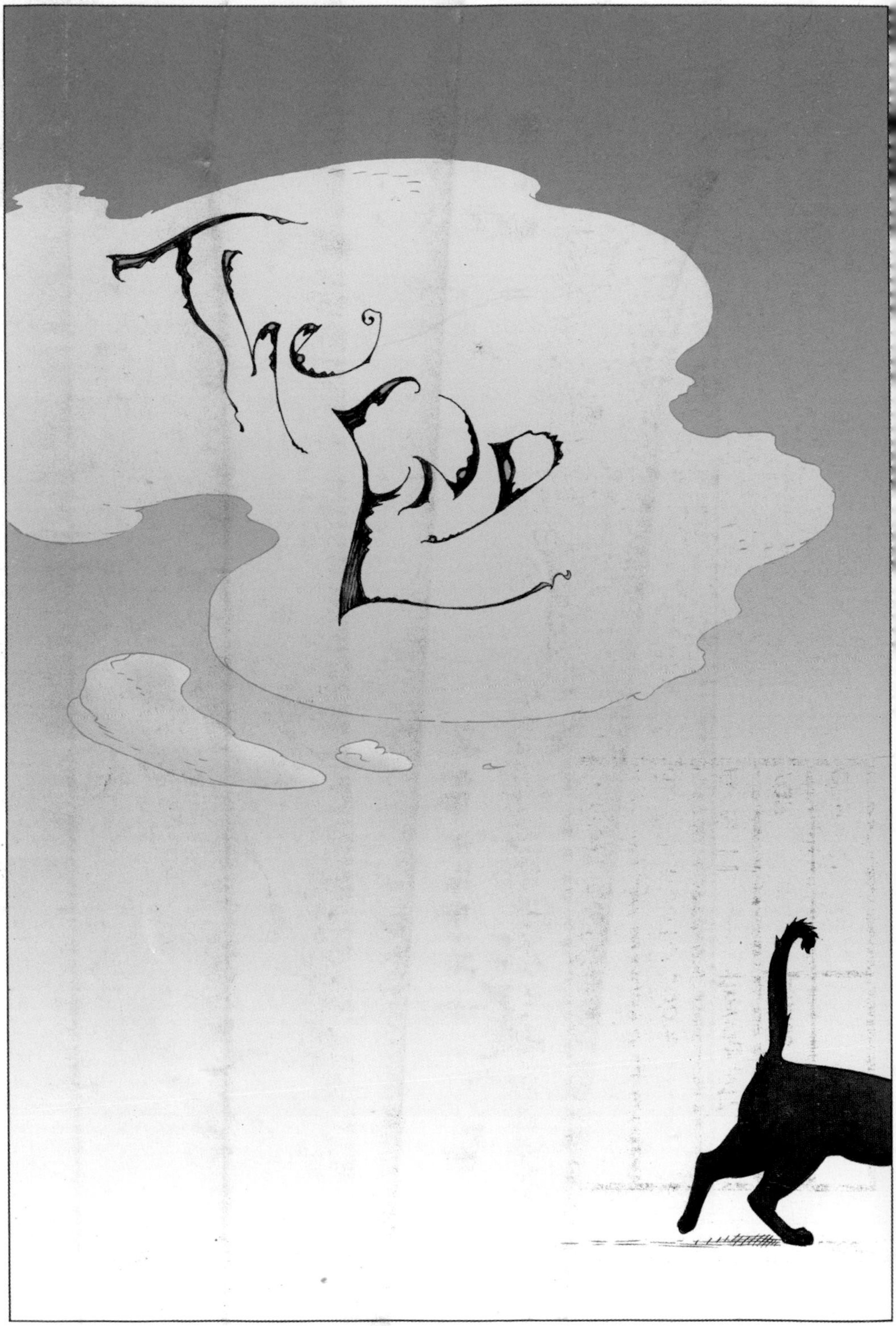
The End